T0321979

Empowering Businesses With Collaborative Enterprise Architecture Frameworks

Tiko Iyamu
Cape Peninsula University of Technology, South Africa

A volume in the Advances in
Business Information Systems and
Analytics (ABISA) Book Series

Published in the United States of America by
>   IGI Global
>   Business Science Reference (an imprint of IGI Global)
>   701 E. Chocolate Avenue
>   Hershey PA, USA 17033
>   Tel: 717-533-8845
>   Fax: 717-533-8661
>   E-mail: cust@igi-global.com
>   Web site: http://www.igi-global.com

Library of Congress Cataloging-in-Publication Data

Names: Iyamu, Tiko, editor.
Title: Empowering businesses with collaborative enterprise architecture
    frameworks / Tiko Iyamu, editor.
Description: Hershey, PA : Business Science Reference, [2019] | Summary:
    "This book provides a long-term view on collaborative enterprise
    architecture framework in adopting disruptive technology. It also
    explores the applications of enterprise architecture in the business
    world"-- Provided by publisher.
Identifiers: LCCN 2018051651 | ISBN 9781522582298 (hardcover) | ISBN
    9781522582304 (ebook)
Subjects: LCSH: Technological innovations--Management. | Information
    technology--Management. | Computer network architectures.
Classification: LCC HD45 .E368 2019 | DDC 658/.05--dc23
LC record available at https://lccn.loc.gov/2018051651

This book is published in the IGI Global book series Advances in Business Information Systems and Analytics (ABISA) (ISSN: 2327-3275; eISSN: 2327-3283)

British Cataloguing in Publication Data
A Cataloguing in Publication record for this book is available from the British Library.

For electronic access to this publication, please contact: eresources@igi-global.com.

Advances in Business Information Systems and Analytics (ABISA) Book Series

ISSN:2327-3275
EISSN:2327-3283

Editor-in-Chief: Madjid Tavana, La Salle University, USA

MISSION

The successful development and management of information systems and business analytics is crucial to the success of an organization. New technological developments and methods for data analysis have allowed organizations to not only improve their processes and allow for greater productivity, but have also provided businesses with a venue through which to cut costs, plan for the future, and maintain competitive advantage in the information age.

The **Advances in Business Information Systems and Analytics (ABISA) Book Series** aims to present diverse and timely research in the development, deployment, and management of business information systems and business analytics for continued organizational development and improved business value.

COVERAGE

- Data Management
- Business Information Security
- Forecasting
- Algorithms
- Data Strategy
- Decision Support Systems
- Management Information Systems
- Business Intelligence
- Big Data
- Strategic Information Systems

IGI Global is currently accepting manuscripts for publication within this series. To submit a proposal for a volume in this series, please contact our Acquisition Editors at Acquisitions@igi-global.com or visit: http://www.igi-global.com/publish/.

Titles in this Series

For a list of additional titles in this series, please visit:
https://www.igi-global.com/book-series/advances-business-information-systems-analytics/37155

Managing Business in the Civil Construction Sector Through Information Communication Tehnologies
Bithal Das Mundhra (Simplex Infrastructures Ltd, India) and Rajesh Bose (Simplex Infrastructures Ltd, India)
Business Science Reference • © 2021 • 250pp • H/C (ISBN: 9781799852919) • US $195.00

Applications of Big Data and Business Analytics in Management
Sneha Kumari (Vaikunth Mehta National Institute of Cooperative Management, India) K. K. Tripathy (Vaikunth Mehta National Institute of Cooperative Management, India) and Vidya Kumbhar (Symbiosis International University (Deemed), India)
Business Science Reference • © 2020 • 300pp • H/C (ISBN: 9781799832614) • US $225.00

Handbook of Research on Integrating Industry 4.0 in Business and Manufacturing
Isak Karabegović (Academy of Sciences and Arts of Bosnia and Herzegovina, Bosnia and Herzegovina) Ahmed Kovačević (City, University London, UK) Lejla Banjanović-Mehmedović (University of Tuzla, Bosnia and Herzegovina) and Predrag Dašić (High Technical Mechanical School of Professional Studies in Trstenik, Serbia)
Business Science Reference • © 2020 • 661pp • H/C (ISBN: 9781799827252) • US $265.00

Internet of Things (IoT) Applications for Enterprise Productivity
Erdinç Koç (Bingol University, Turkey)
Business Science Reference • © 2020 • 357pp • H/C (ISBN: 9781799831754) • US $215.00

Trends and Issues in International Planning for Businesses
Babayemi Adekunle (Arden University, UK) Husam Helmi Alharahsheh (University of Wales Trinity Saint David, UK) and Abraham Pius (Arden University, UK)
Business Science Reference • © 2020 • 225pp • H/C (ISBN: 9781799825470) • US $225.00

Institutional Assistance Support for Small and Medium Enterprise Development in Africa
Isaac Oluwajoba Abereijo (Obafemi Awolowo University, Nigeria)
Business Science Reference • © 2020 • 280pp • H/C (ISBN: 9781522594819) • US $205.00

701 East Chocolate Avenue, Hershey, PA 17033, USA
Tel: 717-533-8845 x100 • Fax: 717-533-8661
E-Mail: cust@igi-global.com • www.igi-global.com

Table of Contents

Detailed Table of Contents

Chapter 1

The AMM is supported by a real-life case of a business transformation architecture in the domain of enterprise asset management (EAM) that is supported by the alignment of a standardized enterprise architecture blueprint. This chapter proposes an assets alignment pattern (AAP) and offers a set of solutions in the form of design, technical, and managerial recommendations to be used by the target company's asset analysts and enterprise architects to implement EAM solutions in the context of business transformation projects (BTP). Heuristics is applied in real-world complex problems that are very similar to transformation projects. The EAM-based AAP is not influenced by any specific business domain and has a holistic approach that uses a neural networks processor.

Chapter 2

Big data has gained popularity in recent years, with increased interest from both public and private organisations including academics. The automation of business processes led to the proliferation of different types of data at various speeds through information systems. Big data is generated at a high rate from multiple sources that can become complex to manage with challenges to collect, manipulate, and store data with traditional IS/IT. Big data has been associated with technical non-technical challenges. Due to these challenges, organisations deploy enterprise architecture as an approach to holistically manage and mitigate challenges associated with business and technology. An exploratory study was done to determine how EA could be used to manage big data in healthcare facilities. This study employs the interpretive approach with documentation as the analysis. Findings were governance, internal and external big data sources, information technology infrastructure development, and big data skills. Through the different EA domains, big data challenges could be mitigated.

Chapter 3
Antoine Trad, IBISTM, France

This chapter on an optimal and adaptable enterprise architecture for business systems is one of a series of research chapters on enterprise architecture and business transformations. This one is about estimating the risk for transforming a business environment. It is a conclusion of many years of research, architecture, consulting, and development efforts. The model is based on an applied holistic mathematical model (AHMM) for business transformations. In this chapter, the CSFs are tuned to support the intelligent architecture concepts for business integration in the form of an applied pattern that is also a part or a chapter in this research series. This chapter is related to the feasibility and prototype of the business engineering and risk management pattern (BE&RMP) that should (or shouldn't) prove whether business transformation projects can optimize enterprise business capabilities and how microartefact implementation can offer a sustainable enterprise business system.

Chapter 4
Tandokazi Zondani, Cape Peninsula University of Technology, South
Africa
Tiko Iyamu, Cape Peninsula University of Technology, South Africa

Often at times many organisations fail to achieve the objectives of their enterprise business architecture (EBA). This can be attributed to lack of assessment of readiness. This is also because there are no models specific to EBA readiness assessment. The lack of readiness assessment before deployment often results to challenges such as uncoordinated business designs, lack of flow in processes, derailment of activities, which make cost of operations prohibitive, increase complexity in managing potential risks, and service stagnancy. These challenges led to this study whose aim was to propose a solution that can be used to assess the readiness of EBA in an organisation. From the interpretivist perspective, the case study approach was employed to gain better understanding of the factors that influence the readiness of EBA in an organisation. The hermeneutics approach was applied in the analysis of the data. The sudy reveals the factors that influence the deployment of business architecture in organisations.

Chapter 5

Irja N. Shaanika, Namibia University of Science and Technology, Namibia

Many cities are adopting information and communication technologies (ICT) to add value to business process. This has led to the realisation of smart cities making them dependable on ICT. In Namibia, the focus is to transform Windhoek into a smart city. However, it is not easy as Windhoek continues to face many challenges, for example lack of collaboration among stakeholders. The challenges could be attributed by lack of approaches such as enterprise architecture (EA). As a management and design approach, EA provides a system view of all components and their relationship. In the absence of EA, realisation of Windhoek smart city will continue to be challenging, impeding the city from providing smart services. The study's aim was to develop EA framework for Windhoek smart city realisation. A qualitative case study approach was employed. Data was interpretively analysed to enable a deeper understating of the influencing factors. Based on the findings, a conceptual EA framework was developed. The framework aims to guide and govern Windhoek city transformation towards its smart objectives.

Chapter 6

Metin Uyar, Istanbul Gelişim University, Turkey

The chapter aims to explain the relationship between the management accounting system and enterprise innovation ability in the context of collaborative enterprise architecture. The study explains modeling the transformation process and outlining why and how the management accounting affects enterprise innovation ability through accounting information which is focused on the decision-making process. The study uses a survey designed and administered to accountants and managers who work in Turkish manufacturing enterprises as a data provider and decision-maker. The hypotheses were tested using multivariable data analysis techniques, and additional analyses were conducted for more details. The statistical findings show that management accounting affects innovation ability positively. Both product and process innovations are positively affected by managerial accounting. There is also a significant relationship between collaborative enterprise and innovation ability. The harmony between organizational architecture and management accounting increases the company's ability to innovate.

A lot of research has been done using Data Envelopment Analysis (DEA) to measure efficiency in Education. DEA has also been used in the field of Information and Communication Technology for Development (ICT4D) to investigate and measure the efficiency of Information and Communication Technology (ICT) investments on Human Development. Education is one of the major components of the Human Development Index (HDI) which affects the core of Human Development. This research investigates the relative efficiency of ICT Infrastructure Utilization on the educational component of the HDI in order to determine the viability of Learning Analytics using DEA for policy direction and decision making. A conceptual model taking the form of a Linear Equation was used and the Constant Returns to Scale (CRS) and Variable Returns to Scale (VRS) models of the Data Envelopment Analysis were employed to measure the relative efficiency of the components of ICT Infrastructure (Inputs) and the components of Education (Outputs). Results show a generally high relative efficiency of ICT Infrastructure utilization on Educational Attainment and Adult Literacy rates, a strong correlation between this Infrastructure and Literacy rates as well, provide an empirical support for the argument of increasing ICT infrastructure to provide an increase in Human Development, especially within the educational context. The research concludes that DEA as a methodology can be used for macroeconomic decision making and policy direction within developmental research.

Chapter 8

Within the South African government, there is an increasing amount of data. The problem is that the South African government is struggling to employ the concept of big data analytics (BDA) for the analysis of its big data. This could be attributed to know-how from both technical and nontechnical perspectives. Failure to implement BDA and ensure appropriate use hinders government enterprises and agencies in their drive to deliver quality service. A government enterprise was selected and used as a case in this study primarily because the concept of BDA is new to many South African government departments. Data was collected through in-depth interviews. From the analysis, four factors—knowledge, process, differentiation, and skillset—that can influence implementation of BDA for government enterprises were revealed. Based on the factors, a set of criteria in the form of a model was developed.

The goals of every organisation are unique. It is difficult to find a single information technology governance framework that will embrace the functions of every organisation. This is attributed to the primary reason why organisations tend to select multiple IT governance frameworks, for their processes and activities. However, many organisations later realised that some of the frameworks are very similar and others are inappropriate. This evidently and inevitably causes complexities and negatively impacts return on investment in organisations. This highlights the need for an architectural framework that guides the selection and implementation of an appropriate framework, as presented and discussed in this chapter. The qualitative case study and interpretive method and approach are followed in conducting this research, which is to develop an architectural framework for the implementation of IT governance in organisations. A South African organisation was used as a case, focusing on the IT division. The data collection method presented in this research was semi-structured interviews.

In the last three decades, two fundamental things have happened to the concept of the enterprise architecture (EA). One, the interest on EA continues to increase, which enacts popular debate and discourse at both academic and business platforms. Two, the pace of deployment within government enterprises is slow, which affects actualisation of the benefits towards service delivery. This can be attributed to confusions and misunderstandings about the concept, which manifests from the fact that the influential factors of the concept are not clear. As a result, many enterprises continue to be hesitant or dismissive about the concept. Thus, the purpose of this study was to develop a conceptual an EA framework that can be used to guide government enterprises towards transformative goal. The framework is intended to guide the fundamental components, which causes confusion about the deployment of EA as agent of change within government enterprises.

Preface

There are two primary fundamental challenges for many organizations, which are return on investment, and the constrains and complexities in the deployment of information technology (IT) solutions toward achieving aims and objectives. These are widely shared problems that have remained within organizations across the globe for many years. This book focuses on these challenges from the perspectives of pragmaticism, implementable strategies, and direction to create IT solutions with collaborative capabilities by employing the concept of enterprise architecture (EA).

In the midst increasing demands and competitiveness, private organizations across spectrum of industries and government institutions in both developing and developed countries continue to seek approaches and methods to improve services to their clients and citizens, respectively. As a result, there has been significant steady increase of investment in IT solutions in the last two decades. Despite the huge investments, and approaches and methods that has been employed, the challenges persist. It is worst in that some of the challenges derail business processes, information exchange and management, and IT solutions deployment and use.

As revealed in this book, better IT solutions and improved business returns can be found through active collaboration within and across organizations and government institutions. The collaboration efforts range from passive information sharing to active and participative decision making, enabled by the EA. This includes aggregation of individual analysis, and big data analytics to enhance collaborative information services, business processes, and deployment of IT solutions for competitive advantage.

This book presents details of how the EA can be used to guide the deployment and use of various IT solutions for an organization's purposes. It presents readers with an understanding of the need for collaboration in adopting disruptive technology, and provide them with a collaborative EA framework (CEAF) adoption. It draws on contributors' experience, to assist organizations with a pragmatic roadmaps in adopting IT solutions including disruptive technologies effectively and efficiently. The adoption of technology requires standardisation, which this book offer guidelines to organizations.

Empirically, the book reveals that the deployment and practice of the EA are not as straightforward as sometimes claimed by agents. This complexity is attributed to the unique nature of organizations and institutions, and the different approaches employed by various actors. Another aspect of complexity is the continued disconnectedness between what is a business need and what is an architectural constraint. This has negatively affected alignment and collaborative initiatives between the business and IT units in many organizations. The book pays great attention to collaboration and alignment using the EA to empower organizations in the delivering of services. Interest in collaborative use of the EA continue to increase in both private and public organizations in developing and developed countries, in their quest to improve service delivery.

The book presents a combination of the factors, context and relevance related to business, service, and IT solutions from the perspectives of in-depth theory and practice, employing how the EA can be used to add value to development in a bid to continually improve services. The quality, credibility, and response time that are instilled in the delivery of services to clients and citizens through rigour and relevance increase the level of stakeholder confidence. This book will therefore benefit both academics and professionals in the organizations, government institutions, and IT sector in the continued process of improving the services through the EA.

The book is truly international with contributors from *Croatia*, France, Namibia, South Africa, and Turkey. Also, the chapters cover a diverse set of issues ranging from business collaborative solutions and big data analytics to the deployment and use of the EA in both organizations and government institutions.

The audience of this book are both academics and business people. This includes IS researchers, Government and industry policy and decision makers, Directors and other decision makes in organizations, business architects, information architects, technical architects, and enterprise architects. Furthermore, this book will be written for adoption by Masters Programs at University levels, making it an ideal text book for students of enterprise architecture and information management. Thus, this book should have immense appeal for classroom teaching of postgraduate programs in information and communication technologies.

The first chapter: 'The Business Transformation Framework and Enterprise Architecture Framework for Managers in Business Innovation' was contributed by Antoine Trad from Institute of Business and Information Systems Transformation Management, France and Damir Kalpić from University of Zagreb Faculty of Electrical Engineering and Computing, Croatia. The chapter is based on an authentic mixed multidisciplinary research method that is supported by intelligent neural networks and a heuristics module, named the Applied Holistic Mathematical Model for Enterprise Asset Management, which can be applied to financial, governance and infrastructural services engineering, to support the detection of financial irregularities and eventual irregularities. This chapter proposes an Assets Alignment Pattern (AAP) which delivers sets of solutions, in the form of design, technical and managerial recommendations. These AAP recommendations can be used by the target company's asset analysts and enterprise architects to implement EAM solutions in the specific context of Business Transformation Projects (BTP). It is supported by a real-life case of a business transformation architecture in the domain of Enterprise Asset Management (EAM).

Next chapter, 'The use of an Enterprise Architecture Framework to guide the Management of Big Data in Healthcare organizations' is contributed by Monica Nehemia from Cape Peninsula University of Technology, South Africa. The chapter discusses the automation of business operations as an aspect of the essentiality, which leads to the proliferation of large amounts of digital information and how many organizations are structured into different divisions and units of distinctive functionalities and mandates through which they deploy information systems and information technology (IS/IT) solutions to automate business processes, and ultimately render effective and efficient services to its stakeholders. This includes how the EA through its different domains can be used to manage big data and the challenges of IT solutions in an organization.

The chapter 'An Applied Mathematical Model for Business Transformation and Enterprise Architecture' is by Antoine Trad from Institute of Business and Information Systems Transformation Management, France. The chapter focuses on an optimal and adaptability of the EA concept, for critical business systems, and business transformations. This chapter is about the estimation of risks related to transformations of business environment(s). The author propose a model that can be used to support transformation and business process reengineering through the use of Artificial Intelligence (AI). The chapter concludes with feasibility of the business engineering and risk management pattern (BE&RMP) for optimisation and transformation of business capabilities.

Tandokazi Zondani from Cape Peninsula University of Technology, South Africa offers: 'Towards an Enterprise Business Architecture Readiness Assessment model'. The chapter discusses the fact that often at times many organizations fail to achieve the objectives of their Enterprise Business Architecture (EBA), which is attributed to lack of assessment of readiness. The examined the root-cause of this challenge, and revealed that the lack of readiness assessment before deployment of EBA often results to challenges such as uncoordinated business designs, lack of flow in processes, derailment of activities, which make cost of operations prohibitive, increase complexity in managing potential risks, and service stagnancy. Based on which some factors were identified, to help gain better understanding of EBA readiness in an organization. The chapter is purportedly for both business and IT managers, in advancing the development of the EBA.

'Enterprise architecture framework for Windhoek smart city realization' by Irja Shaanika from the Namibia University of Science and Technology, Windhoek, Namibia focuses on smart city from a developing country context. The City of Windhoek strives towards becoming a smart city. However, there are numerous challenges which are mainly about governance of IT solutions and business processes. The chapter empirically revealed the challenges that confront the city of Windhoek in the drive towards a smart city. The chapter discusses the challenges, which are both technical and non-technical factors. The proposes the deployment of the EA in addressing the challenges of non-technical and complexities of technical factors, in achieving the goal of a smart city. In conclusion, the chapter explains how the EA can be used as guidelines towards the realization of Windhoek smart city, which include stakeholder's collaboration in alignment with the city's vision.

Metin Uyar from İstanbul Gelişim University, Turkey discusses: 'The Management Accounting System and Enterprise Innovation ability'. The chapter provides an in-depth explanation about the relationship between management accounting and enterprise innovation ability in the context of collaborative enterprise architecture. While innovation is considered to be important for businesses, the role of management accounting in the context of collaborative enterprise architecture has not been adequately studied, which this chapter addresses. The conceptual perspective denotes specific insights into the critical outcomes that influence the success of innovations made by enterprises which is intended to help enterprises to enhance their competitive power. It also explains to determine the key variables that enterprises should concentrate to develop the relationship between innovation and accounting.

Yinka Oyerinde and Felix Bankole from University of South Africa, South Africa next present a chapter titled: 'Influence of Constant Returns to Scale and Variable Returns to Scale Data Envelopment Analysis Models in ICT Infrastructure Efficiency Utilization'. A lot of research has been done using Data Envelopment Analysis (DEA) to measure efficiency in Education. The DEA has also been used in the field of Information and Communication Technology for Development (ICT4D) to investigate and measure the efficiency of Information and Communication Technology (ICT) investments on Human Development. Education is one of the major components of the Human Development Index (HDI) which affects the core of Human Development. This chapter presents the efficiency of ICT Infrastructure Utilization on the educational component of the HDI in order to determine the viability of Learning Analytics using DEA for policy direction and decision making. A conceptual model taking the form of a Linear Equation was used and the Constant Returns to Scale (CRS) and Variable Returns to Scale (VRS) models of the Data Envelopment Analysis were employed to measure the relative efficiency of the components of ICT Infrastructure (Inputs) and the components of Education (Outputs). Results show a generally high relative efficiency of ICT Infrastructure utilization on Educational Attainment and Adult Literacy rates, a strong correlation between this Infrastructure and Literacy rates as well, provide an empirical support for the argument of increasing ICT infrastructure to provide an increase in Human Development, especially within the educational context. The chapter concludes that DEA as a methodology can be used for macroeconomic decision making and policy direction within developmental research.

Namhla Matiwane from the Cape Peninsula University of Technology, Cape Town, South Africa notes: 'Implementation of Big Data Analytics for Government Enterprise'. Within the South African government, there is big data continuous to increase in volume, variety, and speed. Despite the availability of the big data, some government enterprises are struggling to improve services owing to inability to critically conduct analyze. This could be attributed to know-how, in the use of analytics application. Failure to implement big data analytics (BDA) to ensure appropriate analysis hinders the drive to deliver quality service. Qualitative data was collected, and analyzed using the hermeneutics approach. From the analysis, four factors: Knowledge, Process, Differentiation, and Skill-set that can influence implementation of BDA for government enterprises were revealed. Based on the factors, a set of criteria in the form of a model was developed.

The following chapter: 'Deployment of Information Technology Governance using Architectural Framework' is by Nomathamsanqa (Thami) Batyashe of the Department of Communication and Digital Technologies, Pretoria, South Africa. The goals of every organization are unique. As a result, it is difficult to find a single IT governance framework that will embrace functions of every organization. This is attributed to the primary reason why organizations tend to select various IT governance frameworks, for your processes and activities. However, many organizations later realized that some of the frameworks are very similar, and others are inappropriate. This evidently and inevitably cause complexities, and negatively impact return on investment in organizations. This highlights the need for an architectural framework which guides the selection and implementation of an appropriate framework, as presented and discussed in this chapter. Through a framework, the chapter presents and discusses the fundamental factors, which influences the selection and implementation of IT governance in organizations. The factors include organizational needs, managing, assessment and innovation.

The final chapter: 'The Enterprise Architecture as agent of change for government enterprises' by Tiko Iyamu from Cape Peninsula University of Technology, South Africa. In the last three decades, two fundamental things have happened to the concept of the EA. One, the interest on EA continues to increase, which enacts popular debate and discourse at both academic and business platforms. Two, the pace of deployment within government enterprises is slow, which affects actualization of the benefits toward service delivery. This can be attributed to confusions and misunderstandings about the concept, which manifests from the fact that the influential factors of the concept are not clear. As a result, many enterprises continue to be hesitant or dismissive of the concept. This chapter reveals the factors that cause the confusion. This was done by gathering qualitative day, and using actor-network theory (ANT) as a lens to in the analysis. From the analysis, criticality of networks, structural collaboration, transformative process, and iterative approach were found to be of influence to the development, implementation and practice of the EA. Based on the findings, a conceptual framework was developed, which is intended to guide how the EA can be used to facilitate government's activities, in providing services to the communities, and towards transformative goal.

It is important to provide empirical insights on the deployment of the EA as a collaborative effort and approach in support and enhance service delivery in both private and public organisations particularly in developing countries. The goal of this book is to consider various aspects of the EA and collaborative approach, ranging from uptake of EA domains, big data analytics to the deployment and use of IT solutions in general. This includes the development, implementation and diffusion of technologies guided the governance of the EA, for service delivery purposes.

The recent contributions of the EA to both private organisations and government institutions in developed and developing countries have been enormous. As result, large and medium organisations increasingly show interest in the concept of EA. This is attributed to the fact that the EA continues to offer huge opportunities for improved service. This includes areas of IT solutions' selection, standardization, deployment, integration, use, support, and management. I hope that this book will encourage even greater use of the EA in order to further improve service delivery particularly in the areas of business processes, business transformation, information management, and IT solutions' governance.

Chapter 1

The Business Transformation Framework and Enterprise Architecture Framework for Managers in Business Innovation:
The Alignment of Enterprise Asset Management and Enterprise Architecture Methodologies

Antoine Trad

iD https://orcid.org/0000-0002-4199-6970
IBISTM, France

ABSTRACT

The AMM is supported by a real-life case of a business transformation architecture in the domain of enterprise asset management (EAM) that is supported by the alignment of a standardized enterprise architecture blueprint. This chapter proposes an assets alignment pattern (AAP) and offers a set of solutions in the form of design, technical, and managerial recommendations to be used by the target company's asset analysts and enterprise architects to implement EAM solutions in the context of business transformation projects (BTP). Heuristics is applied in real-world complex problems that are very similar to transformation projects. The EAM-based AAP is not influenced by any specific business domain and has a holistic approach that uses a neural networks processor.

DOI: 10.4018/978-1-5225-8229-8.ch001

INTRODUCTION

Today, business enterprises are encountering massive pressure to manage their enterprise assets proactively and holistically in order to insure their business sustainability, reduce costs, and to integrate the continuously transformed assets related legal, regulatory and economic environments. For a BTP, there is a need for a just in time decision making, planning and optimization activities; and to achieve that the designed transformation process can manage the inventory of the EAM. Heuristics is applied in real world complex problems that are very similar to iterative transformation projects. The EAM based AAP, is not influenced by any specific business (or other) domain and has a holistic approach that uses an authentic neural networks processor. The AAP is based on a reasoning concept that is basically a qualitative research method that manages, weights and qualifies Critical Success Factor (CSF) sets, actions to final solutions (Capecchi, Buscema, Contucci, D'Amore, 2010). The AAP's underlined system supports BTPs or Enterprise Architecture Project (EAP) (simply the *Project*) in integrating scenarios that are sets of interactive services (Trad & Kalpić, 2018a; Trad & Kalpić, 2018b).

BACKGROUND

This chapter's background combines: asset management, patterns design, enterprise architecture, mathematical models, heuristics, technology management, business transformation and business engineering fields; where the main focus is on how to integrate EAM solutions. Building an AAP for an EAM system is probably, the most strategic goal for a business company. Fast transformations for efficient business environments have to be supported by a holistic and intelligent AAP based EAM systems (Cearley, Walker, Burke, 2016). The AAP is business driven and is agnostic to a specific technology, financial, business, architecture or any other pattern concept. As shown in Figure 1, AAP, is founded on a research framework that in turn is based on industry standards, like the Architecture Development Method (ADM) (The Open Group, 2011a). Enterprise Architecture (EA), is a methodology, which can be used to develop *Projects*: 1) requirements; 2) business architecture; 3) EAM interfaces and integration; and 4) its Information and Communication System's (ICS) components. The Business Transformation Manager (BTM), EAM responsible, or an Enterprise Architect (simply the *Manager*) can use the APP and EA to integrate the EAM in the business interprise (Trad & Kalpić, 2017b; Trad & Kalpić, 2017c; Thomas & Gartner (2015); Tidd, 2006). This AAP proposal's aim is to deliver recommendations for managing aligned EAM's enterprise architecture integration. The applied research methodology is based on literature review, a qualitative methodology and on a Proof of Concept (PoC) that is used to prove the RQ and the related hypotheses. For the EAM, the *Manager*'s role is important and his or her (for simplicity, in further text – his) decisions are aided by using CSFs within the AHMM4EAM. A large set of CSFs can influence the AHMM4EAM, like: 1) the role of the EAM and control by mechanisms; 2) global enterprise CSFs; 3) enterprise resources planning sources; 4) level of the team's skills; 5) audit and technological conditions; 6) financial and governance predispositions; and 7) security, financial and legal control mechanisms. A holistic system's approach is the optimal to model such EAM controls (Daellenbach & McNickle, 2005; Trad & Kalpić, 2016a). As shown in Figure 1, the decision model interacts with the external world via an implemented framework to manage the EAM's factors and that is this chapter's focus.

Figure 1. The research framework's concept (Trad & Kalpić, 2016a)

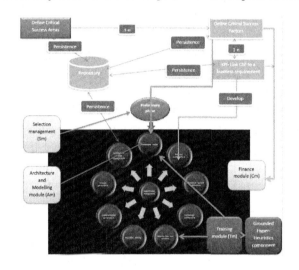

MAIN FOCUS OF THE CHAPTER

The AAP proposes, Financial Technology (FinTech) components that are part of the Financial management module (Fm); Fm is also a part of this Research & Development Project's (RDP) framework, the Transformation, Research and Architecture Development framework (*TRADf),* will be used), that is the major support for of *Project*'s activities; in fact the proposed *TRADf* is a leader in this market (Trad, 2017a; 2017b; Trad & Kalpić, 2020a). This chapter is strongly bonded to two other articles and together they create a research whole on financial engineering risk and technology management related works. These articles are: 1) the intelligent Atomic Service based Decision Making Systems (iASbDMS) (Trad, 2020b); 2) the intelligent Strategic Atomic Service Development (iSASDev) (Trad, 2020c); and 3) he Financial Risk Management with a Strategic Vision (FRMSV) (Trad, 2020d), which describes the usage/instantiation of the AAP. Which makes these two chapters strongly bounded and should read together (Trad, 2020c). The *TRADf* and its AAP which supports FinTech components, needs a specific engineering and technology integration concept, based on agile business engineering methodologies and aBB microartefacts, which in turn are based on an anti-fragile concept. This research project's main focus is on: 1) the AAP's to support an risk management for *Project's* subsystems; 2) the use with existing standard market enterprise architecture frameworks; 3) to support various types of *Projects*; 4) for the selection of the AAP based *Project's* management profile; 5) the use of a AHMM4EAM; 6) the neural networks concept in the form of an NLP; 7) holisms, generics and global concept; 8) the application of risk management to support financial systems; 9) the AAP as the kernel of the future strategy for financial systems; 10) Artificial Intelligence (AI) as a generic interface; 11) the intelligent Atomic Services based Knowledge Management System (iASbKMS) as a holistic strategic knowledge environment to support a financial strategy; and 12) continuous development, deployment, transformation and innovation, using agile iterative development and operations approaches. Searching with the scholar engine, within Google's online search portal, in which the author combined the previously mentioned keywords and key topics; the results show very clearly the uniqueness and the absolute lead of the author's works/ framework, methodology, research and recommendations in the mentioned scientific fields and that can be considered as an important jumpstart for the future industrial use (Trad, 2019a, 2019c). From this point of view and facts, the author considers his long-life works on the mentioned topics as innovative, credible and ultimately useful; to support the chapter's topic. The AHMM4EAM based AAP for *Projects,* where the NLP, can be used for scripting and prototyping FinTech environments using a set of atomic Building Blocks (aBB) in the form of microartefacts.

THE RESEARCH DEVELOPMENT PROCESS

The Research and Development Processes

This research's main topic is related to *Project*s and the ultimate research question is: "Which Manager characteristics and which type of support should be assured in the implementation phase of a business transformation project?" Decision making concepts based on critical success areas are their main research component. Where this chapter's research question is: "Can an assets alignment pattern, support a business transformation project or an intelligent decision making system and minimize the risks of failure ?"

Related Research Works

The AAP supports classical assets' implementation constructs as well as complex ones in order to support business sustainability (Trad & Kalpić, 2018c, 2018d). The AAP is business-driven and is founded on a research framework that is presented using a business case.

The Research's Literature Review and Gap

The outcome is that very little relevant scholar or even general literature and research resources exist on the selected subject; of course with the exception of some frameworks similar to Open Group Architecture Framework (TOGAF) which covers the ADM cyclic part; where *TRADf* has many advantages but lacks the kernel AI mechanisms and a holistic approach. The authors consider their work as a pioneering undertaking; the most relevant EAM and AAP information found in literature was that there is an immense gap, between *Projects* objectives and the existing reality; these facts explain the high failure rates. The knowledge gap was confirmed, mainly because the existing literature on failure rates and on various methodologies treating *asset management*, where practically there is no insight into a holistic approach to designing an EAM. In this chapter: 1) the authors use many of their own referenced and accepted works (managed by an internal review/ weighting system); 2) they consider that these topics are somehow ignored and not sufficiently researched; 3) *TRADf*, uses many abbreviations, which is frequent in complex framework; and 4) that their work is an original pioneering work that is based mainly on empirical requirements engineering disciplines.

Empirical Engineering Research Model

The used RDP is based on an empirical engineering research approach, which is optimal for engineering or cross-functional projects (Easterbrook, Singer, Storey, & Damian, 2008). The RDP uses an authentic mixed method (where mixed research is a simplistic synonym) that can be considered as a natural complement to conventional siloed qualitative and quantitative research methodologies. The main goal of such a mixed method, to deliver empirical pragmatism concepts as a possible holistic approach for interactive mixed methods research. Empirical validity checks if the RDP's are acceptable as a contribution to existing scientific knowledge. The authors want to convince the valuable readers that this chapter's recommendations and that the related PoC are valid. A controlled experiment or a PoC is a concept that contains design artefacts and a software prototype of a testable RQ (and its related hypothesis). For this PoC one or more CSFs (or independent variables) are processed to evaluate their influence on the model's dependent variables. PoCs evaluates, with high precision the CSFs (and KPIs) and checks if they are related, like if the cause–effect relationship exists between these CSFs. The PoC applies the AAP in an Applied Case Study (ACS) (The Open Group, 2011a).

Critical Success Areas, Factors and Related Decision Making Processes

Critical Success Area (CSA) is a category of CSFs where in turn a CSF is a set of KPIs, where a KPI corresponds to a single *Project* requirement or feature. For a given problem, an EAM analyst must identify the initial set of CSFs to be used for the Decision Making System for EAM (DMS4EAM). Hence the CSFs are the most important mapping/relation between the EAM construct, financial status, organisational predisposition and DMS4EAM (Peterson, 2011). Therefore, CSFs reflect performance areas that must meet strategic goals and defined AHMM4EAM constraints. Measurements are used to evaluate performance in each CSA, where CSFs can be internal and/or external; like for example: 1) budget gap analysis is an internal CSF; and 2) percent of market share is an external CSF. The *TRADf* method to select the CSA category and the corresponding CSFs is to audit the EAM vision and strategic planning process. Once the initial set of CSFs has been identified, then the *Project* has to use the decision-making module to verify the CSFs and to give them the right weightings. The AAP delivers a set of recommendations and solutions for an aligned architecture that is a part of the *TRADf* (Trad & Kalpić, 2017b; Trad, & Kalpić, 2017c).

The Authors' Applied Framework

The *Manager* decisions can be made in a just-in-time manner by using outputs from various credible ICS logging sources. The AAP based strategy should asses and govern global enterprise assets that are formalized with an AAP based architecture blueprint. *TRADf* support such an undertaking, as shown Figure 2. Unfortunately, an immense set of archaic factors can influence such a process, like: 1) the influence of EAM on *Projects*; 2) working with complex systems with a very strict financial, audit and legal frameworks; and 3) the holistic EA and design standards for such *Projects* are non-existent, or are too complex to implement. A global concept and the management of related EAM approach is optimal for such complex mechanisms

(Daellenbach & McNickle, 2005). The AAP can be applied to many *Project*s and general fields in *TRADf* and it is a part of the Financial management module (Fm) and the Architecture and modelling module (Am), to be described on the next page (Trad 2018a; Trad 2018b).

Figure 2. The implementation environment that enables asset management

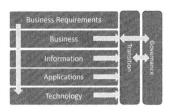

The AAP component is managed by TOGAF's ADM's phases, where each AAP microartefact circulates through its phases. The AAP microartefacts contain their private set of CSFs. These CSFs can be applied to (Peterson, 2011): 1) select the important asset management factors; 2) detect the EAM's most important assets; 3) estimate the actual assets of the *Project* using the decision support system's interface; and to eventually take a decision on *Project*'s continuation; 4) control and monitor the needed AAP instances; 5) upgrade the *Project*'s team asset management skills; and 6) support the architecture and *Project* management activities. The Framework or the *TRADf* is composed of the following modules:

- "Sm": for the selection management of the Framework.
- "Am": for the architecture and modelling strategy that can be applied by the Framework.
- "Cm" for the control and monitoring strategy that can be applied by the Framework.
- "Dm" for the decision-making strategy that can be applied by the Framework.
- "Tm" for the training management of the Framework.
- "Pm" for the project management strategy that can be applied by the Framework.
- "Fm" for the financial management's support to the Framework.
- "Gm" for the Geopolitical mind-mining to the Framework.
- "F" for Framework

This chapter is a part of the RDP cluster that has produced many articles, literature reviews, usable items and research artefacts. In this chapter, sections from previous works are (re)used to improve the understanding of this complex subject in the context of *TRADf*. For this chapter the research question is: "Which enterprise architecture pattern is needed to evaluate and support an enterprise assets' management?".

Enterprise Asset Management

EAM's integration is complex and the massive use of tools and technology to radically improve the performance and achieve hyper-fast business benefits through asset management scripting. Scripting, makes it even very complex. Accountant oriented EAM scripting that promotes off-shoring and rapid ruthless growth has a grave negative effect on *Projects* and business environments, because they promote fast and dirty conclusions and or decisions. EAMs are of extreme strategic importance for companies. If an EAM is successful, the business company and the economical ecosystem will excel, but when it fails, the business company might face important problems and multiplication of such phenomenon would hurt the overall growth. Today, businesses that have been transformed need EAMs to automate the management of their assets through the use of patterns like the AAP. The AAP is based on the ADM, Knowledge Management System (KMS) and the DMS4EAM.

The EAM Knowledge Management System

The KMS for EAM (KMS4EAM) goal, is to manage information items by using a holistic management concept that offers also the possibility to access distributed heterogeneous knowledge. Where the knowledge items are associated with the CSFs and the KMS4EAM's characteristics are:

- The AAP based KMS4EAM is based on a set of multiple coordinated services. AAP microartefacts are responsible for the manipulation and processing. Weightings' concept enables the AAP supports the asset subsystem that delivers answers in the form of asset values, known as items. In many cases, fast change requests may generate an important set of corresponding EAM solutions that can be ambiguous and make AAP's actions uncertain and complex to implement. The AAP is responsible for a rational heuristic approach for KMS4EAM accesses (Clark, Fletcher, Hanson, Irani, Waterhouse & Thelin, 2013).
- The AAP actions map to the various KMS4EAM processes, which are responsible for the implementation of mechanisms needed to deliver knowledge items. The KMS4EAM interfaces all EAM components and the implementation of AAP's mechanisms should be able to deliver the requested asset knowledge items.

- The KMS4EAM manages asset Knowledge Items (aKI); where aKIs and microartefact scripts are responsible for the manipulation of intelligence and control various KMS4EAM processes. The KMS4EAM supports the EAM underlying mechanics to manage aKI microartefacts; and is responsible for access and aKI's extraction, using holistic systemic approach (Daellenbach & McNickle, 2005; Trad & Kalpić, 2016a).
- aKIs map to CSFs and microartefact(s) and are classified in specific CSAs. AAP's fundamental structural supports the KMS4EAM/aKI implementation; which enables a holistic approach to KMS4EAM mapping to CSFs.

The Holistic Decision Making System

The DMS4EAM is conceptually based on a mixed method, combining Action Research (AR), tree heuristics, neural networks and directed quantitative analysis. The authors believe that qualitative, quantitative and other methods can be united in a single reasoning method. AR is applied majorly in education research and this fact supports the *Project*'s capability to build intelligence microartefacts in a continuous learning and experiences improvement processes. This process inspects and learns from configurable intelligent microartefacts that are the basis of the DMS4EAM. The DMS4EAM is generic and can be applied to any business domain and is easily adaptable to various types of problems (Trad & Kalpić, 2017c; Peterson, 2011) and if there is a need, it can launch a precise quantitative analysis to refine the recommended solutions. A DMS4EAM must be managed by existing audit or governance frameworks, where the *Manager*'s configuration of various types of risks is required; these risks are estimated by the *Manager*, by applying DMS4EAM' actions to deliver possible solutions. The DMS4EAM actions' map to the governance processes, found in TOGAF's phase G, which is responsible for the implementation of governance needed to adjust the business objectives. DMS4EAM' microartefacts are implemented in all the *Project*'s components and the implementation of governance mechanisms should be able to identify critical risks. They are to be managed as CSFs, what might need many iterations to contain the risks; such a chain of activities can be modeled and managed by the AHMM4EAM (The Open Group, 2011a).

The Applied Mathematical Model for Assets' Management

The proposed AHMM4EAM is domain agnostic and is not related to any specific methodology and contains a configurable reasoning module that uses CSFs sets and a selected set of actions (Peterson, 2011). As shown in Figure 3, the applied

Figure 3. The TRADf's microartefact concept (Trad, A. & Kalpić, 2017b)

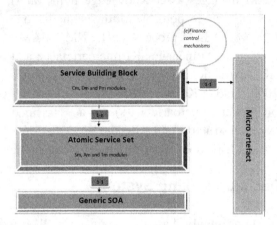

AHMM4EAM supports a microartefact based architecture, which uses a business-driven approach and integrates the ADM (Trad & Kalpić, 2017b).

The AAP takes into account the following CSAs:

- EAM's concept.
- ICS' integration.
- Legal and governance aspects.
- Financial background.

Adapting just the underlined existing silos of technologies is not enough and the main problem in such *Project*s is the lack of a holistic (centralized) EAM (Trad, 2015a). EAM's integration in the very complex and needs and integration pattern that uses CSA which represent EAM' sub-systems like:

- Information Technology Asset Management (ITAM).
- Hardware Asset Management (HAM).
- Software Asset Management (SAM).

For asset related activities we can find tools which have different structures and interfaces, like the Oracle SAM one. The problem lies in integrating these tools in the ICS, which might create an unmanageable hairball. Building the right EA/ADM using an AAP, facilitates such an integration. Knowing that ADM has a governance phase which optimal for an EAM integration. In turn, the CSAs contains selected CSFs that relate to unique standardized tags like the Asset ID (AID) that managed by the EAM.

Scientific vs Business Aspects

The uniqueness and the market lead of the author's proposed AHMM4EAM based *TRADf*, promotes a holistic cohesive EAM and implementation model that supports complex *Projects* integrations using a targeted and genuine PoC (Farhoomand, 2004). Using the scholar engine, within Google's online search portal, in which the author combines the previously mentioned keywords and key topics; the results have shown very clearly the uniqueness and the absolute lead of the author's framework, methodology, research and works (Trad, 2019a). From this point of view and facts, the author considers his works on the mentioned topics as innovative, credible and useful; so the main topics will be introduced.

THE BUSINESS APPLIED CASE STUDY

Information and Communication Infrastructure

The APP uses an ACS, developed by the Open Group as a reference study for its TOGAF environment, it offers the capability to implement *Project* components and is related to an insurance company named ArchiSurance (Jonkers, Band & Quartel, 2012a). The authors recommend that the readers refer to the original ACS, because it is used in the PoC. The AAP 's goals are:

- Offer an ICS to support feasible solutions; in the sense of robustness and performance.
- To apply AAP based solutions.
- Select a jump start objective from the ACS; and use as template architecture blueprint.
- Build EAM microartefacts to support the architecture blueprint.
- Prepare *TRADf's* phase one and if successful, select a problem from the ACS to prove phase two.

Managing the Business Case

AAP instances are used by the ACS, which presents the possibilities on how to integrate an EAM, and is related to an insurance company named ArchiSurance (Trad & Kalpić, 2018f).

Integrating Critical Success Factors

A CSF and its KPI enumerations are measurable and mapped to a weightings that are roughly estimated in the RDP's first iteration and then tuned through ADM iterations, to support the EAM (Felfel, Ayadi, & Masmoudi, 2017; Trad & Kalpić, 2019d). The problem is how to define AAP goals, in order to integrate the EAM and how to interrelate the different business, ICS and other *Project's* components; where the ADM is the *Project's* skeleton.

The Architecture Development Method and Projects

This ADM supports *Projects'* integration and presents the influence of an AAP to support the EAM (Trad & Kalpić, 2019e). Currently, distributed intelligence, complexity, knowledge, economy, complex business models and technology; which are supported by a hyper-heuristics tree in the RDP's Phase 2 (Markides, 2015). *TRADf's* modules synchronize with the ADM, where the EAM and its internal components are interfaced with all ADM phases.

The Business Case Study for Architecture Critical Success Factors and the Link to the Next Section

Based on the CSF review and evaluation processes, the evaluation is done with the relation and influence of architecture on the EAM. The important CSFs that are used and processed by the DMS4EAM are presented in an associated chapter entitled: Business Transformation and Enterprise Architecture-The Resources Management Research and Development Process (RMSRDP) (Trad & Kalpić, 2019e); it is strongly recommended to refer to this chapter in order to understand the reasoning concept. Based on the CSF review process, the important business case's CSFs are used and evaluated as explained below.

In this chapter, the deductions are done by using the analysis of each CSA of a total of 5, where a *TRADf's* NLP script is used, in which all its CSFs are stored and appear in Table's 1 column. The *TRADf's* background scripts, calculate the weightings and ratings (known as the KPIs). KPI values originate from enumerated sets; and they are tuned and stored in column 2. This RDP proposes a standardized and automated manner to evaluate literature reviews that is an evolution in regard to the very subjective method. If the automated literature review's evaluation is successful, only then the experiment can be started. *TRADf* and its RDP, can automate complex RDPs in phase 1, and estimate the values for each selected KPI, as described in the in the associated works; on how to use CSA, CSF, KPI processing in RDPs (Trad, 2019a).

Table 1. The ACS's CSFs that have an average of 9.50

Critical Success Factors	KPIs		Weightings
CSF_RDP_Modelling	HighlyFeasible	▾	From 1 to 10. 09 Selected
CSF_RDP_Factors	PossibleClassification	▾	From 1 to 10. 10 Selected
CSF_RDP_References	AutomatedExists	▾	From 1 to 10. 09 Selected
CSF_RDP_ADM	IntegrationPossible	▾	From 1 to 10. 09 Selected
CSF_RDP_Technologies4iSASDev	AdvancedStage	▾	From 1 to 10. 09 Selected
CSF_RDP_Governance	Advanced	▾	From 1 to 10. 09 Selected
CSF_RDP_Transformation_iASbDMS	IntegrationPossible	▾	From 1 to 10. 10 Selected
CSF_RDP_Leading_TRADf	Possible	▾	From 1 to 10. 10 Selected

valuation

As shown in Table 1, the results justify (average of 9.50) the usage of the ACS in the final PoC (or phase 2). This process is applied to the next six CSAs and their tables. This section's results show clearly the uniqueness *TRADf* in integrating a standard ACS using a mapping structure; the closest comparable framework is TOGAF which does really tackle mapping that is the most complex topic (Trad, 2019a).

ASSET MANAGEMENT BASED TRANSFORMATION

Melvin Conway was cited that: "...organizations which design systems ... are constrained to produce designs which are copies of the communication structures of these organizations", where the EAM produces a set of artefacts based on CSFs that map to the organization's structure and its ICS (James, Grinter, & Grinter, 1999).

A loose AAP concept for EAMs development, is assisted by a holistic and a non-predictive DMS4EAM that depends CSFs, like the types of assets, financial situation, types of business, internal political influences, etc. A *Project* should be adapted to handle complex EAM requirements that can generate complex designs and eventual problems that can be the source of unpredictability... EAM problems can be measured and weighted; while its internal financial risks are not simply measurable. This explains the difficulty of estimating EAM investment risks of a consequential set of requirements. *TRADf* evaluates the EAM values using the DMS4EAM and the globally logged events; which enables prediction, proactive financial risk management; that are the basis of a holistic EAM model (Taleb, 2012).

Figure 4. The neural network enterprise architecture component tree (Capecchi, Buscema, Contucci, & D'Amore, 2010)

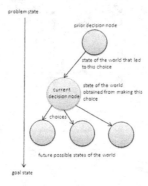

A Holistic Model

EAM's intelligence is a set of multiple coordinated intelligence models that correspond to various just-in-time processing schemes (Cearley, Walker, & Burke, 2016). Intelligence is a holistic human mental capability that combines the ICS and processing that coordinate and control various intelligence activities. Networked information coordination manages data, extracts and correlates them in space and time to detect heuristic patterns for various types of problem solving (Gardner, 1999). These heuristic patterns and their underlined semantics are used to generate sets of weightings for possible actions that are called intelligence artefacts in this research's *TRADf*. Weightings' concept enables the AAP to build an EAM that delivers solutions in the form of assets' management recommendations. In many cases, fast change requests may generate an important set of corresponding solutions that can be ambiguous and makes EAM actions uncertain and complex to implement. The AHMM4EAM is responsible for a rational heuristic approach for EAM problem solving. The EAM is based on a holistic systemic approach (Daellenbach & McNickle, 2005; Trad & Kalpić, 2016a). An EAM can give a company the most important competitive business advantages that may insure its future and it is not a secret that intelligent asset artefacts management are the basis of a successful *Project* (Trad, 2015a; Trad, 2015b). Major research and advisory firms like Gartner, confirm that asset services will leverage business information systems' components from various enterprise departments. Gartner confirms also that services are the dominating business enablers for Fortune 500 companies who need dynamic business intelligence support (Clark, Fletcher, Hanson, Irani, Waterhouse, & Thelin, 2013). AAP's building blocks are based on asset artefacts and services that use a light version of the ADM (Trad, 2015a). AAP is based on the simplification of the EA model, where the ADM is recommended to integrate various development environments like test driven development that is optimal for the management of various EAM's resources and CSFs (Trad & Kalpić, 2018a; Trad & Kalpić, 2018b).

Resources and CSFs

The one-to-one modelling concept is used to assemble the defined units and resources (or assets) of work. This modelling concept is used to manage autonomic AAP instances in the implementation phase; and it is based on a real world iterative model that maps all the EAMs resources in a sequential one-to-one manner that map to CSF (The Open Group, 2011a). The *Project* team has to identify the initial set of CSFs which reflect performance areas that map to strategic *project* goals. As shown in Figure 5, the *Project* must select the needed CSFs to prepare the *Project*; sets of CSFs are stored in CSAs. EAM's integration causes a major paradigm shift and is complex to implement.

Figure 5. The CSFs based framework

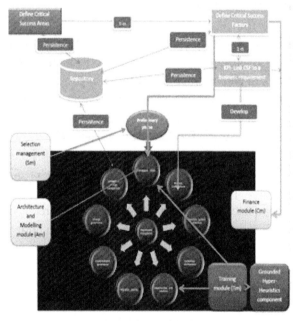

An EAM can give a company the most important competitive business advantages that may insure its future and it is not a secret that intelligent asset artefacts are the basis for such a system. Major research and advisory firms like Gartner, confirm that asset knowledge services will leverage ICS' components tangible and intangible assets from various enterprise departments.

Tangible and Intangible Assets

Tangible Assets

Tangible assets are mainly physical and measurable enterprise assets that are used in research, development and operations management (Murphy, 2019).

Intangible Assets

Intangible assets are nonphysical assets needed in *Projects*, for a long-term and mainly intellectual (knowledge) assets, and are difficult to evaluate them because of the uncertain outcome of *Projects* (Murphy, 2019).

The Role of Assets Management

A *Project* focuses on all aspects like, business transformation, assets management, business engineering, organizational design and enterprise architecture, where all these fields share some kind of choreography layer that is in turn based on microartefacts and one-to-one mapping relationships. A neural network perfectly corresponds to a heuristic tree that is an asset information management paradigm inspired by the biological nervous systems, such as the human brain. The key element of this paradigm is the novel structure of the EAM that is based on the AHMM4EAM. As already mentioned, the AHMM4EAM is composed of a large number of interconnected modules needed to solve specific *Project* and EAM problems, as shown in Figure 6. EAM units are connected to each other like nodes in a tree and there is a real number associated with each connection, which are called weightings used in EAM (Soft Expert, 2018).

Integrated Decision Making

EAM's integration process is supported by the DMS4EAM to support an agile approach to the enterprise's assets and their ADM interfacing (Trad & Kalpić, 2017a, 2017b, 2017c). AAP's structure is based on the following concepts:

Figure 6. Asset management system (Soft Expert, 2018)

- The asset object, which is a conceptual representation of its appearance and its internal functionalities.
- AHMM4EAM is an abstraction of the EAM structure.
- The EAM is a sub-system, responsible for processing, organizing or executing a set of asset related activities.
- The use of existing resources and credible references are prerequisites.

The AAP supports also classical assets' implementation constructs.

Proactive Financial Crimes Detection and Assets' Protection

FinTech Fraud

Using *TRADf, Project* teams can design the EAM that can handle various types of FinTech risks. FinTech would make money more abstract and difficult to trace. Institutions in some countries with the culture of financial secrecy and arbitral confiscation, would be tempted to use FinTech to obfuscate the origins of money, like in the concrete cases:

- Paula Ramada estimated the amount of lost money due to the benchmark of interest rates debacle is estimated at $300 trillion in financial instruments, ranging from mortgages to student loans. Where a trillion represents 1 billion of billions ($10^9 \times 10^9$) or 10^{18}. Therefore, a change or manipulation of a mere 0.1% has a damage of 10^{15} of euros per year; this is the mechanism that banks used to cover the decrease of loans and save their investments at the cost of ruining middle and lower-class households; whereby some banks like the

Swiss UBS got much richer (Ramada, 2013). FinTech would make such operations more embedded and abstract.

- FinTech is the technology that aims to change the traditional financial environment in the delivery of interactive financial services. The usage of intelligent financial endpoints provides some of the technologies intended to make financial services open to many external endpoints. Although FinTech can be used to tackle financial Cybercriminality, it seems that the countries that support massive financial irregularities are making the largest investment in these innovative technologies (Ravanetti, 2016). FinTech companies are transforming the usage of financial services using blockchains and Bitcoin-based technologies very probably for the mere goal of financial profit (Wikipedia, 2017a).

- Blockchains and Bitcoin, Blockchain is a FinTech framework that supports cryptocurrency like the Bitcoin; Bitcoin supports exchange of currencies in a digital encryption form. FinTech automation causes the synchronization of various Cyberfinance services that need specific laws, regulation and cybersecurity mechanisms, knowing that today the most important phenomena are Cybercriminality as an emerging type of Swiss banks' financial irregularities advanced criminality and on the other hand, the apparent disappearance of traditional currencies.

State, Collective Behavior and Culture Oriented Fraud

This section analyzes the notions of fraud organized by global an banks' financial irregularities, like the UBS, which a state in a state, managed by a state. Financial irregularities' tactics can be use to destroy its opponents' assets, and this fact is based on the following scenario:

- Banks, like the UBS, it is not just a bank, it the skeleton of a global financial system and closely related to the Swiss power apparatus.
- Due to the 2008 financial crisis, the Swiss government gives this bank with no return obligations 70 billions Swiss Francs, to help it out of the crisis…
- The Swiss UBS, in which 32 trillion US dollars are *hidden* in only one remote island, so how much has this so called bank illegally detain… (Stupples, Sazonov, & Woolley, 2019).
- The Swiss government ignores international claims on Fraud and even becomes a part of a state organized fraud … Like the tremendous anti-France fraude case…

Anti-Locked in Strategy

Predator's Lock In

This locked-in predator's model combines: 1) the power of (for example Swiss) law; 2) Too Big to Fail banks; 3) Banking secrecy; 4) Ultraliberal economy; 5) Rejection of local and global standards; and 6) A specific political environment. The banks and other Swiss financial institutions are under no supervision what so ever. That makes the country to become the financial industry protector that sets up fortifications against any possible intrusion; even if these institutions execute irregular and illegal activities.

Building Strategy

When building the financial structure of the *Project* team and enterprise architects must be cautious of the financial locked-in situation(s). Even though some predator countries (like Switzerland) offer an attractive financial and tax package, this country applies a legal and financial locked-in trap, it is an unwritten concept that can at any moment sweep out the business environment of its financial resources. This locked-in Swiss model combines: 1) the power of Swiss law; 2) Too Big to Fail banks; 3) Banking secrecy; 4) Ultraliberal economy; 5) Rejection of local and global standards; and 6) A specific political environment. The banks and other Swiss financial institutions are under no supervision what so ever. That makes the country to become the financial industry protector that sets up fortifications against any possible intrusion; even if these institutions execute irregular and illegal activities. The peak of such behavior is the Fraud scandal of UBS bank that was hit with a historic fine and the incredible delict was openly supported and protected by the Swiss Federal Court that makes the Swiss banks' financial irregularities a state model, protect by the law. Here a dilemma and a question can be asked, how such a country can be a synonym of honesty and anti-corruption… (Alderman, 2019; Tagliabuejune, 1986; Trad, & Kalpić, 2019b)

The Asset Management CSFs

Based on the literature review, the most important asset CSFs that are used are:

Table 2. The asset management CSFs

Critical Success Factors	KPIs		Weightings
CSF_AHMM4iASbDMS_TRADf_Integration	Feasible	▼	From 1 to 10. 09 Selected
CSF_AHMM4iASbDMS_InitialPhase	Stable	▼	From 1 to 10. 10 Selected
CSF_AHMM4iASbDMS_PoC	Feasible	▼	From 1 to 10. 09 Selected
CSF_AHMM4iASbDMS_Qualitative&Quantitative	Possible	▼	From 1 to 10. 09 Selected
CSF_AHMM4iASbDMS_Final_Instance	VerifiedModel	▼	From 1 to 10. 10 Selected
CSF_AHMM4iASbDMS_ADM_Integration	Synchronized	▼	From 1 to 10. 10 Selected
CSF_AHMM4iASbDMS_iSASDev_Interfacing	Stable	▼	From 1 to 10. 10 Selected

valuation

The Modules Chained Link to the Legal Aspects

This section's deduction is that the application of a mathematical model is central for the EAM subsystem in which the risks are mitigated.

THE APPLIED MATHEMATICAL MODEL

The AHMM4EAM for *Projects* and in this case the EAM, is based on various mathematical disciplines, development methods and engineering standards.

The Artefacts' Model

The AHMM4EAM nomenclature is presented to the reader in a simplified form to be easily understandable on the cost of a holistic formulation vision. The EAM uses the AHMM4EAM that is formalized as shown in Figure 7.

As shown in Figure 7, the symbol $\sum$ indicates summation of all the relevant named set members, while the indices and the set cardinality have been omitted. The summation should be understood in a broader sense, more like set union.

The Enterprise Mathematical Model

The AHMM4EAM is a part of the *TRADf* that uses service architecture to support the AAP and EAM. The AHMM4EAM is in this RDP, represented in a simplified form, and the symbol $\sum$ indicates the summation of all the relevant elements, while precise cardinality is omitted. The EAM's interfaces, as shown in Figure 8, is based on a light version of the ADM and is a part of the *TRADf* that uses services architecture.

Figure 7. The applied mathematical model's nomenclature (MID, 2014)

AMM

mcRequirement	= KPI	(1)
CSF	= Σ KPI	(2)
CSA	= Σ CSF	(3)
Requirement	= Σ mcRequirement	(4)
(e)neuron	= action + mcIntelligenceArtefact	(5)
mcArtefact	= Σ (e)neurons	(6)
mcEnterprise	= Σ mcArtefact	(7)
(e)Enterprise	= Σ mcEnterprise	(8)
mcArtefactScenario	= Σ mcArtefactDecisionMaking	(9)
IntelligenceComponent	= Σ mcArtefactScenario	(10)
OrganisationalIntelligence	= Σ IntelligenceComponent	(11)
AMM	= ADM + OrganisationalIntelligence	(12)

Figure 8. The architecture development method

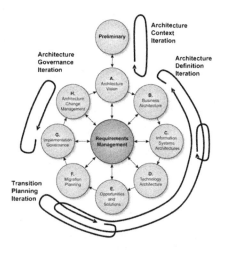

Services architecture enables agility, business benefits and infrastructure scalability. These facts can be formalized in a AHMM4EAM that needs a nomenclature, as shown in Figure 9.

The Enterprise AHMM4EAM (EAHMM4EAM) is the combination of an EA methodology and the AHMM4EAM that can be modelled after the following formula:

$$EAHMM4EAM = Enterprise\ Architecture + AHMM4EAM \tag{1}$$

Figure 9. The enterprise AHMM4EAM's nomenclature

Model's nomenclature

mcEnterprise	A micro enterprise component
mcRequirement	A micro requirement
mcArtefact	A microartefact
action (or action)	An atomic service (or neuron) execution scheme
mcIntelligenceArtefact	A set that contains: dynamic basic intelligence + governance + persistence+ traceability + data_xsd + resources
mcArtefactDecisionMaking	A microartefact_decision making entity
mcArtefactScenario	A microartefact scenario

The EAM Transformation Model

The transformation is the combination of an EA methodology and can be modelled using the following formula:

$$Project = EAHMM4EAM + IterationGap \tag{2}$$

The *Project's* model is based on a concurrent and synchronized infrastructure using threads that make various models run in parallel and exchange dynamically data through a scripting choreography.

Figure 10. Types of asset management (STS, 2018)

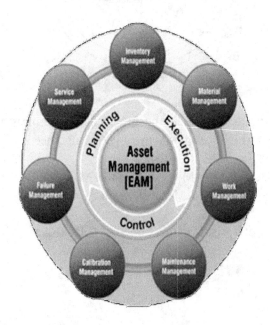

The Role of AHMM4EAM Choreography

A *Project* is related to: transformations, assets management, business engineering, organizational design and enterprise architecture; all these mentioned fields need choreography capability that in turn is based on a neural network based heuristic tree for microartefacts (Wikimedia Foundation, 2016). The AHMM4EAM is composed of a large number of interconnected neurons, to solve a specific EAM or other *Project* problems. EAM units are connected to each other, like nodes of a tree and there is a real number associated with each connection as shown in Figure 10, which are called weightings (Stergiou, & Siganos, 2015).

The Applied Mathematical Model's CSFs

Based on the literature review, the most important AHMM4EAM CSFs that were used are:

Table 3. The AHMM4EAM's CSFs

Critical Success Factors	KPIs	Weightings
CSF_iASbDMS_ACS_Modelling	Complex	From 1 to 10. 09 Selected
CSF_iASbDMS_ACS_Factors	PossibleClassification	From 1 to 10. 10 Selected
CSF_iASbDMS_ACS_References	Exists	From 1 to 10. 09 Selected
CSF_iASbDMS_ACS_ADM	IntegrationPossible	From 1 to 10. 10 Selected
CSF_iASbDMS_ACS_Technologies4iSASDev	AdvancedStage	From 1 to 10. 09 Selected
CSF_iASbDMS_ACS_Governance	Advanced	From 1 to 10. 09 Selected
CSF_iASbDMS_ACS_Transformation_TRADf	IntegrationPossible	From 1 to 10. 10 Selected
CSF_iASbDMS_ACS_Leading	Possible	From 1 to 10. 10 Selected

valuation

The Modules Chained link to the ICS's Integration

This section's deduction is that the EAM depends on the ICS which is the next section.

THE INFORMATION AND COMMUNICATION SYSTEM's INTEGRATION

Global or holistic enterprise agility is achieved by combining various methodologies to promote business and technological agility. Agility is applied to all the *Project's* levels (including EAM) to unbundle the existing business environment and glue its renovated parts using a dynamic ICS's microartefacts as shown in Figure 11. Using a bottom-up approach, the *Project* team can design the optimal ICS's integration concept that can handle various types of subsystems to be used in the standard ADM and technologies.

Figure 11. The information system's interaction with various modules

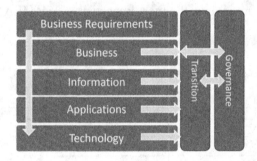

Internet of Things, Telecommunication and Infrastructure Control-the Glue

For EAM distributed communication, a standard from the Institute of Electrical and Electronic Engineers (IEEE) for an architectural framework for the Internet of Things (IoT) can be used. The standard is in its early stages and offers a reference model defining relationships among IoT assets related modules (BSI, 2015).

IoT and mobile infrastructure has expanded to interconnect endpoints of EAM based systems, to create a virtual and holistic environment. In these virtually interconnected EAMs, standard applications, endpoints and mobile apps collaborate in real-time, using standard technology procedures; using reference architecture blue-prints.

Figure 12. Internet supported services (BSI, 2015)

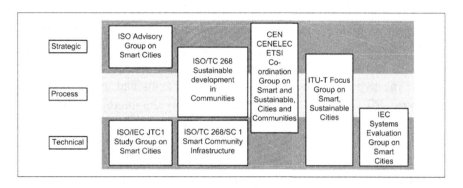

Reference Architecture and its Phases

The intent AAP's reference architecture is to support *Projects* with an implementation and vendor agnostic concept with enhanced interoperable and standards blueprint. Technological and implementation agnostic concept promotes: 1) avoiding locked-in concepts; 2) integrate various asset platforms; 3) certification and compliancy; 4) modularity; and 5) market structure agnostic concept. The ADM manages the *Project's* development iterations and its interaction with the EAM which care also for assets valuations (Trad, 2020e).

EAM's Architecture Blueprint

EAM uses standards that include EA frameworks, microartefacts interoperability… EAM standards are managed by the *TRADf*, which delivers added value, robustness and EA capabilities to establish an architecture principal guideline that defines the *Project's* initial phase and vision; which is based on a "just-enough" architecture (The Open Group, 2011a).

EAM's Standards

To manage agile *Projects* including EAM, an adequate mapping concept must integrate standards. The existing standards have the following levels: 1) strategic; 2) financial; 3) process; and 4) technical. These standards and tooling environments, support the *Projects* through an iterative pseudo-bottom-up approach. Without the use of AAP, a *Project* can: 1) siloed and poor performance; 2) lack scalability; 3) fail, become un-usable and un-maintainable; 4) fail in producing a successful distributed EAM.

Intelligent Static Assets

An intelligent reorganization of *Project*, if possible, makes it ready to integrate the local, regional and global economies, whatever that means. EAM systems are exponentially increasing in number and so the need to interface *Project* data and functions. The hyper-evolution of, new EAM scenarios and applications makes assets centric. IoT supportes scalable EAM; insuring the interoperability between natively incompatible automation technologies, ICS, various asset apps (Miori & Russo, 2014).

Architecture Development Method's Integration

The ADM integration in the EAM and *Project,* enables the automation of all their activities. The ADM encloses cyclic iterations; where all its phases log information to a unified logging system. EAM platforms are not dedicated to any specific business environment and offer information on: 1) assets performance; 2) reliability; and 3) assets security. AAP based platforms are controlled and monitored in real-time using unified logging subsystem and are integrated to support EAM interactions.

AAP's Microartefacts

The AAP expresses a structural concept or schema for *Projects'* implementations: 1) it offers a set of predefined AAP templates to instantiate EAM; 2) it describes their responsibilities and content of asset microartefacts known as items; 3) it defines the software artefacts for these EAM' modules; 4) it defines a EAM engineering model; and 5) it includes the description of the relationships between the different AAP templates. AAP components support the *Project* by offering items to handle various types of EAM endpoints. The usage of endpoints provides some of the mechanisms needed to make AAP tuneable with CSFs. Where an AAP microartefact is an instance of a building block that can interact with other *Project*s microartefacts in a traced and synchronized manner. A microartefact uses the ADM to assist in grouping of the needed services (The Open Group, 2011a). AAP includes microartefact scenarios of interactive atomic service actions. Atomic services make the integration flexible and granular (Trad & Kalpić, 2017a). The APP supports the EAM by offering microartefacts that are instances of financial building blocks.

The Financial Building Blocks

The EAM environment can handle various types of assets' management risks' mitigation, by using FinTech to deliver interactive financial services. The usage of intelligent financial endpoints provides some of the technologies intended to make EAM open to many assets' internal and external information endpoints (Ravanetti, 2016; Wikipedia, 2017a). The main danger effecting assets is organized Fintech fraud.

FinTech Fraud

FinTech transformations can make finance abstract and impossible to trace; institutions in some predator countries that have the culture of financial secrecy and arbitral confiscation. Such predators, would be tempted to use FinTech to obfuscate the origins of money. Paula Ramada estimated the amount of lost money due to the benchmark of interest rates debacle is estimated at $300 trillion in financial instruments, ranging from mortgages to student loans, where a trillion represents 1 billion of billions $(10^9 \times 10^9)$ or 10^{18}. Therefore, a change or manipulation of a mere 0.1% has a damage of $300 * 10^{15}$ of euros per year; this is the mechanism that banks used to cover the decrease of loans and save their investments at the cost of ruining middle and lower-class households; whereby some banks like the UBS got much richer (Ramada, 2013). FinTech would make such operations more embedded and abstract.

Electronic Payments and Finance

Projects use FinTech, to transform EAM, where automating economy and digitalization of financial services are fundamental by transforming the legacy asset sub-system. The evolution of FinTech, is un-linear in different environments. *Projects* need to transform the interaction with banks to automate crucial EAM services, as shown in Figure 13. The technology transformation of Deutsche Bank, Raiffeisenbank, Hana-Bank and Bank Group are good examples of such *Projects* (Makarchenko, Nerkararian & Shmeleva, 2016).

Figure 13. Financial services integration (Makarchenko, Nerkararian & Shmeleva, 2016)

Banking is changing ... with or without the banks. Response to the millennials. Financial services, (2015)
http://oracledigitalbank.com/resources/pdf/DBOF_Industry_Research_Report.pdf

	Important	**Current** capability	Market lag
Mobile device payments	94%	44%	-50%
Market Lag	92%	24%	
Real-time analytics	90%	30%	-60%
Digital advisory service	83%	28%	-55%
Location-driven services	82%	19%	-63%
Offers via social media	78%	34%	-44%
Comparison services based on financial profile	76%	28%	-48%
Social media account management	72%	14%	-58%
Gamification	72%	15%	-57%
Digital personal assistant	67%	12%	-55%

The Legal Aspects and Security Violations

The European commission defines a legislation to govern businesses and their assets; progress has been done in these fields. European commission's member states have implemented and enforced assets management national practices. EAM transactions resulted in value, have to be security, legally asserted, traced, and their periodic summaries are reported to the executive assets managers (Fu & Mittnight, 2015). Businesses and their assets are orthogonal to security requirements, where the business environment's roles define the responsibility for EAM. EAM's legal interests, resources, and accesses, should be managed by *Managers* who are assisted by an EA and a framework. Then, the enterprise structure can integrate assets assertion and access management related to Transaction's execution. The regulation for the transaction's security and law needs qualified time-stamps for robust certifications like those used in the European Union (European Union, 2014; Trad & Kalpić, 2016b).

International Law

The literature review showed that international law on EAM's security is inefficient and archaic. Avant-gardes countries are hesitant to implement EAM related international law that is based on the emergence of non-government norm-making initiatives. These states insist on their traditional central legal system that marginalizes the inter-state governance of the global sphere (Mačák, 2016; Trad & Kalpić, 2016a).

The Accounting Sub-system

The EAM should be supported by a multimodal accounting sub-system that minimizes the dependencies between various business partners with minimized risks (Jin & Zhu, 2011). An important MEA CSF that can be integrated, is the ratio of cost before and after *Project's* completion. *Project's* financial outcomes have to be controlled in real-time and reports must be delivered to the executive *Manager(s)*. The AAP supports automated accounting which uses mapping between EAM activities and the accounting subsystem, as shown in Figure 14 (Xiaohong, 2011).

The accounting sub-system, to support financial, asset management and accountancy activities.

The EAM uses an accounting sub-system for the following types of assets related operations:

- Support day-to-day operations.
- Transaction processing.
- Support the DMS4EAM.

Figure 14. The Accounting Subsystem structure (Xiaohong, 2011)

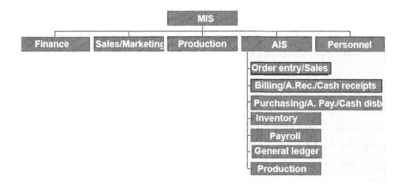

- Trend Analyses.
- Quantitative & Qualitative Data.
- Help fulfil Stewardship Role.

The ICS's CSFs.

Based on the literature review, the most important legal CSFs that are used are:

Figure 15. The Accounting Subsystem interactions (Xiaohong, 2011)

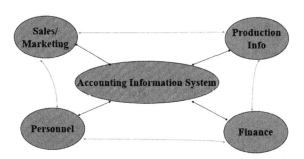

THE MODEL'S IMPLEMENTATION

EAM Design and Implementation

An important prerequisite for the EAM's implementation is the use of existing standards. EAM is to be assisted with existing standards like TOGAF, UML, etc…

These standards include microartefacts to be used to integrate EAM modules in the existing processes, like development and operations, ADM, etc.... The *Project's* main goal, is to support the business results; and that includes the management of EA changes in a synchronous manner to enable tracking and assessment of the underlying EAM (including AAP interfaces) modules.

The Proof of Concept

The PoC was built using the *TRADf* that had been developed using the Microsoft Visual Studio .NET. The PoC is based on the CSFs' binding to a specific research resources, where the EAM was prototyped using *TRADf*. The reasoning model represents the relationships between this RDP's requirements, microartefacts (or building blocks) and selected CSFs.

Table 4. The information system's CSFs

Critical Success Factors	HMM enhances: KPIs	Weightings
CSF_ICS_GUID_IntegrationProcessesModels	Standard	From 1 to 10. 09 Selected
CSF_ICS_TRADf_StandardsIntegration	AdvancedState	From 1 to 10. 10 Selected
CSF_ICS_aBB_Microartefacts	Supported	From 1 to 10. 10 Selected
CSF_ICS_Performance	Exists	From 1 to 10. 08 Selected
CSF_ICS_DistributedCommunication	Stable	From 1 to 10. 10 Selected
CSF_ICS_Finance	ExistingSupport	From 1 to 10. 09 Selected
CSF_ICS_Security	Complex	From 1 to 10. 08 Selected
CSF_ICS_Automation	Supported	From 1 to 10. 09 Selected
CSF_ICS_Pattern_StandardsIntegration	Supported	From 1 to 10. 09 Selected
CSF_ICS_Procedures	Supported	From 1 to 10. 10 Selected

valuation

PoC's interfaces were achieved using Microsoft Visual Studio .NET environment and the research framework that is shown in Figure 16. The EAM uses calls to AAP microartefacts as shown in Figure 17, to execute various actions related to assets.

CSFs were selected and evaluated (using the DMS4EAM) in this chapter's tables; and the results are illustrated in Table 5. Table 5, shows clearly that the EAM is not an independent component and in fact it is strongly bonded to the *Project's* overall risk architecture.

The model's main constraint is that CSAs having an average result below 7.5 will be ignored. This fact leaves the EAM's CSAs (marked in green) to make this work's conclusions; and drops the ICS's CSA marked in red, which means that the biggest challenge in a *Project* is the undulling process of the ICS.

Figure 16. The TRADf frontend

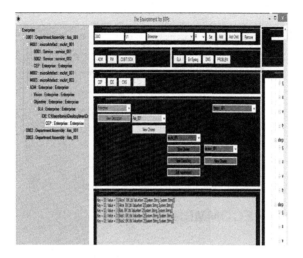

Figure 17. The research flow

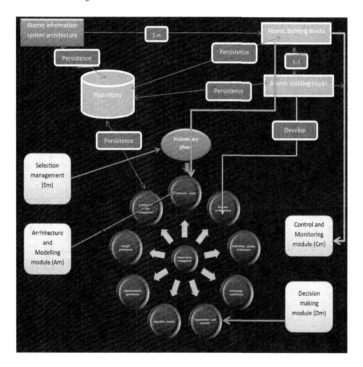

Table 5. The asset management research outcome

Critical Success Factors	HMM enhances: KPIs	Weightings
CSF_ADM_CSF_Initialization&Setup	Feasible	From 1 to 10. 10 Selected
CSF_ADM_aBB_IntegrationProcesses	Supported	From 1 to 10. 10 Selected
CSF_ADM_PhasesSynchronization	Supported	From 1 to 10. 10 Selected
CSF_ADM_Requirements	MappingAutomated	From 1 to 10. 10 Selected
CSF_ADM_Concept4i iASbDMS_Interface	Supported	From 1 to 10. 10 Selected

valuation

SOLUTION AND RECOMMENDATIONS

In this chapter, the authors propose the following set of EAM's architecture, technical and managerial recommendations:

- A *Project* must build a holistic EA concept in order to insure an efficient EAM.
- Enormous efforts must be applied to integrate underlying ICS to support a huge number of assets transactions. Here the main problem is the alignment, because ICSs are silos in reality.
- EAMs should replace traditional assets exchanges in order to improve accountability. By using AAPs interfacing.
- EAM should fit in the company's global EA framework; which is a very difficult task.
- The ADM's integration in an EAM and enables the automation of all its activities.
- Assets are orthogonal to security and legal requirements. Concepts must be built to avoid and block predators.
- Avoid any form of collaboration with doubtful financial and assets management organizations.

FUTURE RESEARCH DIRECTIONS

The *TRADf* future research will focus on the evolution of the system's intelligence.

CONCLUSION

This RDP phase is part of a series of publications related to *Project*s, EAM and EAs. This RDP is based on mixed AR model; where CSFs and areas are offered to help *Managers* to decrease the chances of failure. In this chapter, the focus is on the architecture of alignment of assets. EAM and EA alignment is architecture driven, where it describes a structured relationship between: assets, finance, technical and security solutions to support the long-term needs of the *Project*. The AAP supports EAM's integration in the end system. The most important recommendation that was generated by previous RDP phases was that the *Manager* must be an architect of adaptive business systems. In this chapter, the PoC is based on the CSFs' binding to a specific RDP resources, the DMS4EAM, RQ, and selected CSFs. The result is that EAM is feasible and the main complexity lies in ICS' transformation.

ACKNOWLEDGMENT

In a work as large as this research project, technical, typographical, grammatical, or other kinds of errors are bound to be present. Ultimately, all mistakes are the authors' responsibility. Nevertheless, the authors encourages feedback from readers identifying errors in addition to comments on the work in general. It was our great pleasure to prepare this work. Now our greater hopes are for readers to receive some small measure of that pleasure.

REFERENCES

Alderman, L. (2019). French Court Fines UBS $4.2 Billion for Helping Clients Evade Taxes. *The New York Times*. https://www.nytimes.com/2019/02/20/business/ubs-france-tax-cvasion.html

BSI. (2015). *Architectural framework for the Internet of Things, for Smart Cities*. BSI.

Capecchi, V., Buscema, M., Contucci, P., & D'Amore, D. (2010). *Applications of Mathematics in Models, Artificial Neural Networks and Arts: Mathematics and Society*. Springer Science & Business Media. doi:10.1007/978-90-481-8581-8

Cearley, D., Walker, M., & Burke, B. (2016). *Top 10 Strategic Technology Trends for 2017*. Gartner, ID: G00317560. https://www.gartner.com/doc/3471559?plc=ddp

Clark, M., Fletcher, P., Hanson, J., & Irani, R. (2013). *Web Services Business Strategies and Architectures*. Apress.

Daellenbach, H., McNickle, D., & Dye, Sh. (2012). *Management Science - Decision-making through systems thinking* (2nd ed.). Palgrave Macmillan.

Easterbrook, S., Singer, J., Storey, M., & Damian, D. (2008). *Guide to Advanced Empirical Software Engineering-Selecting Empirical Methods for Software Engineering Research* (F. Shull, Ed.). Springer.

European Union (2014). Regulation (EU) No 910/2014 of the European Par lament and of the Council - on electronic identification and trust services for electronic transactions in the internal market and repealing Directive 1999/93/EC The European Par lament and of the Council – Regulation. European Union.

Felfel, H., Ayadi, O., & Masmoudi, F. (2017). Pareto Optimal Solution Selection for a Multi-Site Supply Chain Planning Problem Using the VIKOR and TOPSIS Methods. *International Journal of Service Science, Management, Engineering, and Technology*. Doi:10.4018/IJSSMET.2017070102

Fu, Zh., & Mittnight, E. (2015). Critical Success Factors for Continually Monitoring, Evaluating and Assessing Management of Enterprise IT. *ICSACA*. https://www.isaca.org/COBIT/focus/Pages/critical-success-factors-for-continually-monitoring-evaluating-and-assessing-management-of-enterprise-it.aspx

Gardner, H. (1999). *Intelligence Reframed: Multiple Intelligences for the 21st Century*. Basic Books.

Gunasekare, U. (2015). *Mixed Research Method as the Third Research Paradigm: A Literature Review*. University of Kelaniya.

James, D., Grinter, H., & Grinter, R. (1999). Splitting the Organization and Integrating the Code: Conway's Law Revisited. Bell Laboratories, Lucent Technologies. *Proceedings, International Conference on Software Engineering*, 85-95.

Jonkers, H., Band, I., & Quartel, D. (2012a). *ArchiSurance Case Study*. The Open Group.

Joseph, Ch. (2014). *Types of eCommerce Business Models*. https://smallbusiness.chron.com/types-ecommerce-business-models-2447.html

Mačák, K. (2016). *Is the International Law of Cyber Security in Crisis? Law School-University of Exeter*. In 8th International Conference on Cyber Conflict. NATO CCD COE Publications.

Makarchenko, M., Nerkararian, S., & Shmeleva, S. (2016). How Traditional Banks Should Work in Smart City. *Communications in Computer and Information Science*. 10.1007/978-3-319-49700-6_13

Markides, C. C. (2015). Research on Business Models: Challenges and Opportunities. *Advances in Strategic Management, 33*, 133–147. doi:10.1108/S0742-332220150000033004

MID. (2014). *Enterprise Architecture Modeling with ArchiMate.* MID GmbH.

Miori, V., & Russo, D. (2014). Domotic Evolution towards the IoT. *IEEE 28th International Conference on Advanced Information Networking and Applications Workshops.* DOI: 10.1109/WAINA.2014.128

Murphy, Ch. (2019). *How do tangible and intangible assets differ?* Investopedia.

Peterson, S. (2011). *Why it Worked: Critical Success Factors of a Financial Reform Project in Africa.* Faculty Research Working Paper Series. Harvard Kennedy School.

Ramada, P. (2013). *How much did allegedly rigged interest rate (Libor) cost?* Academic Press.

Ravanetti, A. (2016). Switzerland Bank on Fintech with Lighter Regulations. *Crowd Valley.* https://news.crowdvalley.com/news/switzerland-bank-on-fintech-with-lighter-regulations

Soft Expert. (2018). *Enterprise Asset Management.* https://www.softexpert.com/solucao/enterprise-asset-management-eam/

Stergiou, Ch., & Siganos, D. (2015). *Neural Networks.* https://www.doc.ic.ac.uk/~nd/surprise_96/journal/vol4/cs11/report.html

STS. (2018). Enterprise asset management. *STS.* http://www.stsolutions-global.com/enterprise-asset-management.html

Stupples, B., Sazonov, A., & Woolley, S. (2019). UBS Whistle-Blower Hunts Trillions Hidden in Treasure Isles. *Bloomberg.* https://www.bloomberg.com/news/articles/2019-07-26/ubs-whistle-blower-hunts-trillions-hidden-in-treasure-islands

Tagliabuejune, J. (1986). The Swiss stop keeping secrets. *The New York Times.* https://www.nytimes.com/1986/06/01/business/the-swiss-stop-keeping-secrets.html

Taleb, N. (2012). *Antifragile: things that gain from disorder. Library of congress catalogging-in-publication data.* Academic Press.

The Open Group. (2011a). Architecture Development Method. *The Open Group.* https://pubs.opengroup.org/architecture/togaf9-doc/arch/chap05.html

Thomas, A., & Gartner, A. (2015). *Innovation Insight for Microservices.* https://www.gartner.com/doc/3157319/innovation-insight-microservices

Tidd, J. (2006). *From Knowledge Management to Strategic Competence* (2nd ed.). Imperial College. doi:10.1142/p439

Trad, A. (2015a). *A Transformation Framework Proposal for Managers in Business Innovation and Business Transformation Projects-Intelligent atomic building block architecture*. Centeris. doi:10.1016/j.procs.2015.08.483

Trad, A. (2015b). *A Transformation Framework Proposal for Managers in Business Innovation and Business Transformation Projects-An information system's atomic architecture vision*. Centeris.

Trad, A. (2018a). *The Business Transformation Framework's Resources Library. Internal project*. IBISTM.

Trad, A. (2018b). *The Transformation Framework Proof of Concept. Internal project and paper*. IBISTM.

Trad, A. (2018c). The Transformation Framework's Resources Library. IBICSTM.

Trad, A. (2018d). *The Transformation Framework Proof of Concept*. IBICSTM.

Trad, A. (2019a). *Applied Mathematical Model for Business Transformation Projects-The intelligent Strategic Decision Making System (iSDMS). Encyclopaedia*. IGI-Global.

Trad, A. (2019b). *An Applied Mathematical Model for Business Transformation and Enterprise Architecture-The Holistic Organisational Intelligence and Knowledge Management Pattern's Integration (HOI&KMPI). International Journal of Organisational and Collective Intelligence*.

Trad, A. (2019c). *Using Google analytics to determine the leading business transformation framework that are based on enterprise architecture*. IBISTM.

Trad, A. (2020b). *The Business Transformation Enterprise Architecture Framework as an Applied Mathematical Model: intelligent Atomic Service based Decision Making Systems (iASbDMS)*. IGI Global.

Trad, A. (2020c). *The Business Transformation Enterprise Architecture Framework as an Applied Mathematical Model: intelligent Strategic Atomic Service Development (iSASDev)*. IGI Global.

Trad, A. (2020d). *The Business Transformation and Enterprise Architecture Framework as an Applied Mathematical Model-The Financial Risk Management with a Strategic Vision (FRMSV)*. IGI Global.

Trad, A. (2020e). *Business Transformation and Enterprise Architecture – The Holistic Project Asset Management Concept (HPAMC).* IGI Global.

Trad, A., & Kalpić, D. (2016a). *A Transformation Framework Proposal for Managers in Business Innovation and Business Transformation Projects - The role of transformation managers in organisational engineering.* Chinese American Scholars Association Conference E-Leader.

Trad, A., & Kalpić, D. (2016b). The Business Transformation Framework and its Business Engineering Law support for Cybertransactions. In Encyclopedia of E-Commerce Development, Implementation, and Management. IGI-Global.

Trad, A., & Kalpić, D. (2017a). *An Intelligent Neural Networks Micro Artefact Patterns' Based Enterprise Architecture Model.* IGI-Global.

Trad, A., & Kalpić, D. (2017b). *A Neural Networks Portable and Agnostic Implementation TRADf for Business Transformation Projects. The Basic Structure.* IEEE.

Trad, A., & Kalpić, D. (2017c). *A Neural Networks Portable and Agnostic Implementation TRADf for Business Transformation Projects. The Framework.* IEEE.

Trad, A., & Kalpić, D. (2018a). Business Transformation Projects-An Enterprise Architecture Applied Mathematical Model / The Basics. *IEEE, CPS, Conference on Applied Mathematics & Computer Science. IEEE, International Conference on Applied Mathematics and Computer Science.*

Trad, A., & Kalpić, D. (2018b). *Business Transformation Projects An Enterprise Architecture Applied Mathematical Model's-The Proof of Concept.* ICAMCS Conference. 10.1109/ICAMCS46079.2018.00015

Trad, A., & Kalpić, D. (2019d). *Business Transformation and Enterprise Architecture-The Resources Management Research and Development Project (RMSRDP). Encyclopaedia.* IGI-Global.

Trad, A., & Kalpić, D. (2019e). *Business Transformation and Enterprise Architecture-The Holistic Project Resources Management Pattern (HPRMP). Encyclopaedia.* IGI-Global.

Trad, A., & Kalpić, D. (2019f). *Business Transformation and Enterprise Architecture-The Resources Management Implementation Concept (RMIC).* IGI-Global.

Trad, A., & Kalpić, D. (2019g). The Business Transformation Framework and the-Application of a Holistic Strategic Security Concept. E-leaders, Check Rep. GCASA.

Trad, A., & Kalpić, D. (2020a). *Using Applied Mathematical Models for Business Transformation*. IGI Global. doi:10.4018/978-1-7998-1009-4

Xiaohong, C. (2011). *Research on E-Commerce Transaction Cost-Benefit Characteristics and Evaluation Approaches*. Management and Service Science (MASS), *2011 International Conference*. Wuhan. China.

ADDITIONAL READING

Capgemini. (2007). *Trends in Business transformation - Survey of European Executives*. Capgemini Consulting and the Economist Intelligence Unit. France.

Farhoomand, A. (2004). *Managing (e)business transformation*. Palgrave Macmillan. doi:10.1007/978-1-137-08380-7

IBM. (2009). TOGAF or not TOGAF: Extending Enterprise Architecture beyond RUP. IBM Developer Works.

KEY TERMS AND DEFINITIONS

Manager: Business transformation manager.
Project: Business transformation project.

Chapter 2

The Use of an Enterprise Architecture Framework to Guide the Management of Big Data in Health Organisations

Monica Nehemia
Cape Peninsula University of Technology, South Africa

Tandokazi Zondani
ⓘ https://orcid.org/0000-0003-0906-2593
Cape Peninsula University of Technology, South Africa

ABSTRACT

Big data has gained popularity in recent years, with increased interest from both public and private organisations including academics. The automation of business processes led to the proliferation of different types of data at various speeds through information systems. Big data is generated at a high rate from multiple sources that can become complex to manage with challenges to collect, manipulate, and store data with traditional IS/IT. Big data has been associated with technical non-technical challenges. Due to these challenges, organisations deploy enterprise architecture as an approach to holistically manage and mitigate challenges associated with business and technology. An exploratory study was done to determine how EA could be used to manage big data in healthcare facilities. This study employs the interpretive approach with documentation as the analysis. Findings were governance, internal and external big data sources, information technology infrastructure development, and big data skills. Through the different EA domains, big data challenges could be mitigated.

DOI: 10.4018/978-1-5225-8229-8.ch002

INTRODUCTION

Many organisations are structured into different divisions and units of distinctive functionalities and mandates. In achieving their objectives, information systems and information technology (IS/IT) are deployed (developed and implemented) to automate business processes, and ultimately render effective and efficient services to its stakeholders (Muladi & Surendro, 2014). This has increased organisations dependence on IS/IT for organisational processes and activities. Van Zijl and Van Belle (2014) posit that IS/IT is an essential part of an organisation. The automation of business operations is one aspect of the essentiality, which leads to the proliferation of large amounts of digital information that is accessible through IS/IT (McAfee, *et al.,* 2012).

Through established organisational functions, different datasets with different sizes are generated from the business operations. Recently, organisational datasets are increasingly generated in varying formats and sizes (Lnenicka & Komarkova, 2019). In the health sector, big data is generated at high volume and rate from multiple sources, which makes it complex to the organisation to manage (Wang, Kung, & Byrd, 2018). This type of data is referred to as big data, and according to Park, Nguyen and Won (2015), big data is hard to collect, manipulate and store with traditional IS/IT. The size of big data is expressed in petabytes and exabyte's, which is challenging to store, manage and analyse by an average database tools and software (Wang, Kung, & Byrd, 2018).

The challenge is also based on the need to integrate the big data from the core business functions. Lnenicka and Komarkova (2019), posits that the combination of quantity, varying source and unstructured data can lead to technology challenges. It is imperative for IS/IT to be deployed holistically in order to ensure cost effective and sustainable solutions for the organisation over an extended period. Without a holistic view of the organisation's data needs, technical solutions can be deployed in isolation. Enterprise architecture (EA) is an approach employed by organisations to holistically manage and mitigate challenges associated with business and technology (Ahmadi et al., 2019). EA is developed to manage organisational complexities that exist between different departments that need to share the same equipment (Lapalme et al., 2016). In addition, EA is used to control and guide the installation of IS/IT based on business needs in order to fulfil the organisation's objectives (Shaanika & Iyamu, 2015). EA is also used to improve the management of complicated business processes and IS/IT in the organisation (Lapalme et al., 2016)

The aim of this paper is to explore how EA can be used manage big data in organisations. The paper will be organised as follows: section two presents literature review on big data and EA. Section three covers the research approach, followed by the analysis and findings. In section five, the guide of EA using big data will be presented. The research is concluded in section six.

RELATED WORK

From the context of this study, a review of literature was conducted on big data in health organisation and EA.

Big Data

Big data emanates from data generated at a rapid rate, exceeding ranges and boundaries that are not regarded as normal in the computing and digital world. Andreu-Perez et al. (2015), posits that big data is characterised by 6V's, value, volume, velocity, variety, veracity and variability. Big data can be unstructured data that is not traditionally database-driven, and derived from multiple sources such as images, videos, documents and audio to mention a few (Zakir et al., 2015). Likewise, big data in healthcare is derived from numerous, large and complex data, which is challenging to analyse and manage with traditional computation (Kankanhalli et al., 2016). Big data is not only restricted to data alone, but includes the associated technology (Oguntimilehin & Ademola, 2014). Hence, the benefit of big data is in its analytics because through computational analysis, big data can reveal new information and value that organisations can use for competitive advantage.

Big data analytics has the benefit of revealing valuable information from complex data, which is difficult to produce without the analytics (Mehat & Pandit, 2018). In healthcare, big data is generated from its clinical and medical operations (Mehta & Pandit, 2018), with big analytics benefits such as increased data availability, improved patient results and healthcare quality can be realised (Lee & Yoon, 2017). Organisations use big data for different reasons, Kangelani and Iyamu (2018) resonates that big data is used to give organisation a comprehension of the data that can assist to forecast the future. Halawe and Massry (2015) on the other hand, claim that big data can assist organisations achieve competitive advantage. In addition, big data has the reputation of producing reliable and correct information after analysis (Oguntimilehin & Ademola, 2014).

Even though big data analysis is associated with many opportunities, it is also associated with challenges in all business fields. Big data is regarded to be complex, because it needs specialized IS/IT equipment and tools for management and analysis. In the same lines, Zaharia et al. (2016), posits that big data is associated with computational challenges. In this context, the complexity to manage big data is based on the fact that traditional computation, storage, IS/IT and methods for data management have become inadequate (Lnenicka & Komarkova, 2019; Tian & Zhao, 2015). Big data is also associated with common technical challenges such as data replication systems, security loopholes as well as non-technical challenges such as data governance and policy establishment (Halaweh & Massry, 2015).

Even though there are tools and technologies in place to address big data challenges, non-techinal factors can still pose as a challenge. Enterprise architecture is an approach deployed to mitigate IS/IT challenges and management in organisations. Supriadi, Kom, and Amalia (2019) defines EA as a conceptual plan of the operation and structure of an organisation. EA enhances the adoption and use of IT solutions in improving organisational performance.

Enterprise Architecture

EA is considered critical in an organisation because it is used for planning and coordinating both the business activities and IT activities (Masuda et al., 2018). According to Bakar and Hussien (2018), EA is a methodology that links the strategy development to strategy execution, achieved with the utilisation of IS/IT, human resources, business processes and the organisation's structure. EA is employed to analyse the current operations in the organisation in order to improve its performance. Kasemsap (2018), suggests that EA enhances the adoption and use of IT solutions in improving organisational performance. In addition, EA improves the efficiency and effectiveness of processes and activities within institutions (Iyamu & Mphahlele, 2014).

EA is also defined as a tool that is used to manage the complexities between business and its information systems (Lapalme et al., 2016). Some of the IS/IT solutions deployed are associated with complexities, making it hard for organisations to realise the benefits of these deployments. The complexities in the organisation are but one of the main driving factors for the use of EA (Al-Kharusi *et al.*, 2017). The associated big data challenges can be eliminated with the use of EA in the organisation. Kasemsap (2018), asserts that EA enhances the adoption and use of IT solutions in improving organisational performance. Benefits such as reduced IS/IT deployment costs, improved business processes, better decisions and improved IT systems have been reported associated with the deployment of EA (Plessius et al., 2018). Aier (2014), claims that organisation that have developed EA effectively enjoys a stable and flexible environment, which are significant benefits.

In managing the big data in an organisation, EA implements the suggestion of a systematic approach of handling and altering organisations in the digital economy where business is hugely reliant on IS/IT (Kudryavtsev et al., 2017). According to Iyamu (2019:1) *"EA is estimated to guide an organisation's practices, such as technology infrastructure management, business process design and information governance, toward sustainability and competitiveness*". EA helps to establish a blueprint of the entire business and technology strategies and objectives and helps to provide a holistic view of the organisational structure (Du Preez et al., 2018).

EA is made up of architectural domains, which covers technical and non-technical activities in an organisation (Iyamu, 2019). EA consits of enterprise business architecture (EBA), enterprise information architecture (EIA), enterprise applications architecture(EAA), and the enterprise technical architecture (ETA) (Chalmeta & Pazos, 2015). Activities are deployed through these domains, to ensure that all departments in the organisation are covered. Shaanika and Iyamu (2018), explain that the technincal and non-technical elements in the organisatio are structured.

RESEARCH APPROACH

This study follows the interpretivist approach, which allows the researcher to have a subjective understanding of the study. Bryman and Bell (2015), posits that interpretivism concerns about the understanding of human actions. Additionally, interpretivism research accommodates different perspectives of reality. Subsequently, the qualitative method was used. Qualitative methods allow researchers to establish a subjective view of the subject, based on the views and opinions of the participants (Kornbluh, 2015). The intention of these methodology is to fulfill the question of the study (i) to investigate the sources of big data, (ii) identify the challenges associated with big data in healthcare facilities (iii), and to explore how EA can be used manage of big data in organisations.

This study also applied the documentation technique for collecting peer-reviewed documents. Documentation was used for data analysis, which is referred to as secondary data analysis. Johnston (2017) refers to secondary data analysis as data that was collected prior for another objective. Documents were searched and gathered from the scholastic databases: IEEE Xplore, Science Direct, AIS, EBSCO and Google Scholar. The search criteria for the documents were done using the following keywords: Big Data and Healthcare. The second criterion was for documents published between 2010 until 2020, which will allow the researcher to collect the latest articles with findings on the subject matter.

A total of 52 documents were collected and thorough scanning was applied to select the most suitable documents. From the existing literature, the following concepts were described: big data source in healthcare, and big data challenges within healthcare. The interpretivist approach was used for data analysis, allowing the researcher to apply subjective analysis. The qualitative method was appropriate because the research intends to solicit information that is based on human perception, such as the challenges experienced with big data. The source and challenges of big data can be affected by human perceptions and views, as described by Berger (2015).

RESULTS AND FINDINGS

In order to achieve the objectives of this study, the articles were structured and grouped according to its content. Two groups were established, the Sources of Big Data and Challenges of Big Data.

Sources of Big Data

The healthcare facilities have multiple stakeholders with interactions that allow sharing of big data. Rouse and Serban (2014), claim that healthcare data is distributed because it comes from different sources. Organisations have different types of IS/IT solutions deployed that sometimes produce different type of data sets. Data gathered from different sources collectively attribute to big data. Administrative databases and electronic health records are regarded as the primary big data source in the healthcare facility. Nedelcu (2013), posits that based on the dimension of data source, data is distinguished as internal data (gathered within the organisation) and external data (gathered from sources outside the organisation).

Challenges of Big Data

Challenges that are not mitigated can hamper the successful deployment of big data, and these challenges can be technical or non-technical factors. Integration of data is a challenge because some of the big data is sourced from various stakeholders each with different datasets (Auffray, et al., 2016). This can even be worsened if the IT infrastructure is not well deployed in the organisation. Fodeh and Zeng (2016), resonates that IT infrastructure is the main challenge for the successful deployment of big data. If these challenges are not mitigated, it can hamper the successful realisation of big data in health facilities.

The preparedness for the use of big data is also a challenge. Zhang et al. (2015), posits that the transition from the use of paper-based records to digital records is a challenge. Likewise, the necessary skills are required that can translate the results from big data. Privacy of health records is a serious factor to be considered when records are shared amongst stakeholders. According to Wu et al. (2016), there is a concern between the different stakeholders that needs to share health records.

BIG DATA EA MANAGEMENT

After the analysis, four factors were identified to have an effect on the design of the framework. The factors identified were governance, big data internal and external sources, information technology infrastructure development and big data skills. Each of these factors makes a difference. The factors are discussed as follows.

Governance

Though governance, standards and policies are established to manage and control services such as big data. Challenges such as privacy are better enforced when governance and policies are established. Privacy in the organisation is a serious factor that needs to be documented and governed seriously. Tungela, Mutudi and Iyamu (2018) resonates that healthcare data is very sensitivity making it a critical element in the healthcare sector. Governance serves as a guide for the operation in the organisation. In addition, the policies and standards set in the organisation will be able to eliminate the challenge experienced with different types of data sets received from healthcare stakeholders. Organisations have deployed EA for the benefit of having a holistic overview of the organisations. Elements of governance and policies, processes and IS/IT are all included in the EA approach.

Big Data Internal and External Sources

Health facilities have many different stakeholders. Some of these stakeholders are internal to the healthcare facility and some of them are external. Frequent communication and interaction exists between these stakeholders in different forms. However, the data sets shared amongst these organisations are not consistent, making integration a challenge. These challenges can be mitigated if policies, standards and guidelines are developed and shared with all stakeholders. Enterprise business architecture (EBA) is one of the EA domains that provide services to the stakeholder, so that they can interact and collaborate in an effective way. Challenges experienced with the stakeholders can be mitigated with the use of EBA.

Information Technology Infrastructure Development

Information system and technology infrastructure is deployed in organisation as an enabler of digital services. However, the deployment of the technical infrastructure can be a challenge if not managed well. Governance and standardisation are some of the important factors to be considered for the deployment of IT infrastructure. Lack of standardisation can complicate the infrastructure deployment, which can lead to isolated infrastructure that does not serve the objective of organisation. Enterprise technical architecture (ETA), as a domain of EA can be deployed to serve as a guide through policies for choices of IS/IT deployment in an organisation (Giachetti, 2016). Through ETA healthcare services can be stable and reliable.

Big Data Skills

The value of big data can only be realised after analysis and interpretation has been done on the data. Consequently, specialised skills are needed for this exercise. The deployment of big data is associated with specialised skills in order to realise its value. A lack of big data specialised skills will derail the usefulness of big data. It is imperative that development of specialised skills be treated as a strategic decision for the healthcare facility, because it is very critical for the business. Since EA is an approach that encompass all elements in the organisation. The aspect of specialised skills will

CONCLUSION

An exploratory study was done to determine how EA could manage big data in healthcare industry. Even though big data in healthcare is associated with many benefits, it is also marred with challenges. These challenges can be both technical and non technical. EA is an approach to mitigate. Through the findings from the analysis, it was theoretical proven how the different domains of EA can manage the challenges. A follow-up study to develop an EA framework to manage big data is encouraged.

REFERENCES

Ahmadi, H., Farahani, B., Aliee, F., & Motlagh, M. (2019). Cross-layer Enterprise Architecture Evaluation: an approach to improve the evaluation of enterprise architecture TO-BE plan. In *Proceedings of COINS conference. COINS* (pp. 1-6). Crete, Greece: ACM. doi:10.1145/3312614.3312659

Aier, S. (2014). The role of organisation culture for grounding, management, guidance and effectiveness of enterprise architecture principles. *Information Systems and e-Business Management*, *12*(1), 43–70. doi:10.100710257-012-0206-8

Auffray, C., Balling, R., Barroso, I., Bencze, L., Benson, M., Bergeron, J., Bernal-Delgado, E., Blomberg, N., Bock, C., Conesa, A., Del Signore, S., Delogne, C., Devilee, P., Di Meglio, A., Eijkemans, M., Flicek, P., Graf, N., Grimm, V., Guchelaar, H.-J., ... Zanetti, G. (2016). Making sense of big data in health research: Towards an EU action plan. *Genome Medicine*, *8*(1), 71. doi:10.118613073-016-0323-y PMID:27338147

Berger, R. (2015). Now I see it, now I don't: Researcher's position and reflexivity in qualitative research. *Qualitative Research*, *15*(2), 219–234. doi:10.1177/1468794112468475

Bryman, A., & Bell, E. (2015). *Business research methods*. Oxford University Press.

Chalmeta, R., & Pazos, V. (2015). A step-by-step methodology for enterprise interoperability projects. *Enterprise Information Systems*, *9*(4), 436–464. doi:10.1 080/17517575.2013.879212

Du Preez, J., Van der Merwe, A., & Matthee, M. (2018). Understanding Enterprise Architects: Different Enterprise Architect Behavioral Styles. *International Conference on Research and Practical Issues of Enterprise Information Systems*, 96-108. 10.1007/978-3-319-99040-8_8

Fodeh, S., & Zeng, Q. (2016). Mining Big Data in biomedicine and health care. *Journal of Biomedical Informatics*, *63*, 400–403. doi:10.1016/j.jbi.2016.09.014 PMID:27670091

Giachetti, R. E. (2016). *Design of enterprise systems: Theory, architecture, and methods*. CRC Press. doi:10.1201/9781439882894

Iyamu, T. (2018). Implementation of the enterprise architecture through the Zachman Framework. *Journal of Systems and Information Technology*, *20*(1), 2–18. doi:10.1108/JSIT-06-2017-0047

Iyamu, T. (2019). What are the implications of theorising the enterprise architecture? *Journal of Enterprise Transformation*, 1-22.

Iyamu, T., & Mgudlwa, S. (2018). Transformation of healthcare big data through the lens of actor network theory. *International Journal of Healthcare Management*, *11*(3), 182–192. doi:10.1080/20479700.2017.1397340

Johnston, M.P. (2017). Secondary data analysis: A method of which the time has come. *Qualitative and Quantitative Methods in Libraries*, *3*(3), 619-626.

Kangelani, P., & Iyamu, T. (2020, April). A Model for Evaluating Big Data Analytics Tools for Organisation Purposes. In *Conference on e-Business, e-Services and e-Society* (pp. 493- 504). Springer.

Kankanhalli, A., Hahn, J., Tan, S., & Gao, G. (2016). Big data and analytics in healthcare: Introduction to the special section. *Information Systems Frontiers*, *18*(2), 233–235. doi:10.100710796-016-9641-2

Kaur, M. J., & Mishra, V. P. (2018, November). Analysis of Big Data Cloud Computing Environment on Healthcare Organisations by implementing Hadoop Clusters. In 2018 Fifth HCT Information Technology Trends (ITT) (pp. 87-90). IEEE.

Kornbluh, M. (2015). Combatting Challenges to Establishing Trustworthiness in Qualitative Research. *Qualitative Research in Psychology*, *12*(4), 397–414. doi:10 .1080/14780887.2015.1021941

Kudryavtsev, D. V., Zaramenskikh, E. P., & Arzumanyan, M. Y. (2017). Development of enterprise architecture management methodology for teaching purposes. *Open Education*, *4*(4), 84–92. doi:10.21686/1818-4243-2017-4-84-92

Lapalme, J., Gerber, A., Van der Merwe, A., Zachman, J., De Vries, M., & Hinkelmann, K. (2016). Exploring the future of enterpirese architecure: A Zachman perspecive. *Computers in Industry*, *79*, 103–113. doi:10.1016/j.compind.2015.06.010

Lee, C. H., & Yoon, H. J. (2017). Medical big data: Promise and challenges. *Kidney Research and Clinical Practice*, *36*(1), 3–11. doi:10.23876/j.krcp.2017.36.1.3 PMID:28392994

Lnenicka, M., & Komarkova, J. (2019). Developing a government enterprise architecture framework to support the requirements of big and open linked data with the use of cloud computing. *International Journal of Information Management*, *46*, 124–141. doi:10.1016/j.ijinfomgt.2018.12.003

McAfee, A., Brynjolfsson, E., Davenport, T. H., Patil, D. J., & Barton, D. (2012). Big Data: The management revolution. *Harvard Business Review*, *90*(10), 60–68. PMID:23074865

Mehta, N., & Pandit, A. (2018). Concurrence of big data analytics and healthcare: A systematic review. *International Journal of Medical Informatics*, *114*, 57–65. doi:10.1016/j.ijmedinf.2018.03.013 PMID:29673604

Mohammed, E. A., Far, B. H., & Naugler, C. (2014). Applications of the MapReduce programming framework to clinical big data analysis: Current landscape and future trends. *BioData Mining*, *7*(1), 22. doi:10.1186/1756-0381-7-22 PMID:25383096

Muladi, N., & Surendro, K. (2014). The Readiness Self-Assessment Model for Green IT Implementation in Organisations. *International Conference of Advanced Informatics: Concept, Theory and Application*, 146-151.

Nedelcu, B. (2013). About big data and its challenges and benefits in manufacturing. *Database System Journal*, *4*(3), 10–19.

Negara, J. G. P., & Emanuel, A. W. R. (2020, May). Enterprise Architecture Design Strategies for UGK Using TOGAF ADM. In *1st Borobudur International Symposium on Humanities, Economics and Social Sciences (BIS-HESS 2019)* (pp. 491-495). Atlantis Press. 10.2991/assehr.k.200529.103

Oguntimilehin, A., & Ademola, E. O. (2014). A review of big data management benefits and challenges. *A Review of Big Data Management. Benefits and Challenges*, *5*(6), 1–7.

Park, K., Nguyen, M. C., & Won, H. (2015, July). Web-based collaborative big data analytics on big data as a service platform. *2015 17th International Conference on Advanced Communication Technology (ICACT)*, 564-567.

Plessius, H., van Steenbergen, M., Slot, R., & Versendaal, J. (2018). *The Enterprise Architecture Value Framework*. ECIS.

Rouse, W. B., & Serban, N. (2014). *Understanding and managing the complexity of healthcare*. MIT Press.

Rumsfeld, J. S., Joynt, K. E., & Maddox, T. M. (2016). Big data analytics to improve cardiovascular care: Promise and challenges. *Nature Reviews. Cardiology*, *13*(6), 350–359. doi:10.1038/nrcardio.2016.42 PMID:27009423

Shaanika, I., & Iyamu, T. (2015). Deployment of enterprise architecture in the Namibian government. The use of activity theory to examine the influencing factors. *The Electronic Journal on Information Systems in Developing Countries*, *71*(1), 1–21. doi:10.1002/j.1681-4835.2015.tb00515.x

Supriadi, H., Kom, M., & Amalia, E. (2019). University's Enterprise Architecture Design Using Enterprise Architecture Planning (EAP) Based on the Zachman's Framework Approach. *International Journal of Higher Education*, *8*(3), 13–28. doi:10.5430/ijhe.v8n3p13

Tungela, N., Mutudi, M., & Iyamu, T. (2018, October). *The Roles of E-Government in Healthcare from the Perspective of Structuration Theory. In 2018 Open Innovations Conference (OI)*. IEEE.

Van Zijl, C., & Van Belle, J. P. (2014). Organisational impact of enterprise architecture and business process capability in South African organisation. *International Journal of Trade. Economics and Finance*, 5(5), 405.

Wang, Y., Kung, L., & Byrd, T. A. (2018). Big data analytics: Understanding its capabilities and potential benefits for healthcare organisations. *Technological Forecasting and Social Change*, *126*, 3–13. doi:10.1016/j.techfore.2015.12.019

We, C., & Kahn, M. G. (2016). Clinical research informatics for big data and precision medicine. *Yearbook of Medical Informatics*, *25*(01), 211–218. doi:10.15265/IY-2016-019 PMID:27830253

Wu, J., Li, H., Cheng, S., & Lin, Z. (2016). The promising future of healthcare services: When big data analytics meets wearable technology. *Information & Management*, *53*(8), 1020–1033. doi:10.1016/j.im.2016.07.003

Zaharia, M., Xin, R. S., Wendell, P., Das, T., Armbrust, M., Dave, A., Meng, X., Rosen, J., Venkataraman, S., Franklin, M. J., Ghodsi, A., Gonzalez, J., Shenker, S., & Stoica, I. (2016). Apache spark: A unified engine for big data processing. *Communications of the ACM*, *59*(11), 56–65. doi:10.1145/2934664

Zhang, F., Cao, J., Khan, S. U., Li, K., & Hwang, K. (2015). A task-level adaptive MapReduce framework for real-time streaming data in healthcare applications. *Future Generation Computer Systems*, *43*, 149–160. doi:10.1016/j.future.2014.06.009

Chapter 3
An Applied Mathematical Model for Business Transformation and Enterprise Architecture:
The Business Engineering and Risk Management Pattern (BE&RMP)

Antoine Trad

(iD) https://orcid.org/0000-0002-4199-6970
IBISTM, France

ABSTRACT

This chapter on an optimal and adaptable enterprise architecture for business systems is one of a series of research chapters on enterprise architecture and business transformations. This one is about estimating the risk for transforming a business environment. It is a conclusion of many years of research, architecture, consulting, and development efforts. The model is based on an applied holistic mathematical model (AHMM) for business transformations. In this chapter, the CSFs are tuned to support the intelligent architecture concepts for business integration in the form of an applied pattern that is also a part or a chapter in this research series. This chapter is related to the feasibility and prototype of the business engineering and risk management pattern (BE&RMP) that should (or shouldn't) prove whether business transformation projects can optimize enterprise business capabilities and how microartefact implementation can offer a sustainable enterprise business system.

DOI: 10.4018/978-1-5225-8229-8.ch003

INTRODUCTION

The BE&RMP is based on research, design and development on: 1) business and technical architecture related to case studies; 2) EA and risk mitigation/optimization processes; 3) continuous business and technical transformations; 4) the AHMM4RM; 5) software architecture; 6) business architecture and implementation; 7) financial/audit intelligent analysis (and not looting initiatives); 8) decision making systems and the use of AI; 9) standardized architecture methodologies; and 10) integrated EA as a central concept. The BE&RMP is based on an authentic and proprietary research method that is supported by a qualitative holistic reasoning module that is explained in this research and development project management (Trad & Kalpić, 2019b). The BE&RMP is an AI/empirical process that uses a natural language environment, which can be easily adapted by the architecture teams (Myers, Pane & Ko, 2004; Kim & Kim, 1999; Della Croce & T'kindt, 2002; Trad & Kalpić, 2017a, 2017b, 2017c, 2017d, 2019b; Gunasekare, 2015). The BE&RMP is implemented to check the feasibility of the proposed pattern, using the AHMM4RM and CSFs approaches. The BE&RMP supports BTP and Enterprise Architecture Projects (EAP) (or simply *Projects*). This chapter is supported mainly by an adapted business case from the insurance domain (Jonkers, Band & Quartel, 2012a). The uniqueness and market lead of the author's proposed AHMM4RM based solutions, promotes a holistic cohesive enterprise architecture, design and implementation model that supports complex *Projects* integrations using a targeted and genuine Proof of Concept (PoC); in this case the BE&RMP's experiment (Farhoomand, 2004). The implementation of the BE&RMP can result in an intelligent Business Management System (iBMS) that uses the iSDMS that can be used in a day to day business, architecture and technology problem solving activities (Trad & Kalpić, 2019f, 2019g; Trad, 2019a). In this chapter, the proposed solutions are supported by a real-life case of a *Project* methodology in the domain of EA that in turn is based on the alignment of various business, architecture and technology standards and avant-garde risk mitigation methodologies. The "i" prefix, which will be used later in this text, does not stand just for the common intelligent agile environments but for a distributed and holistic intelligent architecture concept's approach that identifies this work's background; and "a" will stand for artefacts. This Research and Development Project's (RDP) main focus is on: 1) the BE&RMP's integration with the iSDMS; 2) the use of the existing EA frameworks; 3) *Projects*; 4) selection of the *Project* manager's profile; 5) AHMM4RM; 6) AI; 7) holisms and global concept; 8) risk management; 9) The intelligent Strategic Decision Making System (iSDMS); 10) intelligent Strategic Knowledge Management System (iSKMS); and 11) innovation iterative approaches. Using the scholar engine, within Google's online search portal, in which the author combines the previously mentioned keywords and key topics; the results have shown very clearly the uniqueness and the absolute lead of the author's framework, methodology, research and works (Trad, 2019a). From this point of view and facts, the author considers his works on the mentioned topics as innovative, credible and useful for innovation initiatives. AHMM4RM based BE&RMP for *Projects* offers an internal Natural Language Programming (NLP) (for scripting and prototyping) environment that can be adopted to manage the relationships between the BE&RMP, iSDMS, microartefacts and iBMS, as shown in Figure 2.

Figure 1. The relation between the proposed pattern, microartefacts and end system

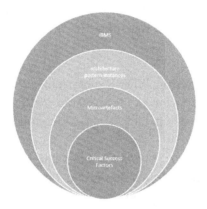

The use of the BE&RMP is done by instantiation (in n instances), using the author's framework; which uses EA concept, to create a reusable blueprint, as shown in Figure 2 (Myers, Pane & Ko, 2004; Neumann, 2002).

Figure 2. The relation between the pattern and architecture blueprint

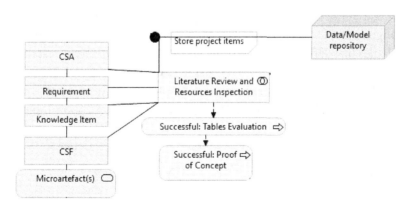

The BE&RMP is supported by an iSDMS and an EA and is proved by a PoC; where the central point is the *Project* of a legacy system to be transformed into a modern iBMS. Such *Projects* are managed by the Business Transformation Managers or an Enterprise Architecture Manager (simply a *Manager*); who, in this case, are supported by a a framework which estimates the risks of the *Projects'* implementation. The iBMS related RDP artefacts are made up of four inter-related approaches:

- The research concept (Trad & Kalpić, 2019d) describing the RDP for the BE&RMP as shown in Figure 3.
- The architecture pattern describes a structural pattern that can be instantiated to create the iBMS.
- The PoC, explains all the steps that are needed to check the BE&RMP' feasibility.

The CSF-based RDP uses the iSDMS subsystem and its unbundling levels that are parts of the proposed framework (Trad, 2018a, 2018b; Trad & Kalpić, 2019d). The RDP phase 1 (represented in tables), checks the following CSAs:

- Business case for the PoC, synthesized in Table 1.
- AHMM4RM as a structure, synthesized in Table 2.
- Information and Communications Systems (ICS), synthesized in Table 3.
- ADM, synthesized in Table 4.
- KMS, synthesized in Table 5.
- iSDMS, synthesized in Table 6.
- The applied domain; which is in this chapter is the BE&RMP, and is synthesized in Table 7.

Table 8, aggregates tables 1 to 7. As shown in Figure 3, the RDP, coloured in brick-orange interfaces the series various parts; include the BE&RMP that uses an Applied Case Study (ACS) (Jonkers, Band & Quartel, 2012a). The ACS is based on the alignment of *Project* microartefacts, various standards and avant-garde methodologies that defines this work's background. The *Manager* is responsible for the implementation of complex *Projects* using EA patterns, RDP and this chapter's BE&RMP, which supports him or her (for simplicity, in further text – him) in a just-in-time manner (Trad & Kalpić, 2016b), which is next section's topic.

Figure 3. The relation between the proposed pattern, artefacts and the research/ development project

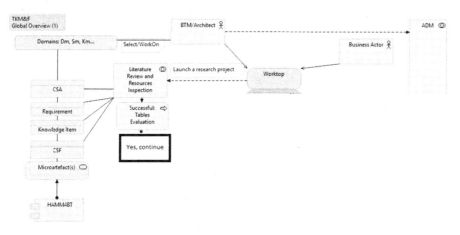

BACKGROUND

The stub of a complex *Project* and its various subsystems, like the iBMS, is the role of the *Manager,* the EA's blueprint (like the BE&RMP), standard technologies and an integration concept; which should be supported by a framework that in turn should support a Global Enterprise Architecture Business Vision and Strategy (GEABV&S) that in turn is the kernel of the meta-implementation of the BE&RMP. The GEABV&S should be also capable of supporting the *Project's* executives, business engineers/analysts, auditors, legal control and integration in a complex interconnected globalized business world that has a jungle like approach. To achieve GEABV&S' goals, global EA, technology (including infrastructure), financial and logistics integration strategy factors should be classified in Critical Success Areas (CSA) categories containing CSFs. CSFs are used to evaluate possible pitfalls and risks, to audit, assert, govern, automate, trace, monitor and control the iBMS (Putri & Yusof, 2009). *Projects* start with the unbundling process, which is initiated by an organizational reengineering process. In the case of the ACS, the first step is to transform the system and to create three departments; once logged-in the system, the BE&RMP is started as shown in Figure 4, on the left side as a tree view, showing the three initial departments; then the *Project* and its iBMS subprojects' CSFs can be configured to manage various activities in local and global eco-systems.

A fully or partially transformed iBMS, must have support of built-in automated scripts in the form of estimation controls, capable of recognizing major changes' and requirements' risks that are classified in a tree, as shown in Figure 5, where the internal subsystems collaborate.

Figure 4. The framework's main graphical interface

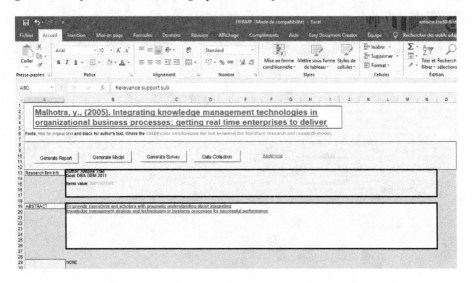

Projects involve the automation of iBMS' processes by using intelligent EA patterns (Felfel, Ayadi & Masmoudi, 2017). This RDP supports the BE&RMP which has a unique approach, and actually, there are no similar frameworks available. The RDP consists of two phases:

- Phase 1, checks the literature review, as shown in Figure 6.
- Phase 2, tries to solve a concrete problem, as shown in Figure 7.

Figure 5. The author framework's main subsystems linking

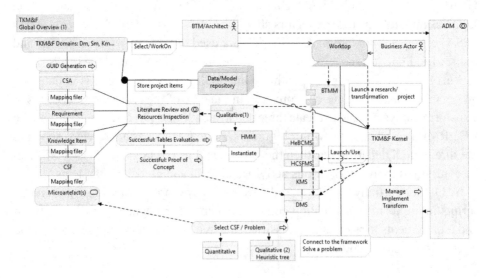

Figure 6. Phase 1 execution steps

Figure 7. Phase 2 execution steps

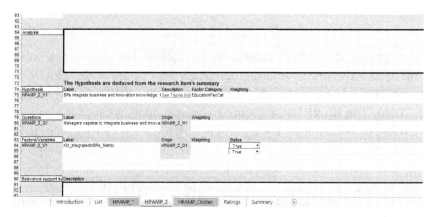

The author he would have a lonely lead that might last more than the next years, mainly in proposing a feasibility check concept to be used for *Projects* in general, and to assist in their design and maintenance phases, which come after the finalization of the implementation phase.

The CSF based BE&RMP is managed by the Transformation, Research, Architecture and Development framework (*TRADf*), and its interface is shown in Figure 8; where the reader has to the *TRADf* user's guide to understand its structure (Trad, 2018a; Trad, 2018b). Figure 6 shows its main modules and components (Trad & Kalpić, 2018f). The BE&RMP CSFs are selected from various iBMS related areas like EA, development, gap valuation, processes, technology/infrastructure, human skills …. and other.

Figure 8. The research framework's concept (Trad, 2019a)

In this chapter, the author presents the BE&RMP that uses an EA pattern in the form of an experiment; offering details on how to apply the *TRADf*, which can be applied to various fields (Trad & Kalpić, 2018a, 2018b; Cearley, Walker & Burke, 2016). The BE&RMP, presents a concrete application of its components that are based on: 1) a holistic EA approach, by interfacing various fields to access microartefacts; 2) Architecture Development Method (ADM) integration; 3) uses AI, where the internal iSDMS and risk management engine(s), using its structure is presented in Figure 8; 4) manages phases, using its structure, which is presented in Figure 8; 5) applies CSF tracking; and 6) it uses the *TRADf's* capabilities (Taleb & Cherkaoui, 2012). The iBMS and the applied BE&RMP are based on the RDP which are agnostic to any specific application, technical or business domain, as shown in Figure 9 (The Open Group, 2011a), but it can use any other existing architecture framework, like for example, Zachman's (The Open Group, 2002).

Figure 9. The architecture method's structure (The Open Group, 2011a)

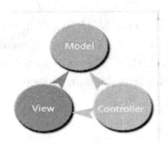

In each of these phases, shown in Figure 9, sets of the CSAs/CSFs are retuned depending on the *Project's* context (Thomas, 2015; Tidd, 2006). In *Projects*, the *Manager*'s role is crucial, and his EA capabilities are needed for the BE&RMP's setup to support a distributed iBMS (Trad & Kalpić, 2019c; Lanubile, Ebert, Prikladnicki, Vizcaíno & Vizcaino, 2010); where the ACS will be used as the BE&RMP's frontend.

Figure 10. Intelligent management system that uses an item/factor management system

The BE&RMP, uses a systemic/holistic approach, where its application interface, as shown in Figure 10, supports the iSDMS/AI interactions with the external world via the *TRADf* (Daellenbach & McNickle, 2005; Trad & Kalpić, 2016a). As shown in Figure 11, the internals of CSF Management System (CSFMS), the CSFs are important for the phase 1, which qualifies the needed CSF set and decides whether there is a need for a BE&RMP solution; in most *Projects* that decision would be called *go or nogo* procedure.

Figure 11. Interaction with critical success factors

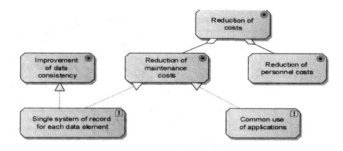

Projects and their internal iBMS' are difficult to implement, because of their complexity and lack of holisticity, archaically distributed and siloed nature, where the biggest part of complexity is encountered in the process of microartefacts classification, technical implementation and integration phases and the linking to sets of CSFs (Gudnason & Scherer, 2012). CSFs are managed from the *TRADf* client Graphical User Interface (GUI) by selecting the active phase from the list box. After selecting the CSF tag and its phase, they are linked to nodes; which are implemented as an items, in an Excel file; where all its details are defined and as shown in Figure 12.

Figure 12. Tuning and linking factors

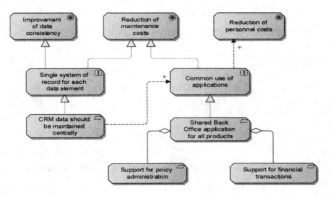

Concerning the internal *TRADf* interaction details, as shown in Figure 13, the *TRADf* can be applied to all types of *Projects* including the iBMS integration using CSFs (Joseph, 2014).

Figure 13. The TRADf's flow and interaction, including factors

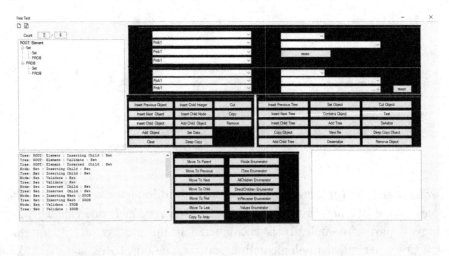

The BE&RMP presents how to check the feasibility of an iBMS which uses access to microartefact based technologies (Sankaralingam, Ferris, Nowatzki, Estan, Wood & Vaish, 2013). In 2013, Gartner, Inc., the leading information technology research and advisory company, announced the fact, that failure rates for projects from now until 2016, ranges in the limits of 20 to 28 percent. Gartner, recommends that *Projects* should prepared to face even more risk of failure; as *Projects* have mainly the focus on cost reduction, they should embrace failure (Gartner, 2013a; Allen, Alleyne, Farmer, McRae, & Turner, 2014).

This iBMS is based on the *TRADf* unique mixed research model; where CSFs and CSAs are offered to help iBMS and *Managers* and resource (and assets) architects to minimize the chances of transformation related failure; while implementing an iBMS (or a *Project)*. This chapter is part of a series of research works related to *Projects*, using iSDMS/AI and iSKMS, based on an AHMM4RM structure. In this chapter that is a part of a research series, the focus is on the iBMS that defines a central pool of CSAs/CSFs to be used throughout all the *Projects* and including subsystem, the iBMS. The BE&RMP, checks mainly the technical implementation phase, which is the major cause of high failure rates in *Projects*; because of the lack of a holistic approach and this fact is this work's focus (Thomas, 2015; Cearley, Walker & Burke, 2016; Trad & Kalpić, 2016b).

FOCUS OF THE CHAPTER

BE&RMP simplifies the *Project's* feasibility and proposes recommendations that can be applied by *Managers* for *Projects* (Desmond, 2013). The BE&RMP, uses the RDP, where this chapter presents an experiment of the BE&RMP based architecture integration and ties to relate a feasibility check process to an experiment and a Research Question (RQ), by using the RDP.

THE RESEARCH DEVELOPMENT PROCESS

Projects failure rates are high and were constantly increasing (Bruce, 1994) what is due to the complexity encountered in the implementation phase (Capgemini, 2009); to enhance the success rate, the author proposes the *TRADf* and a concrete PoC, in the case the BE&RMP is to check the feasibility; (Gartner, 2013a). *TRADf* recommends linking the AHMM4RM to all levels of the iBMS that is in the target level, as shown in Figure 14, where starts at its bottom of the pyramid, in the architecture vision phase (Trad & Kalpić, 2018b; Agievich, 2014; Tidd & Bessant,

Figure 14. Levels of project's interaction (Trad & Kalpić, 2017b; Trad, & Kalpić, 2017c)

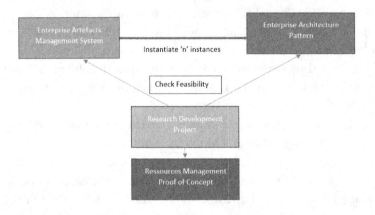

2018). This chapter's RQ is: "Can a holistic architecture concept be applied to an intelligent business system's engineering and minimize the risks of failure ?"

This research is a pioneering work in the mentioned fields and it tries to link the AHMM4RM based iSDMS to all levels of the *Project* and to the underlying infrastructure and its qualification (Trad & Kalpić, 2019c; Trad & Kalpić, 2019d; Agievich, 2014). *Projects* are in general, very risky and have a very high failure rate and one of the concrete reasons is that these *Projects* lack a cross-functional and holistic architecture. That is why the author would like to contribute to enhance these success rates of such *Projects* by the presented *TRADf* that uses CSFs and areas (Tidd & Bessant, 2018).

Critical Success Areas, Factors and Decision Making

A CSA is a selected set of CSFs, where the CSF is a set of Key Performance Indicators (KPI), where each KPI corresponds/maps to a single *Project* requirement and/or problem type. For a given requirement (or problem), an enterprise architect can identify the initial set of CSAs and their CSFs to be managed by the iSDMS (Trad & Kalpić, 2019f; Trad, 2019g). Hence the CSFs are important for the mapping between the problem types, knowledge constructs, organisational items (Peterson, 2011). Therefore, CSFs reflect possible problem types that must meet strategic *Project* goals and predefined constraints. Measurements are used to evaluate performance in each of the CSA sets, where CSFs (and KPIs) can be internal or external to the environment. Once the initial set of CSFs has been identified, then the *Project* can use the iSDMS to propose a set of solution types. The proposed BE&RMP delivers a set of solution instance and recommendations (Trad & Kalpić, 2019c, 2017b, 2017c).

The Applied Research Framework

An integrated iBMS is of strategic importance for the *Project's* problem solving capabilities that should manage and enrich the enterprise's microartefacts' scenarios (Lankhorst, 2009; Trad & Kalpić, 2019b, 2019a). The BE&RMP can be applied to various types of *Projects* and is a part of the Architecture management module (Am) and the Decision module (Dm), that in turn are parts of *TRADf*. In this chapter, the author proposes a set of BE&RMP managerial and technical recommendations on how a reusable real-world framework should be implemented in form of a PoC (Trad 2019c, 2019d, 2018a, 2019b). This chapter and the resultant experiment are also a part of the Selection management, Architecture-modelling, Control-monitoring, Decision-making, Training management, Project management, Finance management, Geopolitical management, Knowledge management, Implementation management and Research management Framework (SmAmCmDmTmPmFmGmKmImRmF, for simplification reasons, in further text the term *TRADf* will be used). The *TRADf* is not a black-box product to be applied as-is, it is rather an transformation, decision making, enterprise architecture, enterprise strategy, recommendations and vision framework that each enterprise should implement a similar framework. A common holistic objective of this chapter on *Projects* in these domains is to deliver solution BE&RMP and recommendations by proposing the *TRADf*, where the author owns the totality of its copyrights; where for this chapter IGI Global holds the copyright, and these two objects are distinct and different. This RQ was formulated after an extensive literature review.

The Research's Literature Review

The outcome is that very little scholar or even general literature and research resources exist on the selected subject (and RQ); of course with the exception of Open Group Architecture Framework (TOGAF), which covers the ADM part. The author considers his work as a pioneering one; the most relevant iSDMS information found in actual literature, was that there is a gap, between *Projects* and iSDMS' realities (Syynimaa, 2015). For various fields there are credible references, but for a holistic approach, credible references, are practically inexistent. In this chapter, RDP and in all its related artefacts, the author uses many of his own referenced and accepted works, because, he considers that this (or these) topics are somehow ignored and not sufficiently researched.

Empirical Engineering Research Model

This RDP is based on an empirical engineering research approach which is optimal for engineering projects (Johnson & Onwuegbuzie, 2004; Easterbrook, Singer, Storey & Damian, 2008), and it uses an authentic mixed method (where mixed research is a simplistic synonym for various methods) that can be considered as a complement to conventional qualitative and quantitative methodologies. Empirical validity checks if RDP works are acceptable as a contribution to existing scientific knowledge, where the aim is to convince the valuable readers that this chapter's recommendations and the related PoC are valid and applicable. A PoC is a software prototype of a testable hypothesis where one or more CSFs (or independent variables) are processed to evaluate their influence on the model's dependent variables on an the ACS (The Open Group, 2011a).

Review's Critical Success Factors

The *Projects* starts with the first phase called the feasibility phase to check if the whole *Project* makes sense. Based on the literature review and related evaluation activities, the most important CSFs are evaluated using the following rules (Trad & Kalpić, 2019f; Trad, 2019g):

- References should be credible and are estimated by the author; the notions of official ranking is less important and ignored.
- *Projects* like mergers are the result of organisational changes in companies to act as a single enterprise with consolidated resources and business interests.
- Applied modelling language should be limited in order to make the *Project* manageable and not too complex to maintain. Whether it is usable or not, can be estimated from a literature review process or from the team's own working experience or credible firm references like Gartner.
- The ADM is considered to be mature, and it has been in use for more than ten years and that it has been reported as successful (Alm & Wissotzki, 2015; Kotusev, 2018).
- The ADM is appropriate for any project's local conditions and manages the *TRADf's* iterations.
- If the aggregations of all the *Project's* CSA/CSF tables is positive and exceeds the defined minimum the *Project* continues to its PoC or can be used for problem solving.

The main reason that methodologies are not used in a holistic manner to achieve organizational alignment, centralized iSDMS and iSKMS (Syynimaa, 2015).

THE BUSINESS APPLIED CASE STUDY

Information and Communication Technology/Infrastructure

The BE&RMP uses an ACS is a reference study for its TOGAF environment, it offers the capability to implement *Project* components and is related to an insurance company named ArchiSurance (Trad & Kalpić, 2018f). The iBMS, like all actual avant-garde systems, uses a distributed ICS which has the following operations and characteristics:

- The ICS offers an infrastructure for feasible solutions.
- Design iBMS architecture solutions, based on EA patterns.
- Select a jump start objective from the ACS; and use it as a template for future EA blueprints.
- Build microartefacts pools to support the EA blueprints.
- Prepare *TRADf's* phase one and if it is successful, then select a problem from the ACS to prove its solvability in phase two.

Managing the Case

EA pattern instances are used by the ACS, with the support of the ADM. Such a construct supports the possibilities to implement the iBMS, and in this chapter is related to an insurance company named ArchiSurance (Trad & Kalpić, 2018f).

Integrating Critical Success Factors

A CSF its KPI enumerations are measurable and mapped to a weighting that is roughly estimated in the first iteration and then tuned through ADM iterations, to support the iBMS; where holistic business and enterprise architecture CSFs are essential (Felfel, Ayadi & Masmoudi, 2017); this process of evaluation is described in various series of RDP works (Trad & Kalpić, 2019d). The main issue here, is how to define the BE&RMP goals to integrate iBMS and how to interrelate the different business, ICS and EA components; where the ADM is its skeleton (KPMG, 2014).

The Architecture Development Method and Projects

This RDP focuses on the EA and design of *Projects'* integration and presents the influence of an architecture pattern to support the iBMS (Trad & Kalpić, 2019e). Currently, distributed intelligence, complexity, knowledge, finance and technology, need an EA pattern that is supported by a hyper-heuristics tree. Such a tree supports a wide class of problem types that are processes in the RDP's Phase 2 (Markides,

2011), where the iSDMS supports the iBMS (Trad & Kalpić, 2014d). The *Project* parts must synchronize with the ADM, where the iBMS and its internal components are interfaced in all the ADM phases.

The Business Case Study for Architecture Critical Success Factors and the Link to the Next Applied Mathematical Model Section

The important business case's CSFs that are used and processed by the internal heuristic engine and are presented in to an associated chapter entitled: Business Transformation and Enterprise Architecture-The Resources Management Research and Development Process (RMSRDP) (Trad & Kalpić, 2019e); it is strongly recommended to refer to this chapter. Based on the CSF review process, the important business case's CSFs are used and evaluated as explained below.

Table 1. The applied case study's critical success factors that have an average of 9.40

Critical Success Factors	KPIs		Weightings
CSF_iBMSCase_Modelling	Complex	▾	From 1 to 10. 09 Selected
CSF_iBMSCase_Factors	PossibleClassification	▾	From 1 to 10. 10 Selected
CSF_iBMSCase_References	Exists	▾	From 1 to 10. 09 Selected
CSF_iBMSCase_ArchitectureDevMethod	IntegrationPossible	▾	From 1 to 10. 09 Selected
CSF_iBMSCase_Technologies	AdvancedStage	▾	From 1 to 10. 09 Selected
CSF_iBMSCase_Governance	Advanced	▾	From 1 to 10. 09 Selected
CSF_iBMSCase_Transformation_TKM&F	IntegrationPossible	▾	From 1 to 10. 10 Selected
CSF_iBMSCase_Leading_Governance	Possible	▾	From 1 to 10. 10 Selected

valuation

As presented in the BE&RMP is based on CSA, CSF and KPIs evaluation (Trad & Kalpić, 2019e) which for the possible operational RDP the sets of CSAs, CSFs and KPIs, iBMS can be used in the architecture ACS' CSAs/CSFs. In this RDP, the deductions are done by using the analysis of each CSA of a total of 7, where a *TRADf's* script is created, in which all its CSFs are stored and appear in Table's 1 column. As shown in Figure 15, the *TRADf's* scripts in the background that are automated to calculate the weightings and ratings; known as the KPIs and a value from the enumerated sets; and they are tuned and stored in column 2. This RDP concept proposes a standardized and automated manner to evaluate literature reviews that is an evolution in regard to the very subjective method, which may or may not make sense, as shown in Figure 15. If the automated literature review's evaluation is successful, only then the experiment can be completed.

Figure 15. The critical success factors and areas (like patterns) stored in workbook sheets

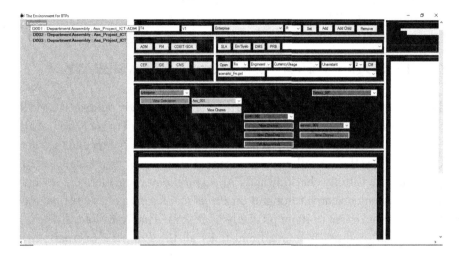

Figure 16. The phase 1 interactions with factors and areas evaluation

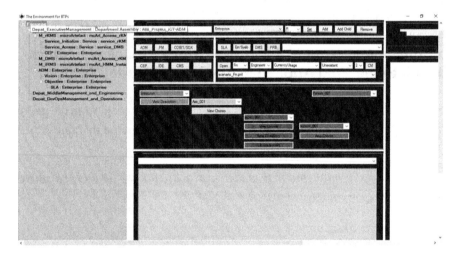

What is unique about the *TRADf* and its RDP, is that it can automate complex RDPs in phase 1, and estimate the values for each selected KPI, as described in the in the associated RMSRDP chapter; on how to use CSA, CSF, KPI processing in the complex research projects (Trad & Kalpić, 2019e).

As shown in Table 1, the results justify (an average of 9.25) the usage of the ACS and how it can be used with the final PoC or phase 2; where the described process is applied to the next six CSAs and their tables. This process enables to go to the next CSA to be analysed that is the AHMM4RM's integration. This section's deduction is that the AHMM4RM is crucial for the BE&RMP's credibility, where it is the basis for its structure.

THE APPLIED MATHEMATICAL MODEL'S FEASIBILITY

As already mentioned, it is recommended to refer to the already published RMSRDP chapter, to understand this chapter and all the author's works (Trad & Kalpić, 2019d). An EA pattern and its links to the ADM are the base of this chapter and they are the basics of the *TRADf.* The author proposes the AHMM4RM as the skeleton of the *TRADf* to solve feasibility checking and *Project* problems . The literature review has shown that existing research resources on *Project* topics, as a mathematical model, are practically inexistent or more precisely irrelevant (Trad & Kalpić, 2019e). This pioneering RDP is cross-functional and links all the *Project*'s microartefacts to the enterprise architecture method. The *Project's* initialization and vision phase, generates the needed CSAs/CSFs and hence creates/proposes the EA pattern types to be used. The AHMM4RM is a part of the *TRADf* that uses microartefacts' scenarios to support EA pattern instantiation requests (Agievich, 2014).

The Holistic Mathematical Model's Critical Success Factors and Link to the Next Applied Mathematical Model Section

Based on the selected and evaluated CSFs, using the same concept from the previous CSA and table (Trad & Kalpić, 2019e), the results are presented in Table 2, below.

Table 2. The holistic mathematical model's critical success factors that have an average of 9.40

Critical Success Factors	KPIs	Weightings
CSF_AHMM4iBMS_TRADf_Integration	Feasible ▾	From 1 to 10. 09 Selected
CSF_AHMM4iBMS_InitialPhase	Stable ▾	From 1 to 10. 10 Selected
CSF_AHMM4iBMS_PoCPhase	Complex ▾	From 1 to 10. 09 Selected
CSF_AHMM4iBMS_Qualitative&Quantitative	Complex ▾	From 1 to 10. 09 Selected
CSF_AHMM4iBMS_Final_AHMM_Instance	VerifiedModel ▾	From 1 to 10. 09 Selected
CSF_AHMM4iBMS_ADM_Integration	Synchronized ▾	From 1 to 10. 10 Selected
CSF_AHMM4iBMS_iBMS_Interfacing	Stable ▾	From 1 to 10. 09 Selected

valuation

As presented in the RMSRDP section (and chapter) the CSA, CSF and KPIs evaluation (Trad & Kalpić, 2019e) which for the possible operational CSAs, CSFs and KPIs, iBMS can be used in ACS' CSAs. As shown in Table 2, the processed results (with an average of 8.72) justify the usage of an AHMM4RM instance and that it can be used with the final PoC or the RDP's Phase 2; and this fact enables the continuation to the next CSA, which is the ICS integration.

THE INTEGRATION OF INFORMATION AND COMMUNICATION TECHNOLOGIES

Technology for Decoupled Information Architecture

Adaptable and loosely coupled atomic Business Logics Block (aBLB) based BE&RMP, can be used to improve the quality and robustness of the iBMS and its integration of the defined business requirements (Trad, 2015c). An optimal aBLB integration is based on the one to one mapping in which each business requirement and its transaction artefact is autonomous. Standardized and transformed EA, enables the *Project* to be iterative, where its design is based on a holistic approach and patterns using interconnection between all implementation phases. The coordination of the pattern is insured by the interaction of: 1) EA patterns; 2) standardised methodologies; and 3) portable tools; like the ADM. *Managers*, business architects and business analysts can use the pattern concept to gain support for business architecture implementations; using aBLBs, and Solution Blocks (SB), for a successful *Project* (Gartner, 2013b). Such a *Project* has to make a choice of the optimal tooling and modelling environment based on a pseudo Model View Control (MVC) pattern (MIS, 2014), as shown in Figure 17. *Project's* complexity lies in its implementation phase, mainly causes high failure rates are very high; the aBLBs and pseudo bottom-up approach can improve succes rates (Bishop, 2009; Shimamoto, 2013; Österle, 1995). The current section presents this CSA in the sense of a literature review and the resultant CSFs that are needed for the BE&RMP, from the following sections:

- Internet of Things (IoT), which is the infrastructure's glue that uses the service-oriented architecture (and microartefacts) to support the *TRADf* ; and are the *Project's* units of work.
- Standard ICS procedures and technology standards, presented in Table 1.
- Global Unique Identifiers Integration (GUID) for resource items, are used to identify and monitor the iBMS.

- Processes, EA patterns and models supported by the *TRADf* to enable interconnected intelligent enterprise architecture (Folinas, 2007); presented in Tables 5 and 6.
- Intelligent microartefacts integration and strategy to relate and assemble the iBMS' and *Project's* resources (The Open Group, 2011a); presented in Table 3.
- Security, has to define a global vision on security by applying holistic qualification procedures that englobe security concepts from many domains used by electronic finance.
- Intelligent static architecture using architecture pattern, which expresses a structural concept or schema for iBMS implementations (Trad & Kalpić, 2019e).

The Information and Communication Technology's Critical Success Factors and Link to the Next Chapter

Based on the literature review process and *TRADf's* processing, the CSFs are evaluated (Trad & Kalpić, 2019e) and are explained below, in this section.

Table 3. The information technology critical success factors that have an average of 9.00

Critical Success Factors	HMM enhances: KPIs	Weightings
CSF_ICS_GUID_IntegrationProcessesModels	Standard	From 1 to 10. 09 Selected
CSF_ICS_TRADf_StandardsIntegration	AdvancedState	From 1 to 10. 10 Selected
CSF_ICS_Services	Supported	From 1 to 10. 09 Selected
CSF_ICS_Performance	Exists	From 1 to 10. 08 Selected
CSF_ICS_DistributedCommunication	Stable	From 1 to 10. 09 Selected
CSF_ICS_Finance	ExistingSupport	From 1 to 10. 09 Selected
CSF_ICS_Security	Complex	From 1 to 10. 08 Selected
CSF_ICS_Automation	Supported	From 1 to 10. 09 Selected
CSF_ICS_Pattern_StandardsIntegration	Supported	From 1 to 10. 09 Selected
CSF_ICS_Procedures	Supported	From 1 to 10. 10 Selected

valuation

As shown in Table 3, the results (an average of 8.70) justify the usage of the ICS integration in the architecture pattern and how it can be used with the final BE&RMP or phase 2; and enable to go to the next CSA to be analysed that is the holistic management of the ADM.

THE INTEGRATION WITH THE ARCHITECTURE DEVELOPMENT METHOD

EA methods, such as the ADM, confirm the importance of requirements engineering strategies in the development of *Projects*. The proposed concept support is needed to specify, document, communicate and experiment the strategy and goals needed to succeed. Actual archaic EA and ICS techniques for *Projects,* focus on the tools, gadgets, ad-hoc services, archaic processes and end-applications of the business enterprise. Added to that, some techniques may be supported to define structured and classified requirements lists and methodological use cases. Minimum support exists for modelling the underlying goals of a *Project,* mainly in terms of stakeholder goals and concerns. These high-level, purely financial goals, address these commercial concerns. This chapter's focus is on a concept that supports the mapping and modelling of linking requirements to all the *Project's* resources. This chapter also illustrates how *Projects* can benefit from holistic analysis techniques in requirements management and proposes an adequate research process (Quartel, Engelsman, Jonkers, & van Sinderen, 2009). The iBMS' integration with ADM, enables the management and automation of iBMS items and considers the following:

- Reference architecture and its phases concept and integration.
- The Unit of Work (in the form of microartefacts) and Enterprise Architecture.
- Business system's architecture blueprint.

TRADf's EA capabilities helps, in establishing an architecture principal guideline that defines the *Project's* initial phase and vision; which is based on a just-enough architecture in the ADM for the iBMS (The Open Group, 2011a).

The Unit of Work

Defining a microartefact granularity and responsibility for a *Project* is a complex process; added to that, there is the complexity in implementing the "1:1" mapping and classification of the discovered microartefacts. The applied design concept uses standard design methodologies like the ADM's. This proposed design and mapping concepts are supported by a set of the *TRADf's* microartefacts where its internal AHMM4RM NLP consists of implementing microartefacts to dynamically evaluate compound expressions, according to the AHMM4RM principles (Neumann, 2002). Defining the unit of work, serves as a concrete microartefact that can be represented by a class diagram, where mapping supports the interoperability between all the *Project's* microartefacts that are compatible with the following standards (Trad, 2019c):

- Decision management and knowledge management XML standard to import and export knowledge items (Feljan, Karapantelakis, Mokrushin, Liang, Inam, Fersman & Souza, 2017).
- The Unified Modelling Language's (UML) and the System Modelling XML (SysML) for the design of the iSDMS specialized microartefacts.
- Design patterns and their XML interfaces for the structural design of the iSDMS microartefacts.
- The Project Management XML (PMXML) for the project coordination of the iSDMS microartefacts.
- The Service Oriented Architecture XML (SoaML) and the Web Services XML (WSDL) for the communication between the iSDMS microartefacts.
- The Business Process Modelling Notation (BPMN) and the Business Process Execution Language (BPEL), can be used for the design of the iSDMS microartefacts.
- The client-side frameworks to build dynamic front-ends using a lifecycle development process.

The Model First Approach

The pseudo bottom up approach of an aBLB strategy used by the *TRADf* is influenced by the microartefacts that are managed by a model strategy, methodology and productivity environments.

Figure 17. The Model-View-Control pattern (Palermo, Bogard, Hexter, Hinze, & Skinner, 2012)

TRADf proposes an upstream pattern that are altered to accommodate traditional services' environments. These services are stored in specialized atomic service repository using the model-view-control pattern, as shown in Figure 17. The author recommends that *Managers* should apply the Open Group's Architecture Framework as a base for their *Project* strategy.

Integration Building Blocks

aBLBs help *Projects* by breaking system components into a set of classified microartefacts. *An aBLB is just another business brick in the enterprise's wall...* The *Manager* builds a prototype to propose a set of aBLBs templates to be used during the unbundling process of the actual monolithic environment. The aBLBs has the following implementation characteristics:

- It unifies implementation and usage, and easily adapts to evolution of technology and standards.
- An aBLBs can be an aggregation of other building blocks, hence a subassembly of other building blocks.
- An aBLBs is a reusable template and easily replaceable.
- An aBLBs can have many implementations.
- An aBLBs has a unique identifier.
- An aBLBs respects the "1:1" mapping concept.
- An aBLBs enables business interoperability and integration.
- GUID Mapping mechanics.

Integration Architecture

Architectures derived from standardized EA, differ greatly, because they depend on the *Project's* requirements quality, *Manager's* skills and the company's overall status. *TRADf* focuses on the development and modelling of architectures, which in turn is based on aBLB services. This approach is about ensuring that *Projects* are under control by the applied strategy; this approach implements a clear alignment between business requirements, organizational (re)structure, governing and business ICS; resulting in a pattern for the actual *Project*. EA models are developed using microartefacts' based architectures and their integration's success can be measured by using CSFs (Ylimäki, 2008).

The Architecture Development Method (ADM) Critical Success Factors and Link to the Next Section

Based on the literature review and associated evaluation processes, the CSFs are evaluated (Trad & Kalpić, 2019e) and are explained below.

As shown in Table 4, the result's (an average of 9.4) justify the usage of the ICS integration concept and how it can be used with the final BE&RMP or phase 2; and enables to go to the next CSA to be analysed is the iSKMS interfacing.

Table 4. The Architecture Development Method's critical success factors that have an average of 9.7

Critical Success Factors	HMM enhances: KPIs		Weightings
CSF_ADM_CSF_Initialization&Setup	Feasible	▾	From 1 to 10. 10 Selected
CSF_ADM_IntegrationProcesses	Supported	▾	From 1 to 10. 10 Selected
CSF_ADM_Phases	Supported	▾	From 1 to 10. 10 Selected
CSF_ADM_Requirements	MappingAutomated	▾	From 1 to 10. 09 Selected
CSF_ADM_Pattern4iBMS_Architecture	Supported	▾	From 1 to 10. 09 Selected

valuation

THE HOLISTIC ASSET iSDMS

For the architecture of the *Project's* iSKMS, the goal is to manage the resource's information items using a holistic management concept that offers the following:

- Architecture of the iSKMS' basics.
- Architecture iSKMS microartefacts.
- The holistic architecture for iSKMS access management.
- The holistic architecture iSKMS strategy.

The Knowledge Management Success Factors

Based on the literature review and associated evaluation processes, the CSFs are evaluated (Trad & Kalpić, 2019e) and are explained below.

Table 5. The knowledge management critical success factors that have an average of 9.20

Critical Success Factors	HMM enhances: KPIs		Weightings
CSF_iBMS_Infrastructure_Integration	Supported	▾	From 1 to 10. 09 Selected
CSF_iBMS_Item_Mapping	ComplexToImpl	▾	From 1 to 10. 09 Selected
CSF_iBMS_Patterns	Implementable	▾	From 1 to 10. 09 Selected
CSF_iBMS_Pattern_Integration	Implementable	▾	From 1 to 10. 09 Selected
CSF_iBMS_Pattern_AccessManagement	StandardIntgeration	▾	From 1 to 10. 10 Selected

valuation

As shown in Table 5, the result's (an average of 9.0) justify the usage of the ICS integration concept and how it can be used with the final BE&RMP or phase 2; and enables to go to the next CSA to be analysed, which is the resources iSDMS.

THE INTEGRATION WITH THE iSDMS

The iSDMS' integration depends on the following facts:

- As mentioned CSFs can be applied in the iBMS and iSDMS' processing (Trad & Kalpić, 2014b).
- Complex iSDMS uses the AHMM4RM.
- An extremely long and risky *Project*.
- The decision making processes.

The iSDMS Critical Success Factors and the Link to the Next Section

Based on the literature review, the CSF are evaluated (Trad & Kalpić, 2019e) and are explained below.

Table 6. The decision making critical success factors that have an average of 9.00

Critical Success Factors	AHMM enhances: KPIs	Weightings
CSF_iSDMS_ComplexSystemsIntegration	Possible	From 1 to 10. 09 Selected
CSF_iSDMS_Pattern4iBMS_Interfacing	Supported	From 1 to 10. 09 Selected
CSF_iSDMS_KMS_Interfacing	Possible	From 1 to 10. 09 Selected
CSF_iSDMS_DMP	IntgeratesAsKernel	From 1 to 10. 10 Selected
CSF_iSDMS_HolisticApproach	Complex	From 1 to 10. 08 Selected

valuation

As shown in Table 6, the result's (an average of 8.80) justify the usage of the ICS integration concept and how it can be used with the final BE&RMP or phase 2; and enables to go to the next CSA to be analysed is the iBMS.

THE ENTERPRISE ARCHITECTURE
INTEGRATION PATTERN BASED SYSTEM

Monolithic business, ICS and teams are the major cause of failure of *Projects;* this fact has motivated the author to research various techniques to promote and recommend solutions like the use of aBLB based architectures for iBMS. Concerning the architecture of the iBMS the following Characteristics are important:

- A deductive approach.
- A recursive structure.
- Tangible and intangible microartefacts evaluation capability.
- Business processing capability, based on services.
- Enterprise artefacts management.
- Artefacts system design and integration.

The Critical Success Factors and Link to the Next Section

Based on the literature review, the CSF are evaluated (Trad & Kalpić, 2019e) and are explained below.

Table 7. The enterprise architecture integration critical success factors that have an average of 9.00

Critical Success Factors	AHMM enhances: KPIs	Weightings
CSF_iBMS_SystemsIntegration	Possible	From 1 to 10. 10 Selected
CSF_iBMS_EA_Structure	Feasible	From 1 to 10. 09 Selected
CSF_iBMS_(in)_Tangible_Values	ManagementEnabled	From 1 to 10. 09 Selected
CSF_iBMS_DMP_Capacities	Feasible	From 1 to 10. 09 Selected
CSF_iBMS_HolisticApproach	Supported	From 1 to 10. 09 Selected
CSF_iBMS_TRADf_Support	ComplexButFeasible	From 1 to 10. 08 Selected
CSF_iBMS_RoleOfPatterns	Possible	From 1 to 10. 09 Selected
CSF_iBMS_Skills	Exisiting	From 1 to 10. 10 Selected
CSF_iBMS_ExistingStatus	Transformable	From 1 to 10. 08 Selected
CSF_iBMS_Automation	Supported	From 1 to 10. 09 Selected
CSF_iBMS_Tracking_Auditing	Feasible	From 1 to 10. 09 Selected

valuation

As shown in Table 7, the results (an average of 8.81) justify the usage of the iBMS integration using architecture patterns and it can be used with the final BE&RMP or phase 2; and enable to go to the next CSA to be analysed is the BE&RMP.

THE PROOF OF CONCEPT OR PROTYPE'S INTEGRATION

The PoC's implementation uses aBLBs based on the granularity approach used to refine the "1:1" mapping concept.

The Implementation Environment and the Grounded Hyper-Heuristic Decision Tree

This PoC is implemented using the *TRADf* which was developed exclusively by the author, who own the total copyrights. In this BE&RMP, the grounded hyper-heuristics to process solutions. Like all heuristics based systems, the iSDMS reasoning engine will not be always perfect and adapted to all possible requirements, but it should be enhanced to make it capable of finding optimal results. The iSDMS applies the positivist action research that is designed on a model identical to the grounded hyper-heuristics model. This BE&RMP uses the iSDMS's heuristics model, which is based on a pseudo beam search tree method (Jaszkiewicz & Sowiñski, 1999). The BE&RMP is based on the AHMM4RM's instance and the iBMS mechanics' interfaces the iSDMS, which uses the internal initial sets of CSFs' that are used in phases 1 and 2.

From Phase 1 to Phase 2

Here is the *Project's* enumeration of CSAs: 1) The Applied Case Study Integration; 2) The Usage of the Architecture Development Method; 3) The Information and Communication Technology System; 4) The Mathematical Model's Integration; 5) The iSDMS; 6) The iSKMS; and 7) The intelligent Resource Management System. The *TRADf* and hence the AHMM4RM's main constraint, is to implement the iBMS using simple *Projects* components, having CSAS average higher than 7.5. In the case, of the current CSA/CSF evaluation, has an average result higher than 8, as shown in Table 8. Once the *TRADf* is setup, the CSAs/CSFs and the related script files are configured; in this chapter's seven tables are presented and the result of processing of the first phase (or phase 1) is illustrated in Table 8, which shows clearly that the iBMS RDP is credible, with an average of 8.89.

Of course, the complexity in integrating the iBMS must be done in multiple iterations, where the first one should try to transform the base iBMS services repository. As already mentioned, the BE&RMP's 1st phase, evaluates CSAs that can be calibrated by the *TRADf's* user(s)). In this research series seven CSAs/Tables qualification is successful using CSFs which are setup from the main client. Afterwards, the KPIs are selected and weighted, then these values are stored in the CSAs/CSFs *TRADf's* scripts; then the BE&RMP's second phase can be conducted. The iBMS uses the

Table 8. The proof of concept's phase 1 outcome, is over 9.30

CSA Category of CSFs/KPIs	Influences transformation management	Average Result
The Applied Case Study Integration	Complex ▾	From 1 to 10. 9.40
The Usage of the Architecture Development Method	FullyIntegrated ▾	From 1 to 10. 9.70
The Information and Communication Technology System	Transformable ▾	From 1 to 10. 9.00
The Mathematical Model's Integration	IsApplicable ▾	From 1 to 10. 9.40
The Decision Making System	Implementable ▾	From 1 to 10. 9.00
The Knowledge Management System	Implementable ▾	From 1 to 10. 9.20
The intelligent Business Management System	Implementable ▾	From 1 to 10. 9.00

Evaluate First Phase

TRADf's functional language development environment to configure the iSDMS/ AI, it uses the Holistic CSF Management System (HCSFMS) to select problems, actions and applicable solutions for the iBMS. The ACS is a concrete case where the demo application is used (Trad & Kalpić, 2018c).

Phase 2

Phase 2, is implemented using the *TRADf*, where the BE&RMP's Phase 2 presents the problem solving mechanics, which interfaces the iSDMS that uses the mixed heuristic methods based on services-oriented microartefacts, having bindings/ mappings to specific *Projects* resources like CSFs.

Mappings and Microartefacts

The used microartefacts are designed using EA methodologies and related tools; these microartefacts are built on service based architectures and their integration's success can be measured by using CSFs (Aier, Bucher, & Winter, 2011). The *TRADf* sets up the relationships between the *Projects* CSAs, CSFs, KPIs, requirements and services-based microartefacts, using global unique identifiers. The *Project* is started by structuring the organisation and linking it to the global unique identifiers by using the client's interface. Once the development setup interface is activated, the scripting language interface can be launched to implement the needed microartefact scripts to process the defined six CSAs. After starting the *TRADf's* graphical interface, the sets of CSFs are selected. Then follows the CSF attachment to a specific node of the *TRADf's* graphical tree (where Phase_R, is an ADM phase); to link later the microartefacts. From the *TRADf* client's interface, the Mathematical Language (ML) development setup and editing interface can be launched to develop the iBMS services to be used in microartefacts. The AHMM4RM uses iBMS services that are called by the iSDMS actions, which manage the edited mathematical language script and flow. This research's architecture pattern instance, the AHMM4RM and its related CSFs were selected as demonstrated previously, for the ACS.

Linking the Applied Case Study - Architecture Unification

The EA pattern and ACS are used in the BE&RMP, which is an experiment (Lebreton, 1957; Ronald, 1961; Spencer, 1955). The ACS is an insurance management system that has an archaic information system, a mainframe, claim files service, customer file service. The ACS manages claims activities where the demo application uses the *TRADf* for the ACS/PoC implementation (Trad & Kalpić, 2018c). The *Project* major achievement is the introduction of microartefacts. This BE&RMP based on the ArchiSurance ACS; analyses a merger, of an old business system's landscape that has become siloed, that results in abundant data and code, knowledge redundancy, functional overlap and archaic integration, using many formats and technologies. For this BE&RMP, a holistic approach is tested to structure the iBMS data using the central data. The data repository structure has to be transformed and to improve data storage and the common use of applications bias data services consistency, quality and robustness, as shown in Figure 18 that can be considered as the CSA set for Phase 2; which has to be assisted by an architecture method.

Figure 18. Transformation goals (Jonkers, Band & Quartel, 2012)

The Architecture Method's Phases' Setup and Related Factors

The Phase 2 implementation setup looks as follows:

- Sub-phase A or the Architecture Vision phase's goals, establishes a data architecture; as shown in Figure 19.
- Sub-phase B or the Business Architecture phase shows how the BE&RMP target architecture realizes the key requirements.
- Sub-phase C or the Gap Analysis phase shows and uses the Application Communication Diagram, which shows the modelled target application landscape.
- Sub-phase D or the Target Technology Architecture and Gap Analysis phase shows the end BE&RMP infrastructure; where here is limited.
- Sub-phases E and F, Implementation and Migration Planning; the transition architecture, proposing possible intermediate situation and evaluates the BE&RMP status.

Figure 19. Data goals and principles (Jonkers, Band & Quartel, 2012)

The data services based microartefacts have bindings/mappings to specific iBMS resources. The used microartefacts are designed using EA methodologies and related tools. The iBMS concept defines relationships between the iBMS requirements and data services based microartefacts (and CSAs/CSFs).

Processing a Concrete Node

The hyper-heuristics approach is used, in order to find a combination of heuristics that solve a complex research question. A specific CSF is linked to a problem type and a related set of actions that starts to be processed at a specific node. For this BE&RMP, the author has selected the CSF_iBMS_SystemsIntegration taken from the Table 7 or iBMS CSA and would like to find solutions related to this CSF's related problems. Such problems can be only researched with a mixed-model that is very similar to the (re)-scheduling of activities model. Solving the given problem involves the determination of actions and related solutions for multiple activities for the ICS integration team. These mixed models are based on quantitative analysis, beam search and grounded hyper-heuristics; that is in fact a dual-objective iSDMS (McMullen, & Tarasewich, 2005). The author has decided to apply the iSDMS to try to solve the CSF_iBMS_SystemsIntegration architecture unification problem or the PRB_iBMS_SystemsIntegration (Vella, Corne, & Murphy, 2009), which is solved by using the following steps:

- Relating the ACS architecture unification resources to CSF_iBMS_SystemsIntegration that is done in Phase 1.
- Link the processing of this node to the pseudo-quantitative modules, then by using qualitative modules, filter and deliver the initial state that is the root node of the iSDMS decision tree.
- The iSDMS heuristics engine is configured, weighted and tuned using configuration information.
- The set of possible solutions results from the hyper-heuristics decision model. The iSDMS starts with the initial CSF_iBMS_SystemsIntegration. Then the iSDMS is launched to find the set of possible solutions in the form of possible improvements.
- Then follows the CSF attachment to a specific node of the *TRADf's* graphical tree; to link later the microartefacts.
- The iSDMS tree (or the qualitative/hyper-heuristics decision tree) is a beam search heuristics model that uses the input from the previous phases to propose an optimal solution by using a common data bus.
- Once the development setup interface is activated, the ML interface can be launched to implement the needed microartefact scripts to process the defined six CSAs. After starting the *TRADf's* graphical interface the script and its sets of CSFs are selected.
- From the *TRADf* client's interface, the ML development setup and editing interface can be launched to develop the data services to be used in microartefacts.

Node Solution

These scripts make up the intelligence basis and the AHMM4RM's instance set of actions that are processed in the background to support data services to be used in microartefacts. The AHMM4RM uses data services that are called by the iSDMS actions, which deliver the solution and flow, as shown in Figure 20.

Figure 20. The heuristics tree configuration

This research series, the AHMM4RM and its related CSAs/CSFs were selected as demonstrated previously.

SOLUTION AND RECOMMENDATIONS

The *Manager* is responsible for the implementation of complex *Projects* using architecture pattern, RDP and their corresponding BE&RMP, where he should have a solid background in architecture patterns/iSDMS based iBMS. The managerial recommendations are needed for finding the solutions to enable an iBMS. The resultant technical and managerial recommendations are:

- The iBMS feasibility was checked by the BE&RMP.
- The ADM's integration in an iBMS enables its automation and automation of its interfaces.
- Setup a central iBMS to be used in *Projects*.
- Define the interface to the iSKMS and iSDMS. The iBMS needs to implement a iSDMS.
- Model the iBMS' and microartefacts' interaction.

iBMS managerial recommendations, and the *TRADf*, round up the approach needed for the complex research activities related to management of resources. .

FUTURE RESEARCH DIRECTIONS

This BE&RMP and related topics, appear to be undiscovered and in fact are very complex, because many of them are based on intangible values that are complex to formulate. Such formulations should be abstracted using the proposed mathematical model. The goal is also to localize fictive bookkeeping or banking secrecy deviations that block real evaluation and promote plundering.

CONCLUSION

Phase 1 proved the feasibility and Phase 2, demonstrated the ability to solve a concrete problem, abstracted by the ACS' architecture unification requirement. The most important managerial recommendation that was generated by the previous research phases was that the *Manager* must be a strong leader and must have in-depth knowledge of transformation projects, enterprise architecture projects, research projects, PoCs and iBMS. The *TRADf* can support an iBMS (and *Projects* in general) by using the iSDMS (and the BE&RMP) to check the feasibility and to deliver a set of managerial recommendations. Concerning financing and preserving *Project* resources and assets, it is strongly recommended to implement an iBMS to avoid any type of approach or models that would allow looting (Trad & Kalpić, 2019g).

ACKNOWLEDGMENT

In a work as large as this research project, technical, typographical, grammatical, or other kinds of errors are bound to be present.

REFERENCES

Agievich, V. (2014). *Mathematical model and multi-criteria analysis of designing large-scale enterprise roadmap*. PhD thesis.

Aier, S., Bucher, T., & Winter, R. (2011). *Critical Success Factors of Service Orientation in Information Systems Engineering. Derivation and Empirical Evaluation of a Causal Model. Business & Information Systems Engineering*. Springer.

Allen, M., Alleyne, D., Farmer, C., McRae, A., & Turner, Ch. (2014, October). A Framework for Project Success. *Journal of IT and Economic Development, 5*(2), 1–17.

Bishop, M. (2009). *CHAOS Report: Worst Project Failure Rate in a Decade.* Standish Group.

Bruce, C. (1994). Research student's early experiences of the dissertation literature review. *Studies in Higher Education, 19*(2), 217-229.

Capgemini. (2009). *Business transformation: From crisis response to radical changes that will create tomorrow's business.* A Capgemini Consulting Survey.

Cearley, D., Walker, M., & Burke, B. (2016). *Top 10 Strategic Technology Trends for 2017.* Gartner, ID: G00317560. https://www.gartner.com/doc/3471559?plc=ddp

Daellenbach, H., McNickle, D., & Dye, Sh. (2012). *Management Science - Decision-making through systems thinking* (2nd ed.). Palgrave Macmillian.

Della Croce, F., & T'kindt, V. (2002). A Recovering Beam Search algorithm for the one-machine dynamic total completion time scheduling problem. *The Journal of the Operational Research Society, 53*(11), 1275–1280. doi:10.1057/palgrave. jors.2601389

Desmond, C. (2013). Management of change. *IEEE Engineering Management Review, 41*(3).

Easterbrook, S., Singer, J., Storey, M., & Damian, D. (2008). *Guide to Advanced Empirical Software Engineering-Selecting Empirical Methods for Software Engineering Research* (F. Shull, Ed.). Springer.

Felfel, H., Ayadi, O., & Masmoudi, F. (2017). Pareto Optimal Solution Selection for a Multi-Site Supply Chain Planning Problem Using the VIKOR and TOPSIS Methods. *International Journal of Service Science, Management, Engineering, and Technology.* Doi:10.4018/IJSSMET.2017070102

Folinas, D. (2007). A conceptual framework for business intelligence based on activities monitoring systems. *Int. J. Intelligent Enterprise, 1*(1), 65. doi:10.1504/IJIE.2007.013811

Gartner, Inc. (2013a). *Gartner Says Smart Organizations Will embrace Fact and Frequent Project Failure in Their Quest for Agility.* Retrieved from https://www.gartner.com/newsroom/id/2477816

Gartner, Inc. (2013b). *Scenario Toolkit: Using EA to Support Business Transformation. ID:G00246943.* Gartner, Inc.

Gudnason, G. & Scherer, R. (2012). *eWork and eBusiness in Architecture, Engineering and Construction: ECPPM 2012.* CRC Press.

Gunasekare, U. (2015). *Mixed Research Method as the Third Research Paradigm: A Literature Review.* University of Kelaniya.

Jaszkiewicz, A., & Sowiñski, R. (1999). The 'Light Beam Search' approach - an overview of methodology and applications. *European Journal of Operational Research, 113*(2), 300–314. doi:10.1016/S0377-2217(98)00218-5

Jonkers, H., Band, I., & Quartel, D. (2012a). *ArchiSurance Case Study.* The Open Group.

Joseph, Ch. (2014). *Types of eCommerce Business Models.* https://smallbusiness.chron.com/types-ecommerce-business-models-2447.html

Kim, K., & Kim, K. (1999). Routing straddle carriers for the loading operation of containers using a beam search algorithm. Elsevier. *Computers & Industrial Engineering, 36*(1), 109–136. doi:10.1016/S0360-8352(99)00005-4

Kornilova, I. (2017). DevOps is a culture, not a role! *Medium.* https://medium.com/@neonrocket/devops-is-a-culture-not-a-role-be1bed149b0

KPMG. (2014). *Over 90 Percent Of U.S. Companies Are Changing Existing Business Models: KPMG Survey.* http://www.kpmg.com/us/en/issuesandinsights/articlespublications/press-releases/pages/over-90-percent-of-us-companies-are-changing-existing-business-models-kpmg-survey.aspx. 2014.

Lanubile, F., Ebert, Ch., Prikladnicki, R., & Vizcaíno, A. (2010). Collaboration Tools for Global Software Engineering. *IEEE Journals & Magazines, 27*(2).

Lebreton, P. (1957). The Case Study Method and the Establishment of Standads of efficiency. Academy of Management Proceedings, 103.

Markides, C. (2011, March). Crossing the Chasm: How to Convert Relevant Research Into Managerially Useful Research. *The Journal of Applied Behavioral Science, 47*(1), 121–134. doi:10.1177/0021886310388162

McMullen, P. R., & Tarasewich, P. (2005). A beam search heuristic method for mixed-model scheduling with setups. *International Journal of Production Economics, 96*(2), 273–283. doi:10.1016/j.ijpe.2003.12.010

MID. (2014). *ArchiMate-Enterprise Architecture Modeling with ArchiMate.* MID GmbH.

Myers, B., Pane, J., & Ko, A. (2004). *Natural programming languages and environments.* ACM New York. doi:10.1145/1015864.1015888

Neumann, G. (2002). Programming Languages in Artificial Intelligence. In Encyclopaedia of Information Systems. Academic Press.

Österle, H. (1995). Business Engineering: Prozess- und Systementwicklung. Band 1: Entwurfstechniken. Springer.

Oxford Dictionaries. (2013). *Heuristics*. http://www.oxforddictionaries.com/definition/english/heuristic

Palermo, J., Bogard, J., Hexter, E., Hinze, M., & Skinner, M. (2012). ASP.NET Model View Control 4. In *Action*. Manning Publisher.

Putri, N., & Yusof, S. M. (2009). Critical success factors for implementing quality engineering tools and techniques in Malaysian's and Indonesian's automotive industries: An Exploratory Study. *Journal Proceedings of the International MultiConference of Engineers and Computer Scientists.*, 2, 18–20.

Ronald, D. (1961). Management Information Crisis. Harvard Business Review, 39(5), 111-121.

Sankaralingam, K., Ferris, M., Nowatzki, T., Estan, C., Wood, D., & Vaish, N. (2013). *Optimization and Mathematical Modeling in Computer Architecture*. Morgan & Claypool Publishers.

Shimamoto, D. (2013). CPA firm technology: Eight keys to success; these steps will increase the odds of effective implementation and deployment. CPA/CITP, CGMA. E.D.G.E.-Sharpening the Next Generation of CPAs Conference, Austin, TX.

Spencer, L. (1955). 10 problems that worry presidents. Harvard Business Review, 33(6), 75-83.

Taleb, M., & Cherkaoui, O. (2012, January). Pattern-Oriented Approach for Enterprise Architecture: TOGAF Framework. *Journal of Software Engineering & Applications*, 5(1), 45–50. doi:10.4236/jsea.2012.51008

The Open Group. (2002). *Mapping the TOGAF ADM to the Zachman Framework*. https://www.opengroup.org/architecture/0210can/togaf8/doc-review/togaf8cr/c/p4/zf/zf_mapping.htm

The Open Group. (2011a). *The Open Group's Architecture Framework*. www.open-group.com/togaf

Thomas, A. (2015). *Innovation Insight for Microservices*. https://www.gartner.com/doc/3157319/innovation-insight-microservices

Tidd, J. (2006). *From Knowledge Management to Strategic Competence* (2nd ed.). Imperial College. doi:10.1142/p439

Tidd, J., & Bessant, J. (2009). *Managing Innovation, Integrating Technological, Market and Organizational Change* (4th ed.). Wiley.

Tidd, J., & Bessant, J. (2018). *Managing Innovation: Integrating Technological, Market and Organizational Change* (6th ed.). Wiley. USA.

Trad, A. (2018a). *The Business Transformation Framework's Resources Library. Internal project.* IBISTM.

Trad, A. (2018b). *The Transformation Framework Proof of Concept. Internal project and paper.* IBISTM.

Trad, A. (2019a). *Applied Mathematical Model for Business Transformation Projects-The intelligent Strategic Decision Making System (iSDMS). Encyclopaedia.* IGI-Global.

Trad, A., & Kalpić, D. (2014b). *The Selection and Training Framework (STF) for Managers in intelligent city Innovation Transformation Projects - Managerial Recommendations.* IEEE.

Trad, A., & Kalpić, D. (2014d). *The Selection and Training Framework (STF) for Managers in Business Innovation and Transformation Projects - The Profile of a Business Transformation Manager.* IMRA.

Trad, A., & Kalpić, D. (2016a). *The intelligent city Transformation Framework for Business (and Financial) Architecture-Modelling Projects. In Encyclopaedia of E-Commerce Development, Implementation, and Management.* IGI-Global.

Trad, A., & Kalpić, D. (2016b). *A Transformation Framework Proposal for Managers in Business Innovation and Business Transformation Projects-A heuristics decision module's background.* ABMR.

Trad, A., & Kalpić, D. (2017a). *An Intelligent Neural Networks Micro Artefact Patterns' Based Enterprise Architecture Model.* IGI-Global.

Trad, A., & Kalpić, D. (2017b). *A Neural Networks Portable and Agnostic Implementation TKM&F for Business Transformation Projects. The Basic Structure.* IEEE.

Trad, A., & Kalpić, D. (2017c). *A Neural Networks Portable and Agnostic Implementation TKM&F for Business Transformation Projects. The Framework.* IEEE.

Trad, A., & Kalpić, D. (2017d). *A Neural Networks Portable and Agnostic Implementation TKM&F for Business Transformation Projects- The Basic Structure. IEEE Conference on Computational Intelligence.* France.

Trad, A., & Kalpić, D. (2017e). *The Business Transformation and Enterprise Architecture Framework / The London Inter Bank Offered Rate Crisis - The Model.* ABMR.

Trad, A., & Kalpić, D. (2018a). *The Business Transformation Framework and Enterprise Architecture Framework for Managers in Business Innovation-Knowledge and Intelligence Driven Development (KIDD). Encyclopaedia.* IGI-Global.

Trad, A., & Kalpić, D. (2018b). *The Business Transformation Framework and Enterprise Architecture Framework for Managers in Business Innovation- Knowledge Management in Global Software Engineering (HKMS). Encyclopaedia.* IGI-Global.

Trad, A., & Kalpić, D. (2018c). *The Business Transformation An applied mathematical model for business transformation-The applied case study. Encyclopaedia.* IGI-Global.

Trad, A., & Kalpić, D. (2018d). *The Business Transformation An applied mathematical model for business transformation-The Research Development Projects Concept (RDPC). Encyclopaedia.* IGI-Global.

Trad, A., & Kalpić, D. (2018e). *The Business Transformation An applied mathematical model for business transformation-Introduction and basics. Encyclopaedia.* IGI-Global.

Trad, A., & Kalpić, D. (2018f). *An applied mathematical model for business transformation-The Holistic Critical Success Factors Management System (HCSFMS). Encyclopaedia of E-Commerce Development, Implementation, and Management.* IGI-Global.

Trad, A., & Kalpić, D. (2019b). *The Business Transformation Framework and Enterprise Architecture Framework for Managers in Business Innovation-An applied holistic mathematical model (AHMM4RM). International Journal of Service Science, Management, Engineering, and Technology.*

Trad, A., & Kalpić, D. (2019c). *A Transformation Model for Assessing Risks of (e) Business/(e)Commerce Projects. International Journal of eBusiness.*

Trad, A., & Kalpić, D. (2019d). *Business Transformation and Enterprise Architecture- The Resources Management Research and Development Project (RMSRDP). Encyclopaedia.* IGI-Global.

Trad, A., & Kalpić, D. (2019e). *Business Transformation and Enterprise Architecture-The Holistic Project Resources Management Pattern (HPRMP). Encyclopaedia*. IGI-Global.

Trad, A., & Kalpić, D. (2019f). *Business Transformation and Enterprise Architecture-The Resources Management Implementation Concept (RMIC). Encyclopaedia*. IGI-Global.

Trad, A., & Kalpić, D. (2019g). The Business Transformation Framework and the-Application of a Holistic Strategic Security Concept. E-Leaders, Check Rep. GCASA.

Uppal, M., & Rahman, T. (2013). *Business Transformation Made Straight-Forward*. QR Systems Inc.

Vella, A., Corne, D., & Murphy, C. (2009). Hyper-heuristic decision tree induction. *NaBIC 2009. World Congress*.

Ylimäki, T. (2008). *Potential Critical Success Factors for Enterprise Architecture*. University of Jyväskylä, Information Technology Research Institute.

ADDITIONAL READING

Farhoomand, A. (2004). *Managing intelligent city transformation*. Palgrave Macmillan.

IBM. (2009). *TOGAF or not TOGAF: Extending Enterprise Architecture beyond RUP*. IBM Developer Works.

KEY TERMS AND DEFINITIONS

Manager: Business transformation manager.
Project: Business transformation project.

Chapter 4
Towards an Enterprise Business Architecture Readiness Assessment Model

Tandokazi Zondani
https://orcid.org/0000-0003-0906-2593
Cape Peninsula University of Technology, South Africa

Tiko Iyamu
https://orcid.org/0000-0002-4949-094X
Cape Peninsula University of Technology, South Africa

ABSTRACT

Often at times many organisations fail to achieve the objectives of their enterprise business architecture (EBA). This can be attributed to lack of assessment of readiness. This is also because there are no models specific to EBA readiness assessment. The lack of readiness assessment before deployment often results to challenges such as uncoordinated business designs, lack of flow in processes, derailment of activities, which make cost of operations prohibitive, increase complexity in managing potential risks, and service stagnancy. These challenges led to this study whose aim was to propose a solution that can be used to assess the readiness of EBA in an organisation. From the interpretivist perspective, the case study approach was employed to gain better understanding of the factors that influence the readiness of EBA in an organisation. The hermeneutics approach was applied in the analysis of the data. The sudy reveals the factors that influence the deployment of business architecture in organisations.

DOI: 10.4018/978-1-5225-8229-8.ch004

INTRODUCTION

The Enterprise Business Architecture (EBA) is one of the domains of Enterprise Architecture (EA) (Dang & Pekkola, 2017). Other domains of EA include Information, Technical and Application Architectures (Iyamu, 2015). According to Whittle and Myrick (2016), EBA provides the blueprint for business processes, events and activities, and focuses on both current and future views of an organisation. In the last two decades, the interest in EBA by both academic and business organisations continues to increase (Hadaya & Gagnon, 2017; Amit & Zott, 2015; Versteeg & Bouwman, 2006). EBA is considered to be the most dominant of the domain of EA, which includes the information, technical and application architectures (Whittle & Myrick, 2016). Based on the interest in the concept of EBA, many projects have been carried out by both academia and practitioners in the areas of development and implementation, as well as in practice (Wikusna, 2018; Sandkuhl et al., 2017).

EBA is used to define the critical aspects of organisational processes, its strategy, polices, monitoring methods and business organisation (Sandkuhl et al., 2017). Versteeg and Bouwman (2006) argue that EBA contributes to governance and the management of activities within the business and computing environments of an organisation. In Shaanika and Iyamu's (2018) view, EBA is used to define an enterprise from a business perspective and then leverages its formalised description to govern and manage change and transformation of environment trends. Minoli (2008) explains EBA as the architectural formulation of the business function, which comprises of documentation that outlines the company's most important business processes. Wikusna (2018) argues that EBA is a domain that contributes towards clarifying the complexities within an organisation whose purpose it is to develop functional, informative, process and application architectures.

Despite the benefits of the concept as discussed above, many organisations experience various challenges with EBA implementation and practice (Hadaya & Gagnon, 2017). According to Whittle and Myrick (2016), some of the challenges arise from the prioritisation of the business activities that always change. Also, some of the challenges of EBA include an understanding of factors such as the risks involved, success factors, as well as the design and implementation of the business for enterprise purposes (Gromoff, Bilinkis & Kazantsev, 2017). The challenges are often experienced at different stages of the concept, from development to implementation and post-implementation (Iyamu, 2015). This is attributable to the lack of a readiness assessment before the process was embarked upon in a specific environment.

An assessment reveals organisational strengths and weaknesses which increase the formidability of readiness in the deployment and manageability of a solution (Hedayati et al., 2014). Ajami et al. (2011) argue that assessment is an essential and critical stage prior to the implementation of solutions. It aims at evaluating preparedness of all the components of an organisation, namely application, information, technical architectures, IT systems and procedures. Based on the outcome of the assessment, organisations are able to make proper and well-informed decisions about whether to go ahead with the implementation or not.

Despite the fact that existing literature recognises the significance of readiness in the computing environment including EA (Andersen & Henriksen, 2005), empirical work remains limited (Abdolvand, Albadvi & Ferdowsi, 2008). Supporting this viewpoint, Alghamdi, Goodwin and Rampersad (2011) proposed readiness assessment solutions dimensions, which include ICT architecture and e-governance. Hedayati et al. (2014) proposed a model that can be used to evaluate organisational readiness in order to implement service-oriented architecture (SOA). Bakar (2014) proposes an EA assessment model for a developing country, with focus on alignment between business and ICT, which integrates the information systems, processes, organisational units and people in public sector.

Even though there are few assessment models, there was no readiness-assessment model specifically for EBA available at the time that this study was in progress. This is a serious challenge, which has affected organisations for many years, in that it either slows implementation of the EBA (Hussein, Mahrin & Maarop, 2017) or derails the implementation and practice of the concept (Aji & Widodo, 2019).

The structure of this paper begin with introduction of the study, followed by review of related literature and discussion of the methodology that was employed. Thereafter, the results are discussed, the data analysis is presented, and finally, a conclusion is drawn.

REVIEW OF RELATED STUDIES

Enterprise Business Architecture (EBA) is a domain of enterprise architecture (EA), which defines the models that represent business processes, operations, interactions and boundaries (Whelan & Meaden, 2016). Karney (2009) argues that EBA shares the artefacts of IT architecture in shaping the goals and objectives of an organisation. According to Iyamu, Nehemia-Maletzky and Shaanika (2016), EBA is applied in an organisation to define its scope and boundaries, its design and how it can develop business process models. Some of the benefits of EBA are to improve decision-making, reduce costs and improve alignment between business and IT units (Dang & Pekkola, 2017; Sandkuhl et al., 2017). According to Karney (2009), EBA focuses on documenting organisational vision, facilitates the formulation of business requirements, towards improving competitiveness.

Even though the interest in EBA has grown over the years, the concept continues to encounter challenges in practice (Hadaya & Gagnon, 2017). According to Versteeg and Bouwman (2006), it is difficult to find an organisation that has successfully deployed EBA. Even though this conclusion was reached over a decade ago, little or nothing has changed. Dang and Pekkola (2017) portray this point by arguing that the challenges of EBA are documented in other studies. According to Whelan and Meaden (2016), given the challenges and trends that organisations face, it is not surprising that the practice of Business Architecture is in the increase. Gromoff et al. (2017) suggest that the complex parameters which are used for unstructured processes during planning is one of EBA's challenges.

In addition to the slow implementation of EBA, it is difficult to find an organisation that has institutionalised the concept (Iyamu, 2015; Versteeg & Bouwman, 2006). This can be attributed to the many challenges that have been identified in literature and in practice (Hedayati et al., 2014; Ajami et al., 2011). The challenges manifest themselves because a readiness assessment has not been conducted before implementation. Adjorlolo (2013) argues that readiness assessment is used to determine success factors. It is one of the ways of reducing the risk of failure in organisational projects. It is an official measurement of the preparedness of an organisation to undergo change but this instrument is currently not available for EBA. As a result, the promoters of EBA struggle to convince management and stakeholders how to mitigate against risk and other challenging factors.

Even though there is an increasing interest in EA from the public sector, the implementation and practice of the concept in organisations remain a concern (Hussein, Mahrin & Maarop, 2017). This is synonymous to the EA domains, and can be associated with lack of readiness assessment, which influence success implementation of the concept. Readiness assessment helpful in reducing potential risks in the implementation of EA (Aji & Widodo, 2019). The assessment model is a useful and cost-effective method for the implementation of the EA (Bakar, Harihodin & Kama, 2016). Bakar (2014) proposes an Enterprise Architecture assessment model for the Malaysian Government, with focus on alignment between business and ICT, which integrates the information systems, processes, organisational units and people in public sector.

In 2001, the Gartner group recommended five factors for measuring the value of Business Architecture in an organisation (Harris, Grey & Rozwell, 2001). Thirteen years later, AL-Malaise AL-Ghamdi (2017) proposed a model that could be used to measure the impact of Business Architecture on an organisation, because the challenges persist. Some of the existing challenges around EBA are due to the fact that organisations tend to focus on processes and services without explicitly understanding the timing factors that may make or break a business model. For example, understanding how the cycles of production are synchronised with sales cycles and cash income is critical to cash flow and the inventory. Analysis of the two separately would be unlikely to reveal the existence or importance of the relationship

(Whelan & Meaden, 2016). Some of the challenges exist primarily because EBA has not undergone a readiness assessment in the environment.

Readiness assessment helps with a smoother transition from the current to a future state (Werner, 2009), which essentially needed in the deployment of the EBA in an organisation. Alshaher (2013) argues that the lack of assessment of an organisation's readiness is the primary reason for the failure of implemented projects, as has been indicated by EBA attempts at many organisations. This is mainly because potential challenges are not fully identified and addressed in accordance with the processes, procedures, events, activities and structure in the course of the development and implementation of EBA. The assessment assists organisations to identify limitations and provide suitable solutions in the implementation, deployment and post-deployment phases of IT solutions. According to Alghamdi et al. (2011), a readiness assessment is purposely used to improve the effectiveness of an organisation's initiatives. Thus, the current state of an organisation's readiness can be evaluated and the desirable state can be managed to enable the transition from the current state to the desirable state (Jahani et al., 2010).

RESEARCH METHODOLOGY

This study followed the interpretivist approach. This was primarily because the approach's rules create signification or meaningful symbolic systems that provide ways for actors to see and interpret events (Iyamu, 2011). According to Myers and Avison (2002), the interpretivist approach generally attempts to understand phenomena through the meanings that people assign to them. Chen and Hirschheim (2004) argue that the interpretivist approach emphasises the subjective meaning of the reality that is constructed through a human and social interaction process. Based on the aim of this study, which is to propose a solution which could be used to assess the readiness of an organisation for the deployment of Business Architecture, the qualitative method was selected from the interpretivist perspective. This is primarily because the opinions and views of individuals, groups and organisational perspectives were required to achieve the research aim. The qualitative method focuses on quality from the perspective of subjectivism (Bradshaw, Atkinson & Doody, 2017), which enables an understanding of what the participants' view and opinions are, and how they come to the conclusions that they reach (Venkatesh et al., 2013). The method is associated with interactive of solutions, which allow complexities to be discussed or explained and, in the process, new topics emerge (Creswell & Poth, 2017).

The case study approach was employed in this research. Other design approaches that were explored are the survey and ethnographic approaches (Yazan, 2015), but the case study was considered most appropriate because of the nature of the research aim. This was primarily because the approach allows an in-depth study of the entity as described by Yin (2017). Also, through the use of the case study approach, theories can be generated and generalised (Creswell & Poth, 2017), which this study aimed to achieve. A set of criteria was used to select an organisation, to ensure appropriateness as follows:

i.   access to the organisation– this means that the organisation allows its employees to participate in the study, and documents about the organisation that relate to this study can be used.
ii.   deploys Business Architecture – the organisation has implemented the concept of Business Architecture in the period of over twelve months. This was to ensure that the employees have hands-on experience.

A Cape Town-based financial institution was selected. A pseudonym, TzFinance, was used to anonymise the company, in accordance with the company's requirements in granting access for academic study.

The semi-structured interview technique was employed in the collection of qualitative data. Individuals were interviewed by using interview guidelines, based on the research objectives. The objectives of the study are: (1) To understand how Business Architecture requirements are defined, identified in an organisation; (2) To understand how Business Architecture is deployed in an organisation; and (3) To examine how the concept of Business Architecture is practised in an organisation. The guidelines were intended to ensure uniformity, and consistency. The interview guidelines were based on the research objectives. Specific criteria were used to select participants in the study. According to Iyamu (2018), criteria are intended to enhance the integrity and richness of the data. The criteria used include:

i.   The participant should have been employed at the organisation for at least one year. This is to ensure that the participant understands the environment well enough, to provide useful information about the organisation.
ii.   The participant must have worked in the area of Business Architecture for at least two years. This was for the purpose of accessing rich data.
iii.   Participants must be employed by either the IT or business unit of the organisation.

A total of four employees were interviewed at the point of saturation, which means that no new information was forthcoming. The interviews were conducted by using the face-to-face approach. They were also conducted in locations chosen by the participants. Where this approach was unfeasible in practical terms, the telephone was used.

The hermeneutics approach was employed from the interpretivist viewpoint for the analysis of the data. The hermeneutics approach is a classical scholarly tradition of how to read, understand and interpret texts (Myers & Avison, 2002). This approach helps to reconstruct the original meaning of a text, namely that the meaning is as it is intended by the author (Suominen & Tuomi, 2015). As prescribed by hermeneutics, the approach was employed by going backwards and forwards with the qualitative data, to enable identification of the factors that influence Business Architecture in an enterprise. This includes examining and understanding how factors manifest themselves in influencing the operations of Business Architecture in an organisation.

RESULTS AND DISCUSSION

From the analysis presented, seven factors were revealed to influence assessment of Business Architecture readiness in an organisation. These factors were based on the result of subjective research from an interpretivist perspective. As shown in Figure 1, the factors are: (1) requirements; (2) alignment between business and IT units; (3) organisational structure; (4) capability; (5) stability; (6) reengineering of organisational activities; and (7) flexibility of activities.

Figure 1. Factors influencing readiness assessment

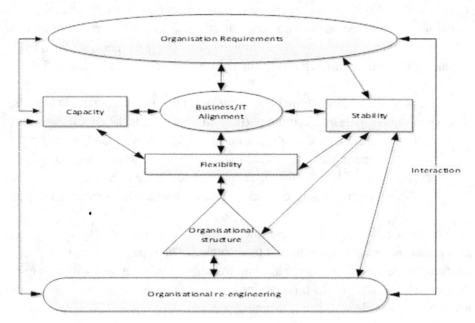

The factors as shown in Figure 1 are discussed as follows:

i. Requirements

The requirements are supposed to address the business initiatives and should be used as a foundation for building effective business solutions. For these reasons, requirements are identified and gathered to ensure the successful development of initiatives (Abai, Yahaya & Deraman, 2013). Based on its criticality, it is paramount that the right (skilled) people are chosen in the process, to gather requirements identified by the most appropriate personnel. Thus, the requirements for the development of the Business Architecture are gathered from the business users, which include managers, team leaders and other employees within the business units of an organisation, working towards Business Architecture, ensuring successful development and deployment in an organisation.

Organisations have different settings with unique objectives, goals and mission and therefore the process of identifying and gathering of requirements-will be unique. As revealed in the analysis, TzFinance did not have any formal approach, such as a template for gathering identified requirements. As a result, the requirements were often not documented. Organisational requirements for Business Architecture need to be documented for the following main reasons: (1) as business changes, the requirements can be revisited; and (2) the output from Business Architecture can be measured and validated against the requirements. Based on these reasons, the relationship and interaction between business and IT units are enacted and facilitated. The interaction results in alignment, which enables sharing and use of the available capacity including participation and common understanding of the organisation's reengineering. The gathering of the identified requirements and documentation is critical for assessing the readiness for Business Architecture in an organisation.

ii. Business/IT alignment

Alignment between the business and IT units is important for effectiveness and efficiency of activities and operations in an organisation (Silvius, 2009). Business Architecture wholly relies on alignment for its development and implementation. In the absence of alignment between the business and IT units, as in the case of TzFinance, the organisation is bound to develop challenges in understanding the factors that influence IT solutions. In the absence of alignment, even if the systems are architected, there will be disparity and incompatibility between business initiatives and IT solutions. According to Connolley, Scholtz and Calitz (2013:1), 'IT is often seen not to meet business expectations and one of the reasons for this is a lack of Business-IT alignment'.

Alignment is enabled through relationships and interaction between units within an organisation. It draws upon a synergy between business processes and IT solutions. Alignment results in flexible execution of events, processes and activities, which, in turn, contribute to creating a stable environment. According to Pandit (2012), the misalignment between IT and business is due to the fact that IT executives lack business knowledge and business leaders lack knowledge or experience of IT, which results in a stumbling block to the attempts to align both business and IT units towards the organisation's goals and objectives. The failure to meet business needs often results in information silos, which affect organisational efficiency, competitiveness and sustainability.

iii. Organisational Structure

Organisational structure refers to the hierarchical structure of the personnel in an organisation. The organisational structure creates a legal recognition of various levels through which roles and responsibilities are assigned, executed and managed. This helps an organisation to achieve its objectives, goals and mission. The roles and responsibilities are the employees' source of power, which are often employed to dictate and influence activities in the organisation. This makes an organisational structure significantly useful for Business Architecture in navigating through the organisation for buy-in purposes. Also, the organisational structure helps to define ownership of tasks and activities in the development and implementation of Business Architecture.

Alignment between business and IT units can be established and practised through the organisational structure. In addition, it can be used to facilitate business performance (Cosh et al., 2010). Despite this important role prior to the implementation of Business Architecture, TzFinance did not explore the usefulness of its organisational structure, which isolated some systems from one another. As a result, TzFinance IT solutions were not aligned with the organisation's objectives, mission and goals. The lack of the organisational structure's influence, leads to ambiguity and uncertainty of roles in the development and implementation of Business Architecture in the organisation. The organisational structure has to interact to allow the organisation to become more flexible in order to promote organisational reengineering.

iv. Capacity

Business capacity refers to available resources, which are both human and non-human, that are handled by an organisation's team, processes, service or tools (Suryani et al., 2010). The human capacity means skilled personnel rather than the presence of a person. Non-human capacity includes finance and governance. The resources can be scaled up or down by adding, reallocating or removing processes and activities.

The development and implementation of Business Architecture depends wholly on capacity. This can be seen in TzFinance, as the organisation struggled in its pursuit to develop and implement the concept of Business Architecture. It is therefore of the utmost importance for the organisation to weigh up available capacity against the requirements of Business Architecture before it proceeds. It is on this basis that interaction between business and IT units is critical in assessing the nature of what capacity is available for the development and implementation of Business Architecture in the organisation.

v.   Stability

In this study, stability refers to a situation where an environment is kept consistent with the minimum of challenges. It is critical to continuously assess business processes and revise business management development in relation to the environment (Vovchenko et al., 2017). The same approach of assessment applies to IT solutions, including the development and implementation of Business Architecture. This is to detect and manage deficiencies as well as risks within the environment.

When the risk management is properly structured, it provides stability and control in an organisation. In TzFinance, the right structure had to be created which allowed and enabled flexibility that created opportunities and increased innovation for competitive advantage. Stability influences the business's requirements, alignment between business and IT units, organisational structure, the flexible reaction of processes and activities, which affects development and implementation of Business Architecture in an environment.

vi.   Organisation Re-engineering

Organisational re-engineering is often referred to as business process reengineering (BPR), which focuses on the recreation of core processes and activities in an organisation (Goksoy et al., 2012). The process also focuses on the analysis and design of workflows and events. The BPR aims at helping an organisation to rethink the improvement of customer service and competitiveness.

It is in this process of re-engineering that inefficiencies are identified and amended, to ensure that all processes are current and relevant in helping the organisation to achieve its objectives. In deploying Business Architecture in TzFinance, process re-engineering and proper documentation of those processes were identified as gaps in the process of identifying requirements. If the processes are not re-engineered in an organisation for the implementation of Business Architecture, organisational performance will not increase, will lack efficiency and competitiveness in a rapidly changing world. Organisational re-engineering entails interaction with the organisational structure and an understanding of the business capacity and stability.

vii. Flexibility

Flexibility is the ability to improve on response time in a business setting. This allows changes which are necessary to respond effectively to the ever-changing environment as quickly as possible. Organisations need to be able to adjust easily to business initiatives with minor or no obstruction to on-going events and activities. According to Bock et al. (2012), flexibility involves responsiveness to pressure and a proactive rather than a reactive approach.

In TzFinance, the Business Architecture concept was a success due to their flexibility which was a result of restructuring to ensure proper skill-sets were aligned with the initiative at hand. Without flexibility, it becomes difficult to assess changing requirements in the light of the implementation of Business Architecture in an organisation. As a result, deficiencies, such as risk, might be detected. The flexibility enables interaction with business/IT alignment and organisational structure.

ANALYSIS OF THE DATA

In carrying out the analysis, a code-format was applied as follows: *[participant_codename, page#: line#]*. For example, TzFin01, Pg 2: 3-5. This means participant 1, page 2 of the interview transcript: from line number 3 to 5. The coding helps referencing from the data appropriately.

The analysis was conducted according to the research objectives, which are (1) to understand how Business Architecture requirements are identified and gathered in an organisation; (2) to understand how Business Architecture is deployed in an organisation; and (3) to examine how the concept of Business Architecture is practised in an organisation.

Identification of Requirements for the Business Architecture of an Organisation

Business Architecture focuses on the design and governance of processes, activities and events in an organisation (Marks, 2008). Thus, the requirements for the development of the architecture are of the utmost importance. As a result, it is critical to determine the appropriate requirements. This means requirements that are unique to the organisation's vision and specific to its goal and objectives.

The process therefore necessitates involvement of the most relevant personnel in determining the requirements. According to Hohmann (2003), the individuals involved must have a good understanding of both the business requirements and the organisation's objectives.

In TzFinance, the idea of Business Architecture came about when a new IT head (CIO) was employed. Before that, the organisation did not have any form of formalised structure or an architecture capability even though its systems had been architected. This means that the architecture of each system had been isolated from one another. Risk and stability were the other two factors that triggered the idea of the Business Architecture concept in the organisation. Both these factors were looked at from the perspective of the business processes and duplication of those processes, so that the organisation could understand how the parts fit together. This has the potentials of being a risk, and the regulatory aspect could alert the organisation to this.

It is crucial that the personnel that are involved in the identification and collection of requirements for Business Architecture have a good understanding of the organisation on the one hand, and, on the other hand, be knowledgeable about the concept of Business Architecture. From the organisation's perspective, there are three main focuses: (1) organisational vision; (2) business processes and events of the organisation; and (3) organisation's relationship with its customers, partners and the environment.

The office of the Chief Information Officer (CIO) communicate the identified requirements of the Business Architecture to the IT Department within TzFinance. There was no formal method for identifying the requirements, such as a template. It was IT initiative to approach the business units about their challenges. There has been a debate in recent years about whether Business Architecture should be driven by the business unit or IT unit (Pandit, 2012). The intention of the TzFinance IT representative was to understand how IT solutions could be used to add more value to the business objectives.

In TzFinance, another member of staff, a business analyst was involved in identifying and gathering of the requirements on behalf of the organisation, for the implementation of Business Architecture. Restructuring in the organisation had taken place to accommodate the concept of Business Architecture. This resulted in the promotion of a business analyst to the position of a business architect in preparation for the implementation of Business Architecture. In the formulation of the requirements, factors that influenced the responses from the business units were considered. These included process fragmentation, systems' interactions and relationships. The requirements were therefore aligned with the strategic intent of the organisation.

Business architecture focuses on business processes, activities and events, also related factors such as people and processes which were also considered in identifying and gathering of requirements for the concept. This was to help understand how these factors fit together, because an organisation cannot have systems if it does not understand how the business units fit together, including the processes that they underpin. Business architecture helps to understand the factors that connect the processes and systems in the organisation.

The requirements for utilising Business Architecture were identified by the IT Department because of two main reasons: first, the business units were not knowledgeable about the concept of business architecture. Generally, the business units considered the Business Architecture as mainly a theory rather than a concept that can be put to practice. This is not unique to TzFinance, as many organisations continue to theorise the concept of Business Architecture (Iyamu, 2019). Second, the business did not know what they wanted. Hence, the IT unit had to take the leadership in identifying and gathering the requirements for the implementation of the Business Architecture.

The Deployment of Business Architecture in an Organisation

The deployment (development and implementation) of Business Architecture aligns with the organisation's needs as they evolve. For this reason, the deployment of Business Architecture is governed by policy, principles and standards, which cover both business and technological requirements. In addition, deployment requires executive-level support, structured decision-making processes and a strategy based on an understanding of the organisation's vision.

The deployment of Business Architecture is influenced by both business and IT factors. The business factors include process design, structure, relationships, interaction, people and management. Some of the IT factors are the integration of processes and enabling collaboration between business units or organisations. Without an understanding and consideration of these factors, it is nearly impossible to assess the value of Business Architecture in an organisation.

The challenge experienced with the deployment of Business Architecture in the organisation could be associated with the lack of proper preparation before the concept was embarked upon. The lack of preparation also affects assessment of the maturity levels of the concept in the organisation.

As a result of poor preparation, the deployment of Business Architecture at TzFinance did not follow all the necessary steps such as conducting readiness assessment, and developing template for collecting requirements. The implementation was considered informal because there was no buy-in from the management and some of the employees. The informal approach can work if it is solely the IT Department's responsibility to make decisions about technology-related solutions and matters in the organisation. The IT Department explores its mandate and imposes solutions such as Business Architecture on the business units. This is irrespective of whether the business understands the concept or not and whether they have the capability of adapting or not. This type of approach has negative implications from both technical and non-technical points of view.

The business unit preferred to drive issues that were related to technological solutions in TzFinance. This is a challenge as many business personnel do not have the technical expertise and know-how to pose technical solutions. The business is not in favour of process documentation, which they consider worthless considering the fact that they have been running the business with current processes. When processes are documented properly, it aids the business to identify the gaps and opportunities.

The implementation of Business Architecture is process-oriented. It follows sequential steps such as documentation of the current situation; formulation of a definition of the concept in the context of the organisation; documentation of the future shape of the organisation; formulation of structure; and upskilling of personnel (Iyamu, 2012). In TzFinance, nothing was documented, which made it difficult to track and trace business activities which are related to processes, coexisting systems and their alignment. Documented processes help to identify gaps, process duplication and opportunities.

Another challenge in the implementation of Business Architecture has to do with the human element. Some of the business architects do not have sufficient experience to take on the task that they were allocated to execute. Also, the main promoter of Business Architecture has a line manager who did not fully support the initiative of implementing Business Architecture in the organisation. The manager's push back is attributed to a lack of knowledge of the concept.

The Practice of the Concept of Business Architecture in an Organisation

For the purpose of improving and mastering business activities, events and business processes, the concept of Business Architecture was deployed at TzFinance. The deployment of the concept included creating standardisation, structure and change management, to foster competitiveness.

The standardisation is intended to ensure the unification of the organisation's documentations, which would enable a more cohesive and comprehensive collection and use of business requirements. The structure covers the hierarchy of the people involved in the practice of Business Architecture in the organisation. In addition, it includes formalising processes and events concerning the practice of Business Architecture within the organisation. This was also the case with change management, where processes and the format of documents were streamlined with the purpose of unification. This helps business units to begin to understand alignment between themselves and the IT unit.

Business architecture does not change the rules of the organisation, but enables it to be flexible so that it can be reengineered. This encourages a dynamic business environment. This includes inclusiveness of about the regulations within which the organisation, TzFinance, operates. An approach that allows flexibility and the reengineering of the processes, rules and regulations, reduces risk. The flexibility and reengineering of business rules and regulations increase stakeholders' confidence in the organisation, which creates stability.

Challenges of fragmentation arise when some of the business units are not part of the Business Architecture deployment. In TzFinance, the retail business unit was not part of the implementation. As a result, a system (customer relationship management) that was deployed to serve the entire organisation began to encounter challenges. This was because IT facilitates solutions, that were defined by the architecture, excluded a business unit in its coverage. Before the implementation of Business Architecture, some of the business units made verbal requests to the IT specialists, to change some services. This was because the business units did not like creating documentation of processes and events. The IT specialists obliged because the requests can potentially contribute towards creating value to the business, even though they were well aware that such undocumented processes were imposing a huge risk to the business environment of the organisation. Through the Business Architecture, the documentation is intended to enable tracing and tracking of incidents and events.

Another aspect is the area of communication, which has improved since the implementation of Business Architecture in the organisation. Personnel from both business and IT units have improved the ways in which they communicate with one other in finding solutions for the organisation. The business has to understand that it is not about systems, but about processes. The processes have to align. The systems then need to align with those processes.

The introduction of documentation processes and formal structures is making employees think and ask questions differently. The implementation of Business Architecture was an eye opener to many of the employees, particularly those in the business units. It makes employees aware of the significance of governance in the processes and activities of the organisation. For this reason, there was more buy-in from the business. Prior to implementation, the business did not know how long their request for change would take to implement. This was because the underpinning processes had not been properly structured, and, most importantly, they were not aware of whether their request had made any impact on organisational activities.

One of the most significant values that Business Architecture added to the business was the ability to make informed decisions, which is aimed at improved sustainability and competitiveness. The value-add can be associated with the formal structure, the documentation approach and flexibility which leads to reengineering processes and activities towards fulfilling the business objectives, goals and mission.

CONCLUSION

The lack of a readiness-assessment model has slowed down the implementation of Business Architecture in organisations, which affects its advancement. This study proposes a solution in the form of a readiness-assessment model to be used specifically for Business Architecture and which can be used by an organisation that is interested in deploying the concept. Figure 1 can be used to assist organisations and managers in their quest to gaining better understanding of the factors that influence readiness assessment. By means of the model, an organisation is able to justify the deployment of the concept, which has been a challenge for many individuals and organisations for many years. The paper adds to literature from both business and IT perspectives. Thus, the study contributes to both business advancement and academic development.

Even though the study fills a significant gap in the concept of Business Architecture, there is room for further studies, to develop a readiness assessment model for business architecture. Requirements can be defined for each of the factors of the readiness-assessment model, based on empirical evidence.

REFERENCES

Abai, N. H. Z., Yahaya, J. H., & Deraman, A. (2013). User requirement analysis in data warehouse design: A review. *Procedia Technology*, *11*, 801–806. doi:10.1016/j.protcy.2013.12.261

Abdolvand, N., Albadvi, A., & Ferdowsi, Z. (2008). Assessing readiness for business process reengineering. *Business Process Management Journal*, *14*(4), 497–511. doi:10.1108/14637150810888046

Adjorlolo, S., & Ellingsen, G. (2013). Readiness assessment for implementation of electronic patient record in Ghana: A case of university of Ghana hospital. *Journal of Health Informatics in Developing Countries*, *7*(2), 128–140.

Ajami, S., Ketabi, S., Isfahani, S. S., & Heidari, A. (2011). Readiness assessment of electronic health records implementation. *Acta Informatica Medica*, *19*(4), 224–227. doi:10.5455/aim.2011.19.224-227 PMID:23407861

Aji, A. S., & Widodo, T. (2019). Measuring enterprise architecture readiness at higher education institutions. *International Journal of Applied Business and Information Systems*, *3*(1), 14–20.

Al-Malaise Al-Ghamdi, A.S. (2017). A proposed model to measure the impact of business architecture. *Cogent Business & Management*, *4*(1), 1–8.

Alghamdi, I. A., Goodwin, R., & Rampersad, G. (2011). E-government readiness assessment for government organizations in developing countries. *Computer and Information Science*, *4*(3), 3–17. doi:10.5539/cis.v4n3p3

Alshaher, A. A. F. (2013). The McKinsey 7S model framework for e-learning system readiness assessment. *International Journal of Advances in Engineering and Technology*, *6*(5), 1948–1966.

Amit, R., & Zott, C. (2015). Crafting business architecture: The antecedents of business model design. *Strategic Entrepreneurship Journal*, *9*(4), 331–350. doi:10.1002ej.1200

Bakar, N. A. (2014). An Assessment Model for Government Enterprise Architecture Establishment Phase. *Journal of Computational and Theoretical Nanoscience*, *20*(10), 1987–1991.

Bakar, N. A. A., Harihodin, S., & Kama, N. (2016). Assessment of enterprise architecture implementation capability and priority in public sector agency. *Procedia Computer Science*, *100*, 198–206. doi:10.1016/j.procs.2016.09.141

Bock, A. J., Opsahl, T., George, G., & Gann, D. M. (2012). The effects of culture and structure on strategic flexibility during business model innovation. *Journal of Management Studies*, *49*(2), 279–305. doi:10.1111/j.1467-6486.2011.01030.x

Bradshaw, C., Atkinson, S., & Doody, O. (2017). Employing a qualitative description approach in health care research. *Global Qualitative Nursing Research*, *4*, 2333393617742282. doi:10.1177/2333393617742282 PMID:29204457

Chen, W., & Hirschheim, R. (2004). A paradigmatic and methodological examination of information systems research from 1991 to 2001. *Information Systems Journal*, *14*(3), 197–235. doi:10.1111/j.1365-2575.2004.00173.x

Connolley, A., Scholtz, B., & Calitz, A. (2013). Achieving the Benefits of Business-IT Alignment Supported by Enterprise Architecture. *Presentado en 7th International Business Conference*.

Creswell, J. W., & Poth, C. N. (2017). *Qualitative inquiry and research design: Choosing among five approaches*. Sage publications, Inc.

Dang, D. D., & Pekkola, S. (2017). Systematic Literature Review on Enterprise Architecture in the Public Sector. *Electronic. Journal of E-Government, 15*(2), 130–154.

Fleck, K., Smythe, E. A., & Hitchen, J. M. (2011). Hermeneutics of self as a research approach. *International Journal of Qualitative Methods, 10*(1), 14–29. doi:10.1177/160940691101000102

Goksoy, A., Ozsoy, B., & Vayvay, O. (2012). Business process reengineering: Strategic tool for managing organizational change an application in a multinational company. *International Journal of Business and Management, 7*(2), 89–112. doi:10.5539/ijbm.v7n2p89

Gromoff, A., Bilinkis, Y., & Kazantsev, N. (2017). Business architecture flexibility as a result of knowledge-intensive process management. *Global Journal of Flexible Systems Managment, 18*(1), 73–86. doi:10.100740171-016-0150-4

Hadaya, P., & Gagnon, B. (2017). *Business Architecture: The Missing Link in Strategy Formulation, Implementation and Execution.* ASATE Publishing.

Harris, K., Grey, M. C., & Rozwell, C. (2001). *Changing the View of ROI to VOI—Value on Investment.* Gartner Research Note, SPA-14-7250.

Hedayati, A., Shirazi, B., & Fazlollahtabar, H. (2014). An Assessment Model for the State of Organizational Readiness Inservice Oriented architecture Implementation Based on Fuzzy Logic. *Computer Science and Information Technology, 2*(1), 1–9.

Hohmann, L. (2003). *Beyond software architecture: creating and sustaining winning solutions.* Addison-Wesley Longman Publishing Co., Inc.

Hussein, S. S., Mahrin, M. N. R., & Maarop, N. (2017). Preliminary study of Malaysian Public Sector (MPS) transformation readiness through Enterprise Architecture (EA) establishment. *Pacific Asia Conference on Information Systems (PACIS).*

Iyamu, T. (2011). Institutionalisation of the enterprise architecture: The actor-network perspective. *International Journal of Actor-Network Theory and Technological Innovation, 3*(1), 27–38. doi:10.4018/jantti.2011010103

Iyamu, T. (2012). A framework for developing and implementing the enterprise technical architecture. *Computer Science and Information Systems, 9*(1), 189–206. doi:10.2298/CSIS101103040I

Iyamu, T. (2015). *Enterprise Architecture: from concept to Practise* (2nd ed.). Heidelberg Press.

Iyamu, T. (2018). Implementation of the enterprise architecture through the Zachman Framework. *Journal of Systems and Information Technology, 20*(1), 2–18. doi:10.1108/JSIT-06-2017-0047

Iyamu, T. (2019). What are the implications of theorizing the enterprise architecture? *Journal of Enterprise Transformation,* 1-22.

Iyamu, T., Nehemia-Maletzky, M., & Shaanika, I. (2016). The overlapping nature of Business Analysis and Business Architecture: What we need to know. *Electronic Journal of Information Systems Evaluation, 19*(3), 169–179.

Jahani, B., Javadein, S. R. S., & Jafari, H. A. (2010). Measurement of enterprise architecture readiness within organizations. *Business Strategy Series, 11*(3), 177–191. doi:10.1108/17515631011043840

Karney, J. (2009). *Introduction to business architecture.* Cengage Learning.

Marks, E. A. (2008). *Service-oriented architecture governance for the services driven enterprise.* John Wiley & Sons.

Minoli, D. (2008). *Enterprise architecture A to Z: frameworks, business process modeling, SOA, and infrastructure technology.* Auerbach Publications. doi:10.1201/9781420013702

Myers, M., & Avison, D. (2002). An introduction to qualitative research in information systems. In Qualitative research in information systems, Introducing Qualitative Methods. SAGE Publications, Ltd. doi:10.4135/9781849209687.n1

Pandit, V. (2012). *Challenges in business and IT alignment: Business and IT consulting project report.* https://www.slideshare.net/panditvidur/challenges-in-business-and-it-alignment

Sandkuhl, K., Seigerroth, U., & Kaidalova, J. (2017). Towards Integration Methods of Product-IT into Enterprise Architectures. In *Enterprise Distributed Object Computing Workshop (EDOCW), 2017 IEEE 21st International.* IEEE. 10.1109/EDOCW.2017.13

Shaanika, I., & Iyamu, T. (2018). Developing the enterprise architecture for the Namibian government. *The Electronic Journal on Information Systems in Developing Countries, 84*(3), 1–11. doi:10.1002/isd2.12028

Silvius, A. G. (2009). Business and IT Alignment. *International conference on information management and engineering (ICIME '09).*

Smith, J. A. (Ed.). (2015). *Qualitative psychology: A practical guide to research methods*. Sage.

Suominen, V. & Tuomi, P. (2015). Literacies, hermeneutics, and literature. *Library Trends, 63*(3), 615-628.

Suryani, E., Chou, S. Y., Hartono, R., & Chen, C. H. (2010). Demand scenario analysis and planned capacity expansion: A system dynamics framework. *Simulation Modelling Practice and Theory, 18*(6), 732–751. doi:10.1016/j.simpat.2010.01.013

Venkatesh, V., Brown, S. A., & Bala, H. (2013). Bridging the qualitative-quantitative divide: Guidelines for conducting mixed methods research in information systems. *Management Information Systems Quarterly, 37*(1), 21–54. doi:10.25300/MISQ/2013/37.1.02

Versteeg, G., & Bouwman, H. (2006). Business architecture: A new paradigm to relate business strategy to ICT. *Information Systems Frontiers, 8*(2), 91–102. doi:10.100710796-006-7973-z

Vovchenko, N. G., Holina, M. G., Orobinskiy, A. S., & Sichev, R. A. (2017). Ensuring financial stability of companies on the basis of international experience in construction of risks maps, internal control and audit. *European Research Studies Journal, 20*(1), 350–368. doi:10.35808/ersj/623

Whelan, J. & Meaden, G. (2016). *Business Architecture: A Practical Guide*. Academic Press.

Whittle, R., & Myrick, C. B. (2016). *Enterprise business architecture: The formal link between strategy and results*. CRC Press. doi:10.1201/9781420000207

Wikusna, W. (2018). Enterprise architecture model for vocational high school. *IJAIT, 2*(1), 22–28. doi:10.25124/ijait.v2i01.925

Yazan, B. (2015). Three approaches to case study methods in education: Yin, Merriam, and Stake. *Qualitative Report, 20*(2), 134–152.

Yin, R. K. (2017). *Case study research and applications: Design and methods*. Sage publications.

Chapter 5
Enterprise Architecture Framework for Windhoek Smart City Realisation

Irja N. Shaanika

(iD) https://orcid.org/0000-0003-4896-2738

Namibia University of Science and Technology, Namibia

ABSTRACT

Many cities are adopting information and communication technologies (ICT) to add value to business process. This has led to the realisation of smart cities making them dependable on ICT. In Namibia, the focus is to transform Windhoek into a smart city. However, it is not easy as Windhoek continues to face many challenges, for example lack of collaboration among stakeholders. The challenges could be attributed by lack of approaches such as enterprise architecture (EA). As a management and design approach, EA provides a system view of all components and their relationship. In the absence of EA, realisation of Windhoek smart city will continue to be challenging, impeding the city from providing smart services. The study's aim was to develop EA framework for Windhoek smart city realisation. A qualitative case study approach was employed. Data was interpretively analysed to enable a deeper understating of the influencing factors. Based on the findings, a conceptual EA framework was developed. The framework aims to guide and govern Windhoek city transformation towards its smart objectives.

DOI: 10.4018/978-1-5225-8229-8.ch005

INTRODUCTION

The Windhoek city aims to become smart. A smart city is one that has developed and implemented information communication and technologies (ICT) to manage its day to day activities and other functions of collaboration. Washburn, Sindhu, Balaouras and Dines (2010) described smart city as the use of smart computing technologies in the development of infrastructures and services of the city which includes its administration, healthcare, public safety and transportation. There are many definitions of what a smart city is in literature, however, it is believed that ICT is considered to be an integral part of city operation (Aurigi, 2016). Schleicher, Vögler, Inzinger and Dustdar (2015) explained that the smart city concept originally started with cities utilising ICT to provide services to their citizens and evolved to the use of ICT in a smart way towards the efficient utilisation resources. Basically, in a smart city physical interaction between service providers and customers is minimised to encourage digital interactions. Thus, processes such as water meter readings, electricity consumption bills, and transport fines are settled through secured e-commerce channels. Visvizi, Lytras, Damiani and Mathkou (2018) advised that when developing a smart city, there is a need to consider emerging technologies, such as internet of things (IoT), cognitive computing, data analytics and business intelligence. However, Meijer and Bolivar (2016) argued that smart cities are not only dependable on sophisticated ICT but also on the collaboration of various stakeholders. Fabry and Blanchet (2019) shared that around the world smart cities share common experiences such as smart development according to local context, resources and abilities to integrate stakeholders. According to Meijer and Bolivar (2016), a smart city is build based on three pillars which are technologies, people and governance. However, for City of Windhoek the intergration of these three has been a challenge as city resources are underpressure leading to housing shortages,water and traffic congestions (Amugongo, Nggada, & Sieck, 2016). In addition, the city continues to be challenged by different factors such as silo systems, processes redundancy and lack of stakeholder's inclusivity.

Meijer and Bolivar (2016) posit that to address challenges of modern cities there is a need for smart technologies, smart collaboration, educated population and effective institutions. However, the design, development and management of resources towards the realisation of a smart city is not any easy process. Bolívar (2016) examined that many of the challenges faced by smart cities are beyond that of their traditional institutions in terms of capacities and capabilities and thus the need for new governance approaches towards their various challenges. To resolve city challenges such as urbanisation, global warming, and power and water consumption, smart solutions are a necessity. According to Amugongo, Nggada and Sieck (2016) cities around the world need to address the challenges they are facing in a smart, efficient and effective manner. Thus, cities of many countries employ approaches such as enterprise architecture to coordinate and control their smart city development process (Bolívar, 2016; Habib, Alsmadi, & Prybutok, 2019).

Enterprise architecture (EA) is a comprehensive approach for business development. According to Ahmadi, Farahani, Aliee and Motlagh (2019), EA provides a holistic view of the organisation processes in its current and future state. EA provides reference models that organisations use to study key business strategies and how to achieve their actual and future objectives (Nogueira, Romero, Espadas, & Molina, 2013). As a management tool, EA ensures the planning and alignment of strategic goals, resources and opportunities that arise in organisations (Song & Song, 2010). Alignment of resources (people, processes and technology) provides a cost-effective operation and ensure proper execution of organisational goals (Lakhrouit, Benhaddi, & Baïna, 2015).

EA is made up of architectural domains, which covers technical and non-technical activities in an organisation (Iyamu, 2019). Lakhrouit, Benhaddi and Baïna (2015) examined business, application, information and technology architecture as architectural domains. According to Iyamu (2015), architectural domains are interdepedent as changes to one affects others.

The development and implementation of EA is achieved through frameworks (Iyamu, 2018). Nogueira, Romero, Espadas and Molina (2013) describe enterprise architecture framework (EAF) as primitive structure that provides the foundation for the enterprise construction. According to Tanaka, de Barros and Mendes (2018), it is critical to have EA framework in order to ensure the mangement of components is being carried out as planned. Kitsios and Kamariotou (2019) asserted that the orientation of the enterprise architecture frameworks is challeged by the lack of intergration among business strategies and supporting tecnologies. Song and Song (2010) argued that for successful EA implementation, EAF must be customised according to organisations culture, policy and procedure.

Similarly, to other cities, the City of Windhoek is striving towards becoming a smart city. However, due to the lack of governance approaches such as EA, the city efforts towards building a smart city continues to be a challenge. Tanaka, de Barros and Mendes (2018) states that ICT has become a part of every organisation but when EA is not implemented it becomes difficult to achieve defined goals. Thus, the study aims to present EA framework that will guide the development and management of Windhoek smart city.

The remainder of this paper is structured as follows. The next section presents the City of Windhoek overview. Then literature review that was conducted is presented in the second section. In the third section, the research approach is discussed. The fourth and fifth section presents the data analysis and Findings discussion respectively. The developed framework is presented in section six and lastly the study is concluded.

WINDHOEK CITY: OVERVIEW

Windhoek is the capital and largest city of Namibia. It is found in the Khomas region, which is centrally located in the country. Due to its central location the city has become the country's business hub. Pendleton, Crush and Nickanor (2014: 195) described Windhoek as "the economic and political hub of Namibia, accounting for more than half of the country's manufacturing activity, over 80% of its finances and business services, and two-thirds of its community and social services". As a result, the city is the fastest growing settlement in Namibia, hosting the country most hospitals, universities, schools and business headquarters.

The city's vision is: "To be a SMART and Caring City by 2022" while its mission is: "To enhance the quality of life for all our people by rendering efficient and effective municipal services". The city is structured into suburbs and townships which represents inhabitant's demarcations and boundaries. According to the City Strategic plan (2017-2022) the city's population is fast approaching to 400 000.

The City of Windhoek is governed by a multi-party municipal council that has fifteen seats (Know your Local authority report, 2015). The council meets once a month and decisions are taken collectively, and councillors are bound by such decisions. The council has complete authority over all administrative affairs in the city. Council members devote their official time to problems of basic policy and act as liaisons between the city and the general public.

The city gets its water and power supply from Namwater and Nampowerr, which are government owned parastatals. Various modes of transport are found in the city namely: road, air and train. From the latter the most commonly used mode of transport is road. This is attributed to two reasons which are: ease of accessibility and affordability. On the other hand, the train is only used for carrying goods and people from the city to neighbouring towns not for daily commuting. The city of Windhoek does not have smart trains that can be used on a daily basis for commuting. Air transport is used for both international and domestic flights via two city airports which are: Hosea Kutako international and Eros airport. However, all modes play a critical role in the transportation of goods and services within and outside the city. In addition, all the institutions of higher learning are found in Windhoek, with various campuses countrywide.

At the time of this study the City of Windhoek managed most of its business processes manually with a minimal integration of ICT. Due to this, the city business processes are considered to be slow and ineffective and as a result distracting the city's strategy towards being a smart city. By becoming a smart, the city is envisioned to have improved transports, education and healthcare systems that are integrated and supported by fourth industrial revolution technological infrastructures such as broadband networks and sensors collecting data. Thus, this study main focus is how an architecture framework to guide City of Windhoek endeavours towards smart city realisation be developed.

LITERATURE REVIEW

Smart City

The concept of smart city has become popular amongst cities of different countries. Hoadjli and Rezeg (2019) describe smart city as a strategic approach that integrate different aspects of a city (transport, energy, water management, governance) into a single system based on the opportunities offered by information and communication technologies (ICT). According to Visvizi, Lytras, Damiani and Mathkou (2018) smart city focus on the integration of ICT with urban services which includes transport networks, water supply and waste-disposal facilities. Zait (2017) stated that cities are driven towards smartness due to competition from other cities and their desire to grow. Letaifa (2015) posits that smart cities development is attributed to the need to balance social development and economic growth due to urbanisation. Urbanisation contributes to challenges such as high population density, air pollution, congestion and difficulties in accessing public services (Dameri & Ricciardi, 2015).

Similar to ordinary cities, smart cities also have social, environment and economic dimensions but with a major focus on ICT integration (Habib, Alsmadi & Prybutok, 2019). Tiwar, Ilavarasan and Punia (2019) argues that ICT implementation is a basic requirement for smart city development. According to Zait (2017) a smart city is made up different compnents which are smart economy, smart people, smart governance, smart mobility, smart environment and smart living. Thus, smart city development have an impact on the environment,sustainability and livability of a city (Alawadhi, Aldama-Nalda, Chourabi, & Gil-Garcia, 2012).

The development of smart cities is an approach that cannot be opposed if it leads to the implementation of effective and efficient solutions to resolve various societal problems (Meijer & Bolivar, 2016). However, the development and implementation of a smart city is a challenging process. Hoadjli and Rezeg (2019) explains that many smart cities encounter challenges of information exchange, knowledge sharing among all entities involved and security concerns. These challenges slow down the city strategic growth leading to bureaucratic process and poor services delivery to citizens and business partners. Letaifa (2015) advices cities to design and implement strategies that will enhance city performance and liveability. Thus, cities seek to implement EA for their operations such as planning and governance of resources.

Enterprise Architecture

Enterprise architecture is a conceptual blueprint that defines the structure and operation of an organisation (Supriadi, Kom, & Amalia, 2019). EA is used to guide and manage organisation practices such as technological infrastructures, business process design, and information governance, towards sustainability and competitiveness (Iyamu, 2019:1). According to Wagter, Proper and Witte (2012) EA manages organisation in a coherent and integral way enabling shared understaing among all stakeholders.

As ICT becomes an intergral part of every business process, organisations are challenged with how to intergrate business and technology strategy (Supriadi, Kom, & Amalia, 2019). Supriadi, Kom and Amalia (2019) argue that by imlementing EA, organisations achieve business agility and systems interoperability.

EA is made up of various domains which includes business, information, application and technology. The business architecture is the first domain of EA. The business architecture is where the business strategies, processes and functional requirements of the organisations are defined (Nogueira, Romero, Espadas, & Molina, 2013). The application architecture provides the model that guides the development and implementation of the applications that executes the business requirements (Nogueira, Romero, Espadas, & Molina, 2013). After their design and development, the applications need to be deployed. Thus, the technology architecture describes the technological hardware capabilities that are required to support business, data and application requirements (Lakhrouit, Benhaddi & Baïna, 2015).

Development and implementation of EA is achieved through architectural frameworks. An enterprise architecture framework (EAF) is an underlying infrastructure providing the groundwork for components to work together (Urbaczewski and Mrdalj, 2006). There are many EAF on the market that are designed to address organisation specific needs. Some of the common architectural frameworks includes Zachman, the open group architectural framework (TOGAF) and Gartner (Urbaczewski & Mrdalj, 2006; Nogueira, Romero, Espadas, & Molina, 2013).

A smart city project is complex and concerns a range of activities in a city (Anthopoulos & Fitsilis, 2010). Thus, the need for EA frameworks as a management tool. Smart cities such as Amsterdam developed EA frameworks that guided their projects (Aurigi, 2016). However, due to the uniqueness of organisations, existing frameworks needs be customised according to organisation goals and environments. Letaifa (2015) opined that due to cities diverse context, size and resources there is a need for a comprehensive framework that will conceptualise different components of smart city.

RESEARCH APPROACH

The study employed the qualitative case study approach. Qualitative case study approach is used for studying phenomenon in their real-life settings. Hyett, Kenny and Dickson-Swift (2014) explained that a case is an object that is identified to be studied for a particular reason and it enable the researcher to gain a deeper understanding of the phenomenon being studied. Tetnowski (2015) supports a qualitative case study research as a valuable tool for answering real world questions as it explores a phenomenon within a context. With qualitative case study approach the researcher ask questions about what happened, how it happened and why it happened (Green & Thorogood, 2018). The what, why and how questions enable the researcher to probe further and gain understanding of the behaviours and concepts of the phenomenon being studied.

Crowe, et al. (2011) advised that the selection of a case must be influenced by its uniqueness which are of interest to the researchers not because of it is general representation. The city of Windhoek was used as a case in this study. This was primarily because the City of Windhoek was transforming into a smart city at the time of this study.

Data was collected from the panel discussion on Smart Cities which took place during the 6th National ICT summit held in Windhoek in October 2019. According to Bucy (2006), panel discussion is a powerful technique to discuss matters and encourage critical thinking. The panel consisted of five (5) participants from different organisations namely: MTC, Huawei, City of Windhoek and Ministry of Information and Communication Technology (MICT). These organisations are city of Windhoek stakeholders that collaborate to support and enable ICT services in the city. The panellists were selected based on their role and knowledge of ICT management in their organisations. Questions were asked around the understanding of smart city, what are the infrastructures needed to realise Windhoek smart city, what are some of the current programs/frameworks that are in place to support Windhoek Smart City development, and what are some of the challenges impeding realisation of smart city.

The panel discussion on smart cities took place in front of an audience of 50 people from academia and different industry organisations such as telecommunications, banking, media and ministries. The researcher was part of the audience.

The panel discussion was facilitated by the moderator whose role was to probe the panellists and guide the discussion in the right direction. The panel discussion session lasted for an hour. After the panel discussion, members of the audience were invited to ask the panellists questions and share their experiences, best-practices and solutions for smart city realisation. The researcher collected data by recording the discussions with the tape recorder. The recorded discussions were later transcribed using Microsoft word document. For analysis purposes the panellists were labelled pan1, pan2, pan3, pan4 and pan5 respectively.

DATA ANALYSIS

As discussed above qualitative data was collected. Data was interpretively analysed. Interpretive analysis allows the researcher to derive in depth meaning about the phenomenon of interest by analysing people's experiences (Melendez-Torres, et al., 2017).

What is Your Understanding of a Smart City?

The understanding of a smart city depends on the individual's knowledge of what constitutes a smart city. Thus, the concept is defined differently by individuals. A panellist from the city traditional authority stated that: *"when talking about a smart city, we are looking at smart ways using technologies to resolve the city challenges. Thus, to us a smart city is a city that is sustainable, liveable and efficient (Pan03)".* Another panellist, an IT manager from a telecommunication company, *shared that: "In a smart city, you have ICT playing as an integral role, whether it's managing transport, whether its governance or whether is e-health, e-education, you find that IT is integrated with that particular process, to enable you to have that smart process that require you to have a smart city* (pan04)*".*

What are the Infrastructures Needed to Realise Windhoek Smart City?

To realise Windhoek smart city, quality and reliable infrastructures are mandatory. Infrastructures are primarily important as they are the mediums through which goods and services are provided to communities. Various types of infrastructures are critical for Windhoek smart city realisation. This include: transport, health, education, telecommunication, power, and water and housing infrastructures. The different types of infrastructures are interdependent as the absence of one lead to unsuccessful operation of the others.

Stakeholders and business partner's communication and collaboration was viewed to be critical for infrastructures acquisition and implementation. However, some panellist revealed stakeholders and business partners are working in silos when implementing infrastructures. As a result, some of the infrastructures are not implemented in alignment with the city strategic goals leading to poor planning and mismanagement of resources. A panellist who is a manager at a telecommunication company shared that *"Collaboration is still a matter of concern among our stakeholders. We need to look at interconnection and infrastructure sharing. And that's the idea, you look at the greater national interest, not just about wasting money at one company* (pan02)".

Also, the development and implementation of infrastructures in the city was not fairly distributed, as the low earning communities do not have adequate infrastructures in comparison to their counterpart higher earning communities. According to one of the panellists, a technical manager "Infrastructures such as *telecommunication differs based on where you live. If you live in Klein Kuppe, it's cheaper, if you are economically challenged than you live in Havana it's much more expensive (pan01)".* Unequal distribution of infrastructures causes frustration among city members and they impede the realisation of a smart city.

At the time of this study the city of Windhoek was faced with infrastructures overcrowding as more people keep flocking to the city for better employment, education and health opportunities. In the view of one of the panellists" *for a city like Windhoek a lot of urbanisation is happening as more people are coming to Windhoek, looking for job opportunities and it's also putting strains on the limited resources (pan03)".* Overcrowded infrastructures hinder quality services provision of leading to slow and ineffective services. Another panellist explained that *"For us to realise our smart city, we need to implement more infrastructures but what is hindering us is working in isolation* (pan01)".

What are Some of the Current Programs/Frameworks That are in Place to Support Windhoek Smart City Development?

The development and implementation of Windhoek smart city is anticipated to enable efficient and effective use city resources. The goal is to integrate all business processes with ICT and promote smart governance of infrastructures. However, developing and implementing a smart city is not easy as it seems. This could be attributed to the different technical and non-technical factors involved. Thus, policies and frameworks are critical and required to provide guidance.

At the time of this study, there was no framework, which can be used as a guiding tool in the realisation of Windhoek smart city. One of the panellists shared that*:" We need to have a legal framework that will help us prepare this smart city (pan03)".* Another panellist expressed the need for a framework as follows*: "putting the correct legislative, correct framework and policies in place is important to enable stakeholders to support smart city projects, because we are going to hit the wall if the central government is not taking the leadership (pan04)".* The lack of framework contributed to leadership and planning difficulties causing stakeholders differences.

In order to realise Windhoek smart city there is a need for implementation of policies that are aligning with ICT and business goals. According to one of the participants:" *Everything that is ICT related needs to be business driven, when I look at it from policies perspective. And when I say business driven, the policies would be incorporated in the business process. If those two gears move together they would actually move into the right direction and an impediment in the policy would actually delay the adoption of technology* (pan04)". The alignment between ICT and business process is fundamental for the city growth and competitiveness. The alignment of policies and business goals is achieved through stakeholder's inclusivity and collaborations.

What are Some of the Challenges Impeding Realisation of Windhoek Smart City?

The realisation of Windhoek smart city is impeded by both technical and non-technical challenges. Technical challenges include infrastructural shortages. Some of the non-technical challenges faced include lack of stakeholder's collaborations, financial resources and skills sets.

Development of a smart city depends on good infrastructure establishment. At the time of this study, it was observed that the city still faces infrastructure shortages. As a result, city development tends to slow down, leading to poor services delivery and potential investors withdrawals. Infrastructure shortages is attributed to many factors which includes mismanagement of resources, lack of governance and urbanisation.

Stakeholders that are part of Windhoek smart city development are not collaborating but rather working in silos. Confirming this a panellist stated that: "*We are finding it very hard to achieve our smart city goals because everyone is working in silo, competing and fighting each other* (pan02)". Collaboration among stakeholders is critical for data and information sharing in order to ensure that stakeholders work towards common goals. In support of stakeholder's collaboration, a participant shared that: "*We need all this regulatory bodies to be together and to identify their challenges so that we can have streamlines processes that speak to each othe*r (pan02) ".

The city was also challenged with getting private investors on-board. A participant shared that: "*when you look at other cities that are embarking on smart cities, they have private partners like IBM, but with us we lack private partnership on board* (pan04)". The lack of private partners on board was viewed as a contributing factor to lack of funds for smart city projects. As a result, due to financial constrains some of the infrastructural projects are put on hold. Thus, there is a need for both private and government investor's participation. The participation and involvement of private investors enables the acquisition of various types of resources such as skills and finances.

In the view of some panellist's realisation of Windhoek smart city requires change in the skill set and empowering local people to take part in the digital transformation. According to one of the participants: *"The skill sets that were valid yesterday, will not be valid in a digital transformed city tomorrow* (pan04)". As ICT becomes integrated in all business process there is a need for new skills and positions that will enable successful operation of business process. Thus, there is a need to invest in human capital and capacitate people towards the digital transformation.

FINDINGS AND DISCUSSION

From the analysis as presented above four factors that can influence the realisation of Windhoek smart city were found. The factors include infrastructure interdependency, stakeholder's collaboration, lack of legal framework and digital skills development. The factors are discussed as follows:

Infrastructural Interdependency

Infrastructure refers to technical resources such as roads, railways, telecommunication and electricity. Each implemented infrastructure serves a unique purpose .However, the various infrastructures do not operate in isolation but are depend on each other to ensure effective operations and service delivery. According to Yilema and Gianoli (2018), infrastructure interdependency refers to the interaction and reliance of the different sectors as part of the complex system which are interconnected. Infrastructure interdependency means there are different networks of actors involved in a smart city development and implementation. Through networks, actors from different areas collaborate towards solving problems (Iyamu, 2015). Subsequently, due to the different networks of actors involved information sharing is critical as decisions in one sector can greatly affect and even jeopardize plans, decisions and strategies of other sectors towards smart city realisation. Thus, infrastructural interdependency calls for stakeholder's collaboration.

Stakeholders Collaboration

Many stakeholders are involved in the development and implementation of Windhoek smart city. This includes community members, private and public enterprises. The collaboration and participation of the stakeholders plays a critical role in the successful implementation of the smart city. Through collaborations, stakeholders share information and knowledge necessary for smart city development such as the deployment of roads, fibre cables and network towers. Alawadhi et al. (2012) shared that smart city initiatives requires collaboration and cooperation through sharing information, resources and sometimes authorities. However, due to various factors such as goals differences, self-interest and political agendas, collaboration among stakeholders was difficult to achieve. Thus, collaborations are dependent on the way stakeholders negotiate their relationships and tensions (Halme, 2020). Consequently, lack of collaboration leads to repetition of efforts and un-integrated efforts. With the advancement in ICT innovations stakeholder's collaboration can be achieved through various mediums such as radios, television, emails and teleconferencing. Collaboration and interaction of stakeholders needs to be guided by legal frameworks to promote acceptable protocols.

Lack of Legal Framework

It will be difficult if not impossible to achieve Windhoek smart city objectives without a legal framework. A legal framework represents an umbrella through which policies and standards are defined and established. Policies and standards are of importance as they guide actor's interactions and ensure process standardisation. The lack of legal frameworks lead to leadership challenges and poor governance across the involved parties. Thus, the need for EA framework to guide and direct various activities involved in the planning, development and implementation of the smart city.

Digital Skills Development

Development and implementation of technological innovations come with a quest for digital skills. Digital skills are instrumental in the development and implementation of ICT innovations as stakeholder's interactions and decision making are informed by such skills. Michelucci, De Marco and Tanda (2016) argued that to develop and implement a smart city, people from different backgrounds and with different skills and competencies must be brought together. Thus, the need to develop digital skills set.

There is a scarcity of digital skills which includes smart governance and enterprise architect's skills. The scarcity of digital skills leads to poor decisions thus creating gaps across business processes. Hence, digital skills are fundamental in the management of resources and achieving fourth industrial revolution. However, due to the uniqueness of each skill set, their development and acquisition can be challenging. Thus, the need for training and development programs through recognised institutions such as colleges and professional bodies. The training and development programs should be developed in collaboration with industry experts to ensure digital skills required.

Digital skills rages from operational, formal, information, communication, content creation and strategic skills (O'Donnell, 2016).

A FRAMEWORK FOR WINDHOEK SMART CITY REALISATION

Based on the findings as presented above this study proposes an architectural framework to guide and enable management of development and implementation activities critical for the realisation of Windhoek smart city. The proposed EA framework consists of four components namely: (1) smart governance, (2) stakeholders inclusivity, (3) connected infrastructures and (4) human capacity building. The components are interconnected and should be read with the figure to enable a better understanding of their relation in the development of Windhoek smart city. Figure 1 is discussed below as follows:

Figure 1. Windhoek Smart city architectural framework

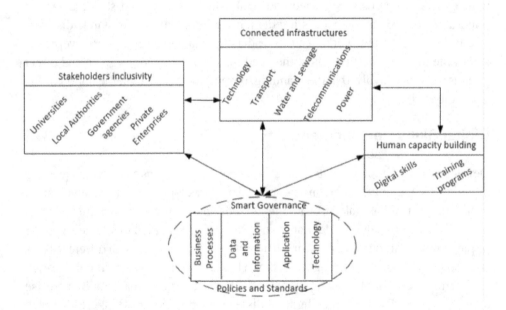

Smart Governance

ICT is pivotal factor for smart city development. Boban and Weber (2018) reported that in a smart city, ICT is a platform through which aggregation of information and data needed to help improve and understand smart city processes is achieved. However, the development and implementation of ICT is not easy but challenging. The challenges could be attributed to the complexity of the main components of ICT which are technology, process and people. The complexity and challenges of the components constrains successful operation of business process thus the need for smart governance. Smart governance Smart governance aims to promote effective use and management of resources to ensure their sustainability.

Smart governance is achieved through the development and implementation of policies and standards. Policies and standards provide boundaries that control actor's engagement and enforces acceptable behaviours across business units. EA is critical for smart city realisation as it provides a comprehensive overview of all the organisation components categorising them into domains. Governance structures need to be imbedded in all architectural domains starting from business to the technology domain. Architectural domains governance ensures transparency and accountability across the organisation structures as well as bridging the gap between business and technology strategies.

Stakeholder's Inclusivity

Every system has stakeholders which are individuals that have interest in the operation of such a system. The inclusivity of various stakeholders in the development and implementation processes of Windhoek smart city is critical to ensure representation of these individuals. Stakeholder's inclusivity can be achieved through meetings and regular engagements in the different stages of the project (Clarke, Waring, & Timmons, 2018). However, stakeholders do not always have common goals but rather different varying interests and opinions. As a result, there is a need for an architectural framework to facilitate communication and align stakeholder's interests with business strategies.

Connected Infrastructures

In this study, connected infrastructures refers to the interconnectivity and linkage between the different infrastructures. Infrastructures interconnectivity and linkage enable communication and sharing of data and information in real time leading to faster decision making. Alawadhi et al. (2012) explained that interconnected infrastructures allow for seamless services delivery. These promotes ease of collaboration leading to business process alignments. Misalignment of business process negatively affects organisation competitiveness, leading to wastage of resources. Thus, infrastructures connectivity needs to be achieved through EA to ensure appropriate governance of the various resources involved.

Human Capacity Building

Technology itself does not make smart city a success. There are many resources which includes human skills. Human skills play a critical role in the smart city development as development and implementation and use technologies and infrastructures are influenced by the individual skills and knowledge. The deployment of various technological innovations creates digital skill gaps within organisation structures that need to be filled to ensure successful operation of business processes. Digital skill development can be a challenging process that is often faced by user's resistance towards change. EA as an agent of change can be used to facilitate training programs to ensure development and management of skills that are aligning city growth and competitiveness.

CONCLUSION

The study has empirically revealed that the city of Windhoek faces many challenges in the development of its smart city. The challenges are both technical and non-technical. In many projects the emphasis is often put on technical factors. However, both factors play a critical role in the success of the smart city. Due to the complexity of the factors involved, this study calls for the development of EA framework. The architectural framework provides guidelines towards the realisation of Windhoek smart city. These guidelines include stakeholder's collaboration as well as development and implementation of infrastructures that are aligned with the city's vision.

The study contributes to the body of knowledge on smart cities and enterprise architecture by providing insights on a phenomenon. Enterprise architecture concept is still at infancy stage in Namibia. Therefore, through this paper, management and academics should recognise the importance of EA and work towards its implementation in organisation structures.

REFERENCES

Ahmadi, H., Farahani, B., Aliee, F., & Motlagh, M. (2019). Cross-layer Enterprise Architecture Evaluation: an approach to improve the evaluation of enterprise architecture TO-BE plan. In *Proceedings of COINS conference. COINS* (pp. 1-6). Crete, Greece: Academic Press.

Alawadhi, S., Aldama-Nalda, A., Chourabi, H., & Gil-Garcia, J. (2012). Building understanding of smart city initiatives. In International conference on electronic government (pp. 40-53). Springer.

Amugongo, L., Nggada, S., & Sieck, J. (2016). Leveraging on open data to solve city challenges: A case study of Windhoek municipality. *3rd MEC International Conference on Big Data and Smart City (ICBDSC)*, 1-6. 10.1109/ICBDSC.2016.7460355

Anthopoulos, L., & Fitsilis, P. (2010). From digital to ubiquitous cities: Defining a common architecture for urban development. In *2010 Sixth International Conference on Intelligent Environments* (pp. 301-306). 10.1109/IE.2010.61

Aurigi, A. (2016). *Making the digital city: the early shaping of urban internet space*. Routledge. doi:10.4324/9781315249964

Boban, M., & Weber, M. (2018). Internet of Things, legal and regulatory framework in digital transformation from smart to intelligent cities. *2018 41st International Convention on Information and Communication Technology, Electronics and Microelectronics (MIPRO)*, 1359-1364

Bolívar, M. (2016). Mapping Dimensions of Governance in Smart Cities. Practitioners versus Prior Research. In *Proceedings of the 17th International Digital Government Research Conference on Digital Government Research* (pp. 1-13). Shanghai, China: Academic Press. 10.1145/2912160.2912176

Bucy, M. (2006). Encouraging Critical Thinking Through Expert Panel. *College Teaching*, *54*(2), 222–224. doi:10.3200/CTCH.54.2.222-224

Clarke, J., Waring, J., & Timmons, S. (2018). The challange of inclusive co-production: The importance of situated rituals and emotional inclusivity in the coproduction of health research projects. *Social Policy and Administration*, *53*(1), 233–248.

Crowe, S., Cresswell, K., Robertson, A., Huby, G., Avery, A., & Sheikh, A. (2011). The case study approach. *BMC Medical Research Methodology*, *11*(100), 2–9. PMID:21707982

Dameri, R., & Ricciardi, F. (2015). Smart city intellectual capital: An emerging view of territorial systems innovation management. *Journal of Intellectual Capital*, *16*(4), 860–887. doi:10.1108/JIC-02-2015-0018

Fabry, N., & Blanchet, C. (2019). Monaco's struggle to become a. *Internationa Journal of Tourism Cities*, *0*(0), 1–13.

Green, J., & Thorogood, N. (2018). *Qualitative methods for health research*. Sage.

Habib, A., Alsmadi, D., & Prybutok, V. (2019). Factors that determine residents' acceptance of smart city technologies. *Behaviour & Information Technology*, 1–14. doi:10.1080/0144929X.2019.1693629

Halme, J. (2020). Constructing consensus and conflicts. *Qualitative Market Research, ahead-of-print*. Advance online publication. doi:10.1108/QMR-12-2017-0172

Hoadjli, A., & Rezeg, K. (2019). A scalable mobile context-aware recommender system for a smart city administration. *International Journal of Parallel, Emergent and Distributed Systems*, 1-20.

Hyett, N., Kenny, A., & Dickson-Swift, V. (2014). Methodology or method? A critical review of qualitative case study reports. *International Journal of Qualitative Studies on Health and Well-being*, 9(1), 23606. doi:10.3402/qhw.v9.23606 PMID:24809980

Iyamu, T. (2018). Implementation of the eneterprise architecture through the Zachman Framework. *Journal of Systems and Information Technology*, 20(1), 2–18. doi:10.1108/JSIT-06-2017-0047

Iyamu, T. (2019). What are the implications of theorizing the enterprise architecture? *Journal of Enterprise Transformation*, 1-22.

Kitsios, F., & Kamariotou, M. (2019). Business strategy modelling based on enterprise architecture: A state of the art review. *Business Process Management Journal*, 25(4), 606–624. doi:10.1108/BPMJ-05-2017-0122

Know Your Local Authority Report. (2015). Retrieved from http://www.windhoekcc.org.na/

Lakhrouit, J., Benhaddi, M., & Baïna, K. (2015). Enterprise architecture approach for agility evaluation. In *International Conference on Cloud Technologies and Applications (CloudTech)* (pp. 1-6). Marrakech, Morocco: Academic Press.

Letaifa, B. (2015). How to strategize smart cities: Revealing the SMART model. *Journal of Business Research*, 68(7), 1414–1419. doi:10.1016/j.jbusres.2015.01.024

Meijer, A., & Bolivar, M. (2016). Governing the smart city: A review of the literature on smart urban governance. *International Review of Administrative Sciences*, 82(2), 392–408. doi:10.1177/0020852314564308

Melendez-Torres, G. J., O'Mara-Eves, A., Thomas, J., Brunton, G., Caird, J., & Petticrew, M. (2017). Interpretive analysis of 85 systematic reviews suggests that narrative syntheses and meta-analyses are incommensurate in argumentation. *Research Synthesis Methods*, 8(1), 109–118. doi:10.1002/jrsm.1231 PMID:27860329

Michelucci, F. V., De Marco, A., & Tanda, A. (2016). Defining the role of the Smart-City manager: An analysis of responsibilities and skills. *Journal of Urban Technology, 23*(3), 23–42. doi:10.1080/10630732.2016.1164439

Nogueira, J., Romero, D., Espadas, J., & Molina, A. (2013). Leveraging the Zachman framework implementation using action – research methodology – a case study: Aligning the enterprise architecture and the business goals. *Journal of Enterprise Information Systems, 7*(1), 100–132. doi:10.1080/17517575.2012.678387

O'Donnell, S. (2016). *Digital skills: unlocking the information society.* Academic Press.

Pendleton, W., Crush, J., & Nickanor, N. (2014). Migrant Windhoek: Rural–Urban Migration and Food Security in Namibia. *Urban Forum, 25*(2), 191-205.

Schleicher, J., Vögler, M., Inzinger, C., & Dustdar, S. (2015). Towards the Internet of Cities: A Research Roadmap for Next-Generation Smart Cities. In *Proceedings of the ACM First International Workshop on Understanding the City with Urban Informatics* (pp. 1-4). Melbourne, Australia: ACM. 10.1145/2811271.2811274

Song, H., & Song, Y.-T. (2010). Enterprise Architecture Institutionalization and Assessment. In *2010 IEEE/ACIS 9th International Conference on Computer and Information Science* (pp. 18-20). Yamagata, Japan: IEEE.

Supriadi, H., Kom, M., & Amalia, E. (2019). University's Enterprise Architecture Design Using Enterprise Architecture Planning (EAP) Based on the Zachman's Framework Approach. *International Journal of Higher Education, 8*(3), 13–28. doi:10.5430/ijhe.v8n3p13

Tanaka, S., de Barros, R., & Mendes, L. (2018). A proposal to a framework for governance of ICT aiming at smart cittes with a focus on enterprise architeccture. In *SBSI'18: XIV Brazilian Symposium on Information Systems* (pp. 1-8). Caxias do Sul, Brazil: ACM.

Tetnowski, J. (2015). Qualitative case study research design. *Perspectives on Fluency and Fluency Disorders, 25*(1), 39–45. doi:10.1044/ffd25.1.39

Tiwar, P., Ilavarasan, P., & Punia, S. (2019). Content analysis of literature on big data in smart cities. *Benchmarking, ahead-of-print,* 1–21. doi:10.1108/BIJ-12-2018-0442

Transformational strategic plan (2017-2022). (n.d.). Retrieved from http://www.windhoekcc.org.na/

Urbaczewski, L., & Mrdalj, S. (2006). A comparison of Enterprise Architecture Frameworks. *Issues in Information Systems, 5*(2), 18–23.

Visvizi, A., Lytras, M., Damiani, E., & Mathkou, H. (2018). Policy making for smart cities: Innovation and social inclusive economic growth for sustainability. *Journal of Science and Technology Policy Management, 9*(2), 126–133. doi:10.1108/JSTPM-07-2018-079

Wagter, R., Proper, H., & Witte, D. (2012). Enterprise Architecture: A strategic specialism. In *14th International Conference on Commerce and Enterprise Computing* (pp. 1-8). Hangzhou, China: Academic Press.

Washburn, D., Sindhu, U., Balaouras, S., & Dines, R. (2010). Helping CIOs understand "smart city" initiatives. *Growth, 17*(2), 1–17.

Yilema, M., & Gianoli, A. (2018). Infrastructure governance: Causes for the poor sectoral coordination among infrastructure sectors of Addis Ababa. *Cities (London, England), 83*(1), 165–172. doi:10.1016/j.cities.2018.06.019

Zait, A. (2017). Exploring the role of civilizational competences for smart cities' development. *Transforming Government: People. Process and Policy, 11*(3), 377–392.

Chapter 6
The Management Accounting System and Enterprise Innovation Ability

Metin Uyar
https://orcid.org/0000-0002-9773-9340
Istanbul Gelişim University, Turkey

ABSTRACT

The chapter aims to explain the relationship between the management accounting system and enterprise innovation ability in the context of collaborative enterprise architecture. The study explains modeling the transformation process and outlining why and how the management accounting affects enterprise innovation ability through accounting information which is focused on the decision-making process. The study uses a survey designed and administered to accountants and managers who work in Turkish manufacturing enterprises as a data provider and decision-maker. The hypotheses were tested using multivariable data analysis techniques, and additional analyses were conducted for more details. The statistical findings show that management accounting affects innovation ability positively. Both product and process innovations are positively affected by managerial accounting. There is also a significant relationship between collaborative enterprise and innovation ability. The harmony between organizational architecture and management accounting increases the company's ability to innovate.

DOI: 10.4018/978-1-5225-8229-8.ch006

INTRODUCTION

In business balance sheets, the increase in the ratio of intangible assets get changed the role of management accounting in the innovation process. Previous studies indicate that the management accounting system has an impact on the performance of innovative companies (Bisbe & Malagueño, 2009). Management accounting, as part of management control systems, helps businesses gain a competitive advantage. This advantage is achieved through innovation. Innovation is defined as the adaptation of new systems, policies, programs, processes, products or services produced internally or externally (Damanpour & Evan, 1984). In general, innovation can be explained as bringing new products or services to customers successfully. Product and process innovation complement each other and increase profitability (Athey & Roberts, 2001). In addition, product and process flexibility contributes to the development of strategies for more efficient manufacturing, thus reducing costs. The importance of innovation in today's competitive conditions is increasing. High technology and innovation open enterprises increase their competitiveness and dominate the market.

There are many internal and external factors in the enterprises affect the innovation. Innovation can be radical and modifying. It is basically a reaction against a similar one. Successful companies do innovate, and their leadership depends on their innovation-based activities. However, doing innovation is very difficult in small and medium-sized enterprises. At this point, the effect of management accounting occurs. Management accounting is primarily a decision support system which it helps the company to use its financial and economic resources efficiently. It contributes to the company allocating more resources for innovation. Managerial accounting contributes to the quantitative and qualitative performance of the enterprise. In particular, increasing resource efficiency increases economic performance. Researchers suggest that organizations can develop more efficient cost management processes by using internal and external knowledge (Adams & Zutshi, 2004). Information encourages the development of new products, the use of more advanced technology processes and the development of cost structures.

The effectiveness of the managerial accounting system is related to the fact that the firm has a collaborative enterprise architecture. The efficiency of the accounting function increases in a business with supportive architecture. The collaborative corporate architecture provides a regular system that reduces operational complexity. It prevents the occurrence of unnecessary processes that repeat each other and increases the communication between the units and provides cooperation. To establish the link between business units and information technologies helps to manage organizational changes. Therefore, collaborative enterprise architecture contributes to the enterprises' ability to innovate while avoiding unnecessary activities. The main objective is to ensure that the information systems and technologies in the enterprise comply with the common standards in line with the objectives and the operation of the company, and in this way to ensure the efficient and effective use of information and communication resources (Minoli, 2008). The basic function of corporate architecture is to provide information about the objectives, structure, operation, systems used in systems (Schekkerman, 2004). On the other hand, collaborative enterprise architecture also depends on organizational culture. Organizational culture shapes the behavior of individuals and organizations. Van Helden & Tillema (2005) points to the importance of value-adding for enterprises to adopt a new technique (innovation). If innovation contributes to the firm's costs, control or economic benefits, it will be easier to adopt.

This study aims to explain the relationship between management accounting and enterprise innovation ability in the context of collaborative enterprise architecture. While innovation is considered to be important for businesses, the role of management accounting in the context of collaborative enterprise architecture has not been adequately studied. The study addresses the lack of this issue. The conceptual perspective denotes specific insights into the critical outcomes that influence the success of innovations made by enterprises which will help enterprises to enhance their competitive power. It also explains to determine the key variables that enterprises should concentrate to develop the relationship between innovation and accounting. The remainder of the study is structured as follows. In the background includes the aim, importance, and contributions of the research. There is a conceptual framework which based on the literature review behind the entrance. First, the concepts of the enterprise architecture, management accounting, and innovation are explained with respect to their construct. Then, a practical research was performed, and the findings were determined. In the discussion and conclusion section, issues and suggestions were expressed.

BACKGROUND

Management accounting, innovation, and enterprise architecture literature used as the theoretical background for the current research. Accounting is a system that provides information to internal and external users through reporting. Pavlatos and Kostakis (2018) states that management accounting innovations will protect businesses against economic crises. It uses specially crafted technologies for this function and prepares documents to understand companies' financial and non-finacial situation (Hull, 2008; Romney & Steinbart, 2017). The data related to financial transactions that cause changes in the assets and resources of the entity should be collected, classified and reported to the related person or groups. Erp et al. (2019) express that the control system and management accounting design have a positive effect on business activities.

Likewise, Johnstone (2020) indicates that management accounting practices will contribute positively to SMEs performance. The management accounting system is one of the main components affecting the success of enterprises. The management accounting helps decision-makers to make the right choices by recording, classifying and reporting on the economic activities of the enterprise. The efficient use of business resources is related to the quality of information generated by the accounting system. Management accounting strengthens the innovation ability of the enterprise by producing information. Accounting establishes the financial relationship between past and future. Managers can understand from their accounting reports what their current products are in demand. New products can be developed using reports. In this context, accounting information provides information flow between firm performance and innovation. The management accounting affects production and new product development processes. By analyzing reports, managers strengthen collaboration between sub-systems. Management accounting system is designed to transform financial and other data into information by gathering resources such as people and equipment (Bodnar and Hopwood, 1998). Previous studies suggest that management accounting may have a significant contribution to product innovation and organization performance (Dunk, 2011). Maletič et al. (2014) emphasize that there is a potential synergy between managerial accounting and sustainable innovation.

For the purposes stated above the research questions examined in this chapter are:

Q1: What are the benefits of management accounting data in the decision-making process.

Q2: What is the relationship between management accounting and the innovation ability of enterprise.

Q3: How an enterprise may turn the management accounting information to innovation.

Q4: What factors facilitate the adoption of the management accounting system in a collaborative enterprise architecture.

Q5: What is the role of the management accounting system at collaborative enterprise architecture.

Q6: What is/are control variable(s) affect the relationship between the management accounting system and enterprise innovation ability.

MANAGEMENT ACCOUNTING

Management accounting is defined as the process of identification, measurement, accumulation, analysis, preparation, interpretation, and communication of information used by management for planning, control and effective use of its resources. The management accounting system refers to the systematic use of accounting tools to achieve organizational goals. As one of the sub-branches of accounting, the main purpose of the management accounting system is to provide information for the managers and employees who are active within the organization and can be defined as internal users. Management accounting is the process of collecting, preparing, recording, measuring, analyzing, interpreting, reporting and communicating the financial information used by the management for planning, control, and evaluation activities within the organization with the accountability and proper use of resources (Crossman, 1985). Managerial accounting is based on data generated by financial accounting to assist the entity in its efficiency and profitability; It helps the management to make decisions by using the data generated in its own subsystems consisting of systems such as costing, decision support, budgeting, and performance appraisal. In terms of both the management and the success and sustainability of the management in the changing competition environment, it also requires the development of new techniques and adaptation of the existing techniques in order for the management accounting system to meet the needs and expectations in the current and future decision-making process (Chenhall & Langfield-Smith, 1998).

Quality development programs, product profitability analysis, benchmarking, customer profitability analysis, stakeholder value analysis (economic value added), target costing, activity-based costing, activity-based management, value chain analysis, product life costing, just-in-time costing, quality costs, and kaizen costing can be considered as tools of management accounting to help improve both the financial and non-financial performance of the company. These tools are used to obtain a strategic competitive advantage when they are used. Many studies have reported that these tools have important implications for achieving competitive advantage. The importance of timely production and costing, quality costs, benchmarking, target and costing kaizen costing in the strategic advantages of the enterprises who have applied more cost planning and cost reduction in the product design stage has been proven in many different studies (Baines & Langfield-Smith, 2003; Cadez & Guilding, 2008, Wijewardena & De Zoysa, 1999).

Strategic management accounting is to manage costs not only in the short term but also in the long term to achieve financial objectives and cost advantage. In other words, to improve the strategic position of enterprises and to minimize the cost of goods/services to implement cost management techniques. This system is based on continuous development which minimizes costs and does not ignore customer demands and demands. Therefore, advanced managerial accounting practices, which are one of the most important tools for achieving a strategic competitive advantage, are indispensable tools for firms (Cooper & Slagmulder, 2003; Yalçın, 2009). Dixon, (1998) states the aim of strategic cost management is to strengthen the strategic position of the company while simultaneously reducing costs and increasing firm performance. Within the framework of researches, it can be said that such advanced managerial accounting practices have a positive effect on organizational performance. From this point of view, it can be said that these tools in advanced management accounting are generally used for two purposes. The first one is the use of these tools for strategic purposes (long-term) and the second one is the use of activities (short term). Although both uses are intended to ultimately improve performance, the strategic priorities will vary depending on their intended use. In line with this, it is expected that advanced managerial accounting practices, in general, will have a positive impact on firm performance. The business benefits from the tools it has in line with its competitive strategy. For this reason, the competitive advantage of the tools to bring the field to the fore. Although it utilizes many of the advanced management accounting tools, it emphasizes the most appropriate ones for its strategy rather than taking advantage of them equally. On the otherhand, traditional management accounting practices such as budgeting and profitability analysis mostly focus on financial and internal organizational issues. The recently developed managerial accounting practices consist of financial and non-financial information that focuses more on strategic aspects (Angelakis et al., 2010). Examples of modern managerial accounting practices include activity-based costing, performance measurement systems, and benchmarking techniques.

An effective management accounting system helps enterprises in many ways. It becomes a vital part of the innovation ability in enterprises, which provides information essential for (i) controlling cost structure; (ii) planning its future strategies, tactics, and operations; (iii) optimizing the use of its resources and budget planning; (iv) measuring and evaluating performance; (v) reducing subjectivity in the decision making process; (vi) improving internal and external communication; and (vii) support innovation process and new product development. The accounting information system provides information to managers for the assessment of the internal strength and weakness. The accounting improves the quality of operations and helps to overcome the complex problems which are the companies met. Management accounting also allows the enterprise to recognize the needs of stakeholders and helps managers to understand the current situation. Management accounting has used a variety of techniques and tools, including traditional volume-based costing systems, budgeting, variance analysis, and responsibility accounting, to meet the needs of managers in traditional manufacturing environments (Chenhall, 2008). Management accounting is used by companies as a decision support mechanism in the determination of managerial decisions and business strategies. Management accounting in today's economic architecture has different implementation areas as follows (Pavlatos & Kostakis, 2015):

- Traditional cost accounting systems

- Cost accounting techniques
- Activity-based techniques
- Planning techniques
- Budgeting techniques
- Decision support systems
- Performance evaluation techniques
- Strategy development
- Strategic management accounting

Management accounting practices are also considered as part of management control systems. Applications enable the use of qualitative and quantitative data in both operational and organizational processes. The effectiveness of management accounting practices helps businesses achieve their goals. The similar results obtained from Duh et al., (2009) and Soobaroyen & Poorundersing (2008) show that managerial accounting practices have a significant contribution to operational performance. More modern managerial accounting practices mostly focus on strategy development and performance (Angelakis et al., 2010). The methods of activity-based costing, target costing, performance analysis, customer profit analysis, customer satisfaction surveys, performance measurement systems, and value engineering are the main applications of modernist management accounting.

Another impact of management accounting is on innovation processes. Innovation activities include risk and uncertainty (Russell & Russell, 1992). To deal with uncertainty, decision makers use more data. The more sophisticated management accounting systems should be used in the enterprise as the innovation is related to uncertainty. Choe (2004) states that the knowledge produced by the management accounting system improves organizational learning and accordingly, production performance increases. Similarly, O'Regan & Sims (2008) found that strategic planning, a management accounting practice, increased corporate performance. The role of the accounting function is to advise an enterprise on how it can trade effectively, profitable and sustainable. Increasing competitiveness is a sub-dimension in this issue, which by definition means that accountants must care about innovation and technological developments. Moreover, the practice of managerial includes recording operations for an organization – not only trucking economic performance, but also by benchmarking progress against a range of financial and non-financial targets and stakeholder expectations. Strategic investments in innovation are hard to track and manage because many of them are typically absorbed in the profit and loss account rather than being shown on the balance sheet. Third, accountants manage business assets. Management and control of intangible assets is a difficult process. Intangible assets are a result of the innovation process and are the hidden value of businesses. A wide range of information will help decision-makers to make better decisions in the process, from the design of products and services to the commercialization. The use of integrated information encourages enterprises by reducing uncertainty in terms of innovation (Bowens & Abernethy, 2000). Timely management accounting information facilitates innovation-oriented businesses to respond to changes in services and products. Reduces delays. In this context, the management accounting system provides an important role in the realization of innovation.

ENTERPRISE INNOVATION ABILITY

Today's manufacturing environment has changed dramatically compared with the past. The use of advanced technology and global competition makes companies more willing to innovate. The innovation is the process of determining the opportunities that generate profitability and ensuring results in these opportunities and ensuring results-oriented activities. The innovation is the level of successful implementation of original ideas in an enterprise. While the original ideas form the beginning of the innovation process, innovation is not enough for itself. Innovation is an economic and social process connected to differentiating and changing the outcome of innovation rather than innovation itself. In other words, innovation refers to the application of a new or significantly modified product (goods or services) or process, a new marketing method or business practices, in the workplace organization or in external relations. The innovation is defined as a process that begins with an invention, continues with the development of the present invention and results in a new product or service introduction into the market. In the broadest sense, innovation is the process of transforming knowledge into economic and social benefit. Therefore, it includes the technical, economic and social processes. The innovation process requires an interactive structure in the enterprise. This process begins with the formation of new knowledge and ends with the discovery of new products and processes and their resulting in commercial gains. For these reasons, innovation is a responsibility of all employees.

Research shows that firms with innovation-based business models achieve faster growth margins and higher sales figures (Ferrari & Parker, 2006; Klomp & Van Leeuwen, 2001). The idea of the process is that the system can be used to implement the process (Damanpour, 1987). Innovations may be radical and incremental; contain high-low risk; or classified as technical or managerial. In this context, it is possible to divide the above classification into two sub-sections as both process and product innovations. Product innovations are understood to mean the development or replacement of an existing product. Process innovation refers to change in internal production and management processes. Organizational structure and supportive systems have an effect on enterprises to be innovative. Innovation of organizational processes contributes to better evaluation and efficiency of firms and it ensures that business strategies are more consistent. Rogers (1995) emphasizes five features of an innovation: relative advantage over existing practice; compatibility with existing culture; complexity; observable, to be able to make a decision to be able to implement (Smith et al, 2008). Innovation process within an enterprise develops in two stages. Figure 1 shows the stages.

Figure 1. The Stage of Innovation Adoption in the Enterprises (Gopalakrishnan & Damanpour, 1997)

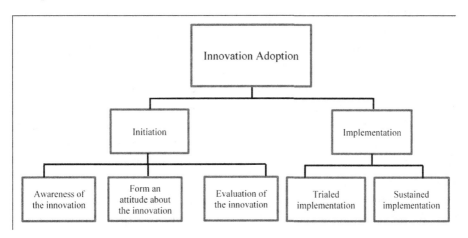

According to the model proposed by Gopalakrishnan & Damanpour (1997), the initiation phase consists of three sub-stages. They are in the form of awareness of the innovation, form an attitude, and evaluation of the innovation. The implementation phase has two sub-stages: trialed implementation and sustained implementation. The preparation of an operation is extremely important for the first use and the continuity of the organizational processes.

COLLABORATIVE ENTERPRISE ARCHITECTURE

Damanpour (1991) states that centralization in decision-making process prevents innovative solutions. In this context, enterprises need a collaborative structure instead of central decision mechanisms. For effective and efficient innovation management, businesses are researching and experimenting with new organizational designs. An organizational architecture that will help overcome the problems encountered can provide a competitive advantage to the company. One of these organizational designs is the collaborative enterprise architecture. Developments in information and communication technologies change both processes and methods for sharing information, storing and processing data, ensuring communication, service, applications, and management of infrastructure. These changes affect the methods and processes of doing business, and the complexity of the system increases when the changes are not managed well. The collaborative corporate architecture provides a regular system by reducing the complexity of organizations. Prevents unnecessary processes from repeating each other. It enhances communication between the units, enabling them to collaborate and makes it useful to manage organizational changes by establishing the link between business units and information technologies. The enterprise structure is a key managerial tool for innovation (Chiaroni et al, 2011; Garicano & Wu, 2012). Because the development of internal networks requires the acquisition of external information effectively. Effective decision and organizational architecture can contribute greatly to innovation success (Lee et al. 2016).

The collaborative enterprise architecture can create an organization in which all components contribute to the company's objectives. Instead of emphasizing individual goals, it is aimed that corporate objectives are at the forefront. The collaborative organizational structure systematically develops "team-shaped" skills to enable employees to contribute more to the organization. This type of organizational structure strengthens the knowledge level of the individual while accelerating the development of other individuals. The strengthening of internal communication also has a positive impact on the employees. The collaborative architecture requires that employees. Innovation is all of the efforts for innovation, improvement, and in order to provide commercial gains. The focus of innovation, improvement and development efforts is the human being, the starting point of new ideas. They are people who are aware of new knowledge about innovation and are able to use it. Therefore, the knowledge, experience, and skills of human capital in enterprises are a decisive element of the innovation process. For the efficiency of the innovation process in enterprises, the human capital, one of the most important innovation capabilities of the enterprise, needs to be supported and developed.

Multidimensional and multidisciplinary activities of innovation increase the importance of collaborative enterprise architecture. Especially high-risk innovation studies can be performed more effectively within the collaborative architecture rather than the static organization. In centralized organizations, individuals are difficult to share their skills and knowledge. Collaborative architecture motivates employees to share their knowledge. Employees share with methods such as knowledge sharing, experience-based learning. Taking part in project teams, joining the problem-solving group, and task rotation can contribute to innovation activities by motivating the employee. The most successful companies when it comes to product and process innovation are those whose organizational structures foster the development of knowledge through formal research and development processes and the development of knowledge based on experience, practice, and interaction between employees, clients, and suppliers (Jensen et al., 2007). More flexible and agile architecture allows the interaction and communication of employee. Accordingly, the innovation capability of the enterprise increases. This organizational configuration provides the ability to cope with unpredictable situations and changes.

The ability to innovate, especially in dynamic environments, results from the collective ability of employees to share and combine knowledge (Nahapiet & Goshal, 1998). The collaborative enterprise architecture focuses on human and technology collaboration. Today, companies use more collaborative technologies such as shared databases, repositories, open-source software. The use of collaborative technologies positively affects the innovation process. Merono-Cerdan et al. (2008) refer to the positive effect of using collaborative technology on innovation. Similarly, it was determined that internet-based knowledge sharing developed innovation processes (Soto-Acosta et al, 2014). In this context, internet technologies are an effective tool for innovation and its diffusion (Bhatt et al., 2005). Xin et al., (2014) points out that there is a significant relationship between certain Internet technologies and firm performance, and draws attention to the collaborative architecture in innovation processes. The ability to innovate new products and service through knowledge sharing may enable enterprises to develop their sustainability performance through innovation. Thus, innovation is becoming an important factor affecting the performance of firms.

RESEARCH METHODS

An empirical study was conducted to determine the relationships between the variables in the study. The data were analyzed using multi-variable statistical techniques.

The Experimental Design and Data Gathering

The Turkish enterprises operating in the cities of Kocaeli and Istanbul constituted the sample of the study. Data were obtained by using the survey method. For this purpose, questionnaires were completed by using face to face interview method. In the first part of the questionnaire, the aim of the study and basic demographic questions are included. In the second part, there are questions about management accounting system, innovation ability and collaborative enterprise structure.

The data were collected from 91 production companies. 28 companies are in the food sector, 53 in the metal sector and 10 in the chemical sector. The number of small and medium sized firms is 72, and the number of large-scale companies is

19. The scales in the measurement tool were created as a result of literature review. Six questions were asked for the effectiveness of management accounting systems. Innovation capability consists of two parts. A total of 8 questions including 4 item for product innovation and 4 item for process innovation were compiled from Ferreira et al., (2010). 7 items were used for collaborative enterprise architecture. There are other factors that strengthen the tendency of innovation within the organization. The size of the business affects innovation ability. One of the factors that have consistently been identified as being associated with innovation is organization size (Askarany & Smith, 2008). They suggest that innovations are adopted more easily in large firms as they have more complex and diverse facilities; it might be expected, therefore, that larger firms will have more innovative sophisticated organization structures. Large-scale enterprises have more innovative tendencies than small-scale firms. The high level of financial resources to be allocated by large enterprises for innovation studies is important. In addition, the employment of highly qualified personnel is also possible for large firms (Mairesse & Mohnen, 2002). The size of the business also strengthens the willingness to use management accounting. Abdel-Kader & Luther (2008) points out that large-scale companies are more suitable to use sophisticated accounting techniques. Large-scale enterprises are coded with "1", and small and medium-sized enterprises are coded with "0". The Likert method used to respond (see annex 2). The hypotheses of the study are as follows.

Hypothesis 1: The collaborative enterprise architecture affects the enterprise innovation ability in the positive direction.
>   **H1a:** The collaborative enterprise architecture affects the product innovation positively.
>   **H1b:** The collaborative enterprise architecture affects the process innovation positively.

Hypothesis 2: The management accounting system effectiveness positively affects the enterprise innovation ability.
>   **H2a:** The management accounting system effectiveness positively affects the product innovation.
>   **H2b:** The management accounting system effectiveness positively affects the process innovation.

Hypothesis 3: There is a positive association between the organization size and the enterprise innovation ability.
>   **H3a:** There is a positive association between the organization size and the product innovation.
>   **H3b:** There is a positive association between the organization size and the process innovation.

Figure 2. The Research Model and Hypoteses

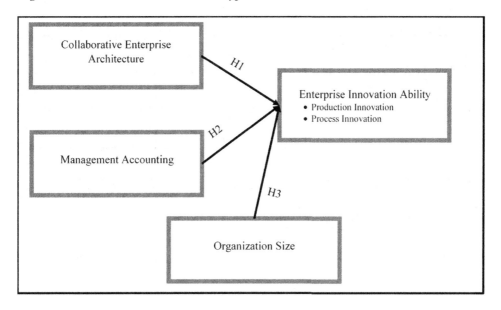

Figure 2 shows the research model and hypotheses.

The data set was evaluated for skewness and kurtosis in order to determine the normal distribution. Table 1 shows the normality of the variables. All three variables are suitable for normal distribution.

Table 1. Normality for Research Variables

	Skewness	Kurtosis
Reference Margin	-1,96 and +1,96	-3 and +3
Collaborative Enterprise Architecture	1,55	1,66
Management Accounting Effectiveness	1,29	1,41
Enterprise Innovation Ability	0,88	1,29
Organization Size	-1,49	-0,11

Analysis and Findings

The statistical analysis process was completed in two stages. In the first stage, the reliability, validity and factor structure of the research variables and the research model are evaluated. In the second stage, hypothesis tests, intermediate variable

Table 2. Metrics for Research Variables

	Mean	Standard Deviation
Collaborative Enterprise Architecture	2,71	0,085
Management Accounting Effectiveness		
Innovation	2,28	0,023
New Product Development	2,16	0,106
Performance Evolution	3,11	0,016
Budget Control	2,66	0,205
Cost Analysis and Management	2,57	0,129
Production Planning	2,29	0,034
Enterprise Innovation Ability		
Product Innovation	2,10	0,059
Process Innovation	2,33	0,230

analysis were performed. The values showing the effectiveness of the management accounting system are found in Table 2.

Performance evaluation is the area where management accounting systems are most effective ($\mu=3,11$). The second order is budget control ($\mu=2,66$). The third activity is cost analysis and management ($\mu=2,57$). It has an average ($\mu=2,28$) value on the contribution of the management accounting system to innovation. The contribution in the new product development process is according to the participants ($\mu=2,16$). Product innovation average ($\mu=2,10$) and process innovation average ($\mu=2,33$). Collaborative enterprise architecture is the mean value of the variable ($=2,28$). Figure 3 shows the levels of variables that affect management accounting effectivenss.

Assuming that the data set is homogeneous, factor analysis was performed by using the covariance matrix. The main components analysis is the method used to determine the factors. The main components method has been chosen in this study since it is frequently preferred in the studies in the field of social sciences. In the main components method, the primary factor explaining the maximum variance between variables is calculated. Varimax method is adopted as rotation. This method increases the ability of the research model to show overall, as it allows the factor loads to be explained as gamma = 1.

Barlett Test (Barlett Test of Sphericity) and Kaiser-Meyer-Olkin (KMO) sample proficiency tests were performed in order to evaluate the suitability of factor analysis for the observed variables (the questions in the survey). Table 3 reflects the results of KMO analysis.

Figure 3. The Variables Affecting The Management Accounting System's Effectivenss

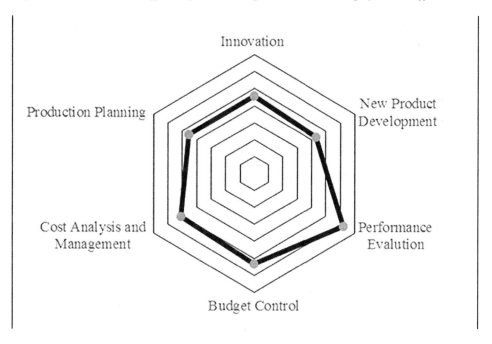

Table 3. KMO and Bartlett Tests for Variables

	Kaiser-Meyer-Olkin		0,822
Management Accounting Effectiveness	Bartlett Test	X^2	2555,806
		Degree of Freedom	139
		Significance	0,001*
	Kaiser-Meyer-Olkin		0,932
Enterprise Innovation Ability	Bartlett Test	X^2	3608,120
		Degree of Freedom	186
		Significance	0,000*
KMO: 0,90 (Perfect); 0,80 (Very well); 0,70 (good); 0,60 (medium); 0,50 (weak).			

*p<0,01**; p<0,05; ***p<0,10

The level of proficiency (KMO = 0,822) is sufficient for the managerial accounting effectiveness variable. The value to be examined for the Barlett test is significant and sufficient (p = 0,001). Enterprise innovation is sufficient for ability (KMO = 0,932). The results of the Barlett test also indicate the adequacy (p = 0,000). Factor loads and reliability (Cronbach α) values of the research components are found in Table 4.

Table 4. Factor Loads and Reliability of Variables

	Loads	Cr. α
Management Accounting Effectiveness		
The management accounting system of the enterprise improves the Innovation ability.	0,817	0,774
The enterprise management accounting system improves the success of the new product development process.	0,824	0,782
The management accounting system positively affects the performance evaluation process conducted by management in the enterprise.	0,863	0,815
The management accounting system positively affects the budget control in the enterprise	0,841	0,808
The management accounting system affects the success of cost Analysis and management in the enterprise.	0,838	0,800
Regarding production planning process, the enterprise is influenced by the management accounting system.	0,795	0,786
Enterprise Innovation Ability		
During the last three years we have launched few/many new products	0,740	0,772
During the last three years we have launched few/many modifications to already existing products	0,766	0,780
Regarding new products, we are very rarely/very often first-to-market	0,705	0,753
The percentage of new products in our product portfolio is much lower/much higher than the industry average	0,673	0,725
During the last three years we have introduced few/many new production processes	0,718	0,758
During the last three years we have introduced few/many modifications to production processes	0,831	0,840
Regarding new production processes, we are very rarely/very often the first to introduce them	0,756	0,775
The frequency of production process improvements in our company is much lower/ much higher than the industry average	0,711	0,756

As a result of the rotation made using the Varimax method, it was determined that the question items of the management accounting system efficiency and enterprise innovation ability variables were reliable. After factor analysis, validity and correlation analysis were performed. Table 5 represents correlation and validity results.

There is sufficient validity value for management accounting efficiency ($\sqrt{AVE}$ = 0,868). The validity parameter for the Collaborative enterprise architecture is valid ($\sqrt{AVE}$=0,880). The validity value for Product innovation is sufficient ($\sqrt{AVE}$=0,893). Process innovation is high ($\sqrt{AVE}$= 0,882). There is a positive correlation between the effectiveness of the management accounting system and the variable of collaborative enterprise architecture (r = 0,332). The linearity between the effectiveness of management accounting and organizational architecture is

Table 5. Validity and Correlations Results

	√AVE	MAE	CEA	PIN	PRI	ORS
MAE	0,868	*1*				
CEA	0,880	*0,323***	*1*			
PIN	0,893	*0,180****	*0,207****	*1*		
PRI	0,882	*0,195****	*0,220****	*0,235****	*1*	
ORS	0,806	*0,169****	*0,372***	*0,282****	*0,325****	*1*

Italic values show the correlation co-efficient among variables.
MAE: Management Accounting Effectiveness; CEA: Collaborative Enterprise Architecture; PIN: Product Innovation; PRI: Process Innovation; ORS: Organization Size; AVE: Average Variance Extracted.

*p<0,01**; p<0,05; ***p<0,10

meaningful. There is a correlation between the effectiveness of management accounting and production innovation (r=0,180). The interaction between process innovation and accounting was also significant (r = 0,119). The correlation between organization size and accounting effectiveness was significant (r=0,163). The correlation coefficient of collaborative enterprise architecture and product innovation is significant (r = 0,207). Process innovation and organization architecture are correlated (r = 0,220). There is significant linearity between organization architecture and organization size (r = 0,372). Process innovation is significantly correlated with production innovation (r = 0,235). The organization size is associated with both product innovation and process innovation (r = 0,282 and r = 0,325).

After correlation analysis, hypothesis testing was performed. Multiple linear regression analysis was performed for hypotheses. The model was analyzed in two stages. In the first stage, an analysis was made about the product innovation. Table 6 shows the effects of independent variables (management accounting efficiency, collaborative enterprise architecture) on product innovation.

Table 6. Regressions for Product Innovation

	β	R^2	Q^2	f^2
Collaborative Enterprise Architecture	0,30*	0,25	0,155	0,179
Management Accounting Effectiveness	0,27**	0,18	0,128	0,154
Organization Size	0,33*	0,29	0,181	0,218

*p<0,01**; p<0,05; ***p<0,10

Collaborative enterprise architecture variable affects production innovation positively (β =0,30). The company has a collaborative architecture and contributes to the company's new product development. In this context, "Hypothesis 1a: The collaborative enterprise architecture affects the product innovation positively" was accepted. The appropriateness of estimation of the related hypothesis is adequate (Q^2=0,155). The fact that this value is above zero (0) indicates that the prediction suitability of the model is sufficient. The effect value was determined as medium (f^2=0,179). Management accounting effectiveness has a significant effect on production innovation (β =0,27). The obtained finding confirms "H2a: Effective management accounting increases the ability of firms to innovate products". The suitability of the hypothesis was determined as moderate (Q^2=0,128 and f^2=0,154). The organization size variable has a significant and positive effect on production innovation ability (β =0,33). "H3a: There is a positive association between the organization size and the product innovation" was accepted. The effect of hypothesis is moderate (Q^2=0,181 and f^2=0,218). Regression analysis results show that organization innovation is the most effective variable of production innovation. In the second stage of the regression analysis, the effect of independent variables on process innovation is examined. Table 7 reflects the results of the second model.

Table 7. Regressions for Process Innovation

	β	R^2	Q^2	f^2
Collaborative Enterprise Architecture	0,34*	0,26	0,178	0,192
Management Accounting Effectiveness	0,31**	0,22	0,150	0,177
Organization Size	0,38*	0,31	0,195	0,235

*p<0,01**; p<0,05; ***p<0,10

Collaborative enterprise architecture affects process innovation positively (β=0,34). The fact that the enterprise has a collaborative architecture makes a positive contribution to the company's process innovation. "H1b: The collaborative enterprise architecture affects the process innovation positively" was accepted. The appropriateness of estimation of the hypothesis is sufficient (Q^2=0,178). Impact value is determined as medium (f^2=0,192). Management accounting effectiveness has a significant impact on process innovation (β=0,31). "H2b: The management accounting system effectiveness positively affects the process innovation" was accepted. Effective managerial accounting increases the process innovation skills of firms. Estimation suitability of hypothesis is determined as medium (Q^2=0,128 and f^2=0,154). Organization size has a significant and positive effect on product innovation ability (β=0,33). "H3b: There is a positive association between the organization size and the process innovation" was confirmed. The effect of hypothesis is moderate (Q^2=0,195 *and* f^2=0,235). The change in level of enterprise innovation ability in terms of industry type has been seen in the findings in Figure 4.

Metal goods sector holds the highest value (μ=2,39). This value is lower for the food industry. However, the lowest average is observed in the chemical industry (μ=1,77).

Figure 4. The Enterprise Innovation Ability by Sectors

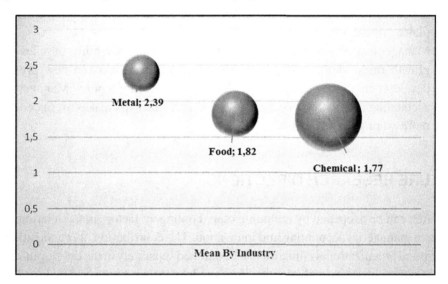

SOLUTIONS AND RECOMMENDATIONS

Based on the above considerations, the following recommendations can be made:

1) The success of businesses is related to innovation skills. A collaborative organizational structure strengthens enterprises' ability to innovate. The integration of a collaborative architecture increases the success of firms in product and process innovation. Correctly designed organizational architecture strengthens the interaction between the employees of the enterprise.

2) Customer and supply chain members' demands affect the policies and procedures of the companies. The fact that firms are in a collaborative structure strengthens the interaction of external stakeholders with the enterprise and encourages the firm to allocate more resources to innovation. As an internal stakeholder,

it is possible for employees to overcome their deficiencies in a collaborative organization and to develop their individual skills.

3) Knowledge sharing is important in the realization of innovations. Management accounting facilitates the flow of knowledge from the inside out. Enterprises must transform the knowledge generated by management accounting into innovations.

4) Management accounting contributes to the effective use of business resources. It prevents waste of resources and allows more budget for innovation. Managers should not ignore the effect of management accounting. In collaborative architecture, the effect of management accounting on innovation increases as the contribution of each unit increases. Management accounting system can play a critical role in enterprise architecture.

5) Management accounting system by reporting the profitability of sales and growth rates warns managers about. Managers can focus on new product development processes by using sales and profitability reports. Management accounting as a control system can also help the decision maker to concentrate more on process innovations.

FUTURE RESEARCH DIRECTIONS

Research can be deepened by including other contingent factors in the relationship between managerial accounting and innovation. The contribution of organizational culture and organizational climate can be examined separately in the development of collaborative enterprise architecture. The sample of the study can be developed and examined in different geographies and cultures. The contribution of the accounting system and technology to the collaborative organizational architecture can also be evaluated in future studies.

CONCLUSION

In this chapter, it is aimed to determine the relationship between management accounting system, collaborative enterprise architecture, and innovation. The data obtained from the companies in Istanbul and Kocaeli were evaluated using multivariate statistical techniques. The managerial accounting system provides financial and non-financial information about the entity's operations and enables the manager to assess enterprise performance. Manages the success and situation of products and processes by reporting managerial accounting. Through this information and reports, the manager starts work on new product development, product innovation, and process innovation. Thus, the company is provided to continue the development. It is very difficult for the manager to do this difficult task alone. Therefore, their management is developing new organizational designs. Collaborative enterprise structure strengthens the relationship between technology and people and enables management to solve problems more easily. Therefore, collaborative enterprise architecture helps the manager by increasing the cooperation between the human resource and technological resource of the enterprise. Collaborative enterprise structure increases the effectiveness of management accounting and contributes to innovation.

It contributes to many organizational components such as management accounting, planning, control, cost, production, and innovation. The managerial accounting system helps control and evaluate organizational activities. Performance measurement makes it easy for the business to determine the successful and unsuccessful aspects. Analyzing weaknesses and strengths for the effectiveness of the company's resources is facilitated by the management accounting system. Thus, the budget that the firm will allocate for innovation reaches higher values. Consequently, research results confirm that the management accounting system contributes to both product and driving innovation. ($\beta=0,27$ and $\beta=0,31$).

In collaborative enterprise architecture, it is important that people and technology are collaborative. Information and technology sharing is a key component of this type of organizational structure. Group work, project teams, task rotations increase the level of collaboration between employees. Sharing the knowledge and experience of individuals strengthens the intellectual capital of the company and contributes to the ability of innovation. Especially product innovation is affected by this situation. Both the correlation analysis and the results of the regression analysis confirm this conclusion ($r=0,207$ and $\beta=0,30$).

Collaborative architecture has high value especially for process innovation ($\beta=0,34$; ($Q^2=0,178$ and $f^2=0,192$). In other words, companies had a collaborative architecture may improve their innovation ability. In this situation, better evaluation and use of the company's human resources is effective.

There is a significant relationship between managerial accounting and collaborative enterprise architecture ($r=0,323$). Therefore, the fact that the firm is in a collaborative structure will increase the effectiveness of management accounting. The effectiveness of managerial accounting will reflect the performance of the company positively. In particular, the contribution of management accounting in process innovation management will be higher.

Organization has a meaningful relationship with innovation. The fact that large firms have more financial and human resources positively affects the amount they use for innovation investments. The findings of this study confirm this view ($\beta = 0,33$ and $\beta = 0,38$). The limited investment in human resources in small and medium-sized companies has a negative impact on in-house cooperation. Information and experience sharing is not sufficient. In addition, small companies are more limited with the use of shared databases and open-source software.

REFERENCES

Abdelkader, M., & Luther, R. (2008). The impact of firm characteristics on management accounting practices: A UK-based empirical analysis. *The British Accounting Review*, *40*(1), 2–27. doi:10.1016/j.bar.2007.11.003

Adams, C., & Zutshi, A. (2004). Corporate social responsibility: Why business should act responsibly and be accountable. *Australian Accounting Review*, *14*(3), 31–40. doi:10.1111/j.1835-2561.2004.tb00238.x

Ahmad, K. (2017). The implementation of management accounting practices and its relationship with performance in small and medium enterprises. *International Review of Management and Marketing*, *7*(1), 342–353.

Angelakis, G., Theriou, N., & Floropoulos, I. (2010). Adoption and benefits of management accounting practices: Evidence from Greece and Finland, *Advances in Accounting, Incorporating. Advances in International Accounting*, *26*(1), 87–96. doi:10.1016/j.adiac.2010.02.003

Askarany, D., & Smith, M. (2008). Diffusion of innovation and business size: A longitudinal study of PACIA. *Managerial Auditing Journal*, *23*(9), 900–916. doi:10.1108/02686900810908445

Athey, S., & Roberts, J. (2001). Organizational design: Decision rights and incentive contracts. *Organizational Economics*, *91*, 200–205.

Baines, A., & Langfield-Smith, K. (2003). Antecedents to management accounting change: A structural equation approach. *Accounting, Organizations and Society*, *28*(7-8), 675–698. doi:10.1016/S0361-3682(02)00102-2

Bhatt, G. D., Gupta, J. N. D., & Kitchens, F. (2005). An exploratory study of groupware use in the knowledge management process. *Journal of Enterprise Information Management*, *8*(1), 28–46. doi:10.1108/17410390510571475

Bisbe, J., & Malagueño, R. (2009). The choice of interactive control systems under different innovation management modes. *European Accounting Review*, *18*(2), 371–405. doi:10.1080/09638180902863803

Bouwens, J., & Abernethy, M. A. (2000). The consequences of customization on management accounting systems design. *Accounting, Organizations and Society*, *25*(3), 221–241. doi:10.1016/S0361-3682(99)00043-4

Cadez, S., & Guilding, C. (2008). An exploratory investigation of an integrated contingency model of strategic management accounting. *Accounting, Organizations and Society*, *33*(7-8), 836–863. doi:10.1016/j.aos.2008.01.003

Chenhall, R. H. (2008). Accounting for the horizontal organisation: A review essay. *Accounting, Organizations and Society*, *33*(4-5), 517–550. doi:10.1016/j. aos.2007.07.004

Chenhall, R. H., & Langfield-Smith, K. (1998). Adoption and benefits of management accounting practices: An Australian study. *Management Accounting Research*, *9*(1), 1–19. doi:10.1006/mare.1997.0060

Chiaroni, D., Chiesa, V., & Frattini, F. (2011). The open innovation journey: How firms dynamically implement the emerging innovation management paradigm. *Technovation*, *31*(1), 34–43. doi:10.1016/j.technovation.2009.08.007

Choe, J. (2004). The relationships among management accounting information, organizational learning and production performance. *The Journal of Strategic Information Systems*, *13*(1), 61–85. doi:10.1016/j.jsis.2004.01.001

Cooper, R., & Slagmulder, R. (2003). Strategic cost management: Expanding scope and boundaries. *Cost and Management*, *17*(1), 23–30.

Crossman, Y. P. (1985). The Nature of Management Accounting. *The Accounting Review*, *33*(2), 222–227.

Damanpour, F. (1987). The adoption of technological, administrative, and ancillary innovations: Impact of organizational factors. *Journal of Management*, *13*(4), 675–688. doi:10.1177/014920638701300408

Damanpour, F. (1991). Organisational innovation: A metaanalysis of effects of determinants and moderators. *Academy of Management Journal*, *34*, 555–590.

Damanpour, F., & Evan, W. (1984). Organizational innovation and performance: The problem of "Organizational Lag". *Administrative Science Quarterly*, *29*(3), 392–409. doi:10.2307/2393031

Dixon, R. (1998). Accounting for strategic management: A practical application. *Long Range Planning*, *31*(2), 272–279. doi:10.1016/S0024-6301(98)00011-9

Duh, R. R., Xiao, J. Z., & Chow, C. W. (2009). Chinese firms' use of management accounting and controls: Facilitators, impediments, and performance effects. *Journal of International Accounting Research*, *8*(1), 1–30. doi:10.2308/jiar.2009.8.1.1

Dunk, A. S. (2011). Product innovation, budgetary control, and the financial performance of firms. *The British Accounting Review*, *43*(2), 102–111. doi:10.1016/j.bar.2011.02.004

Erp, W., Roozen, F., & Vosselman, E. (2019). The performativity of a management accounting and control system: Exploring the dynamic relational consequences of a design. *Scandinavian Journal of Management*, *35*(4). Advance online publication. doi:10.1016/j.scaman.2019.101077

Ferrari, B. & Parker, B. (2006), Digging for innovation, *Supply Chain Management Review*, 48-53.

Ferreira, A., Moulang, C., & Hendro, B. (2010). Environmental management accounting and innovation: An exploratory analysis. *Accounting, Auditing & Accountability Journal*, *23*(7), 920–948. doi:10.1108/09513571011080180

Garicano, L., & Wu, Y. (2012). Knowledge, communication, and organizational capabilities. *Organization Science*, *23*(5), 1382–1397. doi:10.1287/orsc.1110.0723

Gopalakrishnan, S., & Damanpour, F. (1997). 'A Review of innovation research in economics, sociology and technology management', *Omega. International Journal of Management Sciences*, *25*(1), 15–28.

Hull, C. E., & Rothenberg, S. (2008). Firm performance: The interactions of corporate social performance with innovation and industry differentiation. *Strategic Management Journal*, *29*(7), 781–789. doi:10.1002mj.675

Jensen, M. B., Johnson, B., Lorenz, E., & Lundvall, B. A. (2007). Forms of knowledge and modes of innovation. *Research Policy*, *36*(5), 680–693. doi:10.1016/j.respol.2007.01.006

Johnstone, L. (2020). A systematic analysis of environmental management systems in SMEs: Possible research directions from a management accounting and control stance. *Journal of Cleaner Production*, *244*, 118802. Advance online publication. doi:10.1016/j.jclepro.2019.118802

Klomp, L., & Van Leeuwen, G. (2001). Linking innovation and firm performance: A new approach. *International Journal of the Economics of Business*, *8*(3), 343–364. doi:10.1080/13571510110079612

Lee, J., Min, J., & Lee, H. (2016). The effect of organizational structure on open innovation: A quadratic equation. *Procedia Computer Science, 91,* 492–501. doi:10.1016/j.procs.2016.07.128

Mairesse, J., & Mohnen, P. (2002). Accounting for innovation and measuring innovativeness: An illustrative framework and an application. *The Economics of Technology and Innovation, 92*(2), 226–230. doi:10.1257/000282802320189302

Maletič, M., Maletič, D., Dahlgaard, J. J., Dahlgaard-Park, S. M., & Gomišček, B. (2014). Sustainability exploration and sustainability exploitation: From a literature review towards a conceptual framework. *Journal of Cleaner Production, 79,* 182–194. doi:10.1016/j.jclepro.2014.05.045

Meroño-Cerdan, A., Soto-Acosta, P., & Lopez-Nicolas, C. (2008). Analyzing collaborative technologies' effect on performance through intranet use orientations. *Journal of Enterprise Information Management, 21*(1), 39–51. doi:10.1108/17410390810842246

Minoli, D. (2008). *Enterprise Architecture A to Z: Frameworks, Business Process Modeling, SOA, and Infrastructure Technology.* Auerbach Publications, Taylor & Francis Group. doi:10.1201/9781420013702

Nahapiet, J., & Ghoshal, S. (1998). Social capital, intellectual capital, and the organizational advantage. *Academy of Management Review, 23*(2), 242–266. doi:10.5465/amr.1998.533225

O'Regan, N., Sims, M. A., & Gallear, D. (2008). Leaders, loungers, laggards: The strategic-planning-environment performance relationship re-visited in manufacturing SMEs. *Journal of Manufacturing Technology Management, 19*(1), 6–21. doi:10.1108/17410380810843426

Pavlatos, O., & Kostakis, H. (2015). Management accounting practices before and during economic crisis: Evidence from Greece. *Advances in Accounting, incorporating. Advances in International Accounting, 31*(1), 150–164. doi:10.1016/j.adiac.2015.03.016

Pavlatos, O., & Kostakis, H. (2018). Management accounting innovations in a time of economic crisis. *Journal of Economic Asymmetries, 18*(3), e00106. Advance online publication. doi:10.1016/j.jeca.2018.e00106

Rogers, E. M. (1995). *Diffusion of Innovation* (4th ed.). Free Press.

Russell, R. D., & Russell, C. J. (1992). An examination of the effects of organizational norms, organizational structure and environmental uncertainty on entrepreneurial strategy. *Journal of Management, 18*(4), 639–656. doi:10.1177/014920639201800403

Schekkerman, J. (2004), How to Survive in the Jungle of Enterprise Arhitecture Frameworks: Creating or Choosing an Enterprise Architecture Framework (2nd ed.). Trafford.

Smith, M., Abdullah, Z., & Abdul-Razak, R. (2008). The diffusion of technological and management accounting. innovation: Malaysian evidence. *Asian Review of Accounting, 16*(3), 197–218. doi:10.1108/13217340810906672

Smith, M., Abdullah, Z., & Razak, R. A. (2008). The diffusion of technological and management accounting innovation: Malaysian evidence. *Asian Review of Accounting, 16*(3), 197–218. doi:10.1108/13217340810906672

Soobaroyen, T., & Poorundersing, B. (2008). The effectiveness of management accounting systems; evidence from functional managers in a developing country. *Managerial Auditing Journal, 23*(2), 187–219. doi:10.1108/02686900810839866

Soto-Acosta, P., Colomo-Palacios, R., & Popa, S. (2014). Web knowledge sharing and its effect on innovation:an empirical investigation in SMEs. *Knowledge Management Research and Practice, 12*(1), 103–113. doi:10.1057/kmrp.2013.31

Steinbart, P., & Romney, M. B. (2017). Accounting Information Systems (14th ed.). Pearson.

Van Helden, G. J., & Tillema, S. (2005). In search of a benchmarking theory for the public sector. *Financial Accountability &Management, 21*(3).

Wijewardena, H., & De Zoysa, A. (1999). A comparative analysis of management accounting practices in Australia and Japan: An empirical investigation. *The International Journal of Accounting, 34*(1), 49–70. doi:10.1016/S0020-7063(99)80003-X

Xin, J. Y., Ramayah, T., Soto-Acosta, P., Popa, S., & Ping, T. A. (2014). Analyzing the use of the Web 2.0 for brand awareness industry and competitive advantage: An empirical study in the Malaysian hospitability. *Information Systems Management, 31*(2), 96–103. doi:10.1080/10580530.2014.890425

Yalçın, S. (2009). Ürün tasarım ve ürün hayat seyrinde maliyetlerin stratejik yönetimi. *Dumlupınar Üniversitesi Sosyal Bilimler Dergisi, 23*, 289–301.

KEY TERMS AND DEFINITIONS

Collaborative Enterprise Architecture: It is the organizational architecture in which the human and technology resource is designed collaboratively for enterprise purposes.

Cost Management: The activities carried out to ensure that the costs are at the most appropriate level for the business purposes in the production process.

Financial Reporting: Financial pictures that give information to internal and external stakeholders about the company's activities.

Innovation: Refers to innovate a new or significantly modified product (goods or services) or the process, a new marketing method or business practices in the organization or external relations.

Innovation Management: All coordinated and effective activities carried out for the accomplishment of innovation in the enterprise.

Management Accounting: The management accounting system refers to the systematic use of accounting data to achieve organizational goals.

APPENDIX: SURVEY OF THE STUDY

Choose the proper item for your business

The number of employee 1) Under 250 () 2) Over 250 ()
    Your Industry
    Metal () Food () Chemical ()
    Your Job Title
    Manager () Vice Manager () Chief () Senior Accountant ()

Indicate the appropriate choices about following ideas

1) Strongly Disagree 2) Partial Disagree 3) Medium 4) Partial Agree 5) Strongly Agree

Management Accounting Effectiveness

The management accounting system of the enterprise improves the Innovation ability.

The enterprise management accounting system improves the success of the new product development process.

The management accounting system positively affects the performance evaluation process conducted by management in the enterprise.

The management accounting system positively affects the budget control in the enterprise

The management accounting system affects the success of cost Analysis and management in the enterprise.

Regarding production planning process, the enterprise is influenced by the management accounting system.

Collaborative Enterprise Architecture

The organizational structure of your business is aimed at increasing the communication between employees.

Sharing knowledge and experience among employees is easy.

Our information technologies are easily accessible and usable by our employees.

In our business, a collaboration organization architecture has been adopted.

Employees have a positive attitude towards team work and innovation.

The suggestions of the employees are taken into consideration in decision-making processes.

Cooperation between the units of our business is high.

Enterprise Innovation Ability

During the last three years we have launched few/many new products

During the last three years we have launched few/many modifications to already existing products

Regarding new products, we are very rarely/very often first-to-market

The percentage of new products in our product portfolio is much lower/much higher than the industry average

During the last three years we have introduced few/many new production processes

During the last three years we have introduced few/many modifications to production processes

Regarding new production processes, we are very rarely/very often the first to introduce them

The frequency of production process improvements in our company is much lower/much higher than the industry average

Chapter 7

Influence of Constant Returns to Scale and Variable Returns to Scale Data Envelopment Analysis Models in ICT Infrastructure Efficiency Utilization

Yinka Oyerinde
University of South Africa, South Africa

Felix Bankole
University of South Africa, South Africa

ABSTRACT

A lot of research has been done using Data Envelopment Analysis (DEA) to measure efficiency in Education. DEA has also been used in the field of Information and Communication Technology for Development (ICT4D) to investigate and measure the efficiency of Information and Communication Technology (ICT) investments on Human Development. Education is one of the major components of the Human Development Index (HDI) which affects the core of Human Development. This research investigates the relative efficiency of ICT Infrastructure Utilization on the educational component of the HDI in order to determine the viability of Learning Analytics using DEA for policy direction and decision making. A conceptual model taking the form of a Linear Equation was used and the Constant Returns to Scale (CRS) and Variable Returns to Scale (VRS) models of the Data Envelopment Analysis were

DOI: 10.4018/978-1-5225-8229-8.ch007

employed to measure the relative efficiency of the components of ICT Infrastructure (Inputs) and the components of Education (Outputs). Results show a generally high relative efficiency of ICT Infrastructure utilization on Educational Attainment and Adult Literacy rates, a strong correlation between this Infrastructure and Literacy rates as well, provide an empirical support for the argument of increasing ICT infrastructure to provide an increase in Human Development, especially within the educational context. The research concludes that DEA as a methodology can be used for macroeconomic decision making and policy direction within developmental research.

INTRODUCTION

The growth of Information and Communication Technology (ICT) in recent years has been remarkable in all countries and sectors throughout the world because of it's transformational power that favours productivity and efficiency (Kayisire & Wei, 2016). Many governments have heeded the call for increased investments in ICT with the aim to improve national development with respect to the Human Development Index (HDI) (Oyerinde & Bankole, 2019a). Over the last three decades, the literature on national development research has grown to encompass certain intervening variables and social factors such as education and some other aspects of human welfare. (Desai, 1991; Anand & Ravallion, 1993; Bankole & Mimbi, 2017). This is ever more evident considering that countries have defined policies that show an emphasis on creating support mechanisms for the use of ICT (Hinostroza, 2018), however, the opinions on the bearings of ICT Infrastructure for development are in two perspectives vis a vis national development: The adoption of ICTs has the potential to empower communities and countries while secondly, the ICT revolution can lead to imbalances and inequalities through lack of ICT adoption, access and usage (Bankole, 2015).

In the on-going discourse on international human development within the Information and Communication for Development (ICT4D) context, the concept of national development has been said to encapsulate the notion of human development as the means of enlarging people's choices to acquire knowledge, amongst others, in order to have access to the resources needed for a decent standard of living (UNDP, 2006; Bankole & Mimbi, 2017). When considering the importance of educational attainment, itself being one of the core indices for measuring development with respect to the Human Development Index (HDI) (UNDP, 2006; Bankole et al., 2011a; Bankole et al., 2015), in the national development discourse, coupled with the considerable successes of data analytics in business for decision making, it is not surprising that data analytics implementations have found their way into main stream ICT4D research. Data analytics in education, otherwise known as Learning Analytics (LA), and other research investigating the constituent components of the HDI are therefore relevant and applicable for ICT4D research as well as for national policy/decision making and implementation.

Data Envelopment Analysis (DEA) is a well-known and established non-parametric linear programming methodology that has been widely used for data analysis within the Information Systems discipline and in quantitative research within the ICT4D context. DEA is used for the assessment and measurement of relative efficiency and performance of organizations (Cooper et al., 2006; Thanassoulis et al., 2008, 2011; Bankole et al., 2011c) and has also been used for understanding the impacts of IT investments on performance and productivity (Hatami-Marbini et al., 2010). It has long been recognized that DEA by its use of mathematical programming is particularly adept at estimating inefficiencies in multiple input and multiple output production correspondences (Banker et al., 2004). In Enterprise Business Architecture, DEA serves as a purposive tool for creating composite indicators according to multiple outputs articulated in different measurement units so as to enable enterprise specific weighting of different objectives (Staessens et al., 2019). For Instance, DEA has been applied for the assessment of efficiency of the school provision at different levels (Färe et al., 2006; Portela et al., 2012), universities and their departments (Avkiran, 2001; Thanassoulis et al., 2011), and the impact of education policies and, as well as welfare and profit oriented decision making (Bradley et al., 2001; Grosskopf & Moutray, 2001).

The value of Data Envelopment Analysis (DEA), as a non-parametric data analysis method, has been shown to lie in its capability to relatively evaluate the individual efficiency or performance of a decision-making unit (DMU) within a target group of interest that operates in a certain application domain (Liu et al., 2013a). According to Golany & Roll (1989), DEA has been adopted in these application domains to evaluate the effectiveness of programs or policies and to create a quantitative basis for reallocating resources (efficiency assessments) amongst other reasons. As Oyerinde & Bankole (2019b) have shown, DEA can also be used for decision making, policy direction and investment/donor grants justifications.

In this chapter, the authors aim to investigate the relative efficiency of ICT Infrastructure utilization on Education as a component of National Development using CRS and VRS models of the DEA. This is intended to show the viability of DEA as a data analytics methodology in policy direction and decision-making for developmental outcomes. The research employs thesame education index employed by Bankole et al. (2011b) introduced by Orbicom (2005) and International Telecommunications Union (ITU) used to emphasize the effect of education on ICT development. The rest of the chapter is organized as follows: Section two provides the background, section three discusses the theoretical framework, section four provides the research methodology and analysis, section five provides discussion of findings, section six provides the limitations, section seven the conclusion and section eight the future research.

BACKGROUND

Data envelopment analysis (DEA) was first developed by Charnes et al. (1978), which assumed a constant returns-to-scale (CRS). It is popularly known as the CCR model and remained the preferred technique for measuring the relative efficiency of decision-making units (DMUs) due to its intuitive ability to prescribe weights from assessments, which depend on multiple inputs and outputs. Banker et al. (1984) further extended the CCR model by accommodating for variable returns-to-scale (VRS) more popularly known as the BCC model. Consequently, these two conventional models have traditionally been employed in DEA studies in all its application domains. The difference between CRS and VRS is such that the number of efficient DMUs of the CRS is a subset of the VRS (Ahn et al., 1988). This means that one expects that a conventional DEA model based on CRS will have lesser number of efficient DMUs as compared to a VRS derived model (Ghasemi et al., 2018).

These returns to scale (RTS) classifications of DMUs in the DEA methodology have been the subject of study by numerous authors, including Banker (1984), who proposed using the most productive scale size concept and letting the sum of lambda values dictate the RTS, and Färe et al. (1994), who proposed applying their scale efficiency index method. A problem in classifying RTS however, is the existence of multiple optima, meaning that the classification may be a function of the solution selected by the optimization software (Cook & Seiford, 2009). Various attempts have been made to provide a more definitive RTS classification assignment for a given DMU, including developing intervals for the various free variables arising from the multiple optima (Cook & Seiford, 2009). Zhu & Shen (1995) suggested a remedy for the CCR RTS method under multiple optima while Seiford & Zhu (1997; 1999) reviewed the various methods and suggested computationally simple methods to characterize RTS thereby circumventing the need for exploring all alternate optimal solutions.

A common challenge with applications of DEA is the low discriminating power of the model used. This is the ability of the DEA models to differentiate between good and bad performing Decision-Making Units (DMUs) by reflecting on their performance in a sufficiently wide range of efficiency scores (Cooper et al., 2007; Thanassoulis et al., 2008; Atici & Podinovski, 2015). It is well-known that the discrimination of a DEA model depends on a number of factors, including the number of inputs and outputs in relation to the number of units, the type (variable or constant) of returns-to-scale assumed (VRS and CRS, respectively) and, more generally, the particular dataset that is under the investigation (Angulo-Meza & Lins, 2002; Podinovski & Thanassoulis 2007). Even, if the true (best practice) technology is assumed to be VRS, the reference, or benchmark, CRS technology is often used as a part of the scale efficiency calculations (Podinovski et al., 2014).

Despite all this, DEA has been successfully used to measure efficiency for well over 3 decades and its applications spread over a wide range of thematic areas (Liu et al., 2013a). Some applications such as education and health care blossomed in the early days of DEA, while other applications, on the other hand, have just begun to apply DEA recently (Liu et al., 2013b). A systematic survey on DEA applications was carried out by Liu et al., (2013b) and the results identified education as being one of the top five major application areas of DEA and prominent in its grand development. This is seen in Bessent & Bessent (1980), Charnes et al. (1981), Bessent et al. (1982), and Bessent et al. (1983). Consequently, DEA as an analytical methodology is a strong candidate for learning analytics implementation as seen in Oyerinde & Bankole (2018).

In addition, there have been some studies that have used DEA to measure efficiency in education with respect to Human Development. Gupta & Verhoeven (2001) measured the efficiency of education in Africa and Clements (2002) measured efficiency of education in Europe. St. Aubyn (2002) and Afonso & St. Aubyn (2005;2006a; 2006b) measured with respect to OECD countries. Tondeur et al., (2007) and Gulbahar, (2008) examined the efficiency of countries in utilizing their ICT resources for educational outputs and the Impact of ICT on education, respectively. Aristovnik, (2012) did a study on the impact of ICT on educational performance and its efficiency in select EU and OECD countries using DEA while Oyerinde & Bankole, (2019a, 2019b) used DEA to measure efficiency of ICT infrastructure utilization within the educational component of the Human Development Index (HDI) with respect to national development.

It is against this backdrop that this study is carried out to investigate the relative efficiency of ICT infrastructure utilization on education with respect to human development using both the CRS and VRS models of Data Envelopment Analysis. The study aims to show the viability of DEA as an enterprise model by using it in learning analytics to provide decision making support for policy direction and decision making within the context of human development.

THEORETICAL FRAMEWORK

Investments in ICT can be thought of as consisting of four facets: hardware, software, internal (investments in labour) spending and telecommunication investments respectively (WITSA, 2008; Bankole et al., 2013). For this study, only three of these aspects which are readily measurable for Infrastructure Utilization are considered. These are:

1. Hardware: Here data available for percentage of Individuals with Computers is taken.
2. Software: Here data available for percentage of Individuals with Internet is taken.
3. Telecommunications: Here data available for percentage of Individuals with Mobile Phones is taken.

This research uses a conceptual model for measuring the efficiency of ICT Infrastructure on Education and is derived from Bankole et al. (2011b) model for measuring Impact of ICT on Human development which expressed Human Development as:

HDI = f[Standard of living (GDP per capita), Education (Literacy rates / Enrolments) and Health (life expectancy)]

For this research, the authors focus solely on the Education component of Human Development. The conceptual model takes the form of a linear equation derived from Bankole et al. (2011b) model for measuring impact on education within the Human Development Index and is rooted in the Cobb-Douglas production function. It can be considered to have the following form where E represents the educational component of the human development index (HDI), H represents Hardware Infrastructure, S represents Software Infrastructure, T represents Telecommunication Infrastructure, derived from Bankole et al. (2011d) and expressed as:

$$Log(E) = \alpha_o + \alpha_{HS} log(H) * log(S) + \alpha_{TH} log(T) * log(H) + \alpha_{TS} log(T) * log(S) + \xi$$

In this model, the authors consider ICT infrastructure available for utilization and not investments made for potential utilization. Therefore, this model now focuses on educational attainment with adult literacy rates and no longer enrolment as used by Bankole et al. (2011b). This is because the data collected was for ICT infrastructure available for utilization over the specified period being investigated, 2011-2017, when the various educational levels were attained and not investments made. Therefore, the model for this study which reflects the above logarithmic expression is:

The impact on Education (Adult Literacy rates/Attainments) = f[Internet Infrastructure (II) + Computer Infrastructure (CI) + Mobile Phone Infrastructure (MPI)].

RESEARCH METHODOLOGY AND ANALYSIS

This research employs a quantitative research methodology using Data Envelopment Analysis (DEA) to analyze archival time series data. DEA is a well-known non-parametric linear programming method for measuring the relative efficiency (Thanassoulis et al., 2011; Bankole et al., 2011c) and has been used across a vast range of disciplines as a multiple criteria decision making (MCDM) tool (Mousavi-Nasab & Sotoudeh-Anvari, 2017; Wardana et al., 2020). Recently, DEA has been used to develop enterprise architecture models for decision support systems (El-Mashaleh et al., 2016), measure the impact of enterprise integration on firm performance (Fazlollahi & Franke, 2018; Pokushko et al., 2019) and also been used for enterprise architecture analysis in order to provide decision making support for large scale Information Technology development planning and efficiency (Fasanghari et al., 2015).

DEA is a data-oriented method for evaluating the performance (efficiency) of entities known as Decision Making Units (DMUs) (Bankole et al., 2011c) which uses input-output data to compute an efficient production frontier produced by the most efficient DMU's. DEA, unlike a parametric method, is context specific with respect to the interpretations of the results of the analysis, which are restricted to the sample and should not be generalized beyond the sample (Samoilenko & Osei-Bryson, 2017). DEA, therefore, can then be viewed as a multiple-criteria evaluation methodology where DMUs are alternatives, and DEA inputs and outputs are two sets of performance criteria where one set (inputs) is to be minimized and the other (outputs) is to be maximized (Cook et al., 2014).

This research considers the two prevalent DEA models, the VRS and CRS models (Podinovski et al., 2014). The CRS model is derived by considering a set on n DMU's each with DMU_j, $(j=1, ..., n)$ using m inputs $x_{ij}(i=1, ..., m)$ and generating s outputs $y_{rj}(r=1, ..., s)$. If the multipliers $\bar{u}_r$, $\bar{v}_i$ associated with outputs r and inputs i, respectively, are known, then borrowing from conventional cost/benefit theory, the efficiency $\bar{e}_j$ of DMU_j can be expressed as the ratio of weighted outputs to weighted inputs:

$$\sum_r k_r y_{rj} \Big/ \sum_i \bar{v}_i x_{ij}$$

However, a common challenge that lies herein, is that often, the multipliers, $\bar{u}_r$ and $\bar{v}_i$ are not known. To resolve this, Charnes et al., (1978), proposed a model for deriving appropriate multipliers for a given DMU. This model, popularly referred to as the CCR (Charnes, Cooper and Rhodes) model is expressed as:

$$e_0 = \max \sum_r u_r y_{r0} \Big/ \sum_i v_i x_{i0}$$

$$s.t. \sum_r u_r y_{rj} - \sum_i v_i x_{ij} \le 0, \quad all \; j$$

$$u_r v_i \ge \varepsilon, \quad all \; r, i$$

where ε is a non-archimedian value designed to enforce strict positivity on the variables and is the solution to a fractional programming problem (Cook & Seiford, 2009). Going forward, however, Banker et al. (1984) (BCC), extended this by providing for variable returns to scale (VRS) model. The BCC ratio model differs from the CRS model, by way of an additional variable as is expressed as:

$$e_0^* = \max \left[\sum_r u_r y_{r0} - u_0\right] \Big/ \sum_i v_i x_{i0}$$

$$s.t. \sum_r u_r y_{rj} - u_0 - \sum_i v_i x_{ij} \le 0, \quad j = 1, \ldots, n$$

$$u_r \ge \varepsilon, \; v_i \ge \varepsilon, \; \forall i, r$$

where u_0 is unrestricted in sign (Cook & Seiford, 2009). For this research, ICT Infrastructure serve as the Inputs and Educational Attainment/Adult Literacy rates serve as the Outputs.

The ICT Infrastructure input variables used will be individuals with access to computers, internet, and mobile phones. This study measures the relative efficiency of ICT Infrastructure with respect to education only as an aspect of human development, the output variables are educational attainment from post-secondary level through to bachelors' level and adult literacy rates. An Input-Oriented Basic Radial Model (BRM) with Constant Returns to Scale (CRS) DEA approach is used and compared with Input-Oriented BRM with Variable Returns to Scale (VRS) approach for this research. The choice of an Input-Oriented BRM is based on the theoretical assumption that the ICT infrastructure (Input) are controllable and increase or decrease in the levels of these inputs is expected to bring about a corresponding increase or decrease in the levels of Educational Attainments and Literacy Rates (Output) respectively for the CRS. Practically, however this may not be the case as effective utilization of the Inputs may or may not be properly controlled and therefore become subjective to users and participants. This is where VRS helps us to be able to measure the relative efficiency without assuming the inputs are controllable. The results from these two DEA models are presented and findings discussed.

In testing the legitimacy of the choices for input and output variables, this research makes use of the Structural Equation Model (SEM). SEMs are multi-equation regression models (Fox, 2002) that extends beyond linear modelling such as ANOVA and multiple regression. SEMs incorporate multiple independent and dependent variables, as well as theoretical latent constructs that the observed variables might represent (Hoe, 2008). The use of SEM therefore allows researchers to posit the presence of relationships between these latent constructs (Samoilenko & Osei-Bryson, 2017a). Figure 1 shows the outcome of the SEM model run. Both the ICTInfra (Input) and EduAtt (Output) indices take up a reflexive model thus allowing for adding and removal of the component indicators as may be required. The SEM analysis was carried out using the WarpPLS 6.0 Software.

Figure 1. Outcome of SEM model on Input and Output Variables

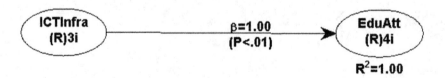

For this study, time series data from the United Nations Educational, Scientific and Cultural Organization (UNESCO); educational attainments; World bank; literacy rates and the International Telecommunication Union (ITU); individuals with computers, internet and mobile phones were obtained. This was done by downloading the data for the years being investigated and sorting it into the aggregates that formed the

DMU's. The available data was then aggregated by taking an average of the data available for the constituent countries within the region for that particular year. For years where data was not available for the countries, the research resolved this by means of extrapolation. Available data was collected for all countries in Sub-Saharan Africa, Northern Africa, and select countries in Europe and Northern America. These were compared with the overall world percentages to measure relative efficiency. Data for 2011-2017 was collected in percentages of the country population, the ratio values computed, and the average values for the years in the study calculated and used for the values representing each region as shown in Table 1.

Table 1. Regional Data Averages (2011 – 2017) in Ratios to Population

Regions	Individuals using Computers	Individuals using Internet	Individuals using Mobile Phones	Educational Attainment (Post-Secondary)	Educational Attainment (Short Cycle Tertiary)	Educational Attainment (Bachelors)	Adult Literacy Rate
	INPUT	INPUT	INPUT	OUTPUT	OUTPUT	OUTPUT	OUTPUT
Sub-Saharan Africa	0.24	0.1399	0.7495	0.1086	0.056	0.0288	0.6287
Northern Africa	0.4257	0.3004	0.8827	0.1235	0.1327	N/A	0.7236
Europe and North America	0.7631	0.7074	0.9134	0.2962	0.2539	0.2168	0.9915
World	0.61	0.4343	0.8772	0.2695	0.2167	0.1507	0.8559

Table 2 shows statistics of the data being analysed. This is the minimum, maximum, mean and standard deviation values for the data.

Table 2. Data Statistics

Index	Minimum	Maximum	Mean	Standard Deviation
Individuals with Computers (Input)	0.24	0.7631	0.51	0.1963
Individuals with Internet (Input)	0.1399	0.7074	0.396	0.2081
Individuals with Mobile Phones (Input)	0.7495	0.9134	0.856	0.0628
Educational Attainment Post-Secondary (Output)	0.1086	0.2962	0.2	0.0841
Educational Attainment Short-cycle Tertiary (Output)	0.056	0.2539	0.165	0.0766
Educational Attainment Bachelors (Output)	0	0.2168	0.099	0.0884
Adult Literacy Rates (Output)	0.6287	0.9915	0.8	0.1369

The Input-Oriented BRM analysis for both the CRS and VRS models of the data collected was calculated using the Data Envelopment Analysis Online Software (D.E.A.O.S.) available online at https://deaos.com Tables 3 shows the BRM weights for the CRS model analysis on the data collected while Table 4 shows that for the VRS model analysis. For more summaries of the outcome of the analysis run and calculations see Tables 7 to 11 in the Appendix.

Table 3. Basic Radial Models (Envelopment Forms) Weights - CRS

Region	Individuals with Computers	Individuals with Internet	Individuals with Mobile Phones	Educational Attainment Post-Secondary	Educational Attainment short cycle tertiary	Educational Attainment Bachelors	Adult Literacy Rates
Sub-Saharan Africa	3.984	0	0.058	9.208	0	0	0
Northern Africa	2.349	0	0	0	4.737	0	0.475
Europe and North America	1.31	0	0	1.073	0	2.159	0.216
World	1.605	0	0.024	3.711	0	0	0

Table 4. Basic Radial Models (Envelopment Forms) Weights – VRS

Region	Individuals with Computers	Individuals with Internet	Individuals with Mobile Phones	Educational Attainment Post-Secondary	Educational Attainment short cycle tertiary	Educational Attainment Bachelors	Adult Literacy Rates
Sub-Saharan Africa	3.984	0	0.058	9.208	0	0	0
Northern Africa	2.349	0	0	0	*5.409*	0	*0*
Europe and North America	1.31	0	0	1.073	0	2.159	0.216
World	1.605	0	0.024	3.711	0	0	0

DISCUSSION OF FINDINGS

From the outcome of both analysis models run as seen in table 5, Northern Africa is 97.2% and 97.8% relatively efficient in its utilization of ICT Infrastructure for the educational component of National Development while Sub-Saharan Africa,

Table 5. Efficiency Summary

Region	Efficiency CRS	Efficiency VRS
Sub-Saharan Africa	100%	100%
Northern Africa	97.20%	97.80%
Europe and North America	100%	100%
World	100%	100%

Europe and North America and the World are optimally relatively efficient. Sub-Saharan Africa has the average lowest percentage of ICT infrastructure utilization, educational attainments, and adult literacy rates, however, both models show that it is optimally relatively efficient in its utilization if ICT Infrastructure for education. This supports the notion that should there be in increase in ICT Infrastructure in this region, whether properly controlled or not, there will be a corresponding increase in educational attainment and Adult Literacy rates. This will bring about an increase in quality of life and Human Development with respect to the Nations HDI. Bankole et al. (2011d) stated that the Human Development Index (HDI) is used to assess the quality of life in a nation and is based on three components: Standard of Living, Knowledge Acquisition (education), and Health. For assessing knowledge acquisition capability (education), national literacy rates and levels of school enrolment/attainment are used (UNDP, 2006).

As expected, Europe and North America have the highest average values for ICT Infrastructure utilization, educational attainments and literacy rates and are optimally relatively efficient in this regard. Continuous increase of ICT Infrastructure utilization in education will continue to yield positive results in educational attainment and adult literacy rates. Although Northern Africa have higher average values than Sub-Saharan Africa across most of the indices, the fact that there was no data available for Educational Attainment (Bachelors) may be a mitigating factor against their relative efficiency frontier thus reducing the efficiency value. This is not to say however that Northern Africa is not efficient, but rather has the lowest relative efficiency in this grouping and within the context of the models used.

In comparing the results of the CRS and VRS models of analysis on this data, the research shows that there is no significant difference in the relative efficiencies of the regions. This therefore means that there is a relatively efficient utilization of ICT infrastructure (Input variables), whether controllable or not, subjective or objective, with respect to educational attainment/adult literacy rates (Output variables) (Oyerinde & Bankole, 2018). In table 6, the research shows that Individuals with computers has the strongest correlation with educational attainment and adult literacy rates while individuals with mobile phones has the weakest correlation. This may

Table 6. Correlation between Input and Output Indices

	Individuals with Computers	Individuals with Internet	Individuals with Mobile Phones
Educational Attainment Post-Secondary	0.9456	0.905	0.6947
Educational Attainment Short-Cycle Tertiary	0.9942	0.951	0.8794
Educational Attainment Bachelors	0.8972	0.8982	0.5709
Adult Literacy Rates	0.9932	0.9913	0.8246
Average	**0.9576**	**0.9364**	**0.7424**

also be a strong indication of the outcome of pedagogical changes in teaching and learning over the years which now include higher usage of computers. This would therefore make a strong case for the continued increase in the introduction of online learning and blended learning environments into education.

LIMITATIONS

The main limitation of this study is the availability of the data for the dataset. The data was collected from the United Nations Educational, Scientific and Cultural Organization (UNESCO) - educational attainments; World bank - literacy rates and the International Telecommunication Union (ITU) - individuals with computers, internet and mobile phones. Considering that the years being investigated are the most recent and the sources of the data are credible and well cited sources for scientific data collection, some countries within each region did not have data available for one or more years being investigated. This may have positive or negative effects on the regional averages calculated as the data collected is represented as a percentage of the population of the countries.

FUTURE RESEARCH DIRECTIONS

An area of future research would be to investigate this outcome further in order to ascertain whether increased spending in computer hardware and availability of these resources to individuals will have any impact on education considering how efficiently these ICT infrastructures are currently being utilized. While noting that the strongest correlation occurs between the individuals with computers and educational attainment post-secondary indices, the further research may choose to consider ICT Infrastructure utilization in secondary and post-secondary education as well and not just tertiary education. Also, it would be interesting to see, as m-learning initiatives pick up, whether the correlation between mobile phones and educational attainments and literacy rates will become stronger and what effect(s), if any, this will have on militating against the challenges currently being encountered in m-learning implementations (Oyerinde, 2014) and consequently Human Development. Another area of future research would be to expand this context by showing how ICT impacts on each of the components of the Human Development Index within the specified DMU's and determine the correlations, if any between them.

CONCLUSION

This research has been able to show that existing ICT infrastructure over the past 7 years are being relatively efficiently utilized with respect to educational attainment and adult literacy rates and thus affecting the HDI of the regions being investigated. The research further shows that Sub-Saharan Africa with significantly lower educational attainment and literacy rates are relatively efficiently utilizing their significantly lower ICT infrastructure and therefore provides an empirical basis for justifying increased spending in ICT infrastructure. Using the CRS and VRS models for the DEA analysis, the research has been able to empirically suggest that there is a relatively efficient utilization of the inputs (ICT Infrastructure) with respect to the outputs (Educational Attainment / Adult Literacy Rates). This can prove useful for policy makers, donors, and macro-economic decision makers. Policy makers can draw up policies to maximize efficiency of ICT infrastructure utilization to justify calls for grants from donor organisations and funders in specific developmental areas i.e. Sustainable Development Goals (SDG) 4.1 amongst others.

Figure 2. Correlation between Input and Output Indices

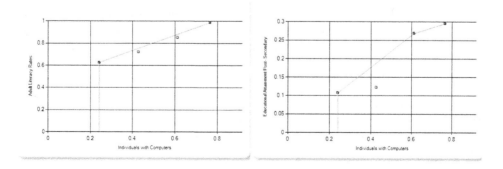

The research has also been able to show that there is a strong correlation between ICT Infrastructure and Educational Attainment / Adult Literacy rates. The correlation is strongest on the individuals with computers index of the ICT Infrastructure as shown in Figure 1. This can provide a basis for understanding why there is a call for increased spending on ICT infrastructure for education.

While acknowledging that that DEA as a methodology is context specific and by its very nature of being non-parametric does not allow for generalization, the research has been able to show that as an enterprise model for decision support, gains can be derived from using it for data analytics decision making at a global level. It has been able to provide insights for determining efficiency which in turn can enable optimal utilization of resources.

REFERENCES

Afonso, A., & St. Aubyn, M. (2005). Non-parametric approaches to education and health efficiency in Oecd countries. *Journal of Applied Econometrics, 8*(2), 227–246.

Afonso, A., & St. Aubyn, M. (2006a). Cross-country efficiency of secondary education provision: A semiparametric analysis with non-discretionary inputs. *Economic Modelling, 23*(3), 476–491. doi:10.1016/j.econmod.2006.02.003

Afonso, A., & St. Aubyn, M. (2006b). Relative efficiency of health provision: a DEA approach with nondiscretionary inputs. *ISEG-UTL, Department of Economics Working Paper n° 33/2006/DE/UECE.*

Ahn, T., Charnes, A., & Cooper, W. W. (1988). Efficiency characterizations in different DEA models. *Socio-Economic Planning Sciences, 22*(6), 253–257. doi:10.1016/0038-0121(88)90007-9

Anand, S., & Ravallion, M. (1993). Human Development in Poor Countries: On the Role of Private Incomes and Public Services. *The Journal of Economic Perspectives, 7*(1), 133–150. doi:10.1257/jep.7.1.133

Angulo-Meza, L., & Lins, M. P. E. (2002). Review of methods for increasing discrimination in data envelopment analysis. *Annals of Operations Research, 116*(1-4), 225–242. doi:10.1023/A:1021340616758

Aristovnik, A. (2012). *The impact of ICT on educational performance and its efficiency in selected EU and OECD countries: a non-parametric analysis.* Available at SSRN: https://ssrn.com/abstract=2187482

Atici, K. B., & Podinovski, V. V. (2015). Using data envelopment analysis for the assessment of technical efficiency of units with different specialisations: An application to agriculture. *Omega, 54,* 72–83. doi:10.1016/j.omega.2015.01.015

Avkiran, N. K. (2001). Investigating technical and scale efficiencies of Australian universities through data envelopment analysis. *Socio-Economic Planning Sciences, 35*(1), 57–80. doi:10.1016/S0038-0121(00)00010-0

Banker, R. D. (1984). Estimating most productive scale size using data envelopment analysis. *European Journal of Operational Research, 17*(1), 35–44. doi:10.1016/0377-2217(84)90006-7

Banker, R. D., Charnes, A., & Cooper, W. W. (1984). Some models for estimating technical and scale inefficiencies in data envelopment analysis. *Management Science, 30*(9), 1078–1092. doi:10.1287/mnsc.30.9.1078

Banker, R. D., Cooper, W. W., Seiford, L. M., Thrall, R. M., & Zhu, J. (2004). Returns to scale in different DEA models. *European Journal of Operational Research, 154*(2), 345–362. doi:10.1016/S0377-2217(03)00174-7

Bankole, F. O. (2015). ICT Infrastructure and Its' Impact on National Development: A Research Direction for Africa Using Analytics. *Proceedings of SIG GlobDev 2015 Pre-ECIS Workshop.*

Bankole, F. O., Brown, I., & Osei-Bryson, K. M. (2011b). The Impact of ICT Infrastructure on Human Development: An Analysis of ICT-Use in SADC Countries. *Proceedings of the 11th International Conference on Social Implications of Computers in Developing Countries.*

Bankole, F. O., Osei-Bryson, K. M., & Brown, I. (2011c). ICT infrastructure utilization in Africa: Data envelopment analysis-based exploration. *Proceeding of special interest group on ICT and global development at Americas Conference on Information System (AMCIS) Workshop.*

Bankole, F. O., Osei-Bryson, K. M., & Brown, I. (2011d). Exploring the Impacts of ICT Investments on Dimensions of Human Development in Different Contexts: A Regression Splines Analysis. *Proceedings of SIG GlobDev Fourth Annual Workshop,* 158.

Bankole, F. O., Osei-Bryson, K. M., & Brown, I. (2013). The impact of ICT investments on human development: A regression splines analysis. *Journal of Global Information Technology Management, 16*(2), 59–85. doi:10.1080/1097198X.2013.10845636

Bankole, F. O., Osei-Bryson, K. M., & Brown, I. (2015). The impact of information and communications technology infrastructure and complementary factors on Intra-African Trade. *Information Technology for Development*, *21*(1), 12–28. doi:10.10 80/02681102.2013.832128

Bankole, F. O., Shirazi, F., & Brown, I. (2011a). Investigating the impact of ICT investments on human development. *The Electronic Journal on Information Systems in Developing Countries*, *48*(1), 1–19. doi:10.1002/j.1681-4835.2011.tb00344.x

Bankole Dr, F., & Mimbi, L. (2017). ICT Infrastructure and It's Impact on National Development: A Research Direction for Africa. *The African Journal of Information Systems*, *9*(2), 1.

Bessent, A., Bessent, W., Kennington, J., & Reagan, B. (1982). An application of mathematical programming to assess productivity in the Houston independent school district. *Management Science*, *28*(12), 1355–1367. doi:10.1287/mnsc.28.12.1355

Bessent, A. M., & Bessent, E. W. (1980). Determining the comparative efficiency of schools through data envelopment analysis. *Educational Administration Quarterly*, *16*(2), 57–75. doi:10.1177/0013161X8001600207

Bessent, A. M., Bessent, E. W., Charnes, A., Cooper, W. W., & Thorogood, N. C. (1983). Evaluation of educational program proposals by means of DEA. *Educational Administration Quarterly*, *19*(2), 82–107. doi:10.1177/0013161X83019002006

Bradley, S., Johnes, G., & Millington, J. (2001). The effect of competition on the efficiency of secondary schools in England. *European Journal of Operational Research*, *135*(3), 545–568. doi:10.1016/S0377-2217(00)00328-3

Charnes, A., Cooper, W. W., & Rhodes, E. (1978). Measuring the efficiency of decision making units. *European Journal of Operational Research*, *2*(6), 429–444. doi:10.1016/0377-2217(78)90138-8

Charnes, A., Cooper, W. W., & Rhodes, E. (1981). Evaluating program and managerial efficiency: An application of data envelopment analysis to program follow through. *Management Science*, *27*(6), 668–697. doi:10.1287/mnsc.27.6.668

Clements, B. (2002). How efficient is education spending in Europe? *European Review of Economics and Finance*, *1*, 3–26.

Cook, W. D., & Seiford, L. M. (2009). Data envelopment analysis (DEA)–Thirty years on. *European Journal of Operational Research*, *192*(1), 1–17. doi:10.1016/j. ejor.2008.01.032

Cook, W. D., Tone, K., & Zhu, J. (2014). Data envelopment analysis: Prior to choosing a model. *Omega*, *44*, 1–4. doi:10.1016/j.omega.2013.09.004

Cooper, W. W., Seiford, L. M., & Tone, K. (2006). *Introduction to data envelopmentanalysis and its uses*. Springer.

Cooper, W. W., Seiford, L. M., & Tone, K. (2007). *Data Envelopment Analysis: A Comprehensive Text with Models*. Applications, References and DEA-Solver Software.

Desai, M. (1991). Human development. *European Economic Review*, *35*(2-3), 350–357. doi:10.1016/0014-2921(91)90136-7 PMID:1717401

Dwyfor Evans, A., Green, C. J., & Murinde, V. (2002). Human capital and financial development in economic growth: New evidence using the translog production function. *International Journal of Finance & Economics*, *7*(2), 123–140. doi:10.1002/ijfe.182

El-Mashaleh, M. S., Hyari, K. H., Bdour, A. N., & Rababeh, S. M. (2016). A multi-attribute decision-making model for construction enterprise resource planning system selection. *International Journal of Construction Education and Research*, *12*(1), 66–79. doi:10.1080/15578771.2015.1015755

Färe, R., Grosskopf, S., Forsund, F. R., Hayes, K., & Heshmati, A. (2006). Measurement of productivity and quality in non-marketable services: With application to schools. *Quality Assurance in Education*, *14*(1), 21–36. doi:10.1108/09684880610643593

Färe, R. S., Grosskopf, S., & Lovell, C. A. K. (1994). *Production Frontiers*. Cambridge University Press.

Fasanghari, M., Amalnick, M. S., Anvari, R. T., & Razmi, J. (2015). A novel credibility-based group decision making method for Enterprise Architecture scenario analysis using Data Envelopment Analysis. *Applied Soft Computing*, *32*, 347–368. doi:10.1016/j.asoc.2015.03.052

Fazlollahi, A., & Franke, U. (2018). Measuring the impact of enterprise integration on firm performance using data envelopment analysis. *International Journal of Production Economics*, *200*, 119–129. doi:10.1016/j.ijpe.2018.02.011

Fox, J. (2002). Structural equation models. *Appendix to an R and S-PLUS Companion to Applied Regression*.

Ghasemi, M. R., Ignatius, J., & Rezaee, B. (2018). Improving discriminating power in data envelopment models based on deviation variables framework. *European Journal of Operational Research*.

Golany, B., & Roll, Y. (1989). An application procedure for DEA. *Omega, 17*(3), 237–250. doi:10.1016/0305-0483(89)90029-7

Grosskopf, S., & Moutray, C. (2001). Evaluating performance in Chicago public highschools in the wake of decentralization. *Economics of Education Review, 20*(1), 1–14. doi:10.1016/S0272-7757(99)00065-5

Gülbahar, Y. (2008). ICT usage in higher education: A case study on preservice teachers and instructors. *The Turkish Online Journal of Educational Technology, 7*(1), 32–37.

Gupta, S., & Verhoeven, M. (2001). The efficiency of government expenditure: Experiences from Africa. *Journal of Policy Modeling, 23*(4), 433–467. doi:10.1016/S0161-8938(00)00036-3

Hinostroza, J. E. (2018). New Challenges for ICT in Education Policies in Developing Countries: The Need to Account for the Widespread Use of ICT for Teaching and Learning Outside the School. In *ICT-Supported Innovations in Small Countries and Developing Regions* (pp. 99–119). Springer. doi:10.1007/978-3-319-67657-9_5

Hoe, S. L. (2008). Issues and procedures in adopting structural equation modeling technique. *Journal of Applied Quantitative Methods, 3*(1), 76–83.

Kayisire, D., & Wei, J. (2016). Information Technology for Development ICT Adoption and Usage in Africa. *Towards an Efficiency Assessment, 1102*. Advance online publication. doi:10.1080/02681102.2015.1081862

Liu, J. S., Lu, L. Y., Lu, W. M., & Lin, B. J. (2013a). Data envelopment analysis 1978–2010: A citation-based literature survey. *Omega, 41*(1), 3–15. doi:10.1016/j.omega.2010.12.006

Liu, J. S., Lu, L. Y., Lu, W. M., & Lin, B. J. (2013b). A survey of DEA applications. *Omega, 41*(5), 893–902. doi:10.1016/j.omega.2012.11.004

Mousavi-Nasab, S. H., & Sotoudeh-Anvari, A. (2017). A comprehensive MCDM-based approach using TOPSIS, COPRAS and DEA as an auxiliary tool for material selection problems. *Materials & Design, 121*, 237–253. doi:10.1016/j.matdes.2017.02.041

Orbicom. (2005) *From The Digital Divide To Digital Opportunities: Measuring Infostates for Development*. Montreal: Claude-Yves Charron.

Oyerinde, O. D. (2014). A Review of Challenges Militating Against Successful E-Learning and M-Learning Implementations in Developing Countries. *International Journal of Science and Advanced Technology, 4*(6).

Oyerinde, Y., & Bankole, F. (2018). Influence of Constant Returns to Scale and Variable Returns to Scale Data Envelopment Analysis Models in ICT Infrastructure Efficiency Utilization. *Proceedings of the 11th Annual Pre-ICIS SIG GlobDev Workshop.*

Oyerinde, Y., & Bankole, F. (2019a). Measuring Efficiency and Productivity of ICT Infrastructure Utilization. *Proceedings of the 24th UK Academy for Information Systems International Conference.*

Oyerinde, Y., & Bankole, F. (2019b). Investigating the Efficiency of ICT Infrastructure Utilization: A Data Envelopment Analysis Approach. In P. Nielsen & H. Kimaro (Eds.), *Information and Communication Technologies for Development. Strengthening Southern-Driven Cooperation as a Catalyst for ICT4D* (Vol. 551). Springer. doi:10.1007/978-3-030-18400-1_52

Podinovski, V. V., Ismail, I., Bouzdine-Chameeva, T., & Zhang, W. (2014). Combining the assumptions of variable and constant returns to scale in the efficiency evaluation of secondary schools. *European Journal of Operational Research, 239*(2), 504–513. doi:10.1016/j.ejor.2014.05.016

Podinovski, V. V., & Thanassoulis, E. (2007). Improving discrimination in data envelopment analysis: Some practical suggestions. *Journal of Productivity Analysis, 28*(1-2), 117–126. doi:10.100711123-007-0042-x

Pokushko, M., Stupina, A., Medina-Bulo, I., Dresvianskii, E., & Karaseva, M. (2019). Application of data envelopment analysis method for assessment of performance of enterprises in fuel and energy complex. *Journal of Physics: Conference Series, 1353*(1), 012140. doi:10.1088/1742-6596/1353/1/012140

Portela, M. C. S., Camanho, A. S., & Borges, D. (2012). Performance assessment of secondary schools: The snapshot of a country taken by DEA. *The Journal of the Operational Research Society, 63*(8), 1098–1115. doi:10.1057/jors.2011.114

Samoilenko, S. V., & Osei-Bryson, K. M. (2017). Creating Theoretical Research Frameworks Using Multiple Methods. *Insight.*

Seiford, L. M., & Zhu, J. (1999). An investigation of returns to scale in data envelopment analysis. *Omega, 27*(1), 1–11. doi:10.1016/S0305-0483(98)00025-5

St Aubyn, M. (2002). Evaluating efficiency in the Portuguese health and education sectors. *Economia, 26.* Available at SSRN: https://ssrn.com/abstract=504942

Staessens, M., Kerstens, P. J., Bruneel, J., & Cherchye, L. (2019). Data envelopment analysis and social enterprises: Analysing performance, strategic orientation, and mission drift. *Journal of Business Ethics*, *159*(2), 325–341. doi:10.100710551-018-4046-4

Thanassoulis, E., Kortelainen, M., Johnes, G., & Johnes, J. (2011). Costs and efficiency of higher education institutions in England: A DEA analysis. *The Journal of the Operational Research Society*, *62*(7), 1282–1297. doi:10.1057/jors.2010.68

Thanassoulis, E., Portela, M. C., & Despic, O. (2008). Data envelopment analysis: the mathematical programming approach to efficiency analysis. *The measurement of productive efficiency and productivity growth*, 251-420.

Tondeur, J., van Braak, J., & Valcke, M. (2007). Towards a typology of computer use in primary education. *Journal of Computer Assisted Learning*, *23*(3), 197–206. doi:10.1111/j.1365-2729.2006.00205.x

UNDP. (2006). *The Millennium Development Goals*. UNDP.

Wardana, R. W., Masudin, I., & Restuputri, D. P. (2020). A novel group decision-making method by P-robust fuzzy DEA credibility constraint for welding process selection. *Cogent Engineering*, *7*(1), 1728057. doi:10.1080/23311916.2020.1728057

WITSA. (2008). *Digital Planet 2008: The Global Information Economy*. The World Information Technology and Services Alliance.

Zhu, J., & Shen, Z. H. (1995). A discussion of testing DMUs' returns to scale. *European Journal of Operational Research*, *81*(3), 590–596. doi:10.1016/0377-2217(93)E0354-Z

KEY TERMS AND DEFINITIONS

Adult Literacy Rates: Percentage of population aged 15 years and over who can both read and write with understanding a short simple statement on his/her everyday life.

Decision Making Unit: A business or organizational entity which is responsible for collectively making decisions.

Educational Attainment: The highest level of education that an individual has completed.

Human Development: The process of enlarging people's freedoms and opportunities and improving their well-being.

Human Development Index: An index/tool for measuring a country's key dimensions of human development.

ICT Infrastructure: Key Information and Communication Technology hardware and software physical stock previously invested in and now available for utilization.

Learning Analytics: Data Analytics on data from the education sector referred to as educational data.

APPENDIX

Table 7. Summary for Sub-Saharan Africa

	Individuals with Computers	Individuals with Internet	Individuals with Mobile Phones	Educational Attainment Post-Secondary	Educational Attainment short cycle tertiary	Educational Attainment Bachelors	Adult Literacy Rates
Slacks	0	0	0	0	0	0	0
Weights	3.984	0	0.058	9.208	0	0	0
Values	0.24	0.14	0.75	0.109	0.056	0.029	0.629
Targets	0.24	0.14	0.75	0.109	0.056	0.029	0.629

Table 8. Summary for Northern Africa

	Individuals with Computers	Individuals with Internet	Individuals with Mobile Phones	Educational Attainment Post-Secondary	Educational Attainment short cycle tertiary	Educational Attainment Bachelors	Adult Literacy Rates
Slacks	0	0.013	0.065	0.061	0	0.087	0
Weights	2.349	0	0	0	4.737	0	0.475
Values	0.426	0.3	0.883	0.124	0.133	0	0.724
Targets	0.414	0.279	0.793	0.184	0.133	0.087	0.724

Table 9. Summary for Europe and North America

	Individuals with Computers	Individuals with Internet	Individuals with Mobile Phones	Educational Attainment Post- Secondary	Educational Attainment short cycle tertiary	Educational Attainment Bachelors	Adult Literacy Rates
Slacks	0	0	0	0	0	0	0
Weights	1.31	0	0	1.073	0	2.159	0.216
Values	0.763	0.707	0.913	0.296	0.254	0.217	0.992
Targets	0.763	0.707	0.913	0.296	0.254	0.217	0.992

Table 10. Summary for World

	Individuals with Computers	Individuals with Internet	Individuals with Mobile Phones	Educational Attainment Post- Secondary	Educational Attainment short cycle tertiary	Educational Attainment Bachelors	Adult Literacy Rates
Slacks	0	0	0	0	0	0	0
Weights	1.605	0	0.024	3.711	0	0	0
Values	0.61	0.434	0.877	0.27	0.217	0.151	0.856
Targets	0.61	0.434	0.877	0.27	0.217	0.151	0.856

Table 11. Summary for Northern Africa - VRS with Difference Highlighted

	Individuals with Computers	Individuals with Internet	Individuals with Mobile Phones	Educational Attainment Post- Secondary	Educational Attainment short cycle tertiary	Educational Attainment Bachelors	Adult Literacy Rates
Slacks	0	*0.014*	*0.053*	*0.062*	0	0.087	*0.014*
Weights	2.349	0	0	0	*5.409*	0	*0*
Values	0.426	0.3	0.883	0.124	0.133	0	0.724
Targets	*0.417*	0.279	*0.81*	*0.185*	0.133	0.087	*0.737*

Chapter 8

Implementation of Big Data Analytics for Government Enterprise

Namhla Matiwane
Cape Peninsula University of Technology, South Africa

Tiko Iyamu
iD https://orcid.org/0000-0002-4949-094X
Cape Peninsula University of Technology, South Africa

ABSTRACT

Within the South African government, there is an increasing amount of data. The problem is that the South African government is struggling to employ the concept of big data analytics (BDA) for the analysis of its big data. This could be attributed to know-how from both technical and nontechnical perspectives. Failure to implement BDA and ensure appropriate use hinders government enterprises and agencies in their drive to deliver quality service. A government enterprise was selected and used as a case in this study primarily because the concept of BDA is new to many South African government departments. Data was collected through in-depth interviews. From the analysis, four factors—knowledge, process, differentiation, and skillset—that can influence implementation of BDA for government enterprises were revealed. Based on the factors, a set of criteria in the form of a model was developed.

DOI: 10.4018/978-1-5225-8229-8.ch008

INTRODUCTION

Big data has attracted attention, not only from private organisations, but major governmental organisations as well (Cao, 2017). As with other sectors of the economy, large amounts of data have been generated by government of many countries (Archenaa & Anita, 2015). Big data is defined as large data sets with characteristics of high volume, variety, and velocity that cannot be easily stored, captured, managed, analysed effectively with traditional database storage software and methods (Ridge et al., 2015). The rate at which data is growing around the world is at a projected rate of 40% per year (Al Nuaimi et al., 2015). According to Berg (2015), big data presents challenges to organisations because of data that are too vast, growing at a very high rate that make it very hard to manage, and difficult to analyse using traditional methods and tools.

The concept of BDA refers to *"the use of advanced data analytic techniques on vast data sets (Big Data) to discover patterns and meaningful use of information"* (Bamiah et al., 2018:231). Thus, it is through the implementation of BDA tools (application) that organisations and government enterprises can derive value and insights from these voluminous datasets (Mehta & Pandit, 2018). (Bumblauskas et al., 2017:703) defined big data analytics (BDA) as *"the ability to analyse meaningful and relevant data and convert data to information, knowledge, and ultimately action in time to favourably influence an organisation is a key competitive differentiator"*. The BDA concept also presents government enterprises with opportunities of analysing the increasing amount of data in its repositories thereby enhancing its operations and decision-making processes (Medaglia, 2014). This includes BDA tools such as Hadoop, HDFS, MapReduce, Cassandra, and PIG to mention the few (Zakir et al., 2015).

This is compounded by the need to integrate the variety of separate legacy systems (silos). Insufficient funding is another challenge that is encountered in attempts to implement the concept in many governments' enterprises. Kim et al. (2014) explained that owing to the expensive nature of some information technology (IT) solutions such as the concept of big data, success is always threatened. Another major challenge pertains to the lack of technical expertise in the areas BDA because of its newness in many countries, particularly in developing world.

Furthermore, implementation of BDA tools requires stable and reliable IT infrastructure (Al Nuaimi et al., 2015). This includes components such as storage, networks, and telecommunications capabilities of these components (Kache & Seuring, 2017). Various organisations, including governments' enterprises have implemented BDA in their environments for various purposes, and with varying degrees of success. For example, countries such as Australia have implemented BDA tools to improve services in the education sector (Bamiah et al., 2018). This has led to enhanced learner performance, improved teaching and assessment methods and techniques (ibid). Whilst there are benefits to implementation of BDA tools, there are challenges from aspects of privacy and confidentiality issues (Hardy & Maurushat, 2017).

The aim of this study was to develop a criteria, which can be used to guide implementation of BDA within the South African government enterprises. In achieving the aim, two objectives were formulated: (1) to understand how big data within government enterprise is analysed; and (2) to examine and understand the factors that can facilitate the implementation of BDA.

CONTEXTUALISING THE RESEARCH PROBLEM

Globally, government enterprises are among the largest and influential companies in an economy (Kowalski et al., 2013). These enterprises occupy key and strategic sectors of the economy and become pillars of national economies whilst having economic, political and social responsibilities (Liu & Zhang, 2016). In South Africa, these enterprises play a vital in the economy and in the delivery of services in energy, transportation and telecommunications sectors (Thomas, 2012). Further, Thomas (2012) discusses that South African government enterprises aim to develop the country by reducing income inequalities, increase employment, and contribute to the development of the country. However, these enterprises have been exposed for their inefficiencies because of corruption, poor governance among the challenges which in turn are a burden to the same economy they seek to vitalize.

Some organisations have benefited from implementing BDA tools in various ways. Adrian et al. (2018) discussed how some organisations incorporated their strategic planning processing in order to enhance organisational performance by shifting their decision-making processes to be data-driven. This has also positively impacted the capabilities of the IT infrastructure by making them sharable and integrated (ibid). However, whilst some organisations have reaped the benefits of implementing BDA tools, many organisations have not been successful, including government enterprises.

The implementation of BDA in many governments' enterprises and agencies have been met with several challenges, such as poor IT infrastructure, bureaucracy, and poor data quality (Adrian et al., 2017). Some of the challenges relate to lack of clear understanding of the benefits and business implications of BDA implementation (Marco, 2016). On the other hand, there is lack of expertise in the area of BDA (ibid).

The South African government is beginning to understand the importance of BDA. However, there is a problem of know-how, in the selection and application of the BDA for government purposes, in improving service delivery (Cervone, 2016).

Also, the lack of know-how affects BDA implementation (Al-Sai et al., 2017). Know-how is critical for innovation, and exploring traditional platforms including infrastructure that will be able to process BDA and generate meaningful information for better decision-making (Lui et al., 2016).

LITERATURE REVIEW

A review of literature was conducted, focusing on the core aspect of the study, which are government as an enterprise, big data analytics and implementation of big data analytics.

Government as an Enterprise

Like other countries, the South African government is well aware that its enterprises are vital to the economy, as they play an important roles in service delivery, such as: electricity, transportation and telecommunications (Adèle, 2012). Furthermore, Kanyane and Sausi (2015) argued that government enterprises are key drivers of the economy, as they play a very big role in economic growth as the major entities that deliver several social goods and facilities to certify the needs of South African citizens. Daiser et al. (2017) mentioned that public sector enterprises frequently take on the duty of providing the citizens with utility facilities, such as water, energy, health, and education.

As with other sectors of the economy, large amounts of data (big data) have been generated by government, and its agencies (Archenaa & Anita, 2015). According to Berg (2015), big data presents challenges to organisation because of data sets that are too vast, growing at a very high rate that make it very hard to manage, and difficult to analyse using traditional methods and tools. Thus, for organisation to gain value from the dataset, the implementation of BDA becomes a necessity. Furthermore, Kim et al. (2014) explained big data as original challenges relating to difficulty, safety, and threats to confidentiality, including a necessity for modern technology equipment and human services. This information supports real time decision-making for the public sector.

The public sector has begun to derive useful information from large volumes of data derived from different sources (Kim et al., 2014). Working on extracting meaningful information from big data that is generated quickly and straightforwardly is challenging. Therefore, analytics has developed to be inextricably vital to comprehend the full value of big data to advance the organisation's performance and service delivery (Zakir, 2015). Archenaa and Anita (2015) discussed the importance of BDA from the viewpoint that it would help government in improving service delivery in the areas of quality education, and to reduce unemployment rate.

Big Data Analytics

Big data analytics are tools (application) used to derive useful information, patterns, or conclusions from big data in making purposeful and quality decisions (Adrian et al., 2017). Gandomi and Haider (2015) explain analytics as methods employed to examine and obtain intellect from big data. Therefore, analysis of big data may be seen as a sub-process of the general process of 'insight extraction' from big data. Furthermore, BDA has the ability to empower organisations with opportunities from the perspectives of operations and effective utilization for useful information, business processes, and enhancement of analytical capabilities, to derive deeper meaningful insights (Mohanty et al., 2013).

The concept has the capacity to manage volumes of incongruent datasets, to permit organisations to implement BDA (Wang & Hajli, 2017). An indication that BDA has competence for improvement is shown through business value should include rapidity of insights, which enable the business to convert raw data into useful information. According to Batarseh et al. (2017), BDA aim to return the intellect and attentive version of big datasets, to deliver rapid insights into information, and assistance with conception and decision-making. The process of analysing big data employs certain methods, such as breaking down the data into 5 different categories: text, audio, video, and predictive analysis. Hence, different BDA tools are used to retrieve insights from different kinds of data (Gandomi & Haider, 2015).

The concept of BDA is employed by government in various areas such as health education, and transport and logistics, to maintain patterns, reveal trends, and ultimately improve services (Raghupathi & Raghupathi, 2014). This means that the concept is crucial in decision-making (Batarseh et al., 2017). In the midst of this premise some organisations have reaped the benefits of implementing BDA tools, while many others have not been successful, including government enterprises. With big data numerous attractive opportunities, there are several challenges organisations encounter in BDA implementation in both private and public sector organisations. BDA has a challenge when a large scale of data need to be analysed in a short period, and with a sensibly decent performance (Cheng et al., 2016). Furthermore, the rapidity of generating big data, leads to fast change of content because the content in big data changes with time, so is BDA targets (Ibid). Challenges on BDA also include inconsistency of data and partial finished, scalable, timeless and safety (Khan et al., 2014).

In the practice of big data analytics, different enterprises are able to derive insights about their businesses to improve the performance of services with data driven decision-making (Lee et al., 2017). This has over the years encouraged many private enterprises to employ data-driven decision-making, and that has an outcome of advancements in big data profits (Adrian et al., 2018). Government facilities might be significantly enhanced through the implementation of BDA in its enterprises as those enterprises are among the largest and influential companies in an economy of a country (Joseph & Johnson, 2013). South African government enterprises encounter challenges when it comes to some factors that could influence the implementation of BDA.

Implementation of Big Data Analytics

Implementation of BDA contains procedure, error handling, competences, capitals, and transforming big data into valuable information (Adrian et al, 2018). *"The model is developed based on three dimensions, performing data strategy (organisation), collaborative knowledge worker (people), and executing data analytics (technology)"* (Adrian et al, 2018:23). Ability to quickly process big data and implement analytics enables an organisation to take well-informed choices in a short period compared to the competitors (Comuzzi & Patel, 2016). Furthermore, to improve excellence of service an organisation should analyse big data effectively to answer new challenges through the information retrieved from those voluminous data sets (Archenaa & Anita, 2015).

The BDA implementation has the ability to benefit strategic long-term planning to support the organisation's growth that will consequently lead to enhanced organisational performance (Adrian et al., 2017). Archenaa and Anita (2015) discussed advantages of implementing BDA in government enterprises, which includes government services provided being reached by all citizens and without unnecessary delays. The factors that may influence implementation of BDA in organisations, include: technology capabilities, human capability, analytics capability, organisation capability, and information quality (Adrian et al., 2018). The Seoul government analysed big data generated from health, transport and residence and produced meaningful information, the benefit to the Seoul government was being able to recognize the patterns and strains, which led to upgraded midnight public services (Lim et al., 2015).

Technology capability in BDA refers to the capability of IT structures and platforms that could be used to analyse data to derive insights form big data for decision making (Adrain et al., 2017). Organisation capability refers to the organisation's readiness with resources to pursue implementation of BDA (Chen et al., 2015). Human competences are the technical IT skill and the managerial skills to coordinate the activities related to methods used in the analysis of big data (Agrawal, 2015).

Information quality is capability to be able to make speed decisions from predictive analytics (Adrain et al., 2018).

RESEARCH METHODOLOGY

The qualitative method, case study approach and semi-structured interview technique were applied in this study. The qualitative method was selected primarily because it helps induce an understandings about the phenomenon being studied (Moser & Krostjens, 2017), which was highly needed to get to know better how the implementation of BDA is done in a government enterprise. Qualitative method is based on opinions and includes examining and reflecting on less physical features of the research focus (Neville, 2007). In achieving the aim of this study, it was critical to understand the reasons, opinions and motives from individuals and groups perspectives, why and how BDA tools are implemented within government enterprises. The case study approach was selected because it allows in-depth understanding of the phenomenon being studied (Kumar, 2011). A government enterprise was selected as a case in the study.

In this study, one organisation was selected as a case. In the process of selecting an organisation there was a criteria that was used. The organisation needed to be one of government enterprises either small, medium or big organisation. Secondly, it had to be an organisation that implements BDA. The selected organisation was not the only organisation that met the criteria that was used but due to time limitations the researcher had to use one organisation as a case for this study. After the organisation was selected, there had to be participant's selection for the study.

The semi-structured interview technique was elected primarily because it allows flexible conversation with the interviewee (Moser & Krostjens, 2017). In the collection of data, the semi-structured technique was used to interview participants on one-on-one basis. The number of interviews was reached at the point of saturation. The interviews were tape-recorded with the permission of the interviewees. Note were also taken in the process of interviews. The hermeneutics technique was used to analyse the qualitative data. Hermeneutics is explained as interpretation of text, or finding meaning in written words by Byrne (2001).

The participants that were selected to participate in this study were a total number of four from the organisation. Also, a certain criteria was followed in selecting who can be a participant. For an individual to be a participant needed to be someone who is currently working in the organisation and must be part of the team that implements BDA. To collect data from the participants there was a data collection technique that was used. The process that took place in data collection was requesting meetings with the participants, then participants responded about their availability. In the meetings that the researcher had with the participants, there were notes taken and recordings of the interview. The records were then transcribed and coded before analysis process of the data commenced.

DATA ANALYSIS

In the analysis of the data, the hermeneutics approach was used following the interpretivist approach. The analysis was done following two objectives as a guide to analyse the data that was collected. The primarily focus was to understand how big data is analysed within government enterprise, and to examine the factors that can facilitate the implementation of BDA. The code of analysis is as follows: participant_codename, page#: line#. EDU_01, Pg2: 3-5 – means that participant 1, page 2 of interview transcript: from line 3 to 5. The organisation that was selected as a case is EduCentre.

How Big Data is Analysed Within Government Enterprise

In EduCentre, big data consists of large volume of data-sets. According to Wielki (2013), big data is not only about size, it include velocity, variety, and volume, often referred to as 3Vs. Volume means the amount or size of data-sets used and managed by the organisation. Variety: the different types of data-sets, which include images, videos, text, and they come from various sources. Velocity: this is the frequency at which the data-sets are accessed or travel between different sources. In EduCentre there are some differences in understanding of big data and whether they do have big data or not. This maybe a contribution to not having same understanding on big data concept.

The first two participants understand that for data to be named as "big data" it has to meet all three Vs. But the other participant seems to have a different understanding on the concept of big data as he explains it as only Volume. These irregularities may affect how the organisation go about analysing the data and the selection of analytics tools. For big data to be useful or add value to the organisation, it needs to be analysed. The method of analysing big data is through the use of analytics tools. There are different types of analytics tools, which include predictive, descriptive, and prescriptive. Predictive analytics tools analyse data-sets using various techniques such as statistics and data mining to predict the future. Descriptive analytics tools are used to describe the past "what has happened?" by analysing data-sets. Prescriptive goes beyond just describing what has happened to go to make some recommendations.

In EduCentre there is not much of analytics that are done as they are still new in big data concept. For now, it is only the IT department that is involved in the big data and analytics and two other people who are not from the IT department. According to Batarseh et al. (2017), government enterprises are still beginning to understand the benefits of BDA that may drive to the direction of better service delivery, enhanced operations and well-informed decision making. The organisation only apply analytics in IT department. The datasets that are analysed are only for the IT department to make better decisions on how they manage and deliver their services in the organisation. In the department they grouped themselves into different sections, and conducted analysis of datasets differently. There are three sections. Section 1: Analyse big data for service delivery. Section 2: Works with organisation applications and do analysis on that. Section 3: analysis students' data and system performance.

The first section apply big data to assess their service delivery to all of its system users. To achieve that the section analysis logs calls or incidences that were reported. Where a certain user calls for assistance in something that the department need to resolve for that individual. That incident will then be sent to the relevant team and assigned to a person to attend it. There are different teams that belong to the section: blackboard team; desktop support team and the printing team. The incidents need to be stored and managed after they have been logged-in to observe and monitor progress of the activities.

In the second section, the organise make use of big data to manage students' special needs. The aim of the organisation is to accept first-time entering students and register them, then make sure that the student graduates as quick as possible. In this section the analysis are done using Splunk analytics tool. To ensure that students graduate, the data analysis is carried out to monitor to students' performances. The organisation also checks other factors such as the students' profile and background to understand the reasons of sudden change in marks.

On the other hand, there is system datasets analysis that is done for system management and security. For EduCentre to ensure the institution's data-sets are secured in various system they need apply analytics on how the systems operate. The organisation consists of various systems that produce log files. Whenever there is an event on each system, the event is recorded on a patchy server. Then from those log files that is where the analysis of big data comes in. They analyse system log files to be able to detect when something unusual happens in their systems.

The third section use big data to develop reports and analytics from the data that is stored in the databases of the organisation. They get requests from different stakeholders to develop reports on certain data that they need to understand and make decisions from. As the organisation have different application which include academic applications and bursary applications. Those applications are analysed to understand the applicant's by groups. For instance, to know how many applications were from local applicants by province or by region and even by nationality.

The Factors That can Facilitate the Implementation of Big Data Analytics

The implementation of BDA is based on three aspects: Organisation, people and technology. The organisation to perform data-sets strategy. People which includes managers and personnel that co-operate with their knowledge on the concept. The technology part of it is where BDA are executed (the platforms). Adrian et al. (2018) described implementation of BDA as procedures of handling BDA capabilities, capitals, and transforming big data valuable information.

There are different factors that contribute to successfulness of the implementation of BDA. These factors include: Knowledge; Skills; Experience; Management support and Access to various data-sets. People or workers need to have at least basic IT skills for them to be able to implement BDA. The understanding of the BDA concept is the most crucial part. As the organisation need to have knowledge on how big data is implemented, the techniques used and analytics tools.

When it comes to experience, the personnel that implements BDA must have a background of working with various databases and using the analytics tools. Management support: the management has to have an understanding on the concept as they are the ones that are responsible to make sure that the analytics are done appropriately. They need to also understand the techniques that are used for BDA to benefit the organisation. Furthermore, the management has to gather all needed resources for implementation of BDA.

The success of BDA implementation is measured by its benefits to the organisation, to help the organisation make better well-informed decisions. For the organisation to reap the benefits of BDA, the organisation itself has to be ready financially and technically. Financial readiness of the organisation means that it will be able to buy license for the analytics tools needed for them to analyse the datasets. Also, the organisations personnel may need more knowledge, skills, and experiences on how to implement the analytics tools. Therefore, the organisation has to invest in its personnel by funding them on short courses and trainings that maybe needed.

FINDINGS AND DISCUSSIONS

Based on the analysis that was done. Four factors were identified. These factors include Knowledge; Process; Differentiation and Skill set.

Knowledge

Knowledge is explained as facts, information and skills. It can be gained by individual's experience or being educated about the subject (Simpson & Weiner, 2015). In EduCentre there are some irregularities when it comes to their knowledge of big data. This is because the organisation is still new on the concept of big data. They are still trying to understand it and its benefits. For an organisation to be able to implement Big Data needs to first understand what is meant by big data. Having full understanding of the concept includes knowledge on how big data can benefit the organisation. Have knowledge on how to achieve those benefits. This leads to understanding the analytics part of it.

The data-sets need to be analysed for them to make sense and be informative. So, it is important for an organisation to also understand BDA. This includes awareness of different analytics tools and how those tools are used. Also, have understanding about the factors that may facilitate the implementation of BDA for them to be successful and gain the benefits of big data.

The full understanding of BDA is very critical. As knowledge is one the factors that contribute in BDA implementation being successful. The successfulness of BDA implementation is measured by gaining its benefits. These benefits of BDA includes being able to make data driven decisions for the organisation. Being able to predict the future. And see where the organisation needs improvements in its service delivery. But if an organisation does not have knowledge on how to turn the data-sets that come in high velocity to meaningful information. That means they will never gain the benefits of big data stored in their databases.

Process

Process is a series of actions taken to achieve desired results at the end (Simpson & Weiner, 2015). For uniformity, there has to be some procedures followed. Having procedures in place helps everyone understand the process and techniques used in BDA. Also, understand the flow of events from one stage to the other. And be able categorize big data for analysis. When there is no process followed, then the intended results will not be achieved.

In EduCentre there is process followed in selecting the analytics tools. They are only using the analytics tools that are available to them. The tools that they are using come as package with the applications that they have as the organisation. For example, the Power BI analytics tool that they use is part of the package of MicroSoft Enterprise suit that the organisation use. And they are still using the demo of the analytic and they still to understand how the tool works. Because it is still a demo, it has limited features.

Differentiation

Differentiation is an action of being able to distinguish between two more subjects (Simpson & Weiner, 2015). It is crucial to be able to differentiate between big data and small data. If the organisation does not understand the difference. There will be impletions in analysing big data. Because, Small Data and Big Data are analysed differently.

Small Data is only about volume. The high quantity of data generated by an organisation and stores in its databases does not make it big data. For "data" to be categorised as big data it has meet the basic 3Vs at least, Volume; Variety and Velocity. This takes us back to the knowledge of big data being a critical factor in BDA implementation. When the organisation understands what makes data to be called big data. Having full understanding of the characteristics of big data. Which are normally called the 3Vs, Volume, Velocity and Variety. This helps an organisation to be able differentiate between Small Data and Big Data.

Skill set

Skill set is an individual's range of abilities (Simpson & Weiner, 2015). It is not easy to get highly skilled people in concept of BDA. As this concept of big data and analytics is new more especially in government enterprises including EduCentre. The skill set needed in BDA implementation includes knowledge and experience. The skills are crucial because for an individual to be able to implement BDA. They need to have some understanding and experience in working databases. Also, be able to understand how to implement the analytics tools. For them to achieve the desired results as an organisation.

CRITERIA FOR THE IMPLEMENTATION OF BIG DATA ANALYTICS

As discussed above, four factors, Knowledge; Process; Differentiation and Skill-set were found to influence the use of BDA tools within the South African government enterprises. The criteria were further interpreted by following the interpretivist approach, which allows research to be subjective in his or her reasoning (Sullivan, 2016).

In order to use BDA tools for improved usefulness and purposefulness, so as to gain results of value, the organisation must have achieved certain level. That level is defined by the factors that influence the use of the tools, which were revealed in this study. There are different, which are determined by the influencing factors and Key Indicators.

The criteria for using the analytics tools are depict in Table 1. The weights are associated with value: 5 as highest, and 1 being the lowest. The weights are briefly defined in the Table.

Table 1. Criteria for Big Data analytics tools

Weight	5	4	3	2	1
Knowledge	Understand BDA tools and able to use the tools	Understand how the BDA tools work but not using them	Understand few BDA tools and have knowledge on how to use the tools	Have basis understanding of the tools but do not know how to apply them	Do not understand the concept of BDA
Process	There is a procedure for selecting tools. it describes the goal and criteria for organisational purposes.	The goal is described with no criteria put in place in selecting BDA tools.	There is no procedure followed in selecting BDA tools. Make use of available BDA tools	Described the goal but do not know how to select the suitable BDA tools	There is no procedure and no BDA tools used
Differentiation	Understands the difference between Small data and Big Data.	Understand characteristics of big data.	Have average understand of big data.	Have little understanding of big data.	Do not understand the difference.
Skill-set	Understands BDA tools. Have experience of using BDA tools.	Understands BDA tools with only basic experience.	Understands BDA tools with no experience.	Have little understanding of BDA tools with no experience.	Do not understand BDA tools.
Total	20	16	12	8	4

Key Indicator

This is calculation of the weights that are associated to the influencing factors. The indications are divided into three categories, Advance, Intermediary, and Foundation as shown in Table 2.

How to employ the criteria:

1.   The organisation assesses or evaluates itself in accordance to the set of criteria.
2.   The weight is added, and the total score is reached.

Table 2. Key Indicator for use of big data analytics tools

Score	Level	Description
16 – 20	Above Average	Advanced in an understanding of BDA tools and implementation. Minimal or error free implementation.
10 – 15	Average	A good understands of BDA tools. Errors and challenges are easily detected and resolved.
0 - 9	Below Average	Have little or no understanding of the BDA tools. Errors and challenges take long or are hardly resolved.

3. The total score is aligned with the Key Indicator as described above.
4. Based on the alignment, a decision is reached.

CONCLUSION

This study explores an area that is vital to both government enterprises and private organisations, in that the phenomenon studied can add value to their processes and activities towards improved sustainability and competitiveness. To be more specific, the findings will help government employees in gaining an understanding of the challenges that they are faced with, in their attempts to employing BDA. Also, the study will assist data scientist in their designs as well as formulating policy and standard, to ensure appropriate use of BDA tools in their organisations. In addition, IT managers can draw their references from the study when developing employee retention strategy in the use of BDA tools. Another area of contribution is that the study adds to the existing literature, particularly, from developing countries perspective.

REFERENCES

Adrian, C., Abdullah, R., Atan, R., & Jusoh, Y. Y. 2017, July. Factors influencing to the implementation success of big data analytics: A systematic literature review. *2017 International Conference on Research and Innovation in Information Systems (ICRIIS)*, 1-6. 10.1109/ICRIIS.2017.8002536

Adrian, C., Abdullah, R., Atan, R., & Jusoh, Y. Y. (2018). Conceptual model development of big data analytics implementation assessment effect on decision-making. *Technology*, 23–24.

Al Nuaimi, E., Al Neyadi, H., Mohamed, N., & Al-Jaroodi, J. (2015). Applications of big data to smart cities. *Journal of Internet Services and Applications*, *6*(1), 25. doi:10.118613174-015-0041-5

Archenaa, J., & Anita, E. A. M. 2015. A Survey of Big Data Analytics in Healthcare and Government. *2nd International Symposium on Big data and Cloud Computing (ISBCC' 15)*, 408–413. 10.1016/j.procs.2015.04.021

Batarseh, F. A., Yang, R., & Deng, L. (2017). A comprehensive model for management and validation of federal big data analytical systems. *Big Data Analytics*, *2*(1), 2. doi:10.118641044-016-0017-x

Bumblauskas, D., Nold, H., Bumblauskas, P., & Igou, A. (2017). Big data analytics: Transforming data to action. *Business Process Management Journal*, *23*(3), 703–720. doi:10.1108/BPMJ-03-2016-0056

Byrne, M. (2001). Hermeneutics as a methodology for textual analysis. *AORN Journal*, *73*(5), 968–968. doi:10.1016/S0001-2092(06)61749-3 PMID:11378953

Cao, L. (2017). Data Science: A Comprehensive Overview. *ACM Computing Surveys*, *50*(3), 1–42. doi:10.1145/3076253

Cervone, H. F. (2016). Organisational considerations initiating a big data and analytics implementation. *Digital Library Perspectives*, *32*(3), 137–141. doi:10.1108/DLP-05-2016-0013

Chen, D. Q., Preston, D. S., & Swink, M. (2005). How the use of big data analytics affects value creation in supply chain management. *Journal of Management Information Systems*, *32*(4), 4–39. doi:10.1080/07421222.2015.1138364

Cheng, S., Zhang, Q., & Qin, Q. (2016). Big data analytics with swarm intelligence. *Industrial Management & Data Systems*, *116*(4), 646–666. doi:10.1108/IMDS-06-2015-0222

Comuzzi, M., & Patel, A. (2016). How organisations leverage big data: A maturity model. *Industrial Management & Data Systems*, *116*(8), 1468–1492. doi:10.1108/IMDS-12-2015-0495

Daiser, P., Ysa, T., & Schmitt, D. (2017). Corporate governance of state-owned enterprises: A systematic analysis of empirical literature. *International Journal of Public Sector Management*, *30*(5), 447–466. doi:10.1108/IJPSM-10-2016-0163

Gandomi, A., & Haider, M. (2015). Beyond the hype: Big data concepts, methods, and analytics. *International Journal of Information Management*, *35*(2), 137–144. doi:10.1016/j.ijinfomgt.2014.10.007

Garlasu, D., Sandulescu, V., Halcu, I., Neculoiu, G., Grigoriu, O., Marinescu, M., & Marinescu, V. (2013, January). A big data implementation based on Grid computing. *2013 11th RoEduNet International Conference*, 1-4.

Hardy, K., & Maurushat, A. (2017). Opening up government data for Big Data analysis and public benefit. *Computer Law & Security Review*, *33*(1), 30–37. doi:10.1016/j.clsr.2016.11.003

Joseph, R. C., & Johnson, N. A. (2013). Big data and transformational government. *IT Professional*, *15*(6), 43–48. doi:10.1109/MITP.2013.61

Kache, F., & Seuring, S. (2017). Challenges and opportunities of digital information at the intersection of Big Data Analytics and supply chain management. *International Journal of Operations & Production Management*, *37*(1), 10–36. doi:10.1108/IJOPM-02-2015-0078

Kanyane, M. H., & Sausi, K. (2015). Reviewing state-owned entities' governance landscape in South Africa. *African Journal of Business Ethics*, *9*(1). Advance online publication. doi:10.15249/9-1-81

Khan, N., Yaqoob, I., Hashem, I. A. T., Inayat, Z., Ali, M., Kamaleldin, W., Alam, M., Shiraz, M., & Gani, A. (2014). Big data: Survey, technologies, opportunities, and challenges. *TheScientificWorldJournal*, *2014*, 2014. doi:10.1155/2014/712826 PMID:25136682

Kim, G. H., Trimi, S., & Chung, J. H. (2014). Big-data applications in the government sector. *Communications of the ACM*, *57*(3), 78–85. doi:10.1145/2500873

Kowalski, P. Büge, M., Sztajerowska, M. & Egeland, M. 2013. State-Owned Enterprises: Trade Effects and Policy Implications. *OECD Trade Policy Papers*, 147.

Kumar, R. (2011). *Research methodology: A step-by-step guide for beginners*. Sage Publications Limited.

Lee, H., Kweon, E., Kim, M., & Chai, S. (2017). Does Implementation of Big Data Analytics Improve Firms' Market Value? Investors' Reaction in Stock Market. *Sustainability*, *9*(6), 978. doi:10.3390u9060978

Lim, C., Kim, K. J., & Maglio, P. P. (2018). Smart cities with big data: Reference models, challenges, and considerations. *Cities (London, England)*, *82*, 82. doi:10.1016/j.cities.2018.04.011

Liu, X., & Zhang, C. (2016). Corporate governance, social responsibility information disclosure, and enterprise value in China. *Journal of Cleaner Production*, 1–10.

Mehta, N., & Pandit, A. (2018). Concurrence of big data analytics and healthcare: A systematic review. *International Journal of Medical Informatics, 114*, 57–65. doi:10.1016/j.ijmedinf.2018.03.013 PMID:29673604

Mohanty, S., Jagadeesh, M., & Srivatsa, H. (2013). *Big data imperatives: Enterprise 'Big Data' warehouse, 'BI' implementations and analytics*. Apress. doi:10.1007/978-1-4302-4873-6

Moser, A., & Korstjens, I. (2018). Series: Practical guidance to qualitative research. Part 3: Sampling, data collection and analysis. *The European Journal of General Practice, 24*(1), 9–18. doi:10.1080/13814788.2017.1375091 PMID:29199486

Neville, C. (2007). *Introduction to research and research methods*. Bradford: Effective learning service.

Raghupathi, W., & Raghupathi, V. (2014). Big data analytics in healthcare: Promise and potential. *Health Information Science and Systems, 2*(1), 3. doi:10.1186/2047-2501-2-3 PMID:25825667

Ridge, M., Johnston, K. A., & O'Donovan, B. (2015). The use of big data analytics in the retail industries in South Africa. *African Journal of Business Management, 9*(19), 688–703. doi:10.5897/AJBM2015.7827

Sullivan, H. (2016). Interpretivism and Public Policy Research. Interpreting Governance High Politics and Public Policy, 184-204.

Thomas, A. (2012). Governance at South African state-owned enterprises: What do annual reports and the print media tell us? *Social Responsibility Journal, 8*(4), 448–470. doi:10.1108/17471111211272057

Thomas, A. (2012). Governance at South African state-owned enterprises: What do annual reports and the print media tell us? *Social Responsibility Journal, 8*(4), 448–470. doi:10.1108/17471111211272057

Wang, Y., & Hajli, N. (2017). Exploring the path to big data analytics success in healthcare. *Journal of Business Research, 70*, 287–299. doi:10.1016/j.jbusres.2016.08.002

Wielki, J. (2013, September). Implementation of the big data concept in organisations-possibilities, impediments and challenges. *2013 Federated Conference on Computer Science and Information Systems*, 985-989.

Zakir, J., Seymour, T., & Berg, K. (2015). Big Data Analytics. *Issues in Information Systems, 16*(2).

Chapter 9

Deployment of Information Technology Governance Using Architectural Framework

Nomathamsanqa (Thami) Rachel Batyashe
ⓘ https://orcid.org/0000-0002-4747-4698
Cape Peninsula University of Technology, South Africa

ABSTRACT

The goals of every organisation are unique. It is difficult to find a single information technology governance framework that will embrace the functions of every organisation. This is attributed to the primary reason why organisations tend to select multiple IT governance frameworks, for their processes and activities. However, many organisations later realised that some of the frameworks are very similar and others are inappropriate. This evidently and inevitably causes complexities and negatively impacts return on investment in organisations. This highlights the need for an architectural framework that guides the selection and implementation of an appropriate framework, as presented and discussed in this chapter. The qualitative case study and interpretive method and approach are followed in conducting this research, which is to develop an architectural framework for the implementation of IT governance in organisations. A South African organisation was used as a case, focusing on the IT division. The data collection method presented in this research was semi-structured interviews.

DOI: 10.4018/978-1-5225-8229-8.ch009

INTRODUCTION

For many organizations, it is not just about information technology (IT), but about governance of systems and technologies, which is inseparable from people and processes. In a similar manner, as business management is governed by generally accepted principled practices, IT must be governed by practices that facilitate and make sure an organization's IT resources are used responsibly and that its risks are managed appropriately. According to Van Grembergen and De Haes (2007), the widespread application of technology has generated a critical reliance on IT, necessitating a special focus on IT governance.

The importance of IT governance for any organization to be successful to provides the mechanism by which the IT and the entire organization's employees can capture the appropriate information and then leverage that information to plan, manage and verify decision making to transform the organization. Most organizations which has inadequate IT governance will face challenges such inefficient processes and practices, lack of standards and principles, and lack of coordination between IT and business. If these challenges are not addressed it will pose a risk to the IT investments and the competitiveness of the organization.

The past decade has seen the term 'governance' moved to the forefront of business thinking in response to instances indicating the importance of good governance of IT. Governance is not an approach by itself, it is guided by architecture. The ISO/IEC/IEEE Std 42010-2011, defined an architecture as the fundamental organization of a system which mainly consists of components and the relationships between them.

Enterprise architecture (EA) consists of four main domains, business, information, technical and application (Iyamu, 2014). Technical architecture means IT architecture in the context of this chapter. This chapter focuses on the technical architecture in the context IT governance. Technical architecture involves the design of systems or sets of systems. Iyamu (2011) defined technical architecture as a logically constant array of principles, standards and models that are originating from business requirements. It guides the engineering of an organization's information systems and technology infrastructure across. According to The Open Group Architecture Forum's (TOGAF) document, IT architecture provides some governance aspects, such as change management and quality assurance. In other words, it is the grouping of systems, represented in components, their relationships to each other and the environment, and the principles governing design and development (Josey, 2016).

IT architecture is driven by the need to bridge the gap between IT and business people and process towards a common goal of the organization. Klein and Gagliardi (2010) described IT architecture as "the logical software and hardware capabilities that are required to support the deployment of business, data and application services. This includes IT infrastructure, middleware, networks, communications, processing and standards". Along the same vain, TOGAF described IT architecture as the hardware, software and network infrastructure needed to support the deployment of core, mission critical applications of an organization. These activities require management and governance in achieving the objectives as well as a return on investment (ROI) for the organizational purposes.

Aligning IT strategy with business strategy requires organizations to have an IT architectural approach which provides a blueprint and roadmap to manage IT. This IT architectural approach provides a guide to direct the growth and changes of organizations with technology (Klein & Gagliardi, 2010). It sequentially gives IT a more strategic advantage to successfully implement new business strategy. The question that is therefore posed by this chapter was "How can architectural framework be developed for the implementation of IT governance in organizations"? This includes understanding of the factors that influence the selection of IT governance in the organization; and how IT governance is implemented in the organization?

BACKGROUND

The prevalence of technology is disrupting organizations of every shape, size and industry. Thus, enterprise architecture becomes pivotal in for organizations for management of organizations to become more enlightened on the benefits and impact that enterprise architectural change has on every business and consumer. Thus, compelling organizations to change organizational dynamics employing enterprise architecture, in particularly, technical architecture to improve business efficiency and competitiveness. Generally, Niemann (2006) viewed enterprise architecture as a structured and aligned collection of plans for the integrated representation of the business and information technology (IT) landscape of the enterprise, in past, current, and future states.

Focusing only on adopting the right technologies may not sustain competitiveness of the organization. Responding to technology adoption requires changing the organization's business processes, standard, practices and culture to be more innovative, agile and tolerant to risk. Kane (2019) state in the today's economy what really drives businesses forward is implementing changes on the processes and standards.

Many organizations from all industries has in recent years conducted various initiatives to analysis different business and IT strategies to take advantage of their benefits. Therefore, requiring organizations to transform crucial business operations, affecting products and processes as well as organizational structure and management perceptions (Matt et al., 2015). In the context of organizational environments, EAs depict the organization of an entire enterprise including all relevant artefacts, such as the organizational structure, business functions and processes, data and information, applications and their technical infrastructure (Wille, et al., 2017). Organizations ought to institute management systems such as business processes, standards and principles to govern complex transformations, that comes with implementing IT governance. Hess et al. (2016) asserted that an important approach is the formulation of an IT strategy that serves as a central concept to integrate the entire coordinates, prioritization, and implementation of IT governance within an organization.

MAIN FOCUS AREA OF THE CHAPTER

The literature section will focus on a more comprehensive review of literature conducted for this study. The key subject areas discussed in this section include information technology governance and architecture, and enterprise architecture.

IT Governance and Architecture

Some organizations view both IT governance and architecture from two different perspectives, in implementation and operationalization. The main and most commonly adopted IT governance frameworks include COBIT, ITIL, ISO/IEC 17799/27002 and TOGAF (Simonsson & Johnson, 2006; Niemann et al., 2008). Enterprise architecture (EA) is the focal point, though some organizations do sometimes focus on one or two domains of EA. Mårten, Lagerström and Johnson (2008) asserted that the aim of IT governance is to support IT's function as a business enabler in order to realize the internal effectiveness in an organization. IT governance enables and improves IT and business strategies gain alignment, including management of risks. Brown (2006) argued that IT governance governs the crafting and execution of the IT strategy, and also help to aligns both IT and business strategies.

The IT Governance Institute (2007) defined IT governance as the "responsibility of executives and the board of directors, and consists of the leadership, organizational structures and processes that ensure that the organization's IT sustains and extends its strategies and objectives". Concurring, Ross, Weill and Robertson (2006) referred to IT governance as "the decision rights and accountability framework for encouraging desirable behavior in the use of IT". IT governance focuses on managing and employing IT to realize corporate performance objectives whilst reflecting the wider corporate governance principles.

Enterprise Architecture

Enterprise architecture (EA) is intended to govern and manage both technical and nontechnical activities of an organization. According to Anaya and Ortiz (2005), "an Enterprise Architecture provides a common view of the primary resources of any enterprise (people, processes and technology) and how they integrate to provide the primary drivers of the enterprise (that is, the strategy)". Enterprise Architecture can be used to guide against business-IT misalignments. This includes coordination of technology investments, to suite business needs, improve the integration between services, and eliminate redundant investments while replacing them with standardized and cost-effective IT services. Becker et al. (2011) stated the purpose of EA is to provide a comprehensive coverage of the organization.

The main purpose of enterprise architecture is to capture the status of the organization's business architecture, information resources, systems and technologies with the aim to identify the differences and weaknesses in the processes and infrastructures and develop corrective actions. Thus, ensuring alignment between the organization's business and information technology units (Dang & Pekkola, 2017). In agreement, Vargas et al. (2016) asserted enterprise architecture presents models, methods and tools that enable organizations to deal with the challenges pertaining to integrating the strategic aspects and business processes with the areas of IT, thus IT generating greater value to business units, improve business's performance, their level of integration. Iyamu (2017) suggested that enterprise architecture an approach that can be used to improve an organization's processes and activities. Therefore, ultimately resulting in creating competitive advantage through effective IT support, achieving the strategies and objectives of the organisation.

Enterprise architecture has a significant role to play in the integrating business processes and IT providing an IT architectural perspective. Enterprise architecture outlines and represent a high-level view of an organization's business processes and IT systems, their interrelationships, and the extent to which these processes and systems are shared by different parts of the organization (Tamm, et al., 2011). Hence, the main purpose of EA is to define the desirable future state of the organization's business processes and IT systems and to provide a roadmap for achieving this target from the current state; thus, an IT architecture is employed.

Weill and Woodman (2002) asserted that IT architecture offers an interrelated set of technical choices to direct the organization in sustaining business needs. According to Hafner and Winter (2008), IT architecture is the sphere of architecture which signifies a combined, enterprise wide model of hardware and communications elements in addition provides support among the technology artefacts. While Iyamu (2011) maintained that it guides the initiation of new technology. IT architecture as defined by Weill and Woodman (2002) is a set of procedures and guidelines that govern the use of IT and design a migration path to the way business will be done. IT architecture consists of standards and guidelines for technology, utilization of data, design of applications and change management processes necessary to use new technologies.

RESEARCH APPROACH

The qualitative, case study and interpretive methods and approach were followed in conducting this research, which was to develop an architectural framework for the implementation of IT governance in the organizations. Qualitative research methods assist researchers to understand people and the social and cultural contexts within which they live. Concurring, Denzin and Lincoln (2011) asserted that qualitative research is often based upon interpretivism, constructivism and inductivism. It is about exploring the subjective meanings through which people interpret the world and the diverse ways in which life is constructed (through language, images and cultural artefacts) in particular settings. Social events and phenomena are understood from the perspective of the people themselves, thus avoiding the imposition of the researcher's own presumptions and definitions.

The case study research approach was followed in this study. A South African organization, RedLeaf Communications was used as the case, with specific focus on the IT division of the company. Case studies are empirical studies that investigate a contemporary phenomenon within its real-life context using multiple sources of evidence (Yin, 2017). Noor (2008) sees case studies as being concerned with "*how*" and "*why*" things happen, allowing the study of appropriate realities and the differences between what was planned and what actually occurred. Thus, case studies are a valuable approach of looking at the world around us. Harrison, et al., (2017) defined a case study as" an examination of a specific phenomenon such as a program, and event, a person, a process, an institution, or a social group". The case study approach, according to Creswell (2013) "explores a single entity or phenomenon bounded by time and activity and collects detailed information by using a variety of data collection procedures during a set period of time".

RedLeaf Communications, the selected case in this study is a postal service organization in South Africa. This organization's primary mandate is to provide postal service to the South African population. The organization's footprint is the largest in the country. The business of the organization is conducted through its operating divisions and its subsidiaries. The IT division is responsible for technology enablement and provide service to the different divisions and subsidiaries to fulfil its mandate. These services are provisioned through a defined structure and associated IT processes aligned to ITIL, COBIT, and TOGAF.

The semi-structured interview approach was employed to collect data. This is mainly because the approach allows the interviewer or interviewee to deviate in order to pursue an idea or response in more detail (Rabinet, 2011). According to Qu and Dumay (2011), the semi-structured interviewee approach helps to reveal important and often hidden aspects of human and organizational behavior. Kvale and Brinkmann (2009) argued that it is often the most effective and suitable method to collect data.

The hermeneutics method, from the perspective of interpretivism, was employed to analyze the data, in order to make sense of the subjective views and opinions of the participants in this study. Hermeneutics is constantly employed within interpretive research. Hermeneutics is the discovery or discipline of interpretation. Its primary concern is questioning the meaning of a text or text-analogue, which can be a book, scholarly article, interview notes or an organization (Myers, 2009). The hermeneutics practice states that in qualitative research, the interpretation is mainly used, no matter how adamantly many researchers may argue the facts speak for themselves (Folwer et al., 2007).

These researchers further stated that hermeneutics is a form of interpretive research where researchers begin with the assumption that interaction to our understanding of reality is gained only through social constructions such as language, consciousness, shared meanings, documents, tools and other artefacts. In Information Systems (IS), interpretive research is aimed at creating an understanding of the context of IS and the process by which IS affects and is affected by its context (Fowler et al., 2007).

ARCHITECTURAL FRAMEWORK FOR IT GOVERNANCE

The data was collected from the case study, RedLeaf Communications was analyzed. The analysis was carried within the context in which data was gathered: (1) What are the factors that influence the selection of IT governance in the organizations? (2) How is IT governance implemented in the organizations? The findings from the case study were combined and presented in Figure 1 below to give a better understanding of the common factors which could influence the implementation of IT governance in organizations.

The critical factors found at RedLeaf Communications, were evaluation of information, technology repository, education and training, organizational strategy and organizational culture. Also found were factors which include environmental assessment, training, knowledge sharing, communicative scheme and organizational culture. The combination of the findings informed the development of the Architectural Framework for IT Governance (AFITG), which can serve as a best practice guide to the implementers of IT governance frameworks in organizations. The framework

(AFITG) is considered a best practice mainly because of the depth and rigor through which empirical evidence was examined, and its organizational relevance.

It is believed that this study could be generalized for the benefit of organizations as the commonalities in the findings from the case. According to Walsham (1995), a generalization can be made to a concept or a theory can be developed or generated from facts or a rich description of a case. Lee and Baskerville (2003) asserted that generalization is important for the purposes of managing and solving problems that corporations and other organizations experience in society. Along the same line of argument, Qureshi, (2005) posited that the insights from a case study can be generalized to reach conclusive or theoretical statements for other organizations' purposes. Further, De Villiers et al. (2019) suggested in a case study, the researcher develops analytic generalizations that support and help generalize theories.

Figure 1. Architectural Framework for IT Governance (AFITG)

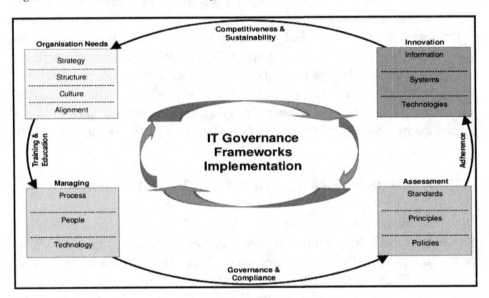

The framework in Figure 1 above depicts four fundamental categories in an organization that must work in concert for the implementation of IT governance to be effective: organizational needs, managing, assessment and innovation. Figure 1 suggests that if a change in IT governance is made in an organization such as the introduction of a new governance framework, this change is likely to affect the other three categories. For example, changes in organization needs can lead to managing changes, and organization needs can drive changes in innovation.

Implementation of IT Governance Frameworks

Figure 1 illustrates the most critical factors which impact and influence the implementation of IT governance frameworks. These factors are categorized into organizational needs, innovation, assessment, and managing. Each category relates to each other and no category stands on its own. Also, each category positively supports the others. The factors are considered critical because of their prevailing and significant roles, as shown in the analysis of the case study. The categories are discussed in more detail below.

Organizational Needs

Organizational needs are made up of strategy, structure, culture and alignment. IT strategy is informed by and aligned to the organizational strategy. An IT structure must support the IT strategy to ensure the organization's objectives are achieved. An organizational culture is shaped by the norms and values of the organization and the management and individual practices.

- **Strategy** - To change its operations, an organization's IT management needs to define a strategy that is aligned with the organizational and business units' strategies. It needs to become a true service provider that operates like a business within a business; the IT strategy should entail an IT governance framework that fully involves the organization's management and individuals in planning and aligning IT initiatives with the organization's priorities. Once the strategy is operational, the structure that supports the strategy should be outlined and implemented with the support of the organization's management.
- **Structure** - Structure is extremely important and a key element in implementing an IT governance framework. The role of the structure within the organization is to define expectations, assign responsibilities and verify performance. This structure also establishes the strategic, operational and technical decision-making processes, which are critical. This helps to manage IT investment; assign trained and capable resources to govern IT resources; put appropriate standards, principles, and policies into place; and create the disciplines around governing and managing IT artefacts. Similar to any major organizational innovation, implementation of IT governance must have an owner and accountabilities. Putting the right IT structure in place is important to support and manage the implementation of IT governance usually requires having an organizational culture that embraces and supports innovation.
- **Culture** - Culture relates to the beliefs and values of the organization, which are generally expressed in its mission statement, and these include ethical

concerns. Management need to understand the influence culture has on the organization's values and behaviors. A strong organizational culture fosters organizational learning capacity to increase awareness of how culture shapes organizational effectiveness by training and educating employees and creating communication programs to address critical cultural weaknesses.

- **Alignment** - Strategic alignment involves making certain that the business and IT plans are connected, and that IT operations are aligned with overall business operations. Alignment is a key element that, if ignored, can lead to serious management issues, sub-standard performance, and even financial problems. Alignment is not easy to achieve. The challenges of creating internal alignment of systems that support appropriate levels of risk-taking include the development of a common language, and an understanding among employees as to the nature and tasks of IT governance. Proper alignment also requires conflicts between functions be addressed. Unnecessary overlaps of jobs and areas of accountability, structure, as well as gaps in responsibility, must be identified and resolved. This may require complex and difficult organizational change.

Innovation

Organizations are continuously challenged to ensure the survival and wellness of their competitiveness and sustainability. Thus, there is a need for continuous innovation. Innovation is intended to provide improved approaches for efficiency and effectiveness in achieving an organization's needs. There are three main factors which represent innovation. They comprise of information, systems and technologies. Information should facilitate making decisions regarding the systems and technologies that are required to implement the innovation.

- **Information** - Information is about the know-how and know-what of the organization's decisions that needs to be made. Information assists decision makers to had an understanding of what needs to be prioritized to ensure that the right systems are implemented to achieve the goals and objectives of the organization. It is also important to ensure that the relevant information is communicated to the relevant stakeholders.
- **Systems** – Although there are various definitions of systems, in this context system refer to the collections of technical and non-technical factors that enable an organization to meet it desired objectives. A system which creates a cohesive work environment, and ensures that implementation of IT governance is understood and adhered to. Technologies are required to enable these systems.

- **Technologies** - Key technologies should be identified to automate and standardized those systems. It should then consider what linking technologies, if any, can be shared across the organization. Organizations dependence on technologies is swiftly and continuously increasing. It is, therefore vital to ensure that IT capability is described and directed by the organization's needs.

Assessment

An environment assessment can be conducted to identify IT objectives and to ensure that the business objectives are aligned with an understanding of management's risk appetite and understanding of the maturity of the existing governance and related processes.

Assessment of the organization environment assists management to identify the gaps in standards, principles, policies. Once they have been reviewed, new business proposals are provided to advice on IT governance compliance issues. As a result, policies are established to ensure compliance with relevant legislation. Policies that govern IT governance and the implementation and management of IT governance frameworks should be familiar with the relevant standards and frameworks and the principles embedded within them.

- **Standards** - Standards are set to ensure uniformity of systems, processes and technologies. However, standards, principles and policies are not permanent solutions as their effectiveness depends on how they have been implemented and kept up to date. Standards are highly valuable when they are used as a set of principles to begin the customization of certain policies. It is therefore important for management and employees to understand what to do, how to do it, and why is it important.
- **Principles** – The organization needs to provide the direction and guidance for the selection and implementation of IT governance based on the capacity and organizational strategy. The guidelines point the organization to the principles that should be reinforced to manage IT governance. These principles are extremely useful to develop policies to manage and control IT governance.
- **Policies** - Policies for IT governance frameworks implementation include best practice framework and standards, stakeholder management, business alignment, knowledge transfer and management of the selected frameworks.

Managing

Managing the implementation of IT governance frameworks consists of three main factors: process, people and technology. The crucial job of implementing these IT governance frameworks is performed by people. All three factors are necessary to get a clear understanding of the IT governance processes, therefore these factors cannot be separated, as they rely on each on the success or failure of implementation IT governance frameworks.

- **Process** – Processes are used to guide the activities of people in the execution of various tasks. Also, processes are applied in the management (selection, implementation, and support) of information systems and technologies in achieving the organizational needs. Without processes, the organizations would face challenges achieving their objectives and managing day-to-day operations. The failure of most IT governance implementation is the lack of well-defined processes.
- **People** - The processes are developed by people, based on their understanding and know-how. People have an integral role in process. People make use of processes at their discretion, either for personal interest or organizational interest, in the selection, implementation and management of information systems and technologies. Different people have different skills and knowledge, which is required in innovations undertakings such as implementing IT governance. This makes their role a determining factor to the success or failure of the organizations' goals and objectives. Thus, it is important to involve the right people, doing the right things, in the right ways, at the rights times.
- **Technology** – The implementation of IT governance frameworks can be complex and involves technology, process and people at all levels of the organization. Technologies are used to enable an organization's goals and objectives. However, technologies can also constrain the organization in the quest for competitiveness. Hence the use of technologies highly depends on its management by people, through processes.

Significance of the AFITG

The architectural framework described in the previous section guides organizations in the selection, implementation and management of frameworks for IT governance. It proposes a strategic plan for IT, which satisfies the current and ongoing needs of an organization's business strategy, and the current and future IT capabilities. It promotes clear decision making, leading to valid reasons for IT acquisitions.

Also, the architectural framework monitors provision of IT services, levels of service and service quality. Thus, it assures that the organization's business processes, people and technology are compliant with relevant IT governance legislation and that the organization operates according to the principles embedded in relevant IT governance frameworks. The AFITG also promotes IT standards, principles and policies, and decisions that recognize the current and changing needs of organizations.

FUTURE RESEARCH

The study was methodically and comprehensively carried out within the objective, which was to develop an architectural framework for the implementation of IT governance in organizations. This includes understanding of the factors that influence the selection and implementation of IT governance in an organization. The findings and analysis reveal that further work with different users and settings will support the research's understanding of the processes that are employed to selecting, implementing and managing IT governance frameworks. In addition, such further research could make use of the framework that is presented in chapter as a point of departure, thereby explores its validity and practicality.

The analysis and interpretation of the case study uncovered participants' concern regarding factors, such as organizational culture and organizational strategy during the selection and implementation of IT governance frameworks. It would be in the interest of scholars to explore and gain a better understanding how organizational culture and strategy influence the selection and implementation of IT governance frameworks.

In addition, further studies could be conducted on the impact that training and educating the implementers and non-implementers has on the implementation and management of IT governance frameworks. Actors need to be knowledgeable on the selected frameworks of IT governance they implement in order for them to make better decisions to innovate.

CONCLUSION

Even though one organization was used in the study, the framework can be generalized. This is mainly because there are many organizations that have similar challenges in the area of IT governance, as revealed in the study. Also, many other organizations that do not yet have challenges, but could potentially do so, now have the privilege of preventing them before they occur. As presented and discussed in this chapter, the use of the AFITG brings a fresh perspective and helps with a deeper understanding of how IT governance can be selected and implemented, through its influencing factors in the organizations. The architectural framework, shown in Figure 1, which was derived from the study, illustrates how non-technical factors can influence and impact the implementation IT governance frameworks in organizations.

The architectural framework developed, based on the outcome of this study can be employed to select and implement IT governance frameworks in an organizational setting. The architectural framework explains how IT governance frameworks can be implemented through different architectural concepts. In addition, it underpins the importance of the organizational strategy, culture, people, process and management (leadership) guidance and support in the selection and implementation of IT governance frameworks.

This study can assist boards of directors, top managers and other employees in organizations to better comprehend the factors which influences or can potentially impact the selection, implementation and management of IT governance frameworks in their organizations. Also, the study can be a useful material to the academics, in twofold: (1) It can be used as a case material, from empirical evidence perspective, and (2) the framework can be used as theoretical foundation.

REFERENCES

Anaya, V., & Ortiz, A. (2005). How enterprise architectures can support integration. In *Proceedings of the first international workshop on Interoperability of heterogeneous information systems*, (pp. 25-30). ACM.

Becker, C., Antunes, G., Barateiro, J., Vieira, R., & Borbinha, J. (2011). Modeling Digital Preservation Capabilities in Enterprise Architecture. In *Proceedings of the 12th Annual International Digital Government Research Conference: Digital Government Innovation in Challenging Times*, (pp. 84-93). ACM. 10.1145/2037556.2037570

Brown, W. C. (2006). IT governance, architectural competency, and the Vasa. *Journal of Information Management and Computer Security*, *14*(2), 140–154. doi:10.1108/09685220610655889

Creswell, J. W. (2013). *Research design: Qualitative, quantitative, and mixed methods approaches*. Sage Publications.

Dang, D. D., & Pekkola, S. (2017). Systematic Literature Review on Enterprise Architecture in the Public Sector. Electronic. *Journal of E-Government*, *15*(2), 130–154.

De Villiers, C., Dumay, J., & Maroun, W. (2019). Qualitative accounting research: Dispelling myths and developing a new research agenda. *Accounting and Finance*, *59*(3), 1459–1487. doi:10.1111/acfi.12487

Denzin, N. K., & Lincoln, Y. S. (2011). *The SAGE Handbook of Qualitative Research 4*. Sage Publications.

Folwer, J., Horan, P., & Cope, C. (2007). How an "Imperative" IS Development was Saved from a Failing Course of Action – A Case Study. *Information and Beyond: Part I: Issues in Informing Science and Information Technology, 4*, 95–406.

Hafner, M., & Winter, R. (2008). Processes for Enterprise Application Architecture Management. In *Hawaii International Conference on System Sciences, Proceedings of the 41st Annual* (pp. 396-396). IEEE.

Harrison, H., Birks, M., Franklin, R., & Mills, J. (2017). Case study research: Foundations and methodological orientations. In *Forum Qualitative Sozialforschung/ Forum: Qualitative. Social Research, 18*(1).

Hess, T., Matt, C., Benlian, A., & Wiesböck, F. (2016). Options for formulating a digital transformation strategy. *MIS Quarterly Executive, 15*(2), 123–139.

ISO/IEC/IEEE. (2011). *Systems and software engineering – Architecture description.* ISO/IEC/IEEE 42010:2011(E), (Dec 2011), 1-46.

IT Governance Institute. (2007). *Unlocking Value: An Executive Primer on the Critical Role of IT Governance.* Information Systems Audit and Control Association. Retrieved from http://www.itgi.org

Iyamu, T. (2011). A Framework for Developing and Implementing the Enterprise Technical Architecture. *Computer Science and Information Systems, 9*(1), 189–206. doi:10.2298/CSIS101103040I

Iyamu, T. (2014). *Information Technology Enterprise Architecture: From Concept to Practice.* Heidelberg Press.

Iyamu, T. (2017). Understanding the complexities of enterprise architecture through structuration theory. *Journal of Computer Information Systems.* Advance online publication. doi:10.1080/08874417.2017.1354341

Johnson, P., Buehring, A., Cassel, C., & Symon, G. (2007). Defining qualitative management research: An empirical investigation. *Qualitative Research in Organisations and Management: An International Journal, 2*(1), 23–42. doi:10.1108/17465640710749108

Josey, A. (2016). *TOGAF® Version 9.1-A Pocket Guide.* Van Haren.

Kane, G. (2019). The Technology Fallacy. *Research Technology Management, 62*(6), 44–49. doi:10.1080/08956308.2019.1661079

Klein, J., & Gagliardi, M. (2010). *A Workshop on Analysis and Evaluation of Enterprise Architectures.* Retrieved from http://www.sei.cmu.edu

Kvale, S., & Brinkmann, S. (2009). *Interviews: Learning the Craft of Qualitative Research Interviewing*. Sage Publications.

Lee, A. S., & Baskerville, R. L. (2003). Generalizing generalizability in information systems research. *Information Systems Research*, *14*(3), 221–243. doi:10.1287/isre.14.3.221.16560

Mårten, S., Lagerström, R., & Johnson, P. (2008). A Bayesian network for IT governance performance prediction. In *Proceedings of the 10th International Conference on Electronic Commerce*. ACM.

Matt, C., Hess, T., & Benlian, A. (2015). Digital transformation strategies. *Business & Information Systems Engineering*, *57*, 339–343.

Maxwell, J. A. (2013). *Qualitative Research Design: An Interactive Approach*. Sage Publications.

Myers, M. D. (2009). *Qualitative Research in Business & Management*. Sage Publications.

Niemann, K. D. (2006). *From Enterprise Architecture to IT Governance—Elements of Effective IT Management*. Vieweg.

Niemann, M., Eckert, J., Repp, N., & Steinmetz, R. (2008). Towards a Generic Governance Model for Service-oriented Architectures. AMCIS 2008 Proceedings, 361.

Noor, K. B. M. (2008). Case Study: A Strategic Research Methodology. *American Journal of Applied Sciences*, *5*(11), 1602–1604. doi:10.3844/ajassp.2008.1602.1604

Qu, S., & Dumay, J. (2011). The Qualitative Research Interview. *Qualitative Research in Accounting & Management*, *8*(3), 238–264. doi:10.1108/11766091111162070

Qureshi, S. (2005). How does Information Technology effect Development? Integrating Theory and Practice into a Process Model. AMCIS 2005 Proceedings, 261.

Rabinet, S. E. (2011). How I Learned to Design and Conduct Semi-Structured Interviews: An Ongoing and Continuous Journey. *Qualitative Report*, *16*(2), 563–566.

Ross, J. W., Weill, P., & Robertson, D. C. (2006). *Enterprise Architecture As Strategy: Creating A Foundation For Business Executives*. Harvard Business School Press.

Simonsson, M., & Johnson, P. (2006). Assessment of IT Governance - A Prioritization of Cobit. In *Proceedings of the Conference on Systems Engineering Research*, (pp. 1-10). Studentlitteratur.

Tamm, T., Seddon, P. B., Shanks, G., & Reynolds, P. (2011). How does enterprise architecture add value to organisations? *Communications of the Association for Information Systems*, *28*(1), 10.

Van Grembergen, W., & De Haes, S. (2007). *Implementing Information Technology Governance: Models, Practices and Cases*. Idea Grouping Publishing.

Vargas, A., Cuenca, L., Boza, A., Sacala, I., & Moisescu, M. (2016). Towards the development of the framework for inter sensing enterprise architecture. *Journal of Intelligent Manufacturing*, *27*(1), 55–72.

Walsham, G. (1995). The Emergence of Interpretivism in IS Research. *Information Systems Research*, *6*(4), 376–394. doi:10.1287/isre.6.4.376

Weill, P., & Woodham, R. (2002). *Don't Just Lead, Govern: Implementing Effective IT Governance*. MIT Sloan Working Paper No. 4237-02. Retrieved from http://ssrn.com/abstract=317319

Wille, D., Wehling, K., Seidl, C., Pluchator, M., & Schaefer, I. (2017). Variability mining of technical architectures. In *Proceedings of the 21st International Systems and Software Product Line Conference*-Volume A (pp. 39-48). Academic Press.

Yin, R. K. (2017). *Case study research and applications: Design and methods*. Sage Publications.

Chapter 10
The Enterprise Architecture as Agent of Change for Government Enterprises

Tiko Iyamu

https://orcid.org/0000-0002-4949-094X

Cape Peninsula University of Technology, South Africa

ABSTRACT

In the last three decades, two fundamental things have happened to the concept of the enterprise architecture (EA). One, the interest on EA continues to increase, which enacts popular debate and discourse at both academic and business platforms. Two, the pace of deployment within government enterprises is slow, which affects actualisation of the benefits towards service delivery. This can be attributed to confusions and misunderstandings about the concept, which manifests from the fact that the influential factors of the concept are not clear. As a result, many enterprises continue to be hesitant or dismissive about the concept. Thus, the purpose of this study was to develop a conceptual an EA framework that can be used to guide government enterprises towards transformative goal. The framework is intended to guide the fundamental components, which causes confusion about the deployment of EA as agent of change within government enterprises.

INTRODUCTION

The concept of enterprise architecture (EA) is not new, it has been adopted in many private organisations (Ross, Weill & Robertson, 2006) and government institutions and agencies for many years (Urbaczewski & Mrdalj, 2006). The views of Cabrera et

DOI: 10.4018/978-1-5225-8229-8.ch010

al. (2016) are that the EA is an approach that enables and supports an organisation's competitive edge by being at the forefront of information systems and technologies (IS/IT), and fulfilling consumers' needs. Governments' reliance on IS/IT to deliver services continue to increase in both developing and developed countries. The reliance on IS/IT is enforced by the need to have better and seamless government service delivery (Olsen & Trelsgård, 2016). According to Al-Nasrawi and Ibrahim (2013), governments around the world increasingly rely on IS/IT in order to accomplish core services and functions, helping some of them to transition into what is known as e-government. Thus, to government of many countries, IS/IT offers unlimited benefits such as ease of access to various governmental services, from online to faster response time (Siddiquee & Siddiquee, 2016). Johnson, Ekstedt and Lagerstrom (2016) argued that irrespective of the level of reliance, the complexity of IS/IT in enterprises continue to increase. According to Shaanika and Iyamu (2018), some of IS/IT challenges include incompatibilities, lack of integration, and lack of scalability. As a result, some governments' enterprises invest in approaches such as the EA, to manage their IS/IT activities including e-government systems (Mohamed et al., 2012).

Since John Zachman introduced the concept of the EA over three decades ago, other frameworks have been developed (Tamm et al., 2011). This includes META Group Inc., Forester, department of defence Architecture Framework (DoDAF), the Federal EA Framework (FEAF), the Treasury EA Framework (TEAF), the open group architecture forum (TOGAF), and the Zachman framework (Lapalme et al., 2016; Urbaczewski & Mrdalj, 2006). The existence of different frameworks have helped to drive various viewpoints about the concept of EA in many organisations and government enterprises (Rouhani et al., 2015). Cameron and McMillan (2013) argue that one of the objectives of the EA is to provide governance for change, from the IS/IT perspectives. Radeke (2011) states that the role of the EA is to guide an organization's strategic goals and facilitate change within which IS/IT activities are governed and managed. Along the same line of viewpoint, Aier (2017) argues that the EA helps to maintain consistency when building, deploying, and managing complexities of IS/IT that are constantly evolving. To both private organisation and government enterprises, the EA facilitates change based on how it is defined, scoped, deployed, and managed, which manifests into its signification in an environment.

The EA promises a different approach through which government institutions and agencies can transform their activities for improved services (Hjort-Madsen & Pries-Heje, 2009). As government enterprises strive to employ EA as an agent of change, and exhume the benefits, so comes the risks and challenges (Safari, Faraji & Majidian, 2016). Some of the challenges were highlighted by Buckle et al., (2011) as follows: gap between requirements and product; unclear time of product delivery; and uncertainty around committed parties. The challenges could be caused by factors such as: how the EA was problematized by the promoters, among various groups (networks) of stakeholders, which attracts different types of interests, and shapes participations (Bui & Levy, 2017).

Another challenge is that many governments' enterprises lack the technical capability in the implementation and practice of EA, to effect, and as an agent of change in their environments. The most common critique of EA is the difficulty of measuring its value, which manifests from the followings: inconsistence of the definitions that are associated with the expected value, which are stakeholders' subjective views (Rodrigues & Almaral, 2010). The complexities of EA value come from both technical and non-technical perspectives, and therefore require deeper understanding of the factors that influence and patent into such intricacies (Iyamu, 2019). The urge to examine and gain an understanding of the factors led to selecting the actor-network theory (ANT). The objective was to propose a framework through which EA can be employed as agent of change within government enterprises.

The ANT brings fresh perspectives in examining and understanding the sociotechnical factors in the deployment of the EA within government computing environments. The theory consists of actors linked together through various interests to form networks. The theory emphasises on the heterogeneous nature of actor-networks which consist of, and link together both human and non-human elements (Callon, 1986). A core assumption in ANT is that no actor is different in kind from another. Instead, how size, power or organisation is generated should be studied in an unprejudiced manner.

Developments and advancements in the areas of EA by academics and IS/IT practitioners have over the years transformed the concept into a field of discipline. However, there are still more questions than answers, particularly within government enterprises. In Shaanika and Iyamu (2018), the question was, what was the purpose of EA to governments? Hjort-Madsen and Pries-Heje (2009) asked, what has driven the use and adoption of the EA concept in governments? This research add a question: how does actor and their networks influence the EA in employing the concept as an agent of change in government enterprises towards transformative goal?

LITERATURE REVIEW

A review of literature relating to this study was conducted, covering EA in the context of government enterprise, and actor-network theory. The review is presented in two subsections as follows:

Government and Enterprise Architecture

Through principles, standards, and governance, the EA have potential to guide organisations towards solving the complexities that resides in their IS/IT environment (Lapalme et al., 2016). At some points, EA's strengths of covering multiple units in an organisation becomes a challenge as the approach gets harder to govern, leading to criticisms (Roth et al., 2013). Löhe and Legner (2014) state that some of the criticisms of the EA include the effort it takes to deploy and manage the activities of the concept; difficulty in measuring its success; and how the benefits often come at a later time than anticipated by the stakeholders. Lagerström et al. (2011) suggested that the aforementioned challenges are ultimately costly to organisation including government institutions and agencies. According to Tamm et al. (2011), some organisations lack understanding of the EA, which leads to failure in justifying their investment in the concept, and how they benefit from it. This relates to Shaanika and Iyamu's (2018) argument where they stated that shortage of skill-set remains a challenge in the deployment of the EA. The shortage of skill-set can be attributed to lack of, or hesitation to investment on EA by government enterprises. However, it is difficult to invest on what you lack knowledge about, and have not skill-set to employ and manage.

Government enterprises seek to implement EA for strategic and operational purposes, such as planning, execution and management of business and IS/IT activities. However, the development, implementation, and support of EA are challenging to many governments' enterprises, from both technical and non-technical viewpoints. Shaanika and Iyamu (2018) discussed some of the factors that influences the deployment of EA from a government in a developing country's angle. In the study of EA deployment for the Indian government, Paul and Paul (2012) found that the administrative structure of the country was far too different from other countries in terms of human diversity, demography, and income, including central, state and local government levels. Lee et al. (2013) explained that with some governments, the challenge is about how to integrate EA practices into the entire views and mission of the government's activities.

Despite the copious challenges, governments of many countries continue to show interest in the concept of EA. The concept is employed in some African countries such as Kenya (Katuu, 2018), Ghana (Kaushik & Raman, 2015), and South Africa (Van Zijl & Van Belle, 2014). According to Olsen and Trelsgård (2016), the Norwegian higher education sector are challenged in the implementation of the EA, which was caused by numerous factors, such as lack of understanding by practitioners, and top management's failure to commit to the concept. The Korean Government enacted a law to mandate the adoption of EA in 2005, in the process, the architects made use of the Zachman framework and Treasure Enterprise Architecture Framework (TEAF) (Lee et al., 2013).

To some degree, government of each country is unique in their rules and resources, which often shape the development, implementation, and practice of EA, toward making the concept contextual and relevance. Al-Nasrawi and Ibrahim (2013) explained that EA is a crucial part in the implementation and management of IS/IT solutions in government enterprises, and the approach guides deployment of systems such as e-government within rules and strategies. The EA facilitates integration of different units within an enterprise, which sometimes becomes a challenge due to the number of stakeholders that require management themselves. Such challenges affect government's service delivery (Roth et al., 2013). Aier (2017) argues that the challenges which the public sector faces may be different from those of private organisations, owing to their objectives and overall goals for the EA. Alwadain et al. (2014) highlighted some of the challenges of EA as evolving of IS/IT activities, and lack of practicality in studies, which often focus on future trends. Lee et al. (2013) argued that the conception of government EA (GEA), and how to implement GEA has become a major challenge among IS/IT policymakers in many countries.

Actor-network Theory

Actor-network theory (ANT) is a socio-technical theory that is embedded within science and technologies (Dwiartama & Rosin, 2014). The main tenets of ANT are actor, network, and translation, which cannot be independent of each other (Thapa, 2011), in that networks exist because there are actors, and actors exist within networks. The existence of networks are results of direct or indirect translation of interest. The actors are both human and non-human entities (Mol, 2010). According to Durepro and Mills (2011), actors must have the ability to make a difference, meaning they act and also can alter one another in their actions. Dery et al. (2013) defined network as a group of actors with allied interest, through which they consciously or unconsciously create link. The theory therefore focuses on the interaction between humans and non-human actors, making them inseparable (Iyamu & Roode, 2010). The inseparability between actor and network enable them to establish negotiation through translation, using four moments as shown in Figure 1.

The theory attempts to elucidate the process of enabling and constraining a variety of networks, which comprises of heterogeneous actors that are involved in the development, implementation and practice of the EA in organisations (Shim & Shin, 2016). According to Gad and Jensen (2010), in spite of its complexities, ANT continues to be widely adopted in studies across disciplines. Cressman (2009) states that even though the theory is difficult to describe and define, it has over the years grown in its popularity across multiple disciplines. However, Díaz Andrade

Figure 1. Moments of translation (Callon, 1986)

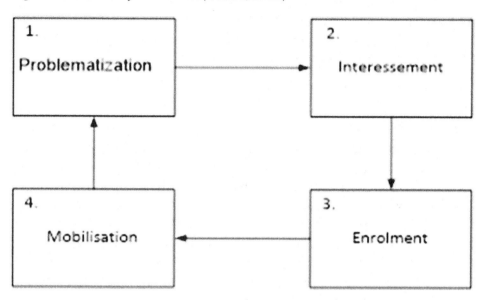

and Urquhart (2010) simplify ANT as a theory which emphasises on how the social and technical actors are equally influential towards one another therefore we cannot detach one from the other.

As shown in Figure 1, the first stage of the moments of translation occurs when an item is problematized by a focal actor (Callon, 1986). At the next stage, which is known as interessement, the problematized item draws various interests from different actors that aligns themselves with the network (Dwiartama & Rosin, 2014). The third moment is when interested actors begin to participate (enrol) in the activity of the problematized item, by accepting the roles or tasks that have been defined and assigned to them by the focal actor (Pollack, Costello & Sankaran, 2013). The fourth and last of the four stages is mobilisation, a state where the network is considered stable in that more actors are attracted to the course, and voluntarily take responsibilities (Baiocchi et al., 2013).

ANT is not only useful to the social sciences, but has found its relevance in IS studies in the last two decades (Wong, 2016). Increasingly, the theory is a popular conceptual approach that focuses on the meaning which human associate with things from sociotechnical perspectives (Müller & Schurr, 2016). The use of ANT as a lens helps to gather more knowledge and understanding of dynamic dimensions of significant complexity in phenomena such the EA. Stanforth (2006) applies ANT as a framework in order to comprehend the process which take place in the implementation of e-government in developing countries. In recent years, the theory has been increasingly applied in research, such as Greenhalgh and Stones (2010), to study technological innovations in the field of healthcare. Iyamu (2018) employs ANT to propose a multilevel approach in the analysis of big data. In Shim and Shin (2016) study, ANT was used as a lens in analysing how the telecommunication industry in China has developed over the years.

METHODOLOGY

In this study, the interpretivist approach was adopted. This is primarily to guide a construction of reality from a sociotechnical perspective (Andrade, 2009), about EA deployment in government. Sociotechnical reality comes from sense making of activities, as well as shared meanings of subjectivity rather than objectivist stance (Walsham, 2006). The qualitative methods were followed from the perspective of interpretivist approach mainly because it assists in the discovering of new knowledge and innovation (Venkatesh, Brown & Bala, 2013). Also, the qualitative methods guide us in our reliance on human perceptions and an understanding within context and relevance (Berger, 2015), which was vital in this study.

The EA is real, meaning the concept exist as an approach, which is constructed through sociotechnical interaction that happen within, and between networks of IS/IT specialists, architects, business (non-IS/IT) employees, and consultants, by using various tools in their constructivism. From qualitative viewpoint, fifty-two articles were collected, based on criteria, from scholar databases, which includes Google Scholar, Scopus, and EBSCO. The criteria: (1) article must be peer-reviewed. As in other subjects, arguable there are more non-academic (peer-reviewed) than academic (peer-reviewed) articles in the areas of EA; (2) articles published in the range of ten years, between 2008 and 2018. This was to ensure wider views from past studies, including the rhetoric background.

From a qualitative methods perspective, existing literature (Myers, 2013) about the EA and government enterprises were gathered and analysed. The interpretive approach was employed through the moments of translation of ANT in the analysis. Another reason for employing ANT is because it is sees the world as a fusion of entities that consist of both human and non-human (Tatnall, 2005), which equally contributes to the deployment of EA. The focus of the analysis was to examine and understand how EA can be deployed as agent of change within government enterprises. This study was thus viewed from ontological perspective, to which epistemology is the end in improving service delivery.

ANALYSIS: ENTERPRISE ARCHITECTURE FOR GOVERNMENT ENTERPRISES

As discussed in previous section, the moments of translation from ANT was applied as a lens to guide the analysis, towards having a better understanding of how government enterprises can employ the EA as agent of change, to improve service delivery. Table 1 provides a summary of the analysis. The discussion that follows should be read with the table in order to gain better understanding of the analysis.

Table 1. Moments of translation in the deployment of EA

Problematisation (1)	Interessement (2)
The concept of EA is problematized (initiated) within an environment by the employees (such as architects) or senior management. Also, consultants initiate the concept on or without invitation (self-volunteerism) from the organisation. The initiation is done based on signification of beneficiary, a motivation which was at the time associated with the concept by the initiator. The basis for problematizing the concept may not necessarily be understood by all the stakeholders at the time of such action.	Consciously or unconsciously the human actors (stakeholders) form networks (groups) on the basis of their divided interests. This shapes how the actors become interested in a problematized item. Individual or group interests are drawn from the premises that is based on how EA was communicated, which influence actors' opinions and views. The opinions of the stakeholders are not end but means to the next stage, which is whether to participate or not in the activities of the EA within the enterprise.
Mobilisation (4)	Enrolment (3)
Actors such as IS/IT managers, architects and consultants are of official appointment or volunteers (self-appointed) as spokespersons in the activities of the EA within their enterprises. The spokespersons exist within the networks that were consciously (within the organisational structure) or unconsciously (within social structure) formed. The spokespersons ensure that the EA is employed to make a difference in their environment. By so doing, the deployment of the EA have been re-problematized, an enactment of iterative process.	Interests of individuals or groups inform actual participations in the development, implementation, and practice of EA in an organisation. The participants, consisting of employees and consultants form participatory networks. The participations are influenced by various factors, such as personal development, know-how, contractual obligations (employment contract), and financial incentive (bonuses). Consultants' interest is mainly on the financial returns.

Actor-Network

In the development, implementation, and practice of the EA, there are human and non-human actors, which include the Chief Information Officer (CIO), enterprise architects, IT managers, business managers, and other business and IT personnel. The non-human actors include rules, regulations, processes, and activities. Within an organisation's rules and regulations, the actors consciously or consciously form groups (networks), based on their interest (Dery et al., 2013) in the activities of the

EA. Through the various networks, some human actors constantly interact with each other, and with the non-human actors (Iyamu & Roode, 2010), making the relationship and interaction the ultimate influence in the success or failure of EA in an environment. This is a bigger challenge in government enterprises in that the employees are often influence by affiliation to political parties in their interactions. Also, the formation of some networks is unconsciously influenced by political affiliations. This makes negotiation between some of the employees or networks to be difficult, which affects the processes and activities of EA during development, implementation, or practice in an environment. This is primarily because each actor has the ability to make a difference, through their intended and unintended actions (Durepro & Mills, 2011).

Moments of Translation: Problematisation

In many governments' enterprises, the concept of EA is problematized by the focal actors, which is often the CIO, towards improving service delivery. The problematization of EA is done through committee (network) of senior management, thereafter, it is filtered across various groups with allied interest, such as the architects and other domains. The interest is centred on EA objectives and deliverables. According to Seppänen (2014), EA is used to improve government service delivery. Nam et al. (2016) suggest that EA enables and supports IS/IT related service delivery to a country's citizens. This premise informs problematization of the concept to engineer a difference (change) in improving provision of services. Within governments' enterprises, problematization of EA is required at two different levels: introduction and definition of the concept.

On the first level, the concept is introduced to the employees, using various medium of communication and interaction. The concept might be new to many of the employees in some governments' enterprises. As a result, some employees consider the concept to be too theoretical or academic (Iyamu, 2015). Hence, preparatory work towards problematisation of the concept is critical, in that it is a point where failure or success potentially began.

The second level of problematisation entails definition of the EA, in the context of the enterprise. This is despite the fact that the concept has been defined in various quarters of both academic studies and by consultants over the years. For example, Ross et al. (2006:9) defined EA as *"the organising logic for business processes and IT infrastructures reflecting the integration and standardisation requirements of the company model"*. It well provides classification of processes and activities of an enterprise into domains, which provides fundamental governance that can be used to manage and bridge the gap between strategic planning and operations, iteratively. As with other many other definitions, although holistic, it is generic. Every environment is unique to certain degree, therefore, EA definition should be contextual.

However, an enterprise's definition should be aligned with the framework that is selected. This helps to refine the scope of EA within the enterprise, in terms of context, relevance, and best practice. Most importantly, it helps the promoters to demonstrate good understanding and ownership of the concept within their environment. Ultimately, it prepares the promoters and other actors in soliciting buy-in from stakeholders through interaction and negotiation.

Moments of Translation: Intressement

By default, employees (IS/IT specialists and managers) are stakeholders in the deployment of the EA in an organisation. The stakeholders directly or indirectly align themselves with networks (Dwiartama & Rosin, 2014), through which various activities of EA are carried out. This type of relationship enacts inseparable interaction between the human actors and EA processes and activities. Interests that are shown in the deployment and practice of EA within the government enterprises come from two main perspectives, personal and organisational. Stakeholders (employees and consultants) interests are influenced by both technical and non-technical factors, which are aligned with EA in order to effect change within the environment (Löhe & Legner, 2014).

Personal interest is often based on human actors' interact with processes. This consequently manifests into know-how, hunger for self-development, voluntarism, and contractual obligations. Some employees make use of their technical know-how as a source of power to make a difference in the deployment as well practice of EA. This type of behaviour and actions often dictates how EA is scoped, developed, implemented, and practiced within an environment (Bui & Levy, 2017), which affects its alignment with the enterprise's goals and objectives. Voluntarism is a hide fact that comes from personal interests, such as job security, financial incentive, and favouritism to a line-manager's approach. The challenge is that it is not easy to detect or foresee how and why personal interests are expressed and applied in the activities of EA. These circumstances have influence on the deployment and practice of EA in an organisation.

Contractual obligation have several implications in the deployment and practice of EA, in that employees are forced to be interested on the subject that they ordinarily wouldn't like to align their views and know-hows with. Primarily, consultants have the best interest of their organisations through EA framework that they present. Some of the consultants have the interest of the clients in order to maintain presence in that environment. Although consultants place emphasis on the fact that EA is intended to add value and contribute to the growth of the enterprise (Cameron & McMillan, 2013), their interest is focused on financial reward.

The interest on EA is founded on its primary aim and strengths, which are considered significant in bridging the gap between business and IS/IT units, in enforcing change from the current to a desired state. In the context of this study, "change" is enacted by strategy, which refers to a new way of working in a government institution or agency. In applying this new approach within an environment, the plan is to improve the chances of success through the practice of EA *as an Agent of Change*. EA helps us to consistently address the activities in the enterprise and many related concerns of IS/IT that support and enables service delivery through business processes and activities. It is on this basis that I consider an understanding of how and why EA is problematized is critical, and why different actors show interest in the concept from various angles. The criticality is to gain better insight of the factors that influence the success or failure of the concept in an environment.

Moments of Translation: Enrolment

The deployment and practice of EA requires participatory efforts by the stakeholders. This is a trajectory that begins with identification of individuals and groups, including their expertise and strengths. By virtue of interest, actors are stakeholders in the concept. However, not every interested persons or stakeholders participate (enrol) in the activities and processes of EA in an environment (Farwick et al., 2016). Enrolment is shaped by personal and contractual obligations, which are influenced by both internal and external factors. Through negotiation, actors accept responsibilities that have been assigned to them by the focal actor (Pollack, Costello & Sankaran, 2013).

The internal factors include both human and non-human actors. The human actors consist of IS/IT and business people. The technical personnel include managers and IT architects whose focus are on the individual domains, for planning and deployments of IS/IT solutions, to enable and support government services (Shaanika & Iyamu, 2018). The non-humans are the processes, procedures, policies which guide the deployment and practice of the concept in an environment.

The external factors consist of consultants and government laws. The consultants are hired for the development and implementation of EA, including the resources such as the framework that are used in the process (Rouhani et al., 2015). The aim is to deploy and operationalize government's activities and services, from information flows to software implementation. The policies influence how EA is defined, developed, and implemented within governments' enterprises. For example, the policies guide how information is operationalized in exchange during interactions. Cognisance of the external factors can be used as determinant in the management of stakeholders' enrolment in the activities of EA.

Moments of Translation: Mobilisation

EA is a process that is iterative in nature. Iyamu (2015) explains that the deployment of the concept is not a project that starts and ends within a period of time. Also, iteration happens only when the network is considered stable (Baiocchi et al., 2013). By virtue of mobilising other actors within and outside of the network, to partake in the plans and operations, problematisation is in itself taking-place. This means that at the point of mobilisation, a new beginning of fresh negotiation takes place.

Through an iterative process, EA is theoretically problematized, and via mobilisation the concept is translated into practice. The results from both current and future states are the outcomes of humans' actions and IS/IT solutions including their interactions, which are produced and reproduced through the domains of EA over a period of time. Giddens (1984) describes the process of reproduction as a duality of structure. In the reproduction of actions, both human and technology act within heterogeneous networks within an enterprise, to develop, implement, and manage EA towards desired outcome. It is difficult or near impossible to separate human actions and IS/IT solutions from each other in the deployment and practice of EA, to significantly transform service delivery within an environment. This is mainly because neither human nor IS/IT operate in a vacuum.

FINDINGS AND DISCUSSION

From the analysis above, four main factors that can influence how the EA is defined, developed, implemented, and practiced in government enterprises were revealed. The factors are (1) criticality of networks, (2) structural collaboration, (3) transformative process, and (4) iterative approach. The findings come from the interactions that happen between actors, human-to-human; human-to-nonhuman; and nonhuman-to-nonhuman. Based on the subjective interpretation of the factors, a framework (Figure 2) was developed.

Figure 2 provides insight how the factors manifest themselves in the use of EA to enable governments' enterprises in providing services to the communities. Criticality of networks – this include health, economic, safety and security, education, and social security. Structural collaboration – municipal, and district governments, provincial government, and national government. Transformative process – EA domains, which are information, service-oriented architecture (SOA), application, security, and technology. Iterative approach – relationship between the structural collaborative effort and critical networks in service delivery. The discussion that follows should be read with Figure 2 in order to comprehend how EA can be employed as agent of change.

Figure 2. EA Conceptual Framework

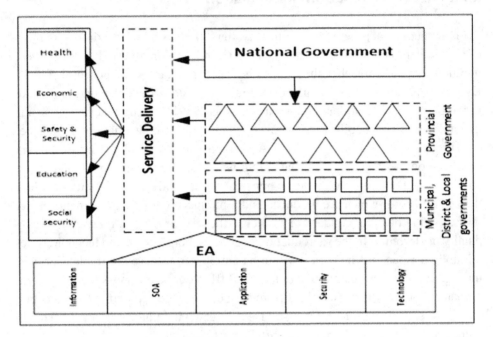

Criticality of Networks

In ANT, a network consists of actors that are consciously or unconsciously allied with common interest, through which they create a link (Dwiartama & Rosin, 2014). Services and government (federation or republic) structures are the two primary networks within a government enterprise, which influences deployment of EA from different viewpoints. Based on service needs networks are created. As shown in Figure 2, some of the networks include healthcare, education, safety and economic growth. Similarly, there are networks within governmental structure, which include national, provincial (state) and local governments. The existence of these networks make it inevitable to have silo processes and deployment of IS/IT solutions. Through silo state, processes and IS/IT solutions are duplicated, inconsistencies are created (Aier, 2017), which manifest into lack of uniformities and standardisation, increase complexities and disparities within an environment.

During the period of applications and infrastructures deployment, requirements often change, and sometimes the change happens so rapidly due to shift in politics or government policies or focuses. Through different networks, IS/IT solutions and processes are employed to respond to the change within the enterprises, for the purposes of service delivery. Through the networks, IS/IT specialist traces and manages how the entire activities within the computing environments change from assembling, disassembling, and reassembling (Baiocchi, Graizbord & Rodríguez-Muñiz, 2013), for improved service delivery. The management of the changes determine success or failure in the deployment and practice of EA in an environment.

Structural Collaboration

Governments are multifaceted structures through ministries or departments and agencies in her provision of services to the society. As shown in Figure 2, services are across different levels of governments' structures. The EA is fundamental to enabling change from strategic planning, systems design, software development, and hardware deployment, to reproduction of multiple systems in improving service delivery. Thus, collaborations is vital to ensure enhanced synergy and synchronisation of services including strategic and operational governance of processes and deployment of IS/IT solutions. This approach enables reuse, which reduces cost, and improve effectiveness and efficiency in service delivery (Seppänen, 2014).

The EA facilitates change through collaboration between units and structures within an organisation (Alwadain et al., 2014). However, there are challenges, one of the factors in collaborative effort is lack of understanding of EA by employees within the government structures (Olsen & Trelsgård, 2016). Some of the challenges that manifests from lack of collaboration within the governments' computing environments include lack of integration, flexibility and governance (Roth et al., 2013; Hjort-Madsen & Pries-Heje, 2009).

Transformative Process

The EA is an agent that drives transformation of strategy into operation through processes and deployment of IS and supporting information technologies, which government enterprises employ in providing services. Ross et al. (2006) described this approach as: EA provides a long-term view of a company's processes, systems, and technologies. As a roadmap, EA promotes knowledge and information sharing across an enterprise through which change happens in the provision of services.

Transformation is a process that starts from point of problematisation (initiation) to practice (mobilisation) through which changes are engineered, in providing services to communities. In every point of transformation there are agents, which include business artefacts, information components, application systems, and technology infrastructures (Lapalme et al., 2016). It is through these ways that EA enables transformation through planning, deployment and operationalization of business process and IS/IT activities towards service delivery (Nam et al., 2016). Transformation brings about stability within networks only when it becomes iterative.

Iterative Approach

Each domain of EA has its objectives, but they depend on each other in order to effect change. Similarly, the structures that exist within governments dependent on each other in the delivering of services. This form of dependency is not project-like, but an iterative process that happens over a period of political shift or end-of-life of an IS/IT solution. Iteratively, the EA is used to manage and govern business processes and IS/IT deployments within an environment (Roth et al., 2013). The iterative approach aims to improve effectiveness, efficiency, and reduction of risk in service delivery, via a new sets of governance and operating models. This includes rationalisation, consolidation, and integration of existing and future IS/IT solutions, in fulfilling societal needs.

Nothing is static, processes and IS/IT infrastructures continue to evolve. The EA therefore employs the iterative approach in order to suit upcoming trends and changes (Alwadain et al., 2014). The iterative approach aids continuity of relationships and connectivity among business processes, application systems, technology infrastructure, and how agents relate and interact with each other in facilitating change towards service delivery (Iyamu, 2019).

EA AS CHANGE AGENT FOR GOVERNMENT ENTERPRISES

Through the deployment of EA as agent of change, the architects provides guides and frameworks, to design and structure the enterprise's components and their relationships, from business processes to IS/IT solutions. The importance of the concept has made many countries to promote their agencies and local governments. According to Lee et al. (2013), the introduction of EA through frameworks and reference models guides standardisation and governance.

The deployment of EA engineer change between business and IS/IT' strategies and processes (Löhe & Legner, 2014). As shown in Figure 3, EA facilitates change from both strategic and operational perspectives, towards delivery of socioeconomic services such as healthcare, education, climate change and safety. The change happens via the business processes, information flow, application systems, and technology infrastructures for service delivery purposes.

The activities of governments' computing environments including the services that they support are influenced by technical and non-technical factors, made up of business processes and IS/IT solutions. In the delivering of services to the society, governments' enterprises rely on support and enablement from IS/IT solutions and other processes, which require architecture and governance if they are to efficiently, effectively, and promptly deliver services to the communities. Iyamu (2015) explains

Figure 3. EA as agent of change

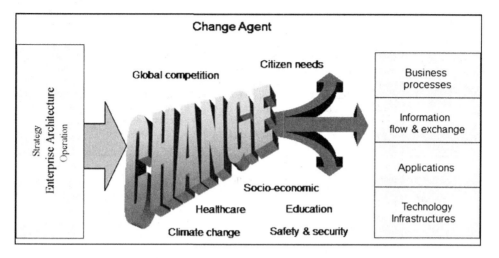

that technologies are selected, developed, and implemented by people through processes, in accordance to structures, rules, and resources.

The deployment and practice of EA supports the integration and dependency between technical and non-technical factors through its domains: business, information, application, and technology towards facilitating change. Having linkages between the domains provide traceability to the relevant stakeholders of EA and the organisation (Lapalme et al., 2016). As an agent of change, EA addresses complexity, integration challenges, lack of collaboration, enabling business processes, and guiding IS/IT solutions' deployment. This allows change from current to future states, in the areas of socioeconomic needs (security, safety, healthcare, and education).

IMPLICATION OF PRACTICE

This study reveals factors of signification in the deployment of EA as agent of change including the criticality of networks, structural collaboration, transformative process, and iterative approach. The factors have implications on the activities that the architects and other stakeholders such as IS/IT specialists and managers carry out. The primary implications are described in Table 2.

Table 2 provides a summary of the implications of practice in the deployment and practice of EA as agent of change, specifically within governments' enterprises. This is primarily to focus on the fact that many employees and their managers find themselves struggling and challenged with factors, such as integration and consolidation of processes and IS/IT solution across levels of government structures (Rodrigues &

Table 2. Implication of practice

Factor	IT	Government Enterprise
Criticality of networks	Some IT specialists act in isolation, and executes their activities in silo, based on their conferment to their individual networks (Seppänen, 2014), which affects the deployment of EA. As a result, many IT specialists know little or nothing about the domains of EA that is outside areas of their immediate responsibilities. This can have negative influence on EA during its deployment in an environment.	Heterogeneity of networks across the various levels of structures within governments. This poses challenges to coordinating activities, deployment, and practice of EA. Some of the challenges from and by actors and networks sometimes have negative effect on service delivery (Farwick et al., 2013).
Government structure	Interactions between the IT and business units are often misconstrued through different subjective interpretations. This is primarily because the interaction is not guided by the objectives of EA. As a result, the power associated with individual authority and structures take preceding.	Interaction requires continuous synergy and training of employees about the concept of EA. This is to solidify enablement of alignment between IT and business units within the enterprise.
Transformative process	Transformative process in the context of IT must be understood, to avoid challenges which can obstruct changes in the deployment and use of technology solutions (Alwadain et al., 2014). Through connectedness of the EA domains, transformation of IT solutions can be appropriately governed, controlled, and managed.	The transformative process can create parallel activities between EA and enterprise' objectives (Siddiquee & Siddiquee, 2016). The implication is that it affects the stability of the environment towards achieving the objectives of the enterprise.
Iterative approach	The iterative process fosters institutionalisation of EA, through which the benefits of the concept is gained (Iyamu, 2015). However, the iterative nature of EA can be challenging and constraining during the deployment and practice of the concept, which can have detrimental effect on IT solutions.	The iterative approach have influence on the type of change that happens, from current to future states. Thus, the approach must be consistent, in order to ensure systems availability, improved performance, scalability, and interoperability.

Almaral, 2010). The challenges remain significant as they are deterministic to the success or failure of an IS/IT environment within an enterprise. The challenges include how software, hardware, and processes are employed to facilitate change from current to future state in service delivery (Farwick et al., 2013).

CONCLUSION

The challenges in the deployment of EA within government enterprises are lacking in academic studies, which this study investigated from both IT and societal perspectives. Therefore, this study can be of interest to government enterprises, academics, and consultants, as many IT specialists within governments' enterprises continue to struggle in resolving challenges in their environments. The study can be of interest to academics in their efforts in advancing the discipline through research, curriculum development. Consultants often rely or complement their efforts with academic research. from that angle, this study will likely be of interest to many consultants.

The contributions of this study can be drawn from both theory and practical perspectives. Theoretical, the study contribute to the existing literature in the areas of EA, government service delivery, and application of ANT. there are little or no study that has applied ANT in EA from both government and developing country viewpoint. In addition, practitioners of EA and other IT personnel within government enterprises can learn from the influencing factors revealed and discussed in section 5, in their quest to implement and practice the concept. Some of the findings in the study might not be entirely new, but the application of ANT brings a fresh perspective on how they manifest, which add to the learning that practitioners gain from the study.

The implementation of EA does not really mean actualisation of the end, in achieving its objectives within government environments. It does require institutionalisation of the practice. Only then the culture can be imbibed, from which the benefits begin to apparent over a period of time. This is a critical area of further studies, because it can help to build reference models for both enterprises and academic domains.

REFERENCES

Aier, A. K. S. (2017). *Enterprise Architecture in public sector: A systematic literature review focusing on hospitals and governance*. Academic Press.

Al-Nasrawi, S., & Ibrahim, M. (2013). An enterprise architecture mapping approach for realizing E-government. In *Communications and Information Technology (ICCIT), 2013 Third International Conference on* (pp. 17–21). IEEE. 10.1109/ICCITechnology.2013.6579515

Alwadain, A., Fielt, E., Korthaus, A., & Rosemann, M. (2014). A critical realist perspective of enterprise architecture evolution: Conditioning and outcomes. *AJIS. Australasian Journal of Information Systems*, *18*(3), 213–226. doi:10.3127/ajis.v18i3.1102

Andrade, A. D. (2009). Interpretive research aiming at theory building: Adopting and adapting the case study design. *Qualitative Report*, *14*(1), 42–60.

Baiocchi, G., Graizbord, D., & Rodríguez-Muñiz, M. (2013). Actor-Network Theory and the ethnographic imagination: An exercise in translation. *Qualitative Sociology*, *36*(4), 323–341. doi:10.100711133-013-9261-9

Berger, R. (2015). Now I see it, now I don't: Researcher's position and reflexivity in qualitative research. *Qualitative Research*, *15*(2), 219–234. doi:10.1177/1468794112468475

Buckle, S., Matthes, F., Monahov, I., Roth, S., Schulz, C., & Schweda, C. M. (2011). Towards an agile design of the enterprise architecture management function. In Enterprise Distributed Object Computing Conference Workshops (EDOCW), 2011 15th IEEE International (pp. 322-329). IEEE. doi:10.1109/EDOCW.2011.33

Bui, Q., & Levy, M. (2017). Institutionalization of Contested Practices: A Case of Enterprise Architecture Implementation in a US State Government. *Proceedings of the 50th Hawaii International Conference on System Sciences*. 10.24251/HICSS.2017.591

Bui, Q. N., Markus, M., & Newell, S. (2015). *Alternative Designs in Widespread Innovation Adoption: Empirical Evidence from Enterprise Architecture Implementation in US State Governments*. Academic Press.

Cabrera, A., Abad, M., Jaramillo, D., Gómez, J., & Verdum, J. C. (2016). Definition and implementation of the enterprise business layer through a business reference model, using the architecture development method ADM-TOGAF. In *Trends and Applications in Software Engineering* (pp. 111–121). Springer. doi:10.1007/978-3-319-26285-7_10

Callon, M. (1986). Some elements of a sociology of translation: domestication of the scallops and the fishermen of St Brieuc Bay. In J. Law (Ed.), *Power, Action & Belief: A New Sociology of Knowledge?* (pp. 196–229). Routledge & Kegan Paul.

Cameron, B. H., & McMillan, E. (2013). Analyzing the current trends in enterprise architecture frameworks. *Journal of Enterprise Architecture*, *9*(1), 60–71.

Cressman, D. (2009). *A brief overview of actor-network theory: Punctualization, heterogeneous engineering & translation*. Academic Press.

Dery, K., Hall, R., Wailes, N., & Wiblen, S. (2013). Lost in translation? An actor-network approach to HRIS implementation. *The Journal of Strategic Information Systems*, *22*(3), 225–237. doi:10.1016/j.jsis.2013.03.002

Díaz Andrade, A., & Urquhart, C. (2010). The affordances of actor network theory in ICT for development research. *Information Technology & People*, *23*(4), 352–374. doi:10.1108/09593841011087806

Dwiartama, A., & Rosin, C. (2014). Exploring agency beyond humans: The compatibility of Actor-Network Theory (ANT) and resilience thinking. *Ecology and Society*, *19*(3), 28–38. doi:10.5751/ES-06805-190328

Farwick, M., Breu, R., Hauder, M., Roth, S., & Matthes, F. (2013). Enterprise architecture documentation: Empirical analysis of information sources for automation. In *System Sciences (HICSS), 2013 46th Hawaii International Conference on* (pp. 3868-3877). IEEE.

Farwick, M., Schweda, C. M., Breu, R., & Hanschke, I. (2016). A situational method for semi-automated Enterprise Architecture Documentation. *Software & Systems Modeling*, *15*(2), 397–426. doi:10.100710270-014-0407-3

Gad, C., & Bruun Jensen, C. (2010). On the consequences of post-ANT. *Science, Technology & Human Values*, *35*(1), 55–80. doi:10.1177/0162243908329567

Giddens, A. (1984). *The Constitution of Society: Outline of the Theory of Structuration*. John Polity Press.

Greenhalgh, T., & Stones, R. (2010). Theorising big IT programmes in healthcare: Strong structuration theory meets actor-network theory. *Social Science & Medicine*, *70*(9), 1285–1294. doi:10.1016/j.socscimed.2009.12.034 PMID:20185218

Hjort-Madsen, K., & Pries-Heje, J. (2009, January). Enterprise architecture in government: Fad or future? In *System Sciences, 2009. HICSS'09. 42nd Hawaii International Conference on* (pp. 1-10). IEEE.

Iyamu, T. (2015). *Enterprise Architecture from Concept to Practice*. Heidelberg press.

Iyamu, T. (2018). A multilevel approach to big data analysis using analytic tools and actor network theory. *South African Journal of Information Management*, *20*(1), a914. doi:10.4102ajim.v20i1.914

Iyamu, T. (2019). Understanding the complexities of enterprise architecture through structuration theory. *Journal of Computer Information Systems*, *59*(3), 287–295. doi:10.1080/08874417.2017.1354341

Iyamu, T., & Roode, D. (2010). The Use of Structuration Theory and Actor Network Theory for Analysis: A case study of a financial institution in South Africa. *International Journal of Actor-Network Theory and Technological Innovation*, *2*(1), 1–26. doi:10.4018/jantti.2010071601

Johnson, P., Ekstedt, M., & Lagerstrom, R. (2016). Automatic Probabilistic Enterprise IT Architecture Modeling: A Dynamic Bayesian Networks Approach. In *Enterprise Distributed Object Computing Workshop (EDOCW), 2016 IEEE 20th International* (pp. 1–8). IEEE. 10.1109/EDOCW.2016.7584351

Katuu, S. (2018). The Utility of Enterprise Architecture to Records and Archives Specialists. *2018 IEEE International Conference on Big Data (Big Data)*, 2702-2710.

Kaushik, A., & Raman, A. (2015). The new data-driven enterprise architecture for e-healthcare: Lessons fromt he Indian public sector. *Government Information Quarterly, 32*(1), 63–74. doi:10.1016/j.giq.2014.11.002

Lagerstrom, R., Sommestad, T., Buschle, M., & Ekstedt, M. (2011). Enterprise architecture management's impact on information technology success. In *System Sciences (HICSS), 2011 44th Hawaii International Conference on* (pp. 1-10). IEEE.

Lapalme, J., Gerber, A., Van der Merwe, A., Zachman, J., De Vries, M., & Hinkelmann, K. (2016). Exploring the future of enterprise architecture: A Zachman perspective. *Computers in Industry, 79*, 103–113. doi:10.1016/j.compind.2015.06.010

Lee, Y.-J., Kwon, Y.-I., Shin, S., & Kim, E.-J. (2013). Advancing government-wide Enterprise Architecture-A meta-model approach. In *Advanced Communication Technology (ICACT), 2013 15th International Conference on* (pp. 886–892). IEEE.

Löhe, J., & Legner, C. (2014). Overcoming implementation challenges in enterprise architecture management: A design theory for architecture-driven IT Management (ADRIMA). *Information Systems and e-Business Management, 12*(1), 101–137. doi:10.100710257-012-0211-y

Mohamed, M. A., Galal-Edeen, G. H., Hassan, H. A., & Hasanien, E. E. (2012). An evaluation of enterprise architecture frameworks for e-government. In *Computer Engineering & Systems (ICCES), 2012 Seventh International Conference on* (pp. 255–260). IEEE 10.1109/ICCES.2012.6408524

Mol, A. (2010). Actor-network theory: Sensitive terms and enduring tensions. *Kölner Zeitschrift für Soziologie und Sozialpsychologie. Sonderheft, 50*, 253–269.

Müller, M., & Schurr, C. (2016). Assemblage thinking and actor-network theory: Conjunctions, disjunctions, cross-fertilisations. *Transactions of the Institute of British Geographers, 41*(3), 217–229. doi:10.1111/tran.12117

Myers, M. (2013). *Qualitative research in business and management* (2nd ed.). Sage.

Nam, K., Oh, S. W., Kim, S. K., Goo, J., & Khan, S. (2016). Dynamics of Enterprise Architecture in the Korean Public Sector: Transformational Change vs. Transactional Change. *Sustainability, 8*(11), 1074. doi:10.3390u8111074

Olsen, D. H., & Trelsgård, K. (2016). Enterprise Architecture Adoption Challenges: An exploratory Case Study of the Norwegian Higher Education Sector. *Procedia Computer Science, 100*, 804–811. doi:10.1016/j.procs.2016.09.228

Paul, A., & Paul, V. (2012). The e-Government interoperability through Enterprise Architecture in Indian perspective. In *World Congress on Information and Communication Technologies* (pp. 646-650). IEEE. 10.1109/WICT.2012.6409155

Pollack, J., Costello, K., & Sankaran, S. (2013). Applying Actor–Network Theory as a sensemaking framework for complex organisational change programs. *International Journal of Project Management, 31*(8), 1118–1128. doi:10.1016/j.ijproman.2012.12.007

Radeke, F. (2011). Toward Understanding Enterprise Architecture Management's Role in Strategic Change: Antecedents, Processes, Outcomes. *Wirtschaftsinformatik, 16*(18), 1–11.

Rodrigues, L. S., & Amaral, L. (2010). Issues in enterprise architecture value. *Journal of Enterprise Architecture, 6*(4), 27–32.

Ross, J., Weill, P., & Robertson, D. (2006). *Enterprise architecture as a strategy: Creating a foundation for business execution.* Havard Business Press.

Roth, S., Hauder, M., Farwick, M., Breu, R., & Matthes, F. (2013). Enterprise Architecture Documentation: Current Practices and Future Directions. In Wirtschaftsinformatik (p. 58). Academic Press.

Rouhani, B. D., Mahrin, M. N., Nikpay, F., & Nikfard, P. (2013). A comparison enterprise architecture implementation methodologies. In *Informatics and Creative Multimedia (ICICM), 2013 International Conference on* (pp. 1-6). IEEE. 10.1109/ICICM.2013.9

Rouhani, B. D., Mahrin, M. N. R., Shirazi, H., Nikpay, F., & Rouhani, B. D. (2015). An Effectiveness Model for Enterprise Architecture Methodologies. *International Journal of Enterprise Information Systems, 11*(2), 50–64. doi:10.4018/IJEIS.2015040103

Safari, H., Faraji, Z., & Majidian, S. (2016). Identifying and evaluating enterprise architecture risks using FMEA and fuzzy VIKOR. *Journal of Intelligent Manufacturing, 27*(2), 475–486. doi:10.100710845-014-0880-0

Seppänen, V. (2014). From problems to critical success factors of enterprise architecture adoption. *Jyväskylä studies in computing; 1456-5390; 201.*

Shaanika, I., & Iyamu, T. (2018). Developing the enterprise architecture for the Namibian government. *The Electronic Journal on Information Systems in Developing Countries, 84*(3), e12028. doi:10.1002/isd2.12028

Shim, Y., & Shin, D. H. (2016). Analyzing China's fintech industry from the perspective of actor–network theory. *Telecommunications Policy*, *40*(2), 168–181. doi:10.1016/j.telpol.2015.11.005

Siddiquee, N. A., & Siddiquee, N. A. (2016). E-government and transformation of service delivery in developing countries: The Bangladesh experience and lessons. *Transforming Government: People. Process and Policy*, *10*(3), 368–390.

Stanforth, C. (2006). Using actor-network theory to analyse e-government implementation in developing countries. *Information Technologies and International Development*, *3*(3), 35–60. doi:10.1162/itid.2007.3.3.35

Tamm, T., Seddon, P. B., Shanks, G. G., & Reynolds, P. (2011). How does enterprise architecture add value to organisations? CAIS, 28, 10.

Tatnall, A. (2005). Actor-network theory in information systems research. In *Encyclopaedia of Information Science and Technology* (1st ed., pp. 42–46). IGI Global. doi:10.4018/978-1-59140-553-5.ch009

Thapa, D. (2011). The role of ICT actors and networks in development: The case study of a wireless project in Nepal. *The Electronic Journal on Information Systems in Developing Countries*, *49*(1), 1–16. doi:10.1002/j.1681-4835.2011.tb00345.x

Urbaczewski, L., & Mrdalj, S. (2006). A Comparison of Enterprise Architecture Frameworks. *Issues in Information Systems*, *7*(2), 18–23.

Van Zijl, C., & Van Belle, J. P. (2014). Organisatinal impact of enterprise architecture and business process capability in South African organisation. *International Journal of Trade. Economics and Finance*, *5*(5), 405.

Venkatesh, V., Brown, S. A., & Bala, H. (2013). Bridging the qualitative-quantitative divide: Guidelines for conducting mixed methods research in information systems. *Management Information Systems Quarterly*, *37*(1), 21–54. doi:10.25300/MISQ/2013/37.1.02

Walsham, G. (2006). Doing interpretive research. *European Journal of Information Systems*, *15*(3), 320–330. doi:10.1057/palgrave.ejis.3000589

Wong, C. M. L. (2016). Assembling interdisciplinary energy research through an actor-network theory (ANT) frame. *Energy Research & Social Science*, *12*, 106–110. doi:10.1016/j.erss.2015.12.024

Zheng, T., & Zheng, L. (2013). Examining e-government enterprise architecture research in China: A systematic approach and research agenda. *Government Information Quarterly*, *30*, S59–S67. doi:10.1016/j.giq.2012.08.005

Compilation of References

Abai, N. H. Z., Yahaya, J. H., & Deraman, A. (2013). User requirement analysis in data warehouse design: A review. *Procedia Technology*, *11*, 801–806. doi:10.1016/j.protcy.2013.12.261

Abdelkader, M., & Luther, R. (2008). The impact of firm characteristics on management accounting practices: A UK-based empirical analysis. *The British Accounting Review*, *40*(1), 2–27. doi:10.1016/j.bar.2007.11.003

Abdolvand, N., Albadvi, A., & Ferdowsi, Z. (2008). Assessing readiness for business process reengineering. *Business Process Management Journal*, *14*(4), 497–511. doi:10.1108/14637150810888046

Adams, C., & Zutshi, A. (2004). Corporate social responsibility: Why business should act responsibly and be accountable. *Australian Accounting Review*, *14*(3), 31–40. doi:10.1111/j.1835-2561.2004. tb00238.x

Adjorlolo, S., & Ellingsen, G. (2013). Readiness assessment for implementation of electronic patient record in Ghana: A case of university of Ghana hospital. *Journal of Health Informatics in Developing Countries*, *7*(2), 128–140.

Adrian, C., Abdullah, R., Atan, R., & Jusoh, Y. Y. (2018). Conceptual model development of big data analytics implementation assessment effect on decision-making. *Technology*, 23–24.

Adrian, C., Abdullah, R., Atan, R., & Jusoh, Y. Y. 2017, July. Factors influencing to the implementation success of big data analytics: A systematic literature review. *2017 International Conference on Research and Innovation in Information Systems (ICRIIS)*, 1-6. 10.1109/ICRIIS.2017.8002536

Afonso, A., & St. Aubyn, M. (2006b). Relative efficiency of health provision: a DEA approach with nondiscretionary inputs. *ISEG-UTL, Department of Economics Working Paper n° 33/2006/ DE/UECE*.

Afonso, A., & St. Aubyn, M. (2005). Non-parametric approaches to education and health efficiency in Oecd countries. *Journal of Applied Econometrics*, *8*(2), 227–246.

Afonso, A., & St. Aubyn, M. (2006a). Cross-country efficiency of secondary education provision: A semiparametric analysis with non-discretionary inputs. *Economic Modelling, 23*(3), 476–491. doi:10.1016/j.econmod.2006.02.003

Agievich, V. (2014). *Mathematical model and multi-criteria analysis of designing large-scale enterprise roadmap*. PhD thesis.

Ahmadi, H., Farahani, B., Aliee, F., & Motlagh, M. (2019). Cross-layer Enterprise Architecture Evaluation: an approach to improve the evaluation of enterprise architecture TO-BE plan. In *Proceedings of COINS conference. COINS* (pp. 1-6). Crete, Greece: Academic Press.

Ahmadi, H., Farahani, B., Aliee, F., & Motlagh, M. (2019). Cross-layer Enterprise Architecture Evaluation: an approach to improve the evaluation of enterprise architecture TO-BE plan. In *Proceedings of COINS conference. COINS* (pp. 1-6). Crete, Greece: ACM. doi:10.1145/3312614.3312659

Ahmad, K. (2017). The implementation of management accounting practices and its relationship with performance in small and medium enterprises. *International Review of Management and Marketing, 7*(1), 342–353.

Ahn, T., Charnes, A., & Cooper, W. W. (1988). Efficiency characterizations in different DEA models. *Socio-Economic Planning Sciences, 22*(6), 253–257. doi:10.1016/0038-0121(88)90007-9

Aier, A. K. S. (2017). *Enterprise Architecture in public sector: A systematic literature review focusing on hospitals and governance*. Academic Press.

Aier, S. (2014). The role of organisation culture for grounding, management, guidance and effectiveness of enterprise architecture principles. *Information Systems and e-Business Management, 12*(1), 43–70. doi:10.100710257-012-0206-8

Aier, S., Bucher, T., & Winter, R. (2011). *Critical Success Factors of Service Orientation in Information Systems Engineering. Derivation and Empirical Evaluation of a Causal Model. Business & Information Systems Engineering*. Springer.

Ajami, S., Ketabi, S., Isfahani, S. S., & Heidari, A. (2011). Readiness assessment of electronic health records implementation. *Acta Informatica Medica, 19*(4), 224–227. doi:10.5455/aim.2011.19.224-227 PMID:23407861

Aji, A. S., & Widodo, T. (2019). Measuring enterprise architecture readiness at higher education institutions. *International Journal of Applied Business and Information Systems, 3*(1), 14–20.

Al Nuaimi, E., Al Neyadi, H., Mohamed, N., & Al-Jaroodi, J. (2015). Applications of big data to smart cities. *Journal of Internet Services and Applications, 6*(1), 25. doi:10.118613174-015-0041-5

Alawadhi, S., Aldama-Nalda, A., Chourabi, H., & Gil-Garcia, J. (2012). Building understanding of smart city initiatives. In International conference on electronic government (pp. 40-53). Springer.

Alderman, L. (2019). French Court Fines UBS $4.2 Billion for Helping Clients Evade Taxes. *The New York Times*. https://www.nytimes.com/2019/02/20/business/ubs-france-tax-evasion.html

Alghamdi, I. A., Goodwin, R., & Rampersad, G. (2011). E-government readiness assessment for government organizations in developing countries. *Computer and Information Science*, *4*(3), 3–17. doi:10.5539/cis.v4n3p3

Allen, M., Alleyne, D., Farmer, C., McRae, A., & Turner, Ch. (2014, October). A Framework for Project Success. *Journal of IT and Economic Development*, *5*(2), 1–17.

Al-Malaise Al-Ghamdi, A.S. (2017). A proposed model to measure the impact of business architecture. *Cogent Business & Management*, *4*(1), 1–8.

Al-Nasrawi, S., & Ibrahim, M. (2013). An enterprise architecture mapping approach for realizing E-government. In *Communications and Information Technology (ICCIT), 2013 Third International Conference on* (pp. 17–21). IEEE. 10.1109/ICCITechnology.2013.6579515

Alshaher, A. A. F. (2013). The McKinsey 7S model framework for e-learning system readiness assessment. *International Journal of Advances in Engineering and Technology*, *6*(5), 1948–1966.

Alwadain, A., Fielt, E., Korthaus, A., & Rosemann, M. (2014). A critical realist perspective of enterprise architecture evolution: Conditioning and outcomes. *AJIS. Australasian Journal of Information Systems*, *18*(3), 213–226. doi:10.3127/ajis.v18i3.1102

Amit, R., & Zott, C. (2015). Crafting business architecture: The antecedents of business model design. *Strategic Entrepreneurship Journal*, *9*(4), 331–350. doi:10.1002ej.1200

Amugongo, L., Nggada, S., & Sieck, J. (2016). Leveraging on open data to solve city challenges: A case study of Windhoek municipality. *3rd MEC International Conference on Big Data and Smart City (ICBDSC)*, 1-6. 10.1109/ICBDSC.2016.7460355

Anand, S., & Ravallion, M. (1993). Human Development in Poor Countries: On the Role of PrivateIncomes and Public Services. *The Journal of Economic Perspectives*, *7*(1), 133–150. doi:10.1257/jep.7.1.133

Anaya, V., & Ortiz, A. (2005). How enterprise architectures can support integration. In *Proceedings of the first international workshop on Interoperability of heterogeneous information systems*, (pp. 25-30). ACM.

Andrade, A. D. (2009). Interpretive research aiming at theory building: Adopting and adapting the case study design. *Qualitative Report*, *14*(1), 42–60.

Angelakis, G., Theriou, N., & Floropoulos, I. (2010). Adoption and benefits of management accounting practices: Evidence from Greece and Finland, *Advances in Accounting, Incorporating. Advances in International Accounting*, *26*(1), 87–96. doi:10.1016/j.adiac.2010.02.003

Angulo-Meza, L., & Lins, M. P. E. (2002). Review of methods for increasing discrimination in data envelopment analysis. *Annals of Operations Research*, *116*(1-4), 225–242. doi:10.1023/A:1021340616758

Anthopoulos, L., & Fitsilis, P. (2010). From digital to ubiquitous cities: Defining a common architecture for urban development. In *2010 Sixth International Conference on Intelligent Environments* (pp. 301-306). 10.1109/IE.2010.61

Archenaa, J., & Anita, E. A. M. 2015. A Survey of Big Data Analytics in Healthcare and Government. *2nd International Symposium on Big data and Cloud Computing (ISBCC' 15)*, 408–413. 10.1016/j.procs.2015.04.021

Aristovnik, A. (2012). *The impact of ICT on educational performance and its efficiency in selected EU and OECD countries: a non-parametric analysis*. Available at SSRN: https://ssrn.com/abstract=2187482

Askarany, D., & Smith, M. (2008). Diffusion of innovation and business size: A longitudinal study of PACIA. *Managerial Auditing Journal, 23*(9), 900–916. doi:10.1108/02686900810908445

Athey, S., & Roberts, J. (2001). Organizational design: Decision rights and incentive contracts. *Organizational Economics, 91*, 200–205.

Atici, K. B., & Podinovski, V. V. (2015). Using data envelopment analysis for the assessment of technical efficiency of units with different specialisations: An application to agriculture. *Omega, 54*, 72–83. doi:10.1016/j.omega.2015.01.015

Auffray, C., Balling, R., Barroso, I., Bencze, L., Benson, M., Bergeron, J., Bernal-Delgado, E., Blomberg, N., Bock, C., Conesa, A., Del Signore, S., Delogne, C., Devilee, P., Di Meglio, A., Eijkemans, M., Flicek, P., Graf, N., Grimm, V., Guchelaar, H.-J., ... Zanetti, G. (2016). Making sense of big data in health research: Towards an EU action plan. *Genome Medicine, 8*(1), 71. doi:10.118613073-016-0323-y PMID:27338147

Aurigi, A. (2016). *Making the digital city: the early shaping of urban internet space*. Routledge. doi:10.4324/9781315249964

Avkiran, N. K. (2001). Investigating technical and scale efficiencies of Australian universities through data envelopment analysis. *Socio-Economic Planning Sciences, 35*(1), 57–80. doi:10.1016/S0038-0121(00)00010-0

Baines, A., & Langfield-Smith, K. (2003). Antecedents to management accounting change: A structural equation approach. *Accounting, Organizations and Society, 28*(7-8), 675–698. doi:10.1016/S0361-3682(02)00102-2

Baiocchi, G., Graizbord, D., & Rodríguez-Muñiz, M. (2013). Actor-Network Theory and the ethnographic imagination: An exercise in translation. *Qualitative Sociology, 36*(4), 323–341. doi:10.100711133-013-9261-9

Bakar, N. A. (2014). An Assessment Model for Government Enterprise Architecture Establishment Phase. *Journal of Computational and Theoretical Nanoscience, 20*(10), 1987–1991.

Bakar, N. A. A., Harihodin, S., & Kama, N. (2016). Assessment of enterprise architecture implementation capability and priority in public sector agency. *Procedia Computer Science, 100*, 198–206. doi:10.1016/j.procs.2016.09.141

Banker, R. D. (1984). Estimating most productive scale size using data envelopment analysis. *European Journal of Operational Research*, *17*(1), 35–44. doi:10.1016/0377-2217(84)90006-7

Banker, R. D., Charnes, A., & Cooper, W. W. (1984). Some models for estimating technical and scale inefficiencies in data envelopment analysis. *Management Science*, *30*(9), 1078–1092. doi:10.1287/mnsc.30.9.1078

Banker, R. D., Cooper, W. W., Seiford, L. M., Thrall, R. M., & Zhu, J. (2004). Returns to scale in different DEA models. *European Journal of Operational Research*, *154*(2), 345–362. doi:10.1016/S0377-2217(03)00174-7

Bankole Dr, F., & Mimbi, L. (2017). ICT Infrastructure and It's Impact on National Development: A Research Direction for Africa. *The African Journal of Information Systems*, *9*(2), 1.

Bankole, F. O., Osei-Bryson, K. M., & Brown, I. (2011c). ICT infrastructure utilization in Africa: Data envelopment analysis-based exploration. *Proceeding of special interest group on ICT and global development at Americas Conference on Information System (AMCIS) Workshop.*

Bankole, F. O. (2015). ICT Infrastructure and Its' Impact on National Development: A Research Direction for Africa Using Analytics. *Proceedings of SIG GlobDev 2015 Pre-ECIS Workshop.*

Bankole, F. O., Brown, I., & Osei-Bryson, K. M. (2011b). The Impact of ICT Infrastructure on Human Development: An Analysis of ICT-Use in SADC Countries. *Proceedings of the 11th International Conference on Social Implications of Computers in Developing Countries.*

Bankole, F. O., Osei-Bryson, K. M., & Brown, I. (2011d). Exploring the Impacts of ICT Investments on Dimensions of Human Development in Different Contexts: A Regression Splines Analysis. *Proceedings of SIG GlobDev Fourth Annual Workshop*, 158.

Bankole, F. O., Osei-Bryson, K. M., & Brown, I. (2013). The impact of ICT investments on human development: A regression splines analysis. *Journal of Global Information Technology Management*, *16*(2), 59–85. doi:10.1080/1097198X.2013.10845636

Bankole, F. O., Osei-Bryson, K. M., & Brown, I. (2015). The impact of information and communications technology infrastructure and complementary factors on Intra-African Trade. *Information Technology for Development*, *21*(1), 12–28. doi:10.1080/02681102.2013.832128

Bankole, F. O., Shirazi, F., & Brown, I. (2011a). Investigating the impact of ICT investments on human development. *The Electronic Journal on Information Systems in Developing Countries*, *48*(1), 1–19. doi:10.1002/j.1681-4835.2011.tb00344.x

Batarseh, F. A., Yang, R., & Deng, L. (2017). A comprehensive model for management and validation of federal big data analytical systems. *Big Data Analytics*, *2*(1), 2. doi:10.118641044-016-0017-x

Becker, C., Antunes, G., Barateiro, J., Vieira, R., & Borbinha, J. (2011). Modeling Digital Preservation Capabilities in Enterprise Architecture. In *Proceedings of the 12th Annual International Digital Government Research Conference: Digital Government Innovation in Challenging Times*, (pp. 84-93). ACM. 10.1145/2037556.2037570

Berger, R. (2015). Now I see it, now I don't: Researcher's position and reflexivity in qualitative research. *Qualitative Research, 15*(2), 219–234. doi:10.1177/1468794112468475

Bessent, A. M., & Bessent, E. W. (1980). Determining the comparative efficiency of schools through data envelopment analysis. *Educational Administration Quarterly, 16*(2), 57–75. doi:10.1177/0013161X8001600207

Bessent, A. M., Bessent, E. W., Charnes, A., Cooper, W. W., & Thorogood, N. C. (1983). Evaluation of educational program proposals by means of DEA. *Educational Administration Quarterly, 19*(2), 82–107. doi:10.1177/0013161X83019002006

Bessent, A., Bessent, W., Kennington, J., & Reagan, B. (1982). An application of mathematical programming to assess productivity in the Houston independent school district. *Management Science, 28*(12), 1355–1367. doi:10.1287/mnsc.28.12.1355

Bhatt, G. D., Gupta, J. N. D., & Kitchens, F. (2005). An exploratory study of groupware use in the knowledge management process. *Journal of Enterprise Information Management, 8*(1), 28–46. doi:10.1108/17410390510571475

Bisbe, J., & Malagueño, R. (2009). The choice of interactive control systems under different innovation management modes. *European Accounting Review, 18*(2), 371–405. doi:10.1080/09638180902863803

Bishop, M. (2009). *CHAOS Report: Worst Project Failure Rate in a Decade*. Standish Group.

Boban, M., & Weber, M. (2018). Internet of Things, legal and regulatory framework in digital transformation from smart to intelligent cities. *2018 41st International Convention on Information and Communication Technology, Electronics and Microelectronics (MIPRO)*, 1359-1364

Bock, A. J., Opsahl, T., George, G., & Gann, D. M. (2012). The effects of culture and structure on strategic flexibility during business model innovation. *Journal of Management Studies, 49*(2), 279–305. doi:10.1111/j.1467-6486.2011.01030.x

Bolívar, M. (2016). Mapping Dimensions of Governance in Smart Cities. Practitioners versus Prior Research. In *Proceedings of the 17th International Digital Government Research Conference on Digital Government Research* (pp. 1-13). Shanghai, China: Academic Press. 10.1145/2912160.2912176

Bouwens, J., & Abernethy, M. A. (2000). The consequences of customization on management accounting systems design. *Accounting, Organizations and Society, 25*(3), 221–241. doi:10.1016/S0361-3682(99)00043-4

Bradley, S., Johnes, G., & Millington, J. (2001). The effect of competition on the efficiency of secondary schools in England. *European Journal of Operational Research, 135*(3), 545–568. doi:10.1016/S0377-2217(00)00328-3

Bradshaw, C., Atkinson, S., & Doody, O. (2017). Employing a qualitative description approach in health care research. *Global Qualitative Nursing Research, 4*, 2333393617742282. doi:10.1177/2333393617742282 PMID:29204457

Brown, W. C. (2006). IT governance, architectural competency, and the Vasa. *Journal of Information Management and Computer Security*, *14*(2), 140–154. doi:10.1108/09685220610655889

Bruce, C. (1994). Research student's early experiences of the dissertation literature review. *Studies in Higher Education, 19*(2), 217-229.

Bryman, A., & Bell, E. (2015). *Business research methods*. Oxford University Press.

BSI. (2015). *Architectural framework for the Internet of Things, for Smart Cities*. BSI.

Buckle, S., Matthes, F., Monahov, I., Roth, S., Schulz, C., & Schweda, C. M. (2011). Towards an agile design of the enterprise architecture management function. In Enterprise Distributed Object Computing Conference Workshops (EDOCW), 2011 15th IEEE International (pp. 322-329). IEEE. doi:10.1109/EDOCW.2011.33

Bucy, M. (2006). Encouraging Critical Thinking Through Expert Panel. *College Teaching, 54*(2), 222–224. doi:10.3200/CTCH.54.2.222-224

Bui, Q. N., Markus, M., & Newell, S. (2015). *Alternative Designs in Widespread Innovation Adoption: Empirical Evidence from Enterprise Architecture Implementation in US State Governments*. Academic Press.

Bui, Q., & Levy, M. (2017). Institutionalization of Contested Practices: A Case of Enterprise Architecture Implementation in a US State Government. *Proceedings of the 50th Hawaii International Conference on System Sciences.* 10.24251/HICSS.2017.591

Bumblauskas, D., Nold, H., Bumblauskas, P., & Igou, A. (2017). Big data analytics: Transforming data to action. *Business Process Management Journal, 23*(3), 703–720. doi:10.1108/BPMJ-03-2016-0056

Byrne, M. (2001). Hermeneutics as a methodology for textual analysis. *AORN Journal, 73*(5), 968–968. doi:10.1016/S0001-2092(06)61749-3 PMID:11378953

Cabrera, A., Abad, M., Jaramillo, D., Gómez, J., & Verdum, J. C. (2016). Definition and implementation of the enterprise business layer through a business reference model, using the architecture development method ADM-TOGAF. In *Trends and Applications in Software Engineering* (pp. 111–121). Springer. doi:10.1007/978-3-319-26285-7_10

Cadez, S., & Guilding, C. (2008). An exploratory investigation of an integrated contingency model of strategic management accounting. *Accounting, Organizations and Society, 33*(7-8), 836–863. doi:10.1016/j.aos.2008.01.003

Callon, M. (1986). Some elements of a sociology of translation: domestication of the scallops and the fishermen of St Brieuc Bay. In J. Law (Ed.), *Power, Action & Belief: A New Sociology of Knowledge?* (pp. 196–229). Routledge & Kegan Paul.

Cameron, B. H., & McMillan, E. (2013). Analyzing the current trends in enterprise architecture frameworks. *Journal of Enterprise Architecture*, *9*(1), 60–71.

Cao, L. (2017). Data Science: A Comprehensive Overview. *ACM Computing Surveys*, *50*(3), 1–42. doi:10.1145/3076253

Capecchi, V., Buscema, M., Contucci, P., & D'Amore, D. (2010). *Applications of Mathematics in Models, Artificial Neural Networks and Arts: Mathematics and Society.* Springer Science & Business Media. doi:10.1007/978-90-481-8581-8

Capgemini. (2009). *Business transformation: From crisis response to radical changes that will create tomorrow's business.* A Capgemini Consulting Survey.

Cearley, D., Walker, M., & Burke, B. (2016). *Top 10 Strategic Technology Trends for 2017.* Gartner, ID: G00317560. https://www.gartner.com/doc/3471559?plc=ddp

Cervone, H. F. (2016). Organisational considerations initiating a big data and analytics implementation. *Digital Library Perspectives*, *32*(3), 137–141. doi:10.1108/DLP-05-2016-0013

Chalmeta, R., & Pazos, V. (2015). A step-by-step methodology for enterprise interoperability projects. *Enterprise Information Systems*, *9*(4), 436–464. doi:10.1080/17517575.2013.879212

Charnes, A., Cooper, W. W., & Rhodes, E. (1978). Measuring the efficiency of decision making units. *European Journal of Operational Research*, *2*(6), 429–444. doi:10.1016/0377-2217(78)90138-8

Charnes, A., Cooper, W. W., & Rhodes, E. (1981). Evaluating program and managerial efficiency: An application of data envelopment analysis to program follow through. *Management Science*, *27*(6), 668–697. doi:10.1287/mnsc.27.6.668

Chen, D. Q., Preston, D. S., & Swink, M. (2005). How the use of big data analytics affects value creation in supply chain management. *Journal of Management Information Systems*, *32*(4), 4–39. doi:10.1080/07421222.2015.1138364

Cheng, S., Zhang, Q., & Qin, Q. (2016). Big data analytics with swarm intelligence. *Industrial Management & Data Systems*, *116*(4), 646–666. doi:10.1108/IMDS-06-2015-0222

Chenhall, R. H. (2008). Accounting for the horizontal organisation: A review essay. *Accounting, Organizations and Society*, *33*(4-5), 517–550. doi:10.1016/j.aos.2007.07.004

Chenhall, R. H., & Langfield-Smith, K. (1998). Adoption and benefits of management accounting practices: An Australian study. *Management Accounting Research*, *9*(1), 1–19. doi:10.1006/mare.1997.0060

Chen, W., & Hirschheim, R. (2004). A paradigmatic and methodological examination of information systems research from 1991 to 2001. *Information Systems Journal*, *14*(3), 197–235. doi:10.1111/j.1365-2575.2004.00173.x

Chiaroni, D., Chiesa, V., & Frattini, F. (2011). The open innovation journey: How firms dynamically implement the emerging innovation management paradigm. *Technovation*, *31*(1), 34–43. doi:10.1016/j.technovation.2009.08.007

Choe, J. (2004). The relationships among management accounting information, organizational learning and production performance. *The Journal of Strategic Information Systems*, *13*(1), 61–85. doi:10.1016/j.jsis.2004.01.001

Clarke, J., Waring, J., & Timmons, S. (2018). The challange of inclusive co-production: The importance of situated rituals and emotional inclusivity in the coproduction of health research projects. *Social Policy and Administration*, *53*(1), 233–248.

Clark, M., Fletcher, P., Hanson, J., & Irani, R. (2013). *Web Services Business Strategies and Architectures*. Apress.

Clements, B. (2002). How efficient is education spending in Europe? *European Review of Economics and Finance*, *1*, 3–26.

Comuzzi, M., & Patel, A. (2016). How organisations leverage big data: A maturity model. *Industrial Management & Data Systems*, *116*(8), 1468–1492. doi:10.1108/IMDS-12-2015-0495

Connolley, A., Scholtz, B., & Calitz, A. (2013). Achieving the Benefits of Business-IT Alignment Supported by Enterprise Architecture. *Presentado en 7th International Business Conference*.

Cook, W. D., & Seiford, L. M. (2009). Data envelopment analysis (DEA)–Thirty years on. *European Journal of Operational Research*, *192*(1), 1–17. doi:10.1016/j.ejor.2008.01.032

Cook, W. D., Tone, K., & Zhu, J. (2014). Data envelopment analysis: Prior to choosing a model. *Omega*, *44*, 1–4. doi:10.1016/j.omega.2013.09.004

Cooper, R., & Slagmulder, R. (2003). Strategic cost management: Expanding scope and boundaries. *Cost and Management*, *17*(1), 23–30.

Cooper, W. W., Seiford, L. M., & Tone, K. (2006). *Introduction to data envelopmentanalysis and its uses*. Springer.

Cooper, W. W., Seiford, L. M., & Tone, K. (2007). *Data Envelopment Analysis: A Comprehensive Text with Models*. Applications, References and DEA-Solver Software.

Cressman, D. (2009). *A brief overview of actor-network theory: Punctualization, heterogeneous engineering & translation*. Academic Press.

Creswell, J. W. (2013). *Research design: Qualitative, quantitative, and mixed methods approaches*. Sage Publications.

Creswell, J. W., & Poth, C. N. (2017). *Qualitative inquiry and research design: Choosing among five approaches*. Sage publications, Inc.

Crossman, Y. P. (1985). The Nature of Management Accounting. *The Accounting Review*, *33*(2), 222–227.

Crowe, S., Cresswell, K., Robertson, A., Huby, G., Avery, A., & Sheikh, A. (2011). The case study approach. *BMC Medical Research Methodology*, *11*(100), 2–9. PMID:21707982

Daellenbach, H., McNickle, D., & Dye, Sh. (2012). *Management Science - Decision-making through systems thinking* (2nd ed.). Palgrave Macmillan.

Daiser, P., Ysa, T., & Schmitt, D. (2017). Corporate governance of state-owned enterprises: A systematic analysis of empirical literature. *International Journal of Public Sector Management*, *30*(5), 447–466. doi:10.1108/IJPSM-10-2016-0163

Damanpour, F. (1987). The adoption of technological, administrative, and ancillary innovations: Impact of organizational factors. *Journal of Management*, *13*(4), 675–688. doi:10.1177/014920638701300408

Damanpour, F. (1991). Organisational innovation: A metaanalysis of effects of determinants and moderators. *Academy of Management Journal*, *34*, 555–590.

Damanpour, F., & Evan, W. (1984). Organizational innovation and performance: The problem of "Organizational Lag". *Administrative Science Quarterly*, *29*(3), 392–409. doi:10.2307/2393031

Dameri, R., & Ricciardi, F. (2015). Smart city intellectual capital: An emerging view of territorial systems innovation management. *Journal of Intellectual Capital*, *16*(4), 860–887. doi:10.1108/JIC-02-2015-0018

Dang, D. D., & Pekkola, S. (2017). Systematic Literature Review on Enterprise Architecture in the Public Sector. *Electronic. Journal of E-Government*, *15*(2), 130–154.

De Villiers, C., Dumay, J., & Maroun, W. (2019). Qualitative accounting research: Dispelling myths and developing a new research agenda. *Accounting and Finance*, *59*(3), 1459–1487. doi:10.1111/acfi.12487

Della Croce, F., & T'kindt, V. (2002). A Recovering Beam Search algorithm for the one-machine dynamic total completion time scheduling problem. *The Journal of the Operational Research Society*, *53*(11), 1275–1280. doi:10.1057/palgrave.jors.2601389

Denzin, N. K., & Lincoln, Y. S. (2011). *The SAGE Handbook of Qualitative Research 4*. Sage Publications.

Dery, K., Hall, R., Wailes, N., & Wiblen, S. (2013). Lost in translation? An actor-network approach to HRIS implementation. *The Journal of Strategic Information Systems*, *22*(3), 225–237. doi:10.1016/j.jsis.2013.03.002

Desai, M. (1991). Human development. *European Economic Review*, *35*(2-3), 350–357. doi:10.1016/0014-2921(91)90136-7 PMID:1717401

Desmond, C. (2013). Management of change. *IEEE Engineering Management Review, 41*(3).

Díaz Andrade, A., & Urquhart, C. (2010). The affordances of actor network theory in ICT for development research. *Information Technology & People*, *23*(4), 352–374. doi:10.1108/09593841011087806

Dixon, R. (1998). Accounting for strategic management: A practical application. *Long Range Planning, 31*(2), 272–279. doi:10.1016/S0024-6301(98)00011-9

Du Preez, J., Van der Merwe, A., & Matthee, M. (2018). Understanding Enterprise Architects: Different Enterprise Architect Behavioral Styles. *International Conference on Research and Practical Issues of Enterprise Information Systems*, 96-108. 10.1007/978-3-319-99040-8_8

Duh, R. R., Xiao, J. Z., & Chow, C. W. (2009). Chinese firms' use of management accounting and controls: Facilitators, impediments, and performance effects. *Journal of International Accounting Research, 8*(1), 1–30. doi:10.2308/jiar.2009.8.1.1

Dunk, A. S. (2011). Product innovation, budgetary control, and the financial performance of firms. *The British Accounting Review, 43*(2), 102–111. doi:10.1016/j.bar.2011.02.004

Dwiartama, A., & Rosin, C. (2014). Exploring agency beyond humans: The compatibility of Actor-Network Theory (ANT) and resilience thinking. *Ecology and Society, 19*(3), 28–38. doi:10.5751/ES-06805-190328

Dwyfor Evans, A., Green, C. J., & Murinde, V. (2002). Human capital and financial development in economic growth: New evidence using the translog production function. *International Journal of Finance & Economics, 7*(2), 123–140. doi:10.1002/ijfe.182

Easterbrook, S., Singer, J., Storey, M., & Damian, D. (2008). *Guide to Advanced Empirical Software Engineering-Selecting Empirical Methods for Software Engineering Research* (F. Shull, Ed.). Springer.

El-Mashaleh, M. S., Hyari, K. H., Bdour, A. N., & Rababeh, S. M. (2016). A multi-attribute decision-making model for construction enterprise resource planning system selection. *International Journal of Construction Education and Research, 12*(1), 66–79. doi:10.1080/15578771.2015.1015755

Erp, W., Roozen, F., & Vosselman, E. (2019). The performativity of a management accounting and control system: Exploring the dynamic relational consequences of a design. *Scandinavian Journal of Management, 35*(4). Advance online publication. doi:10.1016/j.scaman.2019.101077

European Union (2014). Regulation (EU) No 910/2014 of the European Par lament and of the Council - on electronic identification and trust services for electronic transactions in the internal market and repealing Directive 1999/93/EC The European Par lament and of the Council – Regulation. European Union.

Fabry, N., & Blanchet, C. (2019). Monaco's struggle to become a. *Internationa Journal of Tourism Cities, 0*(0), 1–13.

Färe, R. S., Grosskopf, S., & Lovell, C. A. K. (1994). *Production Frontiers*. Cambridge University Press.

Färe, R., Grosskopf, S., Forsund, F. R., Hayes, K., & Heshmati, A. (2006). Measurement of productivity and quality in non-marketable services: With application to schools. *Quality Assurance in Education, 14*(1), 21–36. doi:10.1108/09684880610643593

Farwick, M., Breu, R., Hauder, M., Roth, S., & Matthes, F. (2013). Enterprise architecture documentation: Empirical analysis of information sources for automation. In *System Sciences (HICSS), 2013 46th Hawaii International Conference on* (pp. 3868-3877). IEEE.

Farwick, M., Schweda, C. M., Breu, R., & Hanschke, I. (2016). A situational method for semi-automated Enterprise Architecture Documentation. *Software & Systems Modeling, 15*(2), 397–426. doi:10.100710270-014-0407-3

Fasanghari, M., Amalnick, M. S., Anvari, R. T., & Razmi, J. (2015). A novel credibility-based group decision making method for Enterprise Architecture scenario analysis using Data Envelopment Analysis. *Applied Soft Computing, 32*, 347–368. doi:10.1016/j.asoc.2015.03.052

Fazlollahi, A., & Franke, U. (2018). Measuring the impact of enterprise integration on firm performance using data envelopment analysis. *International Journal of Production Economics, 200*, 119–129. doi:10.1016/j.ijpe.2018.02.011

Felfel, H., Ayadi, O., & Masmoudi, F. (2017). Pareto Optimal Solution Selection for a Multi-Site Supply Chain Planning Problem Using the VIKOR and TOPSIS Methods. *International Journal of Service Science, Management, Engineering, and Technology*. Doi:10.4018/IJSSMET.2017070102

Ferrari, B. & Parker, B. (2006), Digging for innovation, *Supply Chain Management Review*, 48-53.

Ferreira, A., Moulang, C., & Hendro, B. (2010). Environmental management accounting and innovation: An exploratory analysis. *Accounting, Auditing & Accountability Journal, 23*(7), 920–948. doi:10.1108/09513571011080180

Fleck, K., Smythe, E. A., & Hitchen, J. M. (2011). Hermeneutics of self as a research approach. *International Journal of Qualitative Methods, 10*(1), 14–29. doi:10.1177/160940691101000102

Fodeh, S., & Zeng, Q. (2016). Mining Big Data in biomedicine and health care. *Journal of Biomedical Informatics, 63*, 400–403. doi:10.1016/j.jbi.2016.09.014 PMID:27670091

Folinas, D. (2007). A conceptual framework for business intelligence based on activities monitoring systems. *Int. J. Intelligent Enterprise, 1*(1), 65. doi:10.1504/IJIE.2007.013811

Folwer, J., Horan, P., & Cope, C. (2007). How an "Imperative" IS Development was Saved from a Failing Course of Action – A Case Study. *Information and Beyond: Part I: Issues in Informing Science and Information Technology, 4*, 95–406.

Fox, J. (2002). Structural equation models. *Appendix to an R and S-PLUS Companion to Applied Regression*.

Fu, Zh., & Mittnight, E. (2015). Critical Success Factors for Continually Monitoring, Evaluating and Assessing Management of Enterprise IT. *ICSACA*. https://www.isaca.org/COBIT/focus/Pages/critical-success-factors-for-continually-monitoring-evaluating-and-assessing-management-of-enterprise-it.aspx

Gad, C., & Bruun Jensen, C. (2010). On the consequences of post-ANT. *Science, Technology & Human Values, 35*(1), 55–80. doi:10.1177/0162243908329567

Gandomi, A., & Haider, M. (2015). Beyond the hype: Big data concepts, methods, and analytics. *International Journal of Information Management*, *35*(2), 137–144. doi:10.1016/j.ijinfomgt.2014.10.007

Gardner, H. (1999). *Intelligence Reframed: Multiple Intelligences for the 21st Century*. Basic Books.

Garicano, L., & Wu, Y. (2012). Knowledge, communication, and organizational capabilities. *Organization Science*, *23*(5), 1382–1397. doi:10.1287/orsc.1110.0723

Garlasu, D., Sandulescu, V., Halcu, I., Neculoiu, G., Grigoriu, O., Marinescu, M., & Marinescu, V. (2013, January). A big data implementation based on Grid computing. *2013 11th RoEduNet International Conference*, 1-4.

Gartner, Inc. (2013a). *Gartner Says Smart Organizations Will embrace Fact and Frequent Project Failure in Their Quest for Agility*. Retrieved from https://www.gartner.com/newsroom/id/2477816

Gartner, Inc. (2013b). *Scenario Toolkit: Using EA to Support Business Transformation. ID:G00246943*. Gartner, Inc.

Ghasemi, M. R., Ignatius, J., & Rezaee, B. (2018). Improving discriminating power in data envelopment models based on deviation variables framework. *European Journal of Operational Research*.

Giachetti, R. E. (2016). *Design of enterprise systems: Theory, architecture, and methods*. CRC Press. doi:10.1201/9781439882894

Giddens, A. (1984). *The Constitution of Society: Outline of the Theory of Structuration*. John Polity Press.

Goksoy, A., Ozsoy, B., & Vayvay, O. (2012). Business process reengineering: Strategic tool for managing organizational change an application in a multinational company. *International Journal of Business and Management*, *7*(2), 89–112. doi:10.5539/ijbm.v7n2p89

Golany, B., & Roll, Y. (1989). An application procedure for DEA. *Omega*, *17*(3), 237–250. doi:10.1016/0305-0483(89)90029-7

Gopalakrishnan, S., & Damanpour, F. (1997). 'A Review of innovation research in economics, sociology and technology management', *Omega. International Journal of Management Sciences*, *25*(1), 15–28.

Greenhalgh, T., & Stones, R. (2010). Theorising big IT programmes in healthcare: Strong structuration theory meets actor-network theory. *Social Science & Medicine*, *70*(9), 1285–1294. doi:10.1016/j.socscimed.2009.12.034 PMID:20185218

Green, J., & Thorogood, N. (2018). *Qualitative methods for health research*. Sage.

Gromoff, A., Bilinkis, Y., & Kazantsev, N. (2017). Business architecture flexibility as a result of knowledge-intensive process management. *Global Journal of Flexible Systems Managment*, *18*(1), 73–86. doi:10.100740171-016-0150-4

Grosskopf, S., & Moutray, C. (2001). Evaluating performance in Chicago public highschools in the wake of decentralization. *Economics of Education Review*, *20*(1), 1–14. doi:10.1016/S0272-7757(99)00065-5

Gudnason, G. & Scherer, R. (2012). *eWork and eBusiness in Architecture, Engineering and Construction: ECPPM 2012*. CRC Press.

Gülbahar, Y. (2008). ICT usage in higher education: A case study on preservice teachers and instructors. *The Turkish Online Journal of Educational Technology*, *7*(1), 32–37.

Gunasekare, U. (2015). *Mixed Research Method as the Third Research Paradigm: A Literature Review*. University of Kelaniya.

Gupta, S., & Verhoeven, M. (2001). The efficiency of government expenditure: Experiences from Africa. *Journal of Policy Modeling*, *23*(4), 433–467. doi:10.1016/S0161-8938(00)00036-3

Habib, A., Alsmadi, D., & Prybutok, V. (2019). Factors that determine residents' acceptance of smart city technologies. *Behaviour & Information Technology*, 1–14. doi:10.1080/0144929X.2019.1693629

Hadaya, P., & Gagnon, B. (2017). *Business Architecture: The Missing Link in Strategy Formulation, Implementation and Execution*. ASATE Publishing.

Hafner, M., & Winter, R. (2008). Processes for Enterprise Application Architecture Management. In *Hawaii International Conference on System Sciences, Proceedings of the 41st Annual* (pp. 396-396). IEEE.

Halme, J. (2020). Constructing consensus and conflicts. *Qualitative Market Research*, *ahead-of-print*. Advance online publication. doi:10.1108/QMR-12-2017-0172

Hardy, K., & Maurushat, A. (2017). Opening up government data for Big Data analysis and public benefit. *Computer Law & Security Review*, *33*(1), 30–37. doi:10.1016/j.clsr.2016.11.003

Harris, K., Grey, M. C., & Rozwell, C. (2001). *Changing the View of ROI to VOI—Value on Investment*. Gartner Research Note, SPA-14-7250.

Harrison, H., Birks, M., Franklin, R., & Mills, J. (2017). Case study research: Foundations and methodological orientations. In *Forum Qualitative Sozialforschung/Forum: Qualitative. Social Research*, *18*(1).

Hedayati, A., Shirazi, B., & Fazlollahtabar, H. (2014). An Assessment Model for the State of Organizational Readiness Inservice Oriented architecture Implementation Based on Fuzzy Logic. *Computer Science and Information Technology*, *2*(1), 1–9.

Hess, T., Matt, C., Benlian, A., & Wiesböck, F. (2016). Options for formulating a digital transformation strategy. *MIS Quarterly Executive*, *15*(2), 123–139.

Hinostroza, J. E. (2018). New Challenges for ICT in Education Policies in Developing Countries: The Need to Account for the Widespread Use of ICT for Teaching and Learning Outside the School. In *ICT-Supported Innovations in Small Countries and Developing Regions* (pp. 99–119). Springer. doi:10.1007/978-3-319-67657-9_5

Hjort-Madsen, K., & Pries-Heje, J. (2009, January). Enterprise architecture in government: Fad or future? In *System Sciences, 2009. HICSS'09. 42nd Hawaii International Conference on* (pp. 1-10). IEEE.

Hoadjli, A., & Rezeg, K. (2019). A scalable mobile context-aware recommender system for a smart city administration. *International Journal of Parallel, Emergent and Distributed Systems*, 1-20.

Hoe, S. L. (2008). Issues and procedures in adopting structural equation modeling technique. *Journal of Applied Quantitative Methods*, *3*(1), 76–83.

Hohmann, L. (2003). *Beyond software architecture: creating and sustaining winning solutions.* Addison-Wesley Longman Publishing Co., Inc.

Hull, C. E., & Rothenberg, S. (2008). Firm performance: The interactions of corporate social performance with innovation and industry differentiation. *Strategic Management Journal*, *29*(7), 781–789. doi:10.1002mj.675

Hussein, S. S., Mahrin, M. N. R., & Maarop, N. (2017). Preliminary study of Malaysian Public Sector (MPS) transformation readiness through Enterprise Architecture (EA) establishment. *Pacific Asia Conference on Information Systems (PACIS)*.

Hyett, N., Kenny, A., & Dickson-Swift, V. (2014). Methodology or method? A critical review of qualitative case study reports. *International Journal of Qualitative Studies on Health and Well-being*, *9*(1), 23606. doi:10.3402/qhw.v9.23606 PMID:24809980

ISO/IEC/IEEE. (2011). *Systems and software engineering – Architecture description*. ISO/IEC/IEEE 42010:2011(E), (Dec 2011), 1-46.

IT Governance Institute. (2007). *Unlocking Value: An Executive Primer on the Critical Role of IT Governance*. Information Systems Audit and Control Association. Retrieved from http://www.itgi.org

Iyamu, T. (2019). What are the implications of theorising the enterprise architecture? *Journal of Enterprise Transformation,* 1-22.

Iyamu, T. (2019). What are the implications of theorizing the enterprise architecture? *Journal of Enterprise Transformation*, 1-22.

Iyamu, T. (2011). Institutionalisation of the enterprise architecture: The actor-network perspective. *International Journal of Actor-Network Theory and Technological Innovation*, *3*(1), 27–38. doi:10.4018/jantti.2011010103

Iyamu, T. (2012). A framework for developing and implementing the enterprise technical architecture. *Computer Science and Information Systems*, 9(1), 189–206. doi:10.2298/CSIS101103040I

Iyamu, T. (2014). *Information Technology Enterprise Architecture: From Concept to Practice*. Heidelberg Press.

Iyamu, T. (2015). *Enterprise Architecture from Concept to Practice*. Heidelberg press.

Iyamu, T. (2015). *Enterprise Architecture: from concept to Practise* (2nd ed.). Heidelberg Press.

Iyamu, T. (2017). Understanding the complexities of enterprise architecture through structuration theory. *Journal of Computer Information Systems*. Advance online publication. doi:10.1080/08874417.2017.1354341

Iyamu, T. (2018). A multilevel approach to big data analysis using analytic tools and actor network theory. *South African Journal of Information Management*, 20(1), a914. doi:10.4102ajim.v20i1.914

Iyamu, T. (2018). Implementation of the enterprise architecture through the Zachman Framework. *Journal of Systems and Information Technology*, 20(1), 2–18. doi:10.1108/JSIT-06-2017-0047

Iyamu, T., & Mgudlwa, S. (2018). Transformation of healthcare big data through the lens of actor network theory. *International Journal of Healthcare Management*, 11(3), 182–192. doi:10.1080/20479700.2017.1397340

Iyamu, T., Nehemia-Maletzky, M., & Shaanika, I. (2016). The overlapping nature of Business Analysis and Business Architecture: What we need to know. *Electronic Journal of Information Systems Evaluation*, 19(3), 169–179.

Iyamu, T., & Roode, D. (2010). The Use of Structuration Theory and Actor Network Theory for Analysis: A case study of a financial institution in South Africa. *International Journal of Actor-Network Theory and Technological Innovation*, 2(1), 1–26. doi:10.4018/jantti.2010071601

Jahani, B., Javadein, S. R. S., & Jafari, H. A. (2010). Measurement of enterprise architecture readiness within organizations. *Business Strategy Series*, 11(3), 177–191. doi:10.1108/17515631011043840

James, D., Grinter, H., & Grinter, R. (1999). Splitting the Organization and Integrating the Code: Conway's Law Revisited. Bell Laboratories, Lucent Technologies. *Proceedings, International Conference on Software Engineering*, 85-95.

Jaszkiewicz, A., & Sowiñski, R. (1999). The 'Light Beam Search' approach - an overview of methodology and applications. *European Journal of Operational Research*, 113(2), 300–314. doi:10.1016/S0377-2217(98)00218-5

Jensen, M. B., Johnson, B., Lorenz, E., & Lundvall, B. A. (2007). Forms of knowledge and modes of innovation. *Research Policy*, 36(5), 680–693. doi:10.1016/j.respol.2007.01.006

Johnson, P., Buehring, A., Cassel, C., & Symon, G. (2007). Defining qualitative management research: An empirical investigation. *Qualitative Research in Organisations and Management: An International Journal, 2*(1), 23–42. doi:10.1108/17465640710749108

Johnson, P., Ekstedt, M., & Lagerstrom, R. (2016). Automatic Probabilistic Enterprise IT Architecture Modeling: A Dynamic Bayesian Networks Approach. In *Enterprise Distributed Object Computing Workshop (EDOCW), 2016 IEEE 20th International* (pp. 1–8). IEEE. 10.1109/EDOCW.2016.7584351

Johnston, M.P. (2017). Secondary data analysis: A method of which the time has come. *Qualitative and Quantitative Methods in Libraries, 3*(3), 619-626.

Johnstone, L. (2020). A systematic analysis of environmental management systems in SMEs: Possible research directions from a management accounting and control stance. *Journal of Cleaner Production, 244*, 118802. Advance online publication. doi:10.1016/j.jclepro.2019.118802

Jonkers, H., Band, I., & Quartel, D. (2012a). *ArchiSurance Case Study*. The Open Group.

Joseph, Ch. (2014). *Types of eCommerce Business Models*. https://smallbusiness.chron.com/types-ecommerce-business-models-2447.html

Joseph, R. C., & Johnson, N. A. (2013). Big data and transformational government. *IT Professional, 15*(6), 43–48. doi:10.1109/MITP.2013.61

Josey, A. (2016). *TOGAF® Version 9.1-A Pocket Guide*. Van Haren.

Kache, F., & Seuring, S. (2017). Challenges and opportunities of digital information at the intersection of Big Data Analytics and supply chain management. *International Journal of Operations & Production Management, 37*(1), 10–36. doi:10.1108/IJOPM-02-2015-0078

Kane, G. (2019). The Technology Fallacy. *Research Technology Management, 62*(6), 44–49. doi:10.1080/08956308.2019.1661079

Kangelani, P., & Iyamu, T. (2020, April). A Model for Evaluating Big Data Analytics Tools for Organisation Purposes. In *Conference on e-Business, e-Services and e-Society* (pp. 493- 504). Springer.

Kankanhalli, A., Hahn, J., Tan, S., & Gao, G. (2016). Big data and analytics in healthcare: Introduction to the special section. *Information Systems Frontiers, 18*(2), 233–235. doi:10.100710796-016-9641-2

Kanyane, M. H., & Sausi, K. (2015). Reviewing state-owned entities' governance landscape in South Africa. *African Journal of Business Ethics, 9*(1). Advance online publication. doi:10.15249/9-1-81

Karney, J. (2009). *Introduction to business architecture*. Cengage Learning.

Katuu, S. (2018). The Utility of Enterprise Architecture to Records and Archives Specialists. *2018 IEEE International Conference on Big Data (Big Data)*, 2702-2710.

Kaur, M. J., & Mishra, V. P. (2018, November). Analysis of Big Data Cloud Computing Environment on Healthcare Organisations by implementing Hadoop Clusters. In *2018 Fifth HCT Information Technology Trends (ITT)* (pp. 87-90). IEEE.

Kaushik, A., & Raman, A. (2015). The new data-driven enterprise architecture for e-healthcare: Lessons fromt he Indian public sector. *Government Information Quarterly, 32*(1), 63–74. doi:10.1016/j.giq.2014.11.002

Kayisire, D., & Wei, J. (2016). Information Technology for Development ICT Adoption and Usage in Africa. *Towards an Efficiency Assessment, 1102.* Advance online publication. doi:10. 1080/02681102.2015.1081862

Khan, N., Yaqoob, I., Hashem, I. A. T., Inayat, Z., Ali, M., Kamaleldin, W., Alam, M., Shiraz, M., & Gani, A. (2014). Big data: Survey, technologies, opportunities, and challenges. *TheScientificWorldJournal, 2014,* 2014. doi:10.1155/2014/712826 PMID:25136682

Kim, G. H., Trimi, S., & Chung, J. H. (2014). Big-data applications in the government sector. *Communications of the ACM, 57*(3), 78–85. doi:10.1145/2500873

Kim, K., & Kim, K. (1999). Routing straddle carriers for the loading operation of containers using a beam search algorithm. Elsevier. *Computers & Industrial Engineering, 36*(1), 109–136. doi:10.1016/S0360-8352(99)00005-4

Kitsios, F., & Kamariotou, M. (2019). Business strategy modelling based on enterprise architecture: A state of the art review. *Business Process Management Journal, 25*(4), 606–624. doi:10.1108/BPMJ-05-2017-0122

Klein, J., & Gagliardi, M. (2010). *A Workshop on Analysis and Evaluation of Enterprise Architectures.* Retrieved from http://www.sei.cmu.edu

Klomp, L., & Van Leeuwen, G. (2001). Linking innovation and firm performance: A new approach. *International Journal of the Economics of Business, 8*(3), 343–364. doi:10.1080/13571510110079612

Know Your Local Authority Report. (2015). Retrieved from http://www.windhoekcc.org.na/

Kornbluh, M. (2015). Combatting Challenges to Establishing Trustworthiness in Qualitative Research. *Qualitative Research in Psychology, 12*(4), 397–414. doi:10.1080/14780887.2015.1021941

Kornilova, I. (2017). DevOps is a culture, not a role! *Medium.* https://medium.com/@neonrocket/devops-is-a-culture-not-a-role-be1bed149b0

Kowalski, P. Büge, M., Sztajerowska, M. & Egeland, M. 2013. State-Owned Enterprises: Trade Effects and Policy Implications. *OECD Trade Policy Papers, 147.*

KPMG. (2014). *Over 90 Percent Of U.S. Companies Are Changing Existing Business Models: KPMG Survey*. http://www.kpmg.com/us/en/issuesandinsights/articlespublications/press-releases/pages/over-90-percent-of-us-companies-are-changing-existing-business-models-kpmg-survey.aspx. 2014.

Kudryavtsev, D. V., Zaramenskikh, E. P., & Arzumanyan, M. Y. (2017). Development of enterprise architecture management methodology for teaching purposes. *Open Education, 4*(4), 84–92. doi:10.21686/1818-4243-2017-4-84-92

Kumar, R. (2011). *Research methodology: A step-by-step guide for beginners*. Sage Publications Limited.

Kvale, S., & Brinkmann, S. (2009). *Interviews: Learning the Craft of Qualitative Research Interviewing*. Sage Publications.

Lagerstrom, R., Sommestad, T., Buschle, M., & Ekstedt, M. (2011). Enterprise architecture management's impact on information technology success. In *System Sciences (HICSS), 2011 44th Hawaii International Conference on* (pp. 1-10). IEEE.

Lakhrouit, J., Benhaddi, M., & Baïna, K. (2015). Enterprise architecture approach for agility evaluation. In *International Conference on Cloud Technologies and Applications (CloudTech)* (pp. 1-6). Marrakech, Morocco: Academic Press.

Lanubile, F., Ebert, Ch., Prikladnicki, R., & Vizcaíno, A. (2010). Collaboration Tools for Global Software Engineering. *IEEE Journals & Magazines, 27*(2).

Lapalme, J., Gerber, A., Van der Merwe, A., Zachman, J., De Vries, M., & Hinkelmann, K. (2016). Exploring the future of enterpirese architecure: A Zachman perspecive. *Computers in Industry, 79*, 103–113. doi:10.1016/j.compind.2015.06.010

Lebreton, P. (1957). The Case Study Method and the Establishment of Standads of efficiency. Academy of Management Proceedings, 103.

Lee, Y.-J., Kwon, Y.-I., Shin, S., & Kim, E.-J. (2013). Advancing government-wide Enterprise Architecture-A meta-model approach. In *Advanced Communication Technology (ICACT), 2013 15th International Conference on* (pp. 886–892). IEEE.

Lee, A. S., & Baskerville, R. L. (2003). Generalizing generalizability in information systems research. *Information Systems Research, 14*(3), 221–243. doi:10.1287/isre.14.3.221.16560

Lee, C. H., & Yoon, H. J. (2017). Medical big data: Promise and challenges. *Kidney Research and Clinical Practice, 36*(1), 3–11. doi:10.23876/j.krcp.2017.36.1.3 PMID:28392994

Lee, H., Kweon, E., Kim, M., & Chai, S. (2017). Does Implementation of Big Data Analytics Improve Firms' Market Value? Investors' Reaction in Stock Market. *Sustainability, 9*(6), 978. doi:10.3390u9060978

Lee, J., Min, J., & Lee, H. (2016). The effect of organizational structure on open innovation: A quadratic equation. *Procedia Computer Science, 91*, 492–501. doi:10.1016/j.procs.2016.07.128

Letaifa, B. (2015). How to strategize smart cities: Revealing the SMART model. *Journal of Business Research, 68*(7), 1414–1419. doi:10.1016/j.jbusres.2015.01.024

Lim, C., Kim, K. J., & Maglio, P. P. (2018). Smart cities with big data: Reference models, challenges, and considerations. *Cities (London, England), 82*, 82. doi:10.1016/j.cities.2018.04.011

Liu, J. S., Lu, L. Y., Lu, W. M., & Lin, B. J. (2013a). Data envelopment analysis 1978–2010: A citation-based literature survey. *Omega, 41*(1), 3–15. doi:10.1016/j.omega.2010.12.006

Liu, J. S., Lu, L. Y., Lu, W. M., & Lin, B. J. (2013b). A survey of DEA applications. *Omega, 41*(5), 893–902. doi:10.1016/j.omega.2012.11.004

Liu, X., & Zhang, C. (2016). Corporate governance, social responsibility information disclosure, and enterprise value in China. *Journal of Cleaner Production*, 1–10.

Lnenicka, M., & Komarkova, J. (2019). Developing a government enterprise architecture framework to support the requirements of big and open linked data with the use of cloud computing. *International Journal of Information Management, 46*, 124–141. doi:10.1016/j.ijinfomgt.2018.12.003

Löhe, J., & Legner, C. (2014). Overcoming implementation challenges in enterprise architecture management: A design theory for architecture-driven IT Management (ADRIMA). *Information Systems and e-Business Management, 12*(1), 101–137. doi:10.100710257-012-0211-y

Mačák, K. (2016). *Is the International Law of Cyber Security in Crisis? Law School-University of Exeter*. In 8th International Conference on Cyber Conflict. NATO CCD COE Publications.

Mairesse, J., & Mohnen, P. (2002). Accounting for innovation and measuring innovativeness: An illustrative framework and an application. *The Economics of Technology and Innovation, 92*(2), 226–230. doi:10.1257/000282802320189302

Makarchenko, M., Nerkararian, S., & Shmeleva, S. (2016). How Traditional Banks Should Work in Smart City. *Communications in Computer and Information Science*. 10.1007/978-3-319-49700-6_13

Maletič, M., Maletič, D., Dahlgaard, J. J., Dahlgaard-Park, S. M., & Gomišček, B. (2014). Sustainability exploration and sustainability exploitation: From a literature review towards a conceptual framework. *Journal of Cleaner Production, 79*, 182–194. doi:10.1016/j.jclepro.2014.05.045

Markides, C. (2011, March). Crossing the Chasm: How to Convert Relevant Research Into Managerially Useful Research. *The Journal of Applied Behavioral Science, 47*(1), 121–134. doi:10.1177/0021886310388162

Markides, C. C. (2015). Research on Business Models: Challenges and Opportunities. *Advances in Strategic Management, 33*, 133–147. doi:10.1108/S0742-332220150000033004

Marks, E. A. (2008). *Service-oriented architecture governance for the services driven enterprise*. John Wiley & Sons.

Mårten, S., Lagerström, R., & Johnson, P. (2008). A Bayesian network for IT governance performance prediction. In *Proceedings of the 10th International Conference on Electronic Commerce*. ACM.

Matt, C., Hess, T., & Benlian, A. (2015). Digital transformation strategies. *Business & Information Systems Engineering, 57*, 339–343.

Maxwell, J. A. (2013). *Qualitative Research Design: An Interactive Approach*. Sage Publications.

McAfee, A., Brynjolfsson, E., Davenport, T. H., Patil, D. J., & Barton, D. (2012). Big Data: The management revolution. *Harvard Business Review, 90*(10), 60–68. PMID:23074865

McMullen, P. R., & Tarasewich, P. (2005). A beam search heuristic method for mixed-model scheduling with setups. *International Journal of Production Economics, 96*(2), 273–283. doi:10.1016/j.ijpe.2003.12.010

Mehta, N., & Pandit, A. (2018). Concurrence of big data analytics and healthcare: A systematic review. *International Journal of Medical Informatics, 114*, 57–65. doi:10.1016/j.ijmedinf.2018.03.013 PMID:29673604

Meijer, A., & Bolivar, M. (2016). Governing the smart city: A review of the literature on smart urban governance. *International Review of Administrative Sciences, 82*(2), 392–408. doi:10.1177/0020852314564308

Melendez-Torres, G. J., O'Mara-Eves, A., Thomas, J., Brunton, G., Caird, J., & Petticrew, M. (2017). Interpretive analysis of 85 systematic reviews suggests that narrative syntheses and meta-analyses are incommensurate in argumentation. *Research Synthesis Methods, 8*(1), 109–118. doi:10.1002/jrsm.1231 PMID:27860329

Meroño-Cerdan, A., Soto-Acosta, P., & Lopez-Nicolas, C. (2008). Analyzing collaborative technologies' effect on performance through intranet use orientations. *Journal of Enterprise Information Management, 21*(1), 39–51. doi:10.1108/17410390810842246

Michelucci, F. V., De Marco, A., & Tanda, A. (2016). Defining the role of the Smart-City manager: An analysis of responsibilities and skills. *Journal of Urban Technology, 23*(3), 23–42. doi:10.1 080/10630732.2016.1164439

MID. (2014). *ArchiMate-Enterprise Architecture Modeling with ArchiMate*. MID GmbH.

MID. (2014). *Enterprise Architecture Modeling with ArchiMate*. MID GmbH.

Minoli, D. (2008). *Enterprise architecture A to Z: frameworks, business process modeling, SOA, and infrastructure technology*. Auerbach Publications. doi:10.1201/9781420013702

Miori, V., & Russo, D. (2014). Domotic Evolution towards the IoT. *IEEE 28th International Conference on Advanced Information Networking and Applications Workshops*. DOI: 10.1109/WAINA.2014.128

Mohamed, M. A., Galal-Edeen, G. H., Hassan, H. A., & Hasanien, E. E. (2012). An evaluation of enterprise architecture frameworks for e-government. In *Computer Engineering & Systems (ICCES), 2012 Seventh International Conference on* (pp. 255–260). IEEE 10.1109/ICCES.2012.6408524

Mohammed, E. A., Far, B. H., & Naugler, C. (2014). Applications of the MapReduce programming framework to clinical big data analysis: Current landscape and future trends. *BioData Mining, 7*(1), 22. doi:10.1186/1756-0381-7-22 PMID:25383096

Mohanty, S., Jagadeesh, M., & Srivatsa, H. (2013). *Big data imperatives: Enterprise 'Big Data' warehouse, 'BI' implementations and analytics*. Apress. doi:10.1007/978-1-4302-4873-6

Mol, A. (2010). Actor-network theory: Sensitive terms and enduring tensions. *Kölner Zeitschrift für Soziologie und Sozialpsychologie. Sonderheft, 50*, 253–269.

Moser, A., & Korstjens, I. (2018). Series: Practical guidance to qualitative research. Part 3: Sampling, data collection and analysis. *The European Journal of General Practice, 24*(1), 9–18. doi:10.1080/13814788.2017.1375091 PMID:29199486

Mousavi-Nasab, S. H., & Sotoudeh-Anvari, A. (2017). A comprehensive MCDM-based approach using TOPSIS, COPRAS and DEA as an auxiliary tool for material selection problems. *Materials & Design, 121*, 237–253. doi:10.1016/j.matdes.2017.02.041

Muladi, N., & Surendro, K. (2014). The Readiness Self-Assessment Model for Green IT Implementation in Organisations. *International Conference of Advanced Informatics: Concept, Theory and Application*, 146-151.

Müller, M., & Schurr, C. (2016). Assemblage thinking and actor-network theory: Conjunctions, disjunctions, cross-fertilisations. *Transactions of the Institute of British Geographers, 41*(3), 217–229. doi:10.1111/tran.12117

Murphy, Ch. (2019). *How do tangible and intangible assets differ?* Investopedia.

Myers, M., & Avison, D. (2002). An introduction to qualitative research in information systems. In Qualitative research in information systems, Introducing Qualitative Methods. SAGE Publications, Ltd. doi:10.4135/9781849209687.n1

Myers, B., Pane, J., & Ko, A. (2004). *Natural programming languages and environments*. ACM New York. doi:10.1145/1015864.1015888

Myers, M. (2013). *Qualitative research in business and management* (2nd ed.). Sage.

Myers, M. D. (2009). *Qualitative Research in Business & Management*. Sage Publications.

Nahapiet, J., & Ghoshal, S. (1998). Social capital, intellectual capital, and the organizational advantage. *Academy of Management Review, 23*(2), 242–266. doi:10.5465/amr.1998.533225

Nam, K., Oh, S. W., Kim, S. K., Goo, J., & Khan, S. (2016). Dynamics of Enterprise Architecture in the Korean Public Sector: Transformational Change vs. Transactional Change. *Sustainability, 8*(11), 1074. doi:10.3390u8111074

Nedelcu, B. (2013). About big data and its challenges and benefits in manufacturing. *Database System Journal*, *4*(3), 10–19.

Negara, J. G. P., & Emanuel, A. W. R. (2020, May). Enterprise Architecture Design Strategies for UGK Using TOGAF ADM. In *1st Borobudur International Symposium on Humanities, Economics and Social Sciences (BIS-HESS 2019)* (pp. 491-495). Atlantis Press. 10.2991/assehr.k.200529.103

Neumann, G. (2002). Programming Languages in Artificial Intelligence. In Encyclopaedia of Information Systems. Academic Press.

Neville, C. (2007). *Introduction to research and research methods*. Bradford: Effective learning service.

Niemann, M., Eckert, J., Repp, N., & Steinmetz, R. (2008). Towards a Generic Governance Model for Service-oriented Architectures. AMCIS 2008 Proceedings, 361.

Niemann, K. D. (2006). *From Enterprise Architecture to IT Governance—Elements of Effective IT Management*. Vieweg.

Nogueira, J., Romero, D., Espadas, J., & Molina, A. (2013). Leveraging the Zachman framework implementation using action – research methodology – a case study: Aligning the enterprise architecture and the business goals. *Journal of Enterprise Information Systems*, *7*(1), 100–132. doi:10.1080/17517575.2012.678387

Noor, K. B. M. (2008) Case Study: A Strategic Research Methodology. *American Journal of Applied Sciences*, *5*(11), 1602–1604. doi:10.3844/ajassp.2008.1602.1604

O'Donnell, S. (2016). *Digital skills: unlocking the information society*. Academic Press.

O'Regan, N., Sims, M. A., & Gallear, D. (2008). Leaders, loungers, laggards: The strategic-planning-environment performance relationship re-visited in manufacturing SMEs. *Journal of Manufacturing Technology Management*, *19*(1), 6–21. doi:10.1108/17410380810843426

Oguntimilehin, A., & Ademola, E. O. (2014). A review of big data management benefits and challenges. *A Review of Big Data Management. Benefits and Challenges*, *5*(6), 1–7.

Olsen, D. H., & Trelsgård, K. (2016). Enterprise Architecture Adoption Challenges: An exploratory Case Study of the Norwegian Higher Education Sector. *Procedia Computer Science*, *100*, 804–811. doi:10.1016/j.procs.2016.09.228

Orbicom. (2005) *From The Digital Divide To Digital Opportunities: Measuring Infostates for Development*. Montreal: Claude-Yves Charron.

Österle, H. (1995). Business Engineering: Prozess- und Systementwicklung. Band 1: Entwurfstechniken. Springer.

Oxford Dictionaries. (2013). *Heuristics*. http://www.oxforddictionaries.com/definition/english/heuristic

Oyerinde, Y., & Bankole, F. (2018). Influence of Constant Returns to Scale and Variable Returns to Scale Data Envelopment Analysis Models in ICT Infrastructure Efficiency Utilization. *Proceedings of the 11th Annual Pre-ICIS SIG GlobDev Workshop.*

Oyerinde, O. D. (2014). A Review of Challenges Militating Against Successful E-Learning and M-Learning Implementations in Developing Countries. *International Journal of Science and Advanced Technology, 4*(6).

Oyerinde, Y., & Bankole, F. (2019a). Measuring Efficiency and Productivity of ICT Infrastructure Utilization. *Proceedings of the 24th UK Academy for Information Systems International Conference.*

Oyerinde, Y., & Bankole, F. (2019b). Investigating the Efficiency of ICT Infrastructure Utilization: A Data Envelopment Analysis Approach. In P. Nielsen & H. Kimaro (Eds.), *Information and Communication Technologies for Development. Strengthening Southern-Driven Cooperation as a Catalyst for ICT4D* (Vol. 551). Springer. doi:10.1007/978-3-030-18400-1_52

Palermo, J., Bogard, J., Hexter, E., Hinze, M., & Skinner, M. (2012). ASP.NET Model View Control 4. In *Action*. Manning Publisher.

Pandit, V. (2012). *Challenges in business and IT alignment: Business and IT consulting project report.* https://www.slideshare.net/panditvidur/challenges-in-business-and-it-alignment

Park, K., Nguyen, M. C., & Won, H. (2015, July). Web-based collaborative big data analytics on big data as a service platform. *2015 17th International Conference on Advanced Communication Technology (ICACT)*, 564-567.

Paul, A., & Paul, V. (2012). The e-Government interoperability through Enterprise Architecture in Indian perspective. In *World Congress on Information and Communication Technologies* (pp. 646-650). IEEE. 10.1109/WICT.2012.6409155

Pavlatos, O., & Kostakis, H. (2015). Management accounting practices before and during economic crisis: Evidence from Greece. *Advances in Accounting, incorporating. Advances in International Accounting, 31*(1), 150–164. doi:10.1016/j.adiac.2015.03.016

Pavlatos, O., & Kostakis, H. (2018). Management accounting innovations in a time of economic crisis. *Journal of Economic Asymmetries, 18*(3), e00106. Advance online publication. doi:10.1016/j.jeca.2018.e00106

Pendleton, W., Crush, J., & Nickanor, N. (2014). Migrant Windhoek: Rural–Urban Migration and Food Security in Namibia. *Urban Forum, 25*(2), 191-205.

Peterson, S. (2011). *Why it Worked: Critical Success Factors of a Financial Reform Project in Africa.* Faculty Research Working Paper Series. Harvard Kennedy School.

Plessius, H., van Steenbergen, M., Slot, R., & Versendaal, J. (2018). *The Enterprise Architecture Value Framework.* ECIS.

Podinovski, V. V., Ismail, I., Bouzdine-Chameeva, T., & Zhang, W. (2014). Combining the assumptions of variable and constant returns to scale in the efficiency evaluation of secondary schools. *European Journal of Operational Research*, *239*(2), 504–513. doi:10.1016/j.ejor.2014.05.016

Podinovski, V. V., & Thanassoulis, E. (2007). Improving discrimination in data envelopment analysis: Some practical suggestions. *Journal of Productivity Analysis*, *28*(1-2), 117–126. doi:10.100711123-007-0042-x

Pokushko, M., Stupina, A., Medina-Bulo, I., Dresvianskii, E., & Karaseva, M. (2019). Application of data envelopment analysis method for assessment of performance of enterprises in fuel and energy complex. *Journal of Physics: Conference Series*, *1353*(1), 012140. doi:10.1088/1742-6596/1353/1/012140

Pollack, J., Costello, K., & Sankaran, S. (2013). Applying Actor–Network Theory as a sensemaking framework for complex organisational change programs. *International Journal of Project Management*, *31*(8), 1118–1128. doi:10.1016/j.ijproman.2012.12.007

Portela, M. C. S., Camanho, A. S., & Borges, D. (2012). Performance assessment of secondary schools: The snapshot of a country taken by DEA. *The Journal of the Operational Research Society*, *63*(8), 1098–1115. doi:10.1057/jors.2011.114

Putri, N., & Yusof, S. M. (2009). Critical success factors for implementing quality engineering tools and techniques in Malaysian's and Indonesian's automotive industries: An Exploratory Study. *Journal Proceedings of the International MultiConference of Engineers and Computer Scientists.*, *2*, 18–20.

Qureshi, S. (2005). How does Information Technology effect Development? Integrating Theory and Practice into a Process Model. AMCIS 2005 Proceedings, 261.

Qu, S., & Dumay, J. (2011). The Qualitative Research Interview. *Qualitative Research in Accounting & Management*, *8*(3), 238–264. doi:10.1108/11766091111162070

Rabinet, S. E. (2011). How I Learned to Design and Conduct Semi-Structured Interviews: An Ongoing and Continuous Journey. *Qualitative Report*, *16*(2), 563–566.

Radeke, F. (2011). Toward Understanding Enterprise Architecture Management's Role in Strategic Change: Antecedents, Processes, Outcomes. *Wirtschaftsinformatik*, *16*(18), 1–11.

Raghupathi, W., & Raghupathi, V. (2014). Big data analytics in healthcare: Promise and potential. *Health Information Science and Systems*, *2*(1), 3. doi:10.1186/2047-2501-2-3 PMID:25825667

Ramada, P. (2013). *How much did allegedly rigged interest rate (Libor) cost?* Academic Press.

Ravanetti, A. (2016). Switzerland Bank on Fintech with Lighter Regulations. *Crowd Valey*. https://news.crowdvalley.com/news/switzerland-bank-on-fintech-with-lighter-regulations

Ridge, M., Johnston, K. A., & O'Donovan, B. (2015). The use of big data analytics in the retail industries in South Africa. *African Journal of Business Management, 9*(19), 688–703. doi:10.5897/AJBM2015.7827

Rodrigues, L. S., & Amaral, L. (2010). Issues in enterprise architecture value. *Journal of Enterprise Architecture, 6*(4), 27–32.

Rogers, E. M. (1995). *Diffusion of Innovation* (4th ed.). Free Press.

Ronald, D. (1961). Management Information Crisis. Harvard Business Review, 39(5), 111-121.

Ross, J. W., Weill, P., & Robertson, D. C. (2006). *Enterprise Architecture As Strategy: Creating A Foundation For Business Executives.* Harvard Business School Press.

Ross, J., Weill, P., & Robertson, D. (2006). *Enterprise architecture as a strategy: Creating a foundation for business execution.* Havard Business Press.

Roth, S., Hauder, M., Farwick, M., Breu, R., & Matthes, F. (2013). Enterprise Architecture Documentation: Current Practices and Future Directions. In Wirtschaftsinformatik (p. 58). Academic Press.

Rouhani, B. D., Mahrin, M. N., Nikpay, F., & Nikfard, P. (2013). A comparison enterprise architecture implementation methodologies. In *Informatics and Creative Multimedia (ICICM), 2013 International Conference on* (pp. 1-6). IEEE. 10.1109/ICICM.2013.9

Rouhani, B. D., Mahrin, M. N. R., Shirazi, H., Nikpay, F., & Rouhani, B. D. (2015). An Effectiveness Model for Enterprise Architecture Methodologies. *International Journal of Enterprise Information Systems, 11*(2), 50–64. doi:10.4018/IJEIS.2015040103

Rouse, W. B., & Serban, N. (2014). *Understanding and managing the complexity of healthcare.* MIT Press.

Rumsfeld, J. S., Joynt, K. E., & Maddox, T. M. (2016). Big data analytics to improve cardiovascular care: Promise and challenges. *Nature Reviews. Cardiology, 13*(6), 350–359. doi:10.1038/nrcardio.2016.42 PMID:27009423

Russell, R. D., & Russell, C. J. (1992). An examination of the effects of organizational norms, organizational structure and environmental uncertainty on entrepreneurial strategy. *Journal of Management, 18*(4), 639–656. doi:10.1177/014920639201800403

Safari, H., Faraji, Z., & Majidian, S. (2016). Identifying and evaluating enterprise architecture risks using FMEA and fuzzy VIKOR. *Journal of Intelligent Manufacturing, 27*(2), 475–486. doi:10.100710845-014-0880-0

Samoilenko, S. V., & Osei-Bryson, K. M. (2017). Creating Theoretical Research Frameworks Using Multiple Methods. *Insight.*

Sandkuhl, K., Seigerroth, U., & Kaidalova, J. (2017). Towards Integration Methods of Product-IT into Enterprise Architectures. In *Enterprise Distributed Object Computing Workshop (EDOCW), 2017 IEEE 21st International*. IEEE. 10.1109/EDOCW.2017.13

Sankaralingam, K., Ferris, M., Nowatzki, T., Estan, C., Wood, D., & Vaish, N. (2013). *Optimization and Mathematical Modeling in Computer Architecture*. Morgan & Claypool Publishers.

Schekkerman, J. (2004), How to Survive in the Jungle of Enterprise Arhitecture Frameworks: Creating or Choosing an Enterprise Architecture Framework (2nd ed.). Trafford.

Schleicher, J., Vögler, M., Inzinger, C., & Dustdar, S. (2015). Towards the Internet of Cities: A Research Roadmap for Next-Generation Smart Cities. In *Proceedings of the ACM First International Workshop on Understanding the City with Urban Informatics* (pp. 1-4). Melbourne, Australia: ACM. 10.1145/2811271.2811274

Seiford, L. M., & Zhu, J. (1997). An investigation of returns to scale in data envelopment analysis. *Omega*, *27*(1), 1–11. doi:10.1016/S0305-0483(98)00025-5

Seppänen, V. (2014). From problems to critical success factors of enterprise architecture adoption. *Jyväskylä studies in computing; 1456-5390; 201*.

Shaanika, I., & Iyamu, T. (2015). Deployment of enterprise architecture in the Namibian government. The use of activity theory to examine the influencing factors. *The Electronic Journal on Information Systems in Developing Countries*, *71*(1), 1–21. doi:10.1002/j.1681-4835.2015.tb00515.x

Shaanika, I., & Iyamu, T. (2018). Developing the enterprise architecture for the Namibian government. *The Electronic Journal on Information Systems in Developing Countries*, *84*(3), 1–11. doi:10.1002/isd2.12028

Shimamoto, D. (2013). CPA firm technology: Eight keys to success; these steps will increase the odds of effective implementation and deployment. CPA/CITP, CGMA. E.D.G.E.-Sharpening the Next Generation of CPAs Conference, Austin, TX.

Shim, Y., & Shin, D. H. (2016). Analyzing China's fintech industry from the perspective of actor–nctwork theory. *Telecommunications Policy*, *40*(2), 168–181. doi:10.1016/j.telpol.2015.11.005

Siddiquee, N. A., & Siddiquee, N. A. (2016). E-government and transformation of service delivery in developing countries: The Bangladesh experience and lessons. *Transforming Government: People. Process and Policy*, *10*(3), 368–390.

Silvius, A. G. (2009). Business and IT Alignment. *International conference on information management and engineering (ICIME '09)*.

Simonsson, M., & Johnson, P. (2006). Assessment of IT Governance - A Prioritization of Cobit. In *Proceedings of the Conference on Systems Engineering Research*, (pp. 1-10). Studentlitteratur.

Smith, J. A. (Ed.). (2015). *Qualitative psychology: A practical guide to research methods*. Sage.

Smith, M., Abdullah, Z., & Abdul-Razak, R. (2008). The diffusion of technological and management accounting. innovation: Malaysian evidence. *Asian Review of Accounting*, *16*(3), 197–218. doi:10.1108/13217340810906672

Soft Expert. (2018). *Enterprise Asset Management*. https://www.softexpert.com/solucao/enterprise-asset-management-eam/

Song, H., & Song, Y.-T. (2010). Enterprise Architecture Institutionalization and Assessment. In *2010 IEEE/ACIS 9th International Conference on Computer and Information Science* (pp. 18-20). Yamagata, Japan: IEEE.

Soobaroyen, T., & Poorundersing, B. (2008). The effectiveness of management accounting systems; evidence from functional managers in a developing country. *Managerial Auditing Journal*, *23*(2), 187–219. doi:10.1108/02686900810839866

Soto-Acosta, P., Colomo-Palacios, R., & Popa, S. (2014). Web knowledge sharing and its effect on innovation:an empirical investigation in SMEs. *Knowledge Management Research and Practice*, *12*(1), 103–113. doi:10.1057/kmrp.2013.31

Spencer, L. (1955). 10 problems that worry presidents. Harvard Business Review, 33(6), 75-83.

St Aubyn, M. (2002). Evaluating efficiency in the Portuguese health and education sectors. *Economia, 26.* Available at SSRN: https://ssrn.com/abstract=504942

Staessens, M., Kerstens, P. J., Bruneel, J., & Cherchye, L. (2019). Data envelopment analysis and social enterprises: Analysing performance, strategic orientation, and mission drift. *Journal of Business Ethics*, *159*(2), 325–341. doi:10.100710551-018-4046-4

Stanforth, C. (2006). Using actor-network theory to analyse e-government implementation in developing countries. *Information Technologies and International Development*, *3*(3), 35–60. doi:10.1162/itid.2007.3.3.35

Steinbart, P., & Romney, M. B. (2017). Accounting Information Systems (14th ed.). Pearson.

Stergiou, Ch., & Siganos, D. (2015). *Neural Networks*. https://www.doc.ic.ac.uk/~nd/surprise_96/journal/vol4/cs11/report.html

STS. (2018). Enterprise asset management. *STS*. http://www.stsolutions-global.com/enterprise-asset-management.html

Stupples, B., Sazonov, A., & Woolley, S. (2019). UBS Whistle-Blower Hunts Trillions Hidden in Treasure Isles. *Bloomberg*. https://www.bloomberg.com/news/articles/2019-07-26/ubs-whistle-blower-hunts-trillions-hidden-in-treasure-islands

Sullivan, H. (2016). Interpretivism and Public Policy Research. Interpreting Governance High Politics and Public Policy, 184-204.

Suominen, V. & Tuomi, P. (2015). Literacies, hermeneutics, and literature. *Library Trends, 63*(3), 615-628.

Supriadi, H., Kom, M., & Amalia, E. (2019). University's Enterprise Architecture Design Using Enterprise Architecture Planning (EAP) Based on the Zachman's Framework Approach. *International Journal of Higher Education*, 8(3), 13–28. doi:10.5430/ijhe.v8n3p13

Suryani, E., Chou, S. Y., Hartono, R., & Chen, C. H. (2010). Demand scenario analysis and planned capacity expansion: A system dynamics framework. *Simulation Modelling Practice and Theory*, 18(6), 732–751. doi:10.1016/j.simpat.2010.01.013

Tagliabuejune, J. (1986). The Swiss stop keeping secrets. *The New York Times*. https://www.nytimes.com/1986/06/01/business/the-swiss-stop-keeping-secrets.html

Taleb, M., & Cherkaoui, O. (2012, January). Pattern-Oriented Approach for Enterprise Architecture: TOGAF Framework. *Journal of Software Engineering & Applications*, 5(1), 45–50. doi:10.4236/jsea.2012.51008

Taleb, N. (2012). *Antifragile: things that gain from disorder. Library of congress cataloguing-in-publication data*. Academic Press.

Tamm, T., Seddon, P. B., Shanks, G. G., & Reynolds, P. (2011). How does enterprise architecture add value to organisations? CAIS, 28, 10.

Tamm, T., Seddon, P. B., Shanks, G., & Reynolds, P. (2011). How does enterprise architecture add value to organisations? *Communications of the Association for Information Systems*, 28(1), 10.

Tanaka, S., de Barros, R., & Mendes, L. (2018). A proposal to a framework for governance of ICT aiming at smart cities with a focus on enterprise architeccture. In *SBSI'18: XIV Brazilian Symposium on Information Systems* (pp. 1-8). Caxias do Sul, Brazil: ACM.

Tatnall, A. (2005). Actor-network theory in information systems research. In *Encyclopaedia of Information Science and Technology* (1st ed., pp. 42–46). IGI Global. doi:10.4018/978-1-59140-553-5.ch009

Tetnowski, J. (2015). Qualitative case study research design. *Perspectives on Fluency and Fluency Disorders*, 25(1), 39–45. doi:10.1044/ffd25.1.39

Thanassoulis, E., Portela, M. C., & Despic, O. (2008). Data envelopment analysis: the mathematical programming approach to efficiency analysis. *The measurement of productive efficiency and productivity growth*, 251-420.

Thanassoulis, E., Kortelainen, M., Johnes, G., & Johnes, J. (2011). Costs and efficiency of higher education institutions in England: A DEA analysis. *The Journal of the Operational Research Society*, 62(7), 1282–1297. doi:10.1057/jors.2010.68

Thapa, D. (2011). The role of ICT actors and networks in development: The case study of a wireless project in Nepal. *The Electronic Journal on Information Systems in Developing Countries*, 49(1), 1–16. doi:10.1002/j.1681-4835.2011.tb00345.x

The Open Group. (2002). *Mapping the TOGAF ADM to the Zachman Framework*. https://www.opengroup.org/architecture/0210can/togaf8/doc-review/togaf8cr/c/p4/zf/zf_mapping.htm

The Open Group. (2011a). Architecture Development Method. *The Open Group*. https://pubs.opengroup.org/architecture/togaf9-doc/arch/chap05.html

The Open Group. (2011a). *The Open Group's Architecture Framework*. www.open-group.com/togaf

Thomas, A. (2015). *Innovation Insight for Microservices*. https://www.gartner.com/doc/3157319/innovation-insight-microservices

Thomas, A., & Gartner, A. (2015). *Innovation Insight for Microservices*. https://www.gartner.com/doc/3157319/innovation-insight-microservices

Thomas, A. (2012). Governance at South African state-owned enterprises: What do annual reports and the print media tell us? *Social Responsibility Journal*, 8(4), 448–470. doi:10.1108/17471111211272057

Tidd, J. (2006). *From Knowledge Management to Strategic Competence* (2nd ed.). Imperial College. doi:10.1142/p439

Tidd, J., & Bessant, J. (2009). *Managing Innovation, Integrating Technological, Market and Organizational Change* (4th ed.). Wiley.

Tidd, J., & Bessant, J. (2018). *Managing Innovation: Integrating Technological, Market and Organizational Change* (6th ed.). Wiley. USA.

Tiwar, P., Ilavarasan, P., & Punia, S. (2019). Content analysis of literature on big data in smart cities. *Benchmarking, ahead-of-print*, 1–21. doi:10.1108/BIJ-12-2018-0442

Tondeur, J., van Braak, J., & Valcke, M. (2007). Towards a typology of computer use in primary education. *Journal of Computer Assisted Learning*, 23(3), 197–206. doi:10.1111/j.1365-2729.2006.00205.x

Trad, A. (2018c). The Transformation Framework's Resources Library. IBICSTM.

Trad, A., & Kalpić, D. (2016a). *A Transformation Framework Proposal for Managers in Business Innovation and Business Transformation Projects - The role of transformation managers in organisational engineering*. Chinese American Scholars Association Conference E-Leader.

Trad, A., & Kalpić, D. (2016b). The Business Transformation Framework and its Business Engineering Law support for Cybertransactions. In Encyclopedia of E-Commerce Development, Implementation, and Management. IGI-Global.

Trad, A., & Kalpić, D. (2018a). Business Transformation Projects-An Enterprise Architecture Applied Mathematical Model / The Basics. *IEEE, CPS, Conference on Applied Mathematics & Computer Science. IEEE, International Conference on Applied Mathematics and Computer Science.*

Trad, A., & Kalpić, D. (2018b). *Business Transformation Projects An Enterprise Architecture Applied Mathematical Model's-The Proof of Concept*. ICAMCS Conference. 10.1109/ICAMCS46079.2018.00015

Trad, A., & Kalpić, D. (2019g). The Business Transformation Framework and the-Application of a Holistic Strategic Security Concept. E-leaders, Check Rep. GCASA.

Trad, A., & Kalpić, D. (2019g). The Business Transformation Framework and the-Application of a Holistic Strategic Security Concept. E-Leaders, Check Rep. GCASA.

Trad, A. (2015a). *A Transformation Framework Proposal for Managers in Business Innovation and Business Transformation Projects-Intelligent atomic building block architecture.* Centeris. doi:10.1016/j.procs.2015.08.483

Trad, A. (2015b). *A Transformation Framework Proposal for Managers in Business Innovation and Business Transformation Projects-An information system's atomic architecture vision.* Centeris.

Trad, A. (2018a). *The Business Transformation Framework's Resources Library. Internal project.* IBISTM.

Trad, A. (2018b). *The Transformation Framework Proof of Concept. Internal project and paper.* IBISTM.

Trad, A. (2018d). *The Transformation Framework Proof of Concept.* IBICSTM.

Trad, A. (2019a). *Applied Mathematical Model for Business Transformation Projects-The intelligent Strategic Decision Making System (iSDMS). Encyclopaedia.* IGI-Global.

Trad, A. (2019b). *An Applied Mathematical Model for Business Transformation and Enterprise Architecture-The Holistic Organisational Intelligence and Knowledge Management Pattern's Integration (HOI&KMPI). International Journal of Organisational and Collective Intelligence.*

Trad, A. (2019c). *Using Google analytics to determine the leading business transformation framework that are based on enterprise architecture.* IBISTM.

Trad, A. (2020b). *The Business Transformation Enterprise Architecture Framework as an Applied Mathematical Model: intelligent Atomic Service based Decision Making Systems (iASbDMS).* IGI Global.

Trad, A. (2020c). *The Business Transformation Enterprise Architecture Framework as an Applied Mathematical Model: intelligent Strategic Atomic Service Development (iSASDev).* IGI Global.

Trad, A. (2020d). *The Business Transformation and Enterprise Architecture Framework as an Applied Mathematical Model-The Financial Risk Management with a Strategic Vision (FRMSV).* IGI Global.

Trad, A. (2020e). *Business Transformation and Enterprise Architecture –The Holistic Project Asset Management Concept (HPAMC).* IGI Global.

Trad, A., & Kalpić, D. (2014b). *The Selection and Training Framework (STF) for Managers in intelligent city Innovation Transformation Projects - Managerial Recommendations.* IEEE.

Trad, A., & Kalpić, D. (2014d). *The Selection and Training Framework (STF) for Managers in Business Innovation and Transformation Projects - The Profile of a Business Transformation Manager*. IMRA.

Trad, A., & Kalpić, D. (2016a). *The intelligent city Transformation Framework for Business (and Financial) Architecture-Modelling Projects. In Encyclopaedia of E-Commerce Development, Implementation, and Management*. IGI-Global.

Trad, A., & Kalpić, D. (2016b). *A Transformation Framework Proposal for Managers in Business Innovation and Business Transformation Projects-A heuristics decision module's background*. ABMR.

Trad, A., & Kalpić, D. (2017a). *An Intelligent Neural Networks Micro Artefact Patterns' Based Enterprise Architecture Model*. IGI-Global.

Trad, A., & Kalpić, D. (2017b). *A Neural Networks Portable and Agnostic Implementation TKM&F for Business Transformation Projects. The Basic Structure*. IEEE.

Trad, A., & Kalpić, D. (2017b). *A Neural Networks Portable and Agnostic Implementation TRADf for Business Transformation Projects. The Basic Structure*. IEEE.

Trad, A., & Kalpić, D. (2017c). *A Neural Networks Portable and Agnostic Implementation TKM&F for Business Transformation Projects. The Framework*. IEEE.

Trad, A., & Kalpić, D. (2017c). *A Neural Networks Portable and Agnostic Implementation TRADf for Business Transformation Projects. The Framework*. IEEE.

Trad, A., & Kalpić, D. (2017d). *A Neural Networks Portable and Agnostic Implementation TKM&F for Business Transformation Projects- The Basic Structure. IEEE Conference on Computational Intelligence*. France.

Trad, A., & Kalpić, D. (2017e). *The Business Transformation and Enterprise Architecture Framework / The London Inter Bank Offered Rate Crisis - The Model*. ABMR.

Trad, A., & Kalpić, D. (2018a). *The Business Transformation Framework and Enterprise Architecture Framework for Managers in Business Innovation-Knowledge and Intelligence Driven Development (KIDD). Encyclopaedia*. IGI-Global.

Trad, A., & Kalpić, D. (2018b). *The Business Transformation Framework and Enterprise Architecture Framework for Managers in Business Innovation- Knowledge Management in Global Software Engineering (HKMS). Encyclopaedia*. IGI-Global.

Trad, A., & Kalpić, D. (2018c). *The Business Transformation An applied mathematical model for business transformation-The applied case study. Encyclopaedia*. IGI-Global.

Trad, A., & Kalpić, D. (2018d). *The Business Transformation An applied mathematical model for business transformation-The Research Development Projects Concept (RDPC). Encyclopaedia*. IGI-Global.

Trad, A., & Kalpić, D. (2018e). *The Business Transformation An applied mathematical model for business transformation-Introduction and basics. Encyclopaedia.* IGI-Global.

Trad, A., & Kalpić, D. (2018f). *An applied mathematical model for business transformation-The Holistic Critical Success Factors Management System (HCSFMS). Encyclopaedia of E-Commerce Development, Implementation, and Management.* IGI-Global.

Trad, A., & Kalpić, D. (2019b). *The Business Transformation Framework and Enterprise Architecture Framework for Managers in Business Innovation-An applied holistic mathematical model (AHMM4RM). International Journal of Service Science, Management, Engineering, and Technology.*

Trad, A., & Kalpić, D. (2019c). *A Transformation Model for Assessing Risks of (e)Business/(e) Commerce Projects. International Journal of eBusiness.*

Trad, A., & Kalpić, D. (2019d). *Business Transformation and Enterprise Architecture-The Resources Management Research and Development Project (RMSRDP). Encyclopaedia.* IGI-Global.

Trad, A., & Kalpić, D. (2019e). *Business Transformation and Enterprise Architecture-The Holistic Project Resources Management Pattern (HPRMP). Encyclopaedia.* IGI-Global.

Trad, A., & Kalpić, D. (2019f). *Business Transformation and Enterprise Architecture-The Resources Management Implementation Concept (RMIC). Encyclopaedia.* IGI-Global.

Trad, A., & Kalpić, D. (2019f). *Business Transformation and Enterprise Architecture-The Resources Management Implementation Concept (RMIC).* IGI-Global.

Trad, A., & Kalpić, D. (2020a). *Using Applied Mathematical Models for Business Transformation.* IGI Global. doi:10.4018/978-1-7998-1009-4

Transformational strategic plan (2017-2022). (n.d.). Retrieved from http://www.windhoekcc.org.na/

Tungela, N., Mutudi, M., & Iyamu, T. (2018, October). *The Roles of E-Government in Healthcare from the Perspective of Structuration Theory. In 2018 Open Innovations Conference (OI).* IEEE.

UNDP. (2006). *The Millennium Development Goals.* UNDP.

Uppal, M., & Rahman, T. (2013). *Business Transformation Made Straight-Forward.* QR Systems Inc.

Urbaczewski, L., & Mrdalj, S. (2006). A comparison of Enterprise Architecture Frameworks. *Issues in Information Systems, 5*(2), 18–23.

Urbaczewski, L., & Mrdalj, S. (2006). A Comparison of Enterprise Architecture Frameworks. *Issues in Information Systems, 7*(2), 18–23.

Van Grembergen, W., & De Haes, S. (2007). *Implementing Information Technology Governance: Models, Practices and Cases.* Idea Grouping Publishing.

Van Helden, G. J., & Tillema, S. (2005). In search of a benchmarking theory for the public sector. *Financial Accountability &Management, 21*(3).

Van Zijl, C., & Van Belle, J. P. (2014). Organisatinal impact of enterprise architecture and business process capability in South African organisation. *International Journal of Trade. Economics and Finance, 5*(5), 405.

Van Zijl, C., & Van Belle, J. P. (2014). Organisational impact of enterprise architecture and business process capability in South African organisation. *International Journal of Trade. Economics and Finance, 5*(5), 405.

Vargas, A., Cuenca, L., Boza, A., Sacala, I., & Moisescu, M. (2016). Towards the development of the framework for inter sensing enterprise architecture. *Journal of Intelligent Manufacturing, 27*(1), 55–72.

Vella, A., Corne, D., & Murphy, C. (2009). Hyper-heuristic decision tree induction. *NaBIC 2009. World Congress.*

Venkatesh, V., Brown, S. A., & Bala, H. (2013). Bridging the qualitative-quantitative divide: Guidelines for conducting mixed methods research in information systems. *Management Information Systems Quarterly, 37*(1), 21–54. doi:10.25300/MISQ/2013/37.1.02

Versteeg, G., & Bouwman, H. (2006). Business architecture: A new paradigm to relate business strategy to ICT. *Information Systems Frontiers, 8*(2), 91–102. doi:10.100710796-006-7973-z

Visvizi, A., Lytras, M., Damiani, E., & Mathkou, H. (2018). Policy making for smart cities: Innovation and social inclusive economic growth for sustainability. *Journal of Science and Technology Policy Management, 9*(2), 126–133. doi:10.1108/JSTPM-07-2018-079

Vovchenko, N. G., Holina, M. G., Orobinskiy, A. S., & Sichev, R. A. (2017). Ensuring financial stability of companies on the basis of international experience in construction of risks maps, internal control and audit. *European Research Studies Journal, 20*(1), 350–368. doi:10.35808/ersj/623

Wagter, R., Proper, H., & Witte, D. (2012). Enterprise Architecture: A strategic specialism. In *14th International Conference on Commerce and Enterprise Computing* (pp. 1-8). Hangzhou, China: Academic Press.

Walsham, G. (1995). The Emergence of Interpretivism in IS Research. *Information Systems Research, 6*(4), 376–394. doi:10.1287/isre.6.4.376

Walsham, G. (2006). Doing interpretive research. *European Journal of Information Systems, 15*(3), 320–330. doi:10.1057/palgrave.ejis.3000589

Wang, Y., & Hajli, N. (2017). Exploring the path to big data analytics success in healthcare. *Journal of Business Research, 70*, 287–299. doi:10.1016/j.jbusres.2016.08.002

Wang, Y., Kung, L., & Byrd, T. A. (2018). Big data analytics: Understanding its capabilities and potential benefits for healthcare organisations. *Technological Forecasting and Social Change, 126*, 3–13. doi:10.1016/j.techfore.2015.12.019

Wardana, R. W., Masudin, I., & Restuputri, D. P. (2020). A novel group decision-making method by P-robust fuzzy DEA credibility constraint for welding process selection. *Cogent Engineering*, *7*(1), 1728057. doi:10.1080/23311916.2020.1728057

Washburn, D., Sindhu, U., Balaouras, S., & Dines, R. (2010). Helping CIOs understand "smart city" initiatives. *Growth*, *17*(2), 1–17.

We, C., & Kahn, M. G. (2016). Clinical research informatics for big data and precision medicine. *Yearbook of Medical Informatics*, *25*(01), 211–218. doi:10.15265/IY-2016-019 PMID:27830253

Weill, P., & Woodham, R. (2002). *Don't Just Lead, Govern: Implementing Effective IT Governance*. MIT Sloan Working Paper No. 4237-02. Retrieved from http://ssrn.com/abstract=317319

Whelan, J. & Meaden, G. (2016). *Business Architecture: A Practical Guide*. Academic Press.

Whittle, R., & Myrick, C. B. (2016). *Enterprise business architecture: The formal link between strategy and results*. CRC Press. doi:10.1201/9781420000207

Wielki, J. (2013, September). Implementation of the big data concept in organisations-possibilities, impediments and challenges. *2013 Federated Conference on Computer Science and Information Systems*, 985-989.

Wijewardena, H., & De Zoysa, A. (1999). A comparative analysis of management accounting practices in Australia and Japan: An empirical investigation. *The International Journal of Accounting*, *34*(1), 49–70. doi:10.1016/S0020-7063(99)80003-X

Wikusna, W. (2018). Enterprise architecture model for vocational high school. *IJAIT*, *2*(1), 22–28. doi:10.25124/ijait.v2i01.925

Wille, D., Wehling, K., Seidl, C., Pluchator, M., & Schaefer, I. (2017). Variability mining of technical architectures. In *Proceedings of the 21st International Systems and Software Product Line Conference*-Volume A (pp. 39-48). Academic Press.

WITSA. (2008). *Digital Planet 2008: The Global Information Economy*. The World Information Technology and Services Alliance.

Wong, C. M. L. (2016). Assembling interdisciplinary energy research through an actor-network theory (ANT) frame. *Energy Research & Social Science*, *12*, 106–110. doi:10.1016/j.erss.2015.12.024

Wu, J., Li, H., Cheng, S., & Lin, Z. (2016). The promising future of healthcare services: When big data analytics meets wearable technology. *Information & Management*, *53*(8), 1020–1033. doi:10.1016/j.im.2016.07.003

Xiaohong, C. (2011). *Research on E-Commerce Transaction Cost-Benefit Characteristics and Evaluation Approaches*. Management and Service Science (MASS), *2011 International Conference*. Wuhan. China.

Xin, J. Y., Ramayah, T., Soto-Acosta, P., Popa, S., & Ping, T. A. (2014). Analyzing the use of the Web 2.0 for brand awareness industry and competitive advantage: An empirical study in the Malaysian hospitability. *Information Systems Management, 31*(2), 96–103. doi:10.1080/10580 530.2014.890425

Yalçın, S. (2009). Ürün tasarım ve ürün hayat seyrinde maliyetlerin stratejik yönetimi. *Dumlupınar Üniversitesi Sosyal Bilimler Dergisi, 23*, 289–301.

Yazan, B. (2015). Three approaches to case study methods in education: Yin, Merriam, and Stake. *Qualitative Report, 20*(2), 134–152.

Yilema, M., & Gianoli, A. (2018). Infrastructure governance: Causes for the poor sectoral coordination among infrastructure sectors of Addis Ababa. *Cities (London, England), 83*(1), 165–172. doi:10.1016/j.cities.2018.06.019

Yin, R. K. (2017). *Case study research and applications: Design and methods*. Sage publications.

Ylimäki, T. (2008). *Potential Critical Success Factors for Enterprise Architecture*. University of Jyväskylä, Information Technology Research Institute.

Zaharia, M., Xin, R. S., Wendell, P., Das, T., Armbrust, M., Dave, A., Meng, X., Rosen, J., Venkataraman, S., Franklin, M. J., Ghodsi, A., Gonzalez, J., Shenker, S., & Stoica, I. (2016). Apache spark: A unified engine for big data processing. *Communications of the ACM, 59*(11), 56–65. doi:10.1145/2934664

Zait, A. (2017). Exploring the role of civilizational competences for smart cities' development. *Transforming Government: People. Process and Policy, 11*(3), 377–392.

Zakir, J., Seymour, T., & Berg, K. (2015). Big Data Analytics. *Issues in Information Systems, 16*(2).

Zhang, F., Cao, J., Khan, S. U., Li, K., & Hwang, K. (2015). A task-level adaptive MapReduce framework for real-time streaming data in healthcare applications. *Future Generation Computer Systems, 43*, 149–160. doi:10.1016/j.future.2014.06.009

Zheng, T., & Zheng, L. (2013). Examining e-government enterprise architecture research in China: A systematic approach and research agenda. *Government Information Quarterly, 30*, S59–S67. doi:10.1016/j.giq.2012.08.005

Zhu, J., & Shen, Z. H. (1995). A discussion of testing DMUs' returns to scale. *European Journal of Operational Research, 81*(3), 590–596. doi:10.1016/0377-2217(93)E0354-Z

Related References

To continue our tradition of advancing information science and technology research, we have compiled a list of recommended IGI Global readings. These references will provide additional information and guidance to further enrich your knowledge and assist you with your own research and future publications.

Abtahi, M. S., Behboudi, L., & Hasanabad, H. M. (2017). Factors Affecting Internet Advertising Adoption in Ad Agencies. *International Journal of Innovation in the Digital Economy*, 8(4), 18–29. doi:10.4018/IJIDE.2017100102

Agrawal, S. (2017). The Impact of Emerging Technologies and Social Media on Different Business(es): Marketing and Management. In O. Rishi & A. Sharma (Eds.), *Maximizing Business Performance and Efficiency Through Intelligent Systems* (pp. 37–49). Hershey, PA: IGI Global. doi:10.4018/978-1-5225-2234-8.ch002

Alnoukari, M., Razouk, R., & Hanano, A. (2016). BSC-SI: A Framework for Integrating Strategic Intelligence in Corporate Strategic Management. *International Journal of Social and Organizational Dynamics in IT*, 5(2), 1–14. doi:10.4018/IJSODIT.2016070101

Alnoukari, M., Razouk, R., & Hanano, A. (2016). BSC-SI, A Framework for Integrating Strategic Intelligence in Corporate Strategic Management. *International Journal of Strategic Information Technology and Applications*, 7(1), 32–44. doi:10.4018/IJSITA.2016010103

Altındağ, E. (2016). Current Approaches in Change Management. In A. Goksoy (Ed.), *Organizational Change Management Strategies in Modern Business* (pp. 24–51). Hershey, PA: IGI Global. doi:10.4018/978-1-4666-9533-7.ch002

Alvarez-Dionisi, L. E., Turner, R., & Mittra, M. (2016). Global Project Management Trends. *International Journal of Information Technology Project Management*, 7(3), 54–73. doi:10.4018/IJITPM.2016070104

Anantharaman, R. N., Rajeswari, K. S., Angusamy, A., & Kuppusamy, J. (2017). Role of Self-Efficacy and Collective Efficacy as Moderators of Occupational Stress Among Software Development Professionals. *International Journal of Human Capital and Information Technology Professionals*, 8(2), 45–58. doi:10.4018/IJHCITP.2017040103

Aninze, F., El-Gohary, H., & Hussain, J. (2018). The Role of Microfinance to Empower Women: The Case of Developing Countries. *International Journal of Customer Relationship Marketing and Management*, 9(1), 54–78. doi:10.4018/IJCRMM.2018010104

Arsenijević, O. M., Orčić, D., & Kastratović, E. (2017). Development of an Optimization Tool for Intangibles in SMEs: A Case Study from Serbia with a Pilot Research in the Prestige by Milka Company. In M. Vemić (Ed.), *Optimal Management Strategies in Small and Medium Enterprises* (pp. 320–347). Hershey, PA: IGI Global. doi:10.4018/978-1-5225-1949-2.ch015

Aryanto, V. D., Wismantoro, Y., & Widyatmoko, K. (2018). Implementing Eco-Innovation by Utilizing the Internet to Enhance Firm's Marketing Performance: Study of Green Batik Small and Medium Enterprises in Indonesia. *International Journal of E-Business Research*, 14(1), 21–36. doi:10.4018/IJEBR.2018010102

Atiku, S. O., & Fields, Z. (2017). Multicultural Orientations for 21st Century Global Leadership. In N. Baporikar (Ed.), *Management Education for Global Leadership* (pp. 28–51). Hershey, PA: IGI Global. doi:10.4018/978-1-5225-1013-0.ch002

Atiku, S. O., & Fields, Z. (2018). Organisational Learning Dimensions and Talent Retention Strategies for the Service Industries. In N. Baporikar (Ed.), *Global Practices in Knowledge Management for Societal and Organizational Development* (pp. 358–381). Hershey, PA: IGI Global. doi:10.4018/978-1-5225-3009-1.ch017

Ávila, L., & Teixeira, L. (2018). The Main Concepts Behind the Dematerialization of Business Processes. In M. Khosrow-Pour, D.B.A. (Ed.), Encyclopedia of Information Science and Technology, Fourth Edition (pp. 888-898). Hershey, PA: IGI Global. doi:10.4018/978-1-5225-2255-3.ch076

Related References

Bartens, Y., Chunpir, H. I., Schulte, F., & Voß, S. (2017). Business/IT Alignment in Two-Sided Markets: A COBIT 5 Analysis for Media Streaming Business Models. In S. De Haes & W. Van Grembergen (Eds.), *Strategic IT Governance and Alignment in Business Settings* (pp. 82–111). Hershey, PA: IGI Global. doi:10.4018/978-1-5225-0861-8.ch004

Bashayreh, A. M. (2018). Organizational Culture and Organizational Performance. In W. Lee & F. Sabetzadeh (Eds.), *Contemporary Knowledge and Systems Science* (pp. 50–69). Hershey, PA: IGI Global. doi:10.4018/978-1-5225-5655-8.ch003

Bedford, D. A. (2018). Sustainable Knowledge Management Strategies: Aligning Business Capabilities and Knowledge Management Goals. In N. Baporikar (Ed.), *Global Practices in Knowledge Management for Societal and Organizational Development* (pp. 46–73). Hershey, PA: IGI Global. doi:10.4018/978-1-5225-3009-1.ch003

Benmoussa, F., Nakara, W. A., & Jaouen, A. (2016). The Use of Social Media by SMEs in the Tourism Industry. In I. Lee (Ed.), *Encyclopedia of E-Commerce Development, Implementation, and Management* (pp. 2159–2170). Hershey, PA: IGI Global. doi:10.4018/978-1-4666-9787-4.ch155

Berger, R. (2016). Indigenous Management and Bottom of Pyramid Countries: The Role of National Institutions. In U. Aung & P. Ordoñez de Pablos (Eds.), *Managerial Strategies and Practice in the Asian Business Sector* (pp. 107–123). Hershey, PA: IGI Global. doi:10.4018/978-1-4666-9758-4.ch007

Bharwani, S., & Musunuri, D. (2018). Reflection as a Process From Theory to Practice. In M. Khosrow-Pour, D.B.A. (Ed.), Encyclopedia of Information Science and Technology, Fourth Edition (pp. 1529-1539). Hershey, PA: IGI Global. doi:10.4018/978-1-5225-2255-3.ch132

Bhatt, G. D., Wang, Z., & Rodger, J. A. (2017). Information Systems Capabilities and Their Effects on Competitive Advantages: A Study of Chinese Companies. *Information Resources Management Journal*, *30*(3), 41–57. doi:10.4018/IRMJ.2017070103

Bhushan, M., & Yadav, A. (2017). Concept of Cloud Computing in ESB. In R. Bhadoria, N. Chaudhari, G. Tomar, & S. Singh (Eds.), *Exploring Enterprise Service Bus in the Service-Oriented Architecture Paradigm* (pp. 116–127). Hershey, PA: IGI Global. doi:10.4018/978-1-5225-2157-0.ch008

Bhushan, S. (2017). System Dynamics Base-Model of Humanitarian Supply Chain (HSCM) in Disaster Prone Eco-Communities of India: A Discussion on Simulation and Scenario Results. *International Journal of System Dynamics Applications*, *6*(3), 20–37. doi:10.4018/IJSDA.2017070102

Biswas, A., & De, A. K. (2017). On Development of a Fuzzy Stochastic Programming Model with Its Application to Business Management. In S. Trivedi, S. Dey, A. Kumar, & T. Panda (Eds.), *Handbook of Research on Advanced Data Mining Techniques and Applications for Business Intelligence* (pp. 353–378). Hershey, PA: IGI Global. doi:10.4018/978-1-5225-2031-3.ch021

Bücker, J., & Ernste, K. (2018). Use of Brand Heroes in Strategic Reputation Management: The Case of Bacardi, Adidas, and Daimler. In A. Erdemir (Ed.), *Reputation Management Techniques in Public Relations* (pp. 126–150). Hershey, PA: IGI Global. doi:10.4018/978-1-5225-3619-2.ch007

Bureš, V. (2018). Industry 4.0 From the Systems Engineering Perspective: Alternative Holistic Framework Development. In R. Brunet-Thornton & F. Martinez (Eds.), *Analyzing the Impacts of Industry 4.0 in Modern Business Environments* (pp. 199–223). Hershey, PA: IGI Global. doi:10.4018/978-1-5225-3468-6.ch011

Buzady, Z. (2017). Resolving the Magic Cube of Effective Case Teaching: Benchmarking Case Teaching Practices in Emerging Markets – Insights from the Central European University Business School, Hungary. In D. Latusek (Ed.), *Case Studies as a Teaching Tool in Management Education* (pp. 79–103). Hershey, PA: IGI Global. doi:10.4018/978-1-5225-0770-3.ch005

Campatelli, G., Richter, A., & Stocker, A. (2016). Participative Knowledge Management to Empower Manufacturing Workers. *International Journal of Knowledge Management*, 12(4), 37–50. doi:10.4018/IJKM.2016100103

Căpusneanu, S., & Topor, D. I. (2018). Business Ethics and Cost Management in SMEs: Theories of Business Ethics and Cost Management Ethos. In I. Oncioiu (Ed.), *Ethics and Decision-Making for Sustainable Business Practices* (pp. 109–127). Hershey, PA: IGI Global. doi:10.4018/978-1-5225-3773-1.ch007

Carneiro, A. (2016). Maturity in Health Organization Information Systems: Metrics and Privacy Perspectives. *International Journal of Privacy and Health Information Management*, 4(2), 1–18. doi:10.4018/IJPHIM.2016070101

Chan, R. L., Mo, P. L., & Moon, K. K. (2018). Strategic and Tactical Measures in Managing Enterprise Risks: A Study of the Textile and Apparel Industry. In K. Strang, M. Korstanje, & N. Vajjhala (Eds.), *Research, Practices, and Innovations in Global Risk and Contingency Management* (pp. 1–19). Hershey, PA: IGI Global. doi:10.4018/978-1-5225-4754-9.ch001

Chandan, H. C. (2016). Motivations and Challenges of Female Entrepreneurship in Developed and Developing Economies. In N. Baporikar (Ed.), *Handbook of Research on Entrepreneurship in the Contemporary Knowledge-Based Global Economy* (pp. 260–286). Hershey, PA: IGI Global. doi:10.4018/978-1-4666-8798-1.ch012

Charlier, S. D., Burke-Smalley, L. A., & Fisher, S. L. (2018). Undergraduate Programs in the U.S: A Contextual and Content-Based Analysis. In J. Mendy (Ed.), *Teaching Human Resources and Organizational Behavior at the College Level* (pp. 26–57). Hershey, PA: IGI Global. doi:10.4018/978-1-5225-2820-3.ch002

Chaudhuri, S. (2016). Application of Web-Based Geographical Information System (GIS) in E-Business. In U. Panwar, R. Kumar, & N. Ray (Eds.), *Handbook of Research on Promotional Strategies and Consumer Influence in the Service Sector* (pp. 389–405). Hershey, PA: IGI Global. doi:10.4018/978-1-5225-0143-5.ch023

Choudhuri, P. S. (2016). An Empirical Study on the Quality of Services Offered by the Private Life Insurers in Burdwan. In U. Panwar, R. Kumar, & N. Ray (Eds.), *Handbook of Research on Promotional Strategies and Consumer Influence in the Service Sector* (pp. 31–55). Hershey, PA: IGI Global. doi:10.4018/978-1-5225-0143-5.ch002

Dahlberg, T., Kivijärvi, H., & Saarinen, T. (2017). IT Investment Consistency and Other Factors Influencing the Success of IT Performance. In S. De Haes & W. Van Grembergen (Eds.), *Strategic IT Governance and Alignment in Business Settings* (pp. 176–208). Hershey, PA: IGI Global. doi:10.4018/978-1-5225-0861-8.ch007

Damnjanović, A. M. (2017). Knowledge Management Optimization through IT and E-Business Utilization: A Qualitative Study on Serbian SMEs. In M. Vemić (Ed.), *Optimal Management Strategies in Small and Medium Enterprises* (pp. 249–267). Hershey, PA: IGI Global. doi:10.4018/978-1-5225-1949-2.ch012

Daneshpour, H. (2017). Integrating Sustainable Development into Project Portfolio Management through Application of Open Innovation. In M. Vemić (Ed.), *Optimal Management Strategies in Small and Medium Enterprises* (pp. 370–387). Hershey, PA: IGI Global. doi:10.4018/978-1-5225-1949-2.ch017

Daniel, A. D., & Reis de Castro, V. (2018). Entrepreneurship Education: How to Measure the Impact on Nascent Entrepreneurs. In A. Carrizo Moreira, J. Guilherme Leitão Dantas, & F. Manuel Valente (Eds.), *Nascent Entrepreneurship and Successful New Venture Creation* (pp. 85–110). Hershey, PA: IGI Global. doi:10.4018/978-1-5225-2936-1.ch004

David, F., van der Sijde, P., & van den Besselaar, P. (2016). Enterpreneurial Incentives, Obstacles, and Management in University-Business Co-Operation: The Case of Indonesia. In J. Saiz-Álvarez (Ed.), *Handbook of Research on Social Entrepreneurship and Solidarity Economics* (pp. 499–518). Hershey, PA: IGI Global. doi:10.4018/978-1-5225-0097-1.ch024

David, R., Swami, B. N., & Tangirala, S. (2018). Ethics Impact on Knowledge Management in Organizational Development: A Case Study. In N. Baporikar (Ed.), *Global Practices in Knowledge Management for Societal and Organizational Development* (pp. 19–45). Hershey, PA: IGI Global. doi:10.4018/978-1-5225-3009-1.ch002

Delias, P., & Lakiotaki, K. (2018). Discovering Process Horizontal Boundaries to Facilitate Process Comprehension. *International Journal of Operations Research and Information Systems*, 9(2), 1–31. doi:10.4018/IJORIS.2018040101

Denholm, J., & Lee-Davies, L. (2018). Success Factors for Games in Business and Project Management. In *Enhancing Education and Training Initiatives Through Serious Games* (pp. 34–68). Hershey, PA: IGI Global. doi:10.4018/978-1-5225-3689-5.ch002

Deshpande, M. (2017). Best Practices in Management Institutions for Global Leadership: Policy Aspects. In N. Baporikar (Ed.), *Management Education for Global Leadership* (pp. 1–27). Hershey, PA: IGI Global. doi:10.4018/978-1-5225-1013-0.ch001

Deshpande, M. (2018). Policy Perspectives for SMEs Knowledge Management. In N. Baporikar (Ed.), *Knowledge Integration Strategies for Entrepreneurship and Sustainability* (pp. 23–46). Hershey, PA: IGI Global. doi:10.4018/978-1-5225-5115-7.ch002

Dezdar, S. (2017). ERP Implementation Projects in Asian Countries: A Comparative Study on Iran and China. *International Journal of Information Technology Project Management*, 8(3), 52–68. doi:10.4018/IJITPM.2017070104

Domingos, D., Martinho, R., & Varajão, J. (2016). Controlled Flexibility in Healthcare Processes: A BPMN-Extension Approach. In M. Cruz-Cunha, I. Miranda, R. Martinho, & R. Rijo (Eds.), *Encyclopedia of E-Health and Telemedicine* (pp. 521–535). Hershey, PA: IGI Global. doi:10.4018/978-1-4666-9978-6.ch040

Domingos, D., Respício, A., & Martinho, R. (2017). Reliability of IoT-Aware BPMN Healthcare Processes. In C. Reis & M. Maximiano (Eds.), *Internet of Things and Advanced Application in Healthcare* (pp. 214–248). Hershey, PA: IGI Global. doi:10.4018/978-1-5225-1820-4.ch008

Dosumu, O., Hussain, J., & El-Gohary, H. (2017). An Exploratory Study of the Impact of Government Policies on the Development of Small and Medium Enterprises in Developing Countries: The Case of Nigeria. *International Journal of Customer Relationship Marketing and Management*, 8(4), 51–62. doi:10.4018/IJCRMM.2017100104

Durst, S., Bruns, G., & Edvardsson, I. R. (2017). Retaining Knowledge in Smaller Building and Construction Firms. *International Journal of Knowledge and Systems Science*, 8(3), 1–12. doi:10.4018/IJKSS.2017070101

Edvardsson, I. R., & Durst, S. (2017). Outsourcing, Knowledge, and Learning: A Critical Review. *International Journal of Knowledge-Based Organizations*, 7(2), 13–26. doi:10.4018/IJKBO.2017040102

Edwards, J. S. (2018). Integrating Knowledge Management and Business Processes. In M. Khosrow-Pour, D.B.A. (Ed.), Encyclopedia of Information Science and Technology, Fourth Edition (pp. 5046-5055). Hershey, PA: IGI Global. doi:10.4018/978-1-5225-2255-3.ch437

Ejiogu, A. O. (2018). Economics of Farm Management. In *Agricultural Finance and Opportunities for Investment and Expansion* (pp. 56–72). Hershey, PA: IGI Global. doi:10.4018/978-1-5225-3059-6.ch003

Ekanem, I., & Abiade, G. E. (2018). Factors Influencing the Use of E-Commerce by Small Enterprises in Nigeria. *International Journal of ICT Research in Africa and the Middle East*, 7(1), 37–53. doi:10.4018/IJICTRAME.2018010103

Ekanem, I., & Alrossais, L. A. (2017). Succession Challenges Facing Family Businesses in Saudi Arabia. In P. Zgheib (Ed.), *Entrepreneurship and Business Innovation in the Middle East* (pp. 122–146). Hershey, PA: IGI Global. doi:10.4018/978-1-5225-2066-5.ch007

El Faquih, L., & Fredj, M. (2017). Ontology-Based Framework for Quality in Configurable Process Models. *Journal of Electronic Commerce in Organizations*, 15(2), 48–60. doi:10.4018/JECO.2017040104

El-Gohary, H., & El-Gohary, Z. (2016). An Attempt to Explore Electronic Marketing Adoption and Implementation Aspects in Developing Countries: The Case of Egypt. *International Journal of Customer Relationship Marketing and Management*, 7(4), 1–26. doi:10.4018/IJCRMM.2016100101

Entico, G. J. (2016). Knowledge Management and the Medical Health Librarians: A Perception Study. In J. Yap, M. Perez, M. Ayson, & G. Entico (Eds.), *Special Library Administration, Standardization and Technological Integration* (pp. 52–77). Hershey, PA: IGI Global. doi:10.4018/978-1-4666-9542-9.ch003

Faisal, M. N., & Talib, F. (2017). Building Ambidextrous Supply Chains in SMEs: How to Tackle the Barriers? *International Journal of Information Systems and Supply Chain Management, 10*(4), 80–100. doi:10.4018/IJISSCM.2017100105

Fernandes, T. M., Gomes, J., & Romão, M. (2017). Investments in E-Government: A Benefit Management Case Study. *International Journal of Electronic Government Research, 13*(3), 1–17. doi:10.4018/IJEGR.2017070101

Fouda, F. A. (2016). A Suggested Curriculum in Career Education to Develop Business Secondary Schools Students' Career Knowledge Management Domains and Professional Thinking. *International Journal of Technology Diffusion, 7*(2), 42–62. doi:10.4018/IJTD.2016040103

Gallardo-Vázquez, D., & Pajuelo-Moreno, M. L. (2016). How Spanish Universities are Promoting Entrepreneurship through Your Own Lines of Teaching and Research? In L. Carvalho (Ed.), *Handbook of Research on Entrepreneurial Success and its Impact on Regional Development* (pp. 431–454). Hershey, PA: IGI Global. doi:10.4018/978-1-4666-9567-2.ch019

Gao, S. S., Oreal, S., & Zhang, J. (2018). Contemporary Financial Risk Management Perceptions and Practices of Small-Sized Chinese Businesses. In I. Management Association (Ed.), Global Business Expansion: Concepts, Methodologies, Tools, and Applications (pp. 917-931). Hershey, PA: IGI Global. doi:10.4018/978-1-5225-5481-3.ch041

Garg, R., & Berning, S. C. (2017). Indigenous Chinese Management Philosophies: Key Concepts and Relevance for Modern Chinese Firms. In B. Christiansen & G. Koc (Eds.), *Transcontinental Strategies for Industrial Development and Economic Growth* (pp. 43–57). Hershey, PA: IGI Global. doi:10.4018/978-1-5225-2160-0.ch003

Gencer, Y. G. (2017). Supply Chain Management in Retailing Business. In U. Akkucuk (Ed.), *Ethics and Sustainability in Global Supply Chain Management* (pp. 197–210). Hershey, PA: IGI Global. doi:10.4018/978-1-5225-2036-8.ch011

Giacosa, E. (2016). Innovation in Luxury Fashion Businesses as a Means for the Regional Development. In L. Carvalho (Ed.), *Handbook of Research on Entrepreneurial Success and its Impact on Regional Development* (pp. 206–222). Hershey, PA: IGI Global. doi:10.4018/978-1-4666-9567-2.ch010

Giacosa, E. (2018). The Increasing of the Regional Development Thanks to the Luxury Business Innovation. In L. Carvalho (Ed.), *Handbook of Research on Entrepreneurial Ecosystems and Social Dynamics in a Globalized World* (pp. 260–273). Hershey, PA: IGI Global. doi:10.4018/978-1-5225-3525-6.ch011

Gianni, M., & Gotzamani, K. (2016). Integrated Management Systems and Information Management Systems: Common Threads. In P. Papajorgji, F. Pinet, A. Guimarães, & J. Papathanasiou (Eds.), *Automated Enterprise Systems for Maximizing Business Performance* (pp. 195–214). Hershey, PA: IGI Global. doi:10.4018/978-1-4666-8841-4.ch011

Gianni, M., Gotzamani, K., & Linden, I. (2016). How a BI-wise Responsible Integrated Management System May Support Food Traceability. *International Journal of Decision Support System Technology*, 8(2), 1–17. doi:10.4018/IJDSST.2016040101

Glykas, M., & George, J. (2017). Quality and Process Management Systems in the UAE Maritime Industry. *International Journal of Productivity Management and Assessment Technologies*, 5(1), 20–39. doi:10.4018/IJPMAT.2017010102

Glykas, M., Valiris, G., Kokkinaki, A., & Koutsoukou, Z. (2018). Banking Business Process Management Implementation. *International Journal of Productivity Management and Assessment Technologies*, 6(1), 50–69. doi:10.4018/IJPMAT.2018010104

Gomes, J., & Romão, M. (2017). The Balanced Scorecard: Keeping Updated and Aligned with Today's Business Trends. *International Journal of Productivity Management and Assessment Technologies*, 5(2), 1–15. doi:10.4018/IJPMAT.2017070101

Gomes, J., & Romão, M. (2017). Aligning Information Systems and Technology with Benefit Management and Balanced Scorecard. In S. De Haes & W. Van Grembergen (Eds.), *Strategic IT Governance and Alignment in Business Settings* (pp. 112–131). Hershey, PA: IGI Global. doi:10.4018/978-1-5225-0861-8.ch005

Grefen, P., & Turetken, O. (2017). Advanced Business Process Management in Networked E-Business Scenarios. *International Journal of E-Business Research*, 13(4), 70–104. doi:10.4018/IJEBR.2017100105

Haider, A., & Saetang, S. (2017). Strategic IT Alignment in Service Sector. In S. Rozenes & Y. Cohen (Eds.), *Handbook of Research on Strategic Alliances and Value Co-Creation in the Service Industry* (pp. 231–258). Hershey, PA: IGI Global. doi:10.4018/978-1-5225-2084-9.ch012

Haider, A., & Tang, S. S. (2016). Maximising Value Through IT and Business Alignment: A Case of IT Governance Institutionalisation at a Thai Bank. *International Journal of Technology Diffusion, 7*(3), 33–58. doi:10.4018/IJTD.2016070104

Hajilari, A. B., Ghadaksaz, M., & Fasghandis, G. S. (2017). Assessing Organizational Readiness for Implementing ERP System Using Fuzzy Expert System Approach. *International Journal of Enterprise Information Systems, 13*(1), 67–85. doi:10.4018/IJEIS.2017010105

Haldorai, A., Ramu, A., & Murugan, S. (2018). Social Aware Cognitive Radio Networks: Effectiveness of Social Networks as a Strategic Tool for Organizational Business Management. In H. Bansal, G. Shrivastava, G. Nguyen, & L. Stanciu (Eds.), *Social Network Analytics for Contemporary Business Organizations* (pp. 188–202). Hershey, PA: IGI Global. doi:10.4018/978-1-5225-5097-6.ch010

Hall, O. P. Jr. (2017). Social Media Driven Management Education. *International Journal of Knowledge-Based Organizations, 7*(2), 43–59. doi:10.4018/IJKBO.2017040104

Hanifah, H., Halim, H. A., Ahmad, N. H., & Vafaei-Zadeh, A. (2017). Innovation Culture as a Mediator Between Specific Human Capital and Innovation Performance Among Bumiputera SMEs in Malaysia. In N. Ahmad, T. Ramayah, H. Halim, & S. Rahman (Eds.), *Handbook of Research on Small and Medium Enterprises in Developing Countries* (pp. 261–279). Hershey, PA: IGI Global. doi:10.4018/978-1-5225-2165-5.ch012

Hartlieb, S., & Silvius, G. (2017). Handling Uncertainty in Project Management and Business Development: Similarities and Differences. In Y. Raydugin (Ed.), *Handbook of Research on Leveraging Risk and Uncertainties for Effective Project Management* (pp. 337–362). Hershey, PA: IGI Global. doi:10.4018/978-1-5225-1790-0.ch016

Hass, K. B. (2017). Living on the Edge: Managing Project Complexity. In Y. Raydugin (Ed.), *Handbook of Research on Leveraging Risk and Uncertainties for Effective Project Management* (pp. 177–201). Hershey, PA: IGI Global. doi:10.4018/978-1-5225-1790-0.ch009

Hassan, A., & Privitera, D. S. (2016). Google AdSense as a Mobile Technology in Education. In J. Holland (Ed.), *Wearable Technology and Mobile Innovations for Next-Generation Education* (pp. 200–223). Hershey, PA: IGI Global. doi:10.4018/978-1-5225-0069-8.ch011

Hassan, A., & Rahimi, R. (2016). Consuming "Innovation" in Tourism: Augmented Reality as an Innovation Tool in Digital Tourism Marketing. In N. Pappas & I. Bregoli (Eds.), *Global Dynamics in Travel, Tourism, and Hospitality* (pp. 130–147). Hershey, PA: IGI Global. doi:10.4018/978-1-5225-0201-2.ch008

Hawking, P., & Carmine Sellitto, C. (2017). Developing an Effective Strategy for Organizational Business Intelligence. In M. Tavana (Ed.), *Enterprise Information Systems and the Digitalization of Business Functions* (pp. 222–237). Hershey, PA: IGI Global. doi:10.4018/978-1-5225-2382-6.ch010

Hawking, P., & Sellitto, C. (2017). A Fast-Moving Consumer Goods Company and Business Intelligence Strategy Development. *International Journal of Enterprise Information Systems*, *13*(2), 22–33. doi:10.4018/IJEIS.2017040102

Hawking, P., & Sellitto, C. (2017). Business Intelligence Strategy: Two Case Studies. *International Journal of Business Intelligence Research*, *8*(2), 17–30. doi:10.4018/IJBIR.2017070102

Haynes, J. D., Arockiasamy, S., Al Rashdi, M., & Al Rashdi, S. (2016). Business and E Business Strategies for Coopetition and Thematic Management as a Sustained Basis for Ethics and Social Responsibility in Emerging Markets. In M. Al-Shammari & H. Masri (Eds.), *Ethical and Social Perspectives on Global Business Interaction in Emerging Markets* (pp. 25–39). Hershey, PA: IGI Global. doi:10.4018/978-1-4666-9864-2.ch002

Hee, W. J., Jalleh, G., Lai, H., & Lin, C. (2017). E-Commerce and IT Projects: Evaluation and Management Issues in Australian and Taiwanese Hospitals. *International Journal of Public Health Management and Ethics*, *2*(1), 69–90. doi:10.4018/IJPHME.2017010104

Hernandez, A. A. (2018). Exploring the Factors to Green IT Adoption of SMEs in the Philippines. *Journal of Cases on Information Technology*, *20*(2), 49–66. doi:10.4018/JCIT.2018040104

Hernandez, A. A., & Ona, S. E. (2016). Green IT Adoption: Lessons from the Philippines Business Process Outsourcing Industry. *International Journal of Social Ecology and Sustainable Development*, *7*(1), 1–34. doi:10.4018/IJSESD.2016010101

Hollman, A., Bickford, S., & Hollman, T. (2017). Cyber InSecurity: A Post-Mortem Attempt to Assess Cyber Problems from IT and Business Management Perspectives. *Journal of Cases on Information Technology*, *19*(3), 42–70. doi:10.4018/JCIT.2017070104

Igbinakhase, I. (2017). Responsible and Sustainable Management Practices in Developing and Developed Business Environments. In Z. Fields (Ed.), *Collective Creativity for Responsible and Sustainable Business Practice* (pp. 180–207). Hershey, PA: IGI Global. doi:10.4018/978-1-5225-1823-5.ch010

Ilahi, L., Ghannouchi, S. A., & Martinho, R. (2016). A Business Process Management Approach to Home Healthcare Processes: On the Gap between Intention and Reality. In M. Cruz-Cunha, I. Miranda, R. Martinho, & R. Rijo (Eds.), *Encyclopedia of E-Health and Telemedicine* (pp. 439–457). Hershey, PA: IGI Global. doi:10.4018/978-1-4666-9978-6.ch035

Iwata, J. J., & Hoskins, R. G. (2017). Managing Indigenous Knowledge in Tanzania: A Business Perspective. In P. Jain & N. Mnjama (Eds.), *Managing Knowledge Resources and Records in Modern Organizations* (pp. 198–214). Hershey, PA: IGI Global. doi:10.4018/978-1-5225-1965-2.ch012

Jabeen, F., Ahmad, S. Z., & Alkaabi, S. (2016). The Internationalization Decision-Making of United Arab Emirates Family Businesses. In N. Zakaria, A. Abdul-Talib, & N. Osman (Eds.), *Handbook of Research on Impacts of International Business and Political Affairs on the Global Economy* (pp. 1–22). Hershey, PA: IGI Global. doi:10.4018/978-1-4666-9806-2.ch001

Jain, P. (2017). Ethical and Legal Issues in Knowledge Management Life-Cycle in Business. In P. Jain & N. Mnjama (Eds.), *Managing Knowledge Resources and Records in Modern Organizations* (pp. 82–101). Hershey, PA: IGI Global. doi:10.4018/978-1-5225-1965-2.ch006

Jamali, D., Abdallah, H., & Matar, F. (2016). Opportunities and Challenges for CSR Mainstreaming in Business Schools. *International Journal of Technology and Educational Marketing*, *6*(2), 1–29. doi:10.4018/IJTEM.2016070101

James, S., & Hauli, E. (2017). Holistic Management Education at Tanzanian Rural Development Planning Institute. In N. Baporikar (Ed.), *Management Education for Global Leadership* (pp. 112–136). Hershey, PA: IGI Global. doi:10.4018/978-1-5225-1013-0.ch006

Janošková, M., Csikósová, A., & Čulková, K. (2018). Measurement of Company Performance as Part of Its Strategic Management. In R. Leon (Ed.), *Managerial Strategies for Business Sustainability During Turbulent Times* (pp. 309–335). Hershey, PA: IGI Global. doi:10.4018/978-1-5225-2716-9.ch017

Jean-Vasile, A., & Alecu, A. (2017). Theoretical and Practical Approaches in Understanding the Influences of Cost-Productivity-Profit Trinomial in Contemporary Enterprises. In A. Jean Vasile & D. Nicolò (Eds.), *Sustainable Entrepreneurship and Investments in the Green Economy* (pp. 28–62). Hershey, PA: IGI Global. doi:10.4018/978-1-5225-2075-7.ch002

Jha, D. G. (2016). Preparing for Information Technology Driven Changes. In S. Tiwari & L. Nafees (Eds.), *Innovative Management Education Pedagogies for Preparing Next-Generation Leaders* (pp. 258–274). Hershey, PA: IGI Global. doi:10.4018/978-1-4666-9691-4.ch015

Joia, L. A., & Correia, J. C. (2018). CIO Competencies From the IT Professional Perspective: Insights From Brazil. *Journal of Global Information Management*, 26(2), 74–103. doi:10.4018/JGIM.2018040104

Juma, A., & Mzera, N. (2017). Knowledge Management and Records Management and Competitive Advantage in Business. In P. Jain & N. Mnjama (Eds.), *Managing Knowledge Resources and Records in Modern Organizations* (pp. 15–28). Hershey, PA: IGI Global. doi:10.4018/978-1-5225-1965-2.ch002

K., I., & A, V. (2018). Monitoring and Auditing in the Cloud. In K. Munir (Ed.), *Cloud Computing Technologies for Green Enterprises* (pp. 318-350). Hershey, PA: IGI Global. doi:10.4018/978-1-5225-3038-1.ch013

Kabra, G., Ghosh, V., & Ramesh, A. (2018). Enterprise Integrated Business Process Management and Business Intelligence Framework for Business Process Sustainability. In A. Paul, D. Bhattacharyya, & S. Anand (Eds.), *Green Initiatives for Business Sustainability and Value Creation* (pp. 228–238). Hershey, PA: IGI Global. doi:10.4018/978-1-5225-2662-9.ch010

Kaoud, M. (2017). Investigation of Customer Knowledge Management: A Case Study Research. *International Journal of Service Science, Management, Engineering, and Technology*, 8(2), 12–22. doi:10.4018/IJSSMET.2017040102

Kara, M. E., & Fırat, S. Ü. (2016). Sustainability, Risk, and Business Intelligence in Supply Chains. In M. Erdoğdu, T. Arun, & I. Ahmad (Eds.), *Handbook of Research on Green Economic Development Initiatives and Strategies* (pp. 501–538). Hershey, PA: IGI Global. doi:10.4018/978-1-5225-0440-5.ch022

Katuu, S. (2018). A Comparative Assessment of Enterprise Content Management Maturity Models. In N. Gwangwava & M. Mutingi (Eds.), *E-Manufacturing and E-Service Strategies in Contemporary Organizations* (pp. 93–118). Hershey, PA: IGI Global. doi:10.4018/978-1-5225-3628-4.ch005

Khan, M. A. (2016). MNEs Management Strategies in Developing Countries: Establishing the Context. In M. Khan (Ed.), *Multinational Enterprise Management Strategies in Developing Countries* (pp. 1–33). Hershey, PA: IGI Global. doi:10.4018/978-1-5225-0276-0.ch001

Khan, M. A. (2016). Operational Approaches in Organizational Structure: A Case for MNEs in Developing Countries. In M. Khan (Ed.), *Multinational Enterprise Management Strategies in Developing Countries* (pp. 129–151). Hershey, PA: IGI Global. doi:10.4018/978-1-5225-0276-0.ch007

Kinnunen, S., Ylä-Kujala, A., Marttonen-Arola, S., Kärri, T., & Baglee, D. (2018). Internet of Things in Asset Management: Insights from Industrial Professionals and Academia. *International Journal of Service Science, Management, Engineering, and Technology*, 9(2), 104–119. doi:10.4018/IJSSMET.2018040105

Klein, A. Z., Sabino de Freitas, A., Machado, L., Freitas, J. C. Jr, Graziola, P. G. Jr, & Schlemmer, E. (2017). Virtual Worlds Applications for Management Education. In L. Tomei (Ed.), *Exploring the New Era of Technology-Infused Education* (pp. 279–299). Hershey, PA: IGI Global. doi:10.4018/978-1-5225-1709-2.ch017

Kożuch, B., & Jabłoński, A. (2017). Adopting the Concept of Business Models in Public Management. In M. Lewandowski & B. Kożuch (Eds.), *Public Sector Entrepreneurship and the Integration of Innovative Business Models* (pp. 10–46). Hershey, PA: IGI Global. doi:10.4018/978-1-5225-2215-7.ch002

Kumar, J., Adhikary, A., & Jha, A. (2017). Small Active Investors' Perceptions and Preferences Towards Tax Saving Mutual Fund Schemes in Eastern India: An Empirical Note. *International Journal of Asian Business and Information Management*, 8(2), 35–45. doi:10.4018/IJABIM.2017040103

Lassoued, Y., Bouzguenda, L., & Mahmoud, T. (2016). Context-Aware Business Process Versions Management. *International Journal of e-Collaboration*, 12(3), 7–33. doi:10.4018/IJeC.2016070102

Lavassani, K. M., & Movahedi, B. (2017). Applications Driven Information Systems: Beyond Networks toward Business Ecosystems. *International Journal of Innovation in the Digital Economy*, 8(1), 61–75. doi:10.4018/IJIDE.2017010104

Lazzareschi, V. H., & Brito, M. S. (2017). Strategic Information Management: Proposal of Business Project Model. In G. Jamil, A. Soares, & C. Pessoa (Eds.), *Handbook of Research on Information Management for Effective Logistics and Supply Chains* (pp. 59–88). Hershey, PA: IGI Global. doi:10.4018/978-1-5225-0973-8.ch004

Lederer, M., Kurz, M., & Lazarov, P. (2017). Usage and Suitability of Methods for Strategic Business Process Initiatives: A Multi Case Study Research. *International Journal of Productivity Management and Assessment Technologies*, *5*(1), 40–51. doi:10.4018/IJPMAT.2017010103

Lee, I. (2017). A Social Enterprise Business Model and a Case Study of Pacific Community Ventures (PCV). In V. Potocan, M. Ünğan, & Z. Nedelko (Eds.), *Handbook of Research on Managerial Solutions in Non-Profit Organizations* (pp. 182–204). Hershey, PA: IGI Global. doi:10.4018/978-1-5225-0731-4.ch009

Lee, L. J., & Leu, J. (2016). Exploring the Effectiveness of IT Application and Value Method in the Innovation Performance of Enterprise. *International Journal of Enterprise Information Systems*, *12*(2), 47–65. doi:10.4018/IJEIS.2016040104

Lee, Y. (2016). Alignment Effect of Entrepreneurial Orientation and Marketing Orientation on Firm Performance. *International Journal of Customer Relationship Marketing and Management*, *7*(4), 58–69. doi:10.4018/IJCRMM.2016100104

Leon, L. A., Seal, K. C., Przasnyski, Z. H., & Wiedenman, I. (2017). Skills and Competencies Required for Jobs in Business Analytics: A Content Analysis of Job Advertisements Using Text Mining. *International Journal of Business Intelligence Research*, *8*(1), 1–25. doi:10.4018/IJBIR.2017010101

Lcu, J., Lee, L. J., & Krischke, A. (2016). Value Engineering-Based Method for Implementing the ISO14001 System in the Green Supply Chains. *International Journal of Strategic Decision Sciences*, *7*(4), 1–20. doi:10.4018/IJSDS.2016100101

Levy, C. L., & Elias, N. I. (2017). SOHO Users' Perceptions of Reliability and Continuity of Cloud-Based Services. In M. Moore (Ed.), *Cybersecurity Breaches and Issues Surrounding Online Threat Protection* (pp. 248–287). Hershey, PA: IGI Global. doi:10.4018/978-1-5225-1941-6.ch011

Levy, M. (2018). Change Management Serving Knowledge Management and Organizational Development: Reflections and Review. In N. Baporikar (Ed.), *Global Practices in Knowledge Management for Societal and Organizational Development* (pp. 256–270). Hershey, PA: IGI Global. doi:10.4018/978-1-5225-3009-1.ch012

Lewandowski, M. (2017). Public Organizations and Business Model Innovation: The Role of Public Service Design. In M. Lewandowski & B. Kożuch (Eds.), *Public Sector Entrepreneurship and the Integration of Innovative Business Models* (pp. 47–72). Hershey, PA: IGI Global. doi:10.4018/978-1-5225-2215-7.ch003

Lhannaoui, H., Kabbaj, M. I., & Bakkoury, Z. (2017). A Survey of Risk-Aware Business Process Modelling. *International Journal of Risk and Contingency Management*, *6*(3), 14–26. doi:10.4018/IJRCM.2017070102

Li, J., Sun, W., Jiang, W., Yang, H., & Zhang, L. (2017). How the Nature of Exogenous Shocks and Crises Impact Company Performance?: The Effects of Industry Characteristics. *International Journal of Risk and Contingency Management*, *6*(4), 40–55. doi:10.4018/IJRCM.2017100103

Lu, C., & Liu, S. (2016). Cultural Tourism O2O Business Model Innovation-A Case Study of CTrip. *Journal of Electronic Commerce in Organizations*, *14*(2), 16–31. doi:10.4018/JECO.2016040102

Machen, B., Hosseini, M. R., Wood, A., & Bakhshi, J. (2016). An Investigation into using SAP-PS as a Multidimensional Project Control System (MPCS). *International Journal of Enterprise Information Systems*, *12*(2), 66–81. doi:10.4018/IJEIS.2016040105

Malega, P. (2017). Small and Medium Enterprises in the Slovak Republic: Status and Competitiveness of SMEs in the Global Markets and Possibilities of Optimization. In M. Vemić (Ed.), *Optimal Management Strategies in Small and Medium Enterprises* (pp. 102–124). Hershey, PA: IGI Global. doi:10.4018/978-1-5225-1949-2.ch006

Malewska, K. M. (2017). Intuition in Decision-Making on the Example of a Non-Profit Organization. In V. Potocan, M. Üngan, & Z. Nedelko (Eds.), *Handbook of Research on Managerial Solutions in Non-Profit Organizations* (pp. 378–399). Hershey, PA: IGI Global. doi:10.4018/978-1-5225-0731-4.ch018

Maroofi, F. (2017). Entrepreneurial Orientation and Organizational Learning Ability Analysis for Innovation and Firm Performance. In N. Baporikar (Ed.), *Innovation and Shifting Perspectives in Management Education* (pp. 144–165). Hershey, PA: IGI Global. doi:10.4018/978-1-5225-1019-2.ch007

Martins, P. V., & Zacarias, M. (2017). A Web-based Tool for Business Process Improvement. *International Journal of Web Portals*, *9*(2), 68–84. doi:10.4018/IJWP.2017070104

Matthies, B., & Coners, A. (2017). Exploring the Conceptual Nature of e-Business Projects. *Journal of Electronic Commerce in Organizations*, *15*(3), 33–63. doi:10.4018/JECO.2017070103

McKee, J. (2018). Architecture as a Tool to Solve Business Planning Problems. In M. Khosrow-Pour, D.B.A. (Ed.), Encyclopedia of Information Science and Technology, Fourth Edition (pp. 573-586). Hershey, PA: IGI Global. doi:10.4018/978-1-5225-2255-3.ch050

McMurray, A. J., Cross, J., & Caponecchia, C. (2018). The Risk Management Profession in Australia: Business Continuity Plan Practices. In N. Bajgoric (Ed.), *Always-On Enterprise Information Systems for Modern Organizations* (pp. 112–129). Hershey, PA: IGI Global. doi:10.4018/978-1-5225-3704-5.ch006

Meddah, I. H., & Belkadi, K. (2018). Mining Patterns Using Business Process Management. In R. Hamou (Ed.), *Handbook of Research on Biomimicry in Information Retrieval and Knowledge Management* (pp. 78–89). Hershey, PA: IGI Global. doi:10.4018/978-1-5225-3004-6.ch005

Mendes, L. (2017). TQM and Knowledge Management: An Integrated Approach Towards Tacit Knowledge Management. In D. Jaziri-Bouagina & G. Jamil (Eds.), *Handbook of Research on Tacit Knowledge Management for Organizational Success* (pp. 236–263). Hershey, PA: IGI Global. doi:10.4018/978-1-5225-2394-9.ch009

Mnjama, N. M. (2017). Preservation of Recorded Information in Public and Private Sector Organizations. In P. Jain & N. Mnjama (Eds.), *Managing Knowledge Resources and Records in Modern Organizations* (pp. 149–167). Hershey, PA: IGI Global. doi:10.4018/978-1-5225-1965-2.ch009

Mokoqama, M., & Fields, Z. (2017). Principles of Responsible Management Education (PRME): Call for Responsible Management Education. In Z. Fields (Ed.), *Collective Creativity for Responsible and Sustainable Business Practice* (pp. 229–241). Hershey, PA: IGI Global. doi:10.4018/978-1-5225-1823-5.ch012

Muniapan, B. (2017). Philosophy and Management: The Relevance of Vedanta in Management. In P. Ordóñez de Pablos (Ed.), *Managerial Strategies and Solutions for Business Success in Asia* (pp. 124–139). Hershey, PA: IGI Global. doi:10.4018/978-1-5225-1886-0.ch007

Muniapan, B., Gregory, M. L., & Ling, L. A. (2016). Marketing Education in Sarawak: Looking at It from the Employers' Viewpoint. In B. Smith & A. Porath (Eds.), *Global Perspectives on Contemporary Marketing Education* (pp. 112–130). Hershey, PA: IGI Global. doi:10.4018/978-1-4666-9784-3.ch008

Murad, S. E., & Dowaji, S. (2017). Using Value-Based Approach for Managing Cloud-Based Services. In A. Turuk, B. Sahoo, & S. Addya (Eds.), *Resource Management and Efficiency in Cloud Computing Environments* (pp. 33–60). Hershey, PA: IGI Global. doi:10.4018/978-1-5225-1721-4.ch002

Mutahar, A. M., Daud, N. M., Thurasamy, R., Isaac, O., & Abdulsalam, R. (2018). The Mediating of Perceived Usefulness and Perceived Ease of Use: The Case of Mobile Banking in Yemen. *International Journal of Technology Diffusion*, *9*(2), 21–40. doi:10.4018/IJTD.2018040102

Naidoo, V. (2017). E-Learning and Management Education at African Universities. In N. Baporikar (Ed.), *Management Education for Global Leadership* (pp. 181–201). Hershey, PA: IGI Global. doi:10.4018/978-1-5225-1013-0.ch009

Naidoo, V., & Igbinakhase, I. (2018). Opportunities and Challenges of Knowledge Retention in SMEs. In N. Baporikar (Ed.), *Knowledge Integration Strategies for Entrepreneurship and Sustainability* (pp. 70–94). Hershey, PA: IGI Global. doi:10.4018/978-1-5225-5115-7.ch004

Nayak, S., & Prabhu, N. (2017). Paradigm Shift in Management Education: Need for a Cross Functional Perspective. In N. Baporikar (Ed.), *Management Education for Global Leadership* (pp. 241–255). Hershey, PA: IGI Global. doi:10.4018/978-1-5225-1013-0.ch012

Ndede-Amadi, A. A. (2016). Student Interest in the IS Specialization as Predictor of the Success Potential of New Information Systems Programmes within the Schools of Business in Kenyan Public Universities. *International Journal of Information Systems and Social Change*, *7*(2), 63–79. doi:10.4018/IJISSC.2016040104

Nedelko, Z., & Potocan, V. (2016). Management Practices for Processes Optimization: Case of Slovenia. In G. Alor-Hernández, C. Sánchez-Ramírez, & J. García-Alcaraz (Eds.), *Handbook of Research on Managerial Strategies for Achieving Optimal Performance in Industrial Processes* (pp. 545–561). Hershey, PA: IGI Global. doi:10.4018/978-1-5225-0130-5.ch025

Nedelko, Z., & Potocan, V. (2017). Management Solutions in Non-Profit Organizations: Case of Slovenia. In V. Potocan, M. Üngan, & Z. Nedelko (Eds.), *Handbook of Research on Managerial Solutions in Non-Profit Organizations* (pp. 1–22). Hershey, PA: IGI Global. doi:10.4018/978-1-5225-0731-4.ch001

Nedelko, Z., & Potocan, V. (2017). Priority of Management Tools Utilization among Managers: International Comparison. In V. Wang (Ed.), *Encyclopedia of Strategic Leadership and Management* (pp. 1083–1094). Hershey, PA: IGI Global. doi:10.4018/978-1-5225-1049-9.ch075

Nedelko, Z., Raudeliūnienė, J., & Črešnar, R. (2018). Knowledge Dynamics in Supply Chain Management. In N. Baporikar (Ed.), *Knowledge Integration Strategies for Entrepreneurship and Sustainability* (pp. 150–166). Hershey, PA: IGI Global. doi:10.4018/978-1-5225-5115-7.ch008

Nguyen, H. T., & Hipsher, S. A. (2018). Innovation and Creativity Used by Private Sector Firms in a Resources-Constrained Environment. In S. Hipsher (Ed.), *Examining the Private Sector's Role in Wealth Creation and Poverty Reduction* (pp. 219–238). Hershey, PA: IGI Global. doi:10.4018/978-1-5225-3117-3.ch010

Nycz, M., & Pólkowski, Z. (2016). Business Intelligence as a Modern IT Supporting Management of Local Government Units in Poland. *International Journal of Knowledge and Systems Science*, 7(4), 1–18. doi:10.4018/IJKSS.2016100101

Obaji, N. O., Senin, A. A., & Olugu, M. U. (2016). Supportive Government Policy as a Mechanism for Business Incubation Performance in Nigeria. *International Journal of Information Systems and Social Change*, 7(4), 52–66. doi:10.4018/IJISSC.2016100103

Obicci, P. A. (2017). Risk Sharing in a Partnership. In *Risk Management Strategies in Public-Private Partnerships* (pp. 115–152). Hershey, PA: IGI Global. doi:10.4018/978-1-5225-2503-5.ch004

Obidallah, W. J., & Raahemi, B. (2017). Managing Changes in Service Oriented Virtual Organizations: A Structural and Procedural Framework to Facilitate the Process of Change. *Journal of Electronic Commerce in Organizations*, 15(1), 59–83. doi:10.4018/JECO.2017010104

Ojasalo, J., & Ojasalo, K. (2016). Service Logic Business Model Canvas for Lean Development of SMEs and Start-Ups. In N. Baporikar (Ed.), *Handbook of Research on Entrepreneurship in the Contemporary Knowledge-Based Global Economy* (pp. 217–243). Hershey, PA: IGI Global. doi:10.4018/978-1-4666-8798-1.ch010

Ojo, O. (2017). Impact of Innovation on the Entrepreneurial Success in Selected Business Enterprises in South-West Nigeria. *International Journal of Innovation in the Digital Economy*, 8(2), 29–38. doi:10.4018/IJIDE.2017040103

Okdinawati, L., Simatupang, T. M., & Sunitiyoso, Y. (2017). Multi-Agent Reinforcement Learning for Value Co-Creation of Collaborative Transportation Management (CTM). *International Journal of Information Systems and Supply Chain Management*, 10(3), 84–95. doi:10.4018/IJISSCM.2017070105

Ortner, E., Mevius, M., Wiedmann, P., & Kurz, F. (2016). Design of Interactional Decision Support Applications for E-Participation in Smart Cities. *International Journal of Electronic Government Research*, 12(2), 18–38. doi:10.4018/IJEGR.2016040102

Pal, K. (2018). Building High Quality Big Data-Based Applications in Supply Chains. In A. Kumar & S. Saurav (Eds.), *Supply Chain Management Strategies and Risk Assessment in Retail Environments* (pp. 1–24). Hershey, PA: IGI Global. doi:10.4018/978-1-5225-3056-5.ch001

Palos-Sanchez, P. R., & Correia, M. B. (2018). Perspectives of the Adoption of Cloud Computing in the Tourism Sector. In J. Rodrigues, C. Ramos, P. Cardoso, & C. Henriques (Eds.), *Handbook of Research on Technological Developments for Cultural Heritage and eTourism Applications* (pp. 377–400). Hershey, PA: IGI Global. doi:10.4018/978-1-5225-2927-9.ch018

Parry, V. K., & Lind, M. L. (2016). Alignment of Business Strategy and Information Technology Considering Information Technology Governance, Project Portfolio Control, and Risk Management. *International Journal of Information Technology Project Management*, 7(4), 21–37. doi:10.4018/IJITPM.2016100102

Pashkova, N., Trujillo-Barrera, A., Apostolakis, G., Van Dijk, G., Drakos, P. D., & Baourakis, G. (2016). Business Management Models of Microfinance Institutions (MFIs) in Africa: A Study into Their Enabling Environments. *International Journal of Food and Beverage Manufacturing and Business Models*, 1(2), 63–82. doi:10.4018/IJFBMBM.2016070105

Patiño, B. E. (2017). New Generation Management by Convergence and Individual Identity: A Systemic and Human-Oriented Approach. In N. Baporikar (Ed.), *Innovation and Shifting Perspectives in Management Education* (pp. 119–143). Hershey, PA: IGI Global. doi:10.4018/978-1-5225-1019-2.ch006

Pawliczek, A., & Rössler, M. (2017). Knowledge of Management Tools and Systems in SMEs: Knowledge Transfer in Management. In A. Bencsik (Ed.), *Knowledge Management Initiatives and Strategies in Small and Medium Enterprises* (pp. 180–203). Hershey, PA: IGI Global. doi:10.4018/978-1-5225-1642-2.ch009

Pejic-Bach, M., Omazic, M. A., Aleksic, A., & Zoroja, J. (2018). Knowledge-Based Decision Making: A Multi-Case Analysis. In R. Leon (Ed.), *Managerial Strategies for Business Sustainability During Turbulent Times* (pp. 160–184). Hershey, PA: IGI Global. doi:10.4018/978-1-5225-2716-9.ch009

Perano, M., Hysa, X., & Calabrese, M. (2018). Strategic Planning, Cultural Context, and Business Continuity Management: Business Cases in the City of Shkoder. In A. Presenza & L. Sheehan (Eds.), *Geopolitics and Strategic Management in the Global Economy* (pp. 57–77). Hershey, PA: IGI Global. doi:10.4018/978-1-5225-2673-5.ch004

Related References

Pereira, R., Mira da Silva, M., & Lapão, L. V. (2017). IT Governance Maturity Patterns in Portuguese Healthcare. In S. De Haes & W. Van Grembergen (Eds.), *Strategic IT Governance and Alignment in Business Settings* (pp. 24–52). Hershey, PA: IGI Global. doi:10.4018/978-1-5225-0861-8.ch002

Perez-Uribe, R., & Ocampo-Guzman, D. (2016). Conflict within Colombian Family Owned SMEs: An Explosive Blend between Feelings and Business. In J. Saiz-Álvarez (Ed.), *Handbook of Research on Social Entrepreneurship and Solidarity Economics* (pp. 329–354). Hershey, PA: IGI Global. doi:10.4018/978-1-5225-0097-1.ch017

Pérez-Uribe, R. I., Torres, D. A., Jurado, S. P., & Prada, D. M. (2018). Cloud Tools for the Development of Project Management in SMEs. In R. Perez-Uribe, C. Salcedo-Perez, & D. Ocampo-Guzman (Eds.), *Handbook of Research on Intrapreneurship and Organizational Sustainability in SMEs* (pp. 95–120). Hershey, PA: IGI Global. doi:10.4018/978-1-5225-3543-0.ch005

Petrisor, I., & Cozmiuc, D. (2017). Global Supply Chain Management Organization at Siemens in the Advent of Industry 4.0. In L. Saglietto & C. Cezanne (Eds.), *Global Intermediation and Logistics Service Providers* (pp. 123–142). Hershey, PA: IGI Global. doi:10.4018/978-1-5225-2133-4.ch007

Pierce, J. M., Velliaris, D. M., & Edwards, J. (2017). A Living Case Study: A Journey Not a Destination. In N. Silton (Ed.), *Exploring the Benefits of Creativity in Education, Media, and the Arts* (pp. 158–178). Hershey, PA: IGI Global. doi:10.4018/978-1-5225-0504-4.ch008

Radosavljevic, M., & Andjelkovic, A. (2017). Multi-Criteria Decision Making Approach for Choosing Business Process for the Improvement: Upgrading of the Six Sigma Methodology. In J. Stanković, P. Delias, S. Marinković, & S. Rochhia (Eds.), *Tools and Techniques for Economic Decision Analysis* (pp. 225–247). Hershey, PA: IGI Global. doi:10.4018/978-1-5225-0959-2.ch011

Radovic, V. M. (2017). Corporate Sustainability and Responsibility and Disaster Risk Reduction: A Serbian Overview. In M. Camilleri (Ed.), *CSR 2.0 and the New Era of Corporate Citizenship* (pp. 147–164). Hershey, PA: IGI Global. doi:10.4018/978-1-5225-1842-6.ch008

Raghunath, K. M., Devi, S. L., & Patro, C. S. (2018). Impact of Risk Assessment Models on Risk Factors: A Holistic Outlook. In K. Strang, M. Korstanje, & N. Vajjhala (Eds.), *Research, Practices, and Innovations in Global Risk and Contingency Management* (pp. 134–153). Hershey, PA: IGI Global. doi:10.4018/978-1-5225-4754-9.ch008

Raman, A., & Goyal, D. P. (2017). Extending IMPLEMENT Framework for Enterprise Information Systems Implementation to Information System Innovation. In M. Tavana (Ed.), *Enterprise Information Systems and the Digitalization of Business Functions* (pp. 137–177). Hershey, PA: IGI Global. doi:10.4018/978-1-5225-2382-6.ch007

Rao, Y., & Zhang, Y. (2017). The Construction and Development of Academic Library Digital Special Subject Databases. In L. Ruan, Q. Zhu, & Y. Ye (Eds.), *Academic Library Development and Administration in China* (pp. 163–183). Hershey, PA: IGI Global. doi:10.4018/978-1-5225-0550-1.ch010

Ravasan, A. Z., Mohammadi, M. M., & Hamidi, H. (2018). An Investigation Into the Critical Success Factors of Implementing Information Technology Service Management Frameworks. In K. Jakobs (Ed.), *Corporate and Global Standardization Initiatives in Contemporary Society* (pp. 200–218). Hershey, PA: IGI Global. doi:10.4018/978-1-5225-5320-5.ch009

Renna, P., Izzo, C., & Romaniello, T. (2016). The Business Process Management Systems to Support Continuous Improvements. In W. Nuninger & J. Châtelet (Eds.), *Handbook of Research on Quality Assurance and Value Management in Higher Education* (pp. 237–256). Hershey, PA: IGI Global. doi:10.4018/978-1-5225-0024-7.ch009

Rezaie, S., Mirabedini, S. J., & Abtahi, A. (2018). Designing a Model for Implementation of Business Intelligence in the Banking Industry. *International Journal of Enterprise Information Systems*, *14*(1), 77–103. doi:10.4018/IJEIS.2018010105

Riccò, R. (2016). Diversity Management: Bringing Equality, Equity, and Inclusion in the Workplace. In J. Prescott (Ed.), *Handbook of Research on Race, Gender, and the Fight for Equality* (pp. 335–359). Hershey, PA: IGI Global. doi:10.4018/978-1-5225-0047-6.ch015

Romano, L., Grimaldi, R., & Colasuonno, F. S. (2017). Demand Management as a Success Factor in Project Portfolio Management. In L. Romano (Ed.), *Project Portfolio Management Strategies for Effective Organizational Operations* (pp. 202–219). Hershey, PA: IGI Global. doi:10.4018/978-1-5225-2151-8.ch008

Rostek, K. B. (2016). Risk Management: Role and Importance in Business Organization. In D. Jakóbczak (Ed.), *Analyzing Risk through Probabilistic Modeling in Operations Research* (pp. 149–178). Hershey, PA: IGI Global. doi:10.4018/978-1-4666-9458-3.ch007

Rouhani, S., & Savoji, S. R. (2016). A Success Assessment Model for BI Tools Implementation: An Empirical Study of Banking Industry. *International Journal of Business Intelligence Research*, *7*(1), 25–44. doi:10.4018/IJBIR.2016010103

Ruan, Z. (2016). A Corpus-Based Functional Analysis of Complex Nominal Groups in Written Business Discourse: The Case of "Business". *International Journal of Computer-Assisted Language Learning and Teaching*, 6(2), 74–90. doi:10.4018/IJCALLT.2016040105

Ruhi, U. (2018). Towards an Interdisciplinary Socio-Technical Definition of Virtual Communities. In M. Khosrow-Pour, D.B.A. (Ed.), Encyclopedia of Information Science and Technology, Fourth Edition (pp. 4278-4295). Hershey, PA: IGI Global. doi:10.4018/978-1-5225-2255-3.ch371

Ryan, J., Doster, B., Daily, S., & Lewis, C. (2016). A Case Study Perspective for Balanced Perioperative Workflow Achievement through Data-Driven Process Improvement. *International Journal of Healthcare Information Systems and Informatics*, 11(3), 19–41. doi:10.4018/IJHISI.2016070102

Safari, M. R., & Jiang, Q. (2018). The Theory and Practice of IT Governance Maturity and Strategies Alignment: Evidence From Banking Industry. *Journal of Global Information Management*, 26(2), 127–146. doi:10.4018/JGIM.2018040106

Sahoo, J., Pati, B., & Mohanty, B. (2017). Knowledge Management as an Academic Discipline: An Assessment. In B. Gunjal (Ed.), *Managing Knowledge and Scholarly Assets in Academic Libraries* (pp. 99–126). Hershey, PA: IGI Global. doi:10.4018/978-1-5225-1741-2.ch005

Saini, D. (2017). Relevance of Teaching Values and Ethics in Management Education. In N. Baporikar (Ed.), *Management Education for Global Leadership* (pp. 90–111). Hershey, PA: IGI Global. doi:10.4018/978-1-5225-1013-0.ch005

Sambhanthan, A. (2017). Assessing and Benchmarking Sustainability in Organisations: An Integrated Conceptual Model. *International Journal of Systems and Service-Oriented Engineering*, 7(4), 22–43. doi:10.4018/IJSSOE.2017100102

Sambhanthan, A., & Potdar, V. (2017). A Study of the Parameters Impacting Sustainability in Information Technology Organizations. *International Journal of Knowledge-Based Organizations*, 7(3), 27–39. doi:10.4018/IJKBO.2017070103

Sánchez-Fernández, M. D., & Manríquez, M. R. (2018). The Entrepreneurial Spirit Based on Social Values: The Digital Generation. In P. Isaias & L. Carvalho (Eds.), *User Innovation and the Entrepreneurship Phenomenon in the Digital Economy* (pp. 173–193). Hershey, PA: IGI Global. doi:10.4018/978-1-5225-2826-5.ch009

Sanchez-Ruiz, L., & Blanco, B. (2017). Process Management for SMEs: Barriers, Enablers, and Benefits. In M. Vemić (Ed.), *Optimal Management Strategies in Small and Medium Enterprises* (pp. 293–319). Hershey, PA: IGI Global. doi:10.4018/978-1-5225-1949-2.ch014

Sanz, L. F., Gómez-Pérez, J., & Castillo-Martinez, A. (2018). Analysis of the European ICT Competence Frameworks. In V. Ahuja & S. Rathore (Eds.), *Multidisciplinary Perspectives on Human Capital and Information Technology Professionals* (pp. 225–245). Hershey, PA: IGI Global. doi:10.4018/978-1-5225-5297-0.ch012

Sarvepalli, A., & Godin, J. (2017). Business Process Management in the Classroom. *Journal of Cases on Information Technology*, *19*(2), 17–28. doi:10.4018/JCIT.2017040102

Satpathy, B., & Muniapan, B. (2016). Ancient Wisdom for Transformational Leadership and Its Insights from the Bhagavad-Gita. In U. Aung & P. Ordoñez de Pablos (Eds.), *Managerial Strategies and Practice in the Asian Business Sector* (pp. 1–10). Hershey, PA: IGI Global. doi:10.4018/978-1-4666-9758-4.ch001

Saygili, E. E., Ozturkoglu, Y., & Kocakulah, M. C. (2017). End Users' Perceptions of Critical Success Factors in ERP Applications. *International Journal of Enterprise Information Systems*, *13*(4), 58–75. doi:10.4018/IJEIS.2017100104

Saygili, E. E., & Saygili, A. T. (2017). Contemporary Issues in Enterprise Information Systems: A Critical Review of CSFs in ERP Implementations. In M. Tavana (Ed.), *Enterprise Information Systems and the Digitalization of Business Functions* (pp. 120–136). Hershey, PA: IGI Global. doi:10.4018/978-1-5225-2382-6.ch006

Seidenstricker, S., & Antonino, A. (2018). Business Model Innovation-Oriented Technology Management for Emergent Technologies. In M. Khosrow-Pour, D.B.A. (Ed.), Encyclopedia of Information Science and Technology, Fourth Edition (pp. 4560-4569). Hershey, PA: IGI Global. doi:10.4018/978-1-5225-2255-3.ch396

Senaratne, S., & Gunarathne, A. D. (2017). Excellence Perspective for Management Education from a Global Accountants' Hub in Asia. In N. Baporikar (Ed.), *Management Education for Global Leadership* (pp. 158–180). Hershey, PA: IGI Global. doi:10.4018/978-1-5225-1013-0.ch008

Sensuse, D. I., & Cahyaningsih, E. (2018). Knowledge Management Models: A Summative Review. *International Journal of Information Systems in the Service Sector*, *10*(1), 71–100. doi:10.4018/IJISSS.2018010105

Sensuse, D. I., Wibowo, W. C., & Cahyaningsih, E. (2016). Indonesian Government Knowledge Management Model: A Theoretical Model. *Information Resources Management Journal, 29*(1), 91–108. doi:10.4018/irmj.2016010106

Seth, M., Goyal, D., & Kiran, R. (2017). Diminution of Impediments in Implementation of Supply Chain Management Information System for Enhancing its Effectiveness in Indian Automobile Industry. *Journal of Global Information Management, 25*(3), 1–20. doi:10.4018/JGIM.2017070101

Seyal, A. H., & Rahman, M. N. (2017). Investigating Impact of Inter-Organizational Factors in Measuring ERP Systems Success: Bruneian Perspectives. In M. Tavana (Ed.), *Enterprise Information Systems and the Digitalization of Business Functions* (pp. 178–204). Hershey, PA: IGI Global. doi:10.4018/978-1-5225-2382-6.ch008

Shaikh, A. A., & Karjaluoto, H. (2016). On Some Misconceptions Concerning Digital Banking and Alternative Delivery Channels. *International Journal of E-Business Research, 12*(3), 1–16. doi:10.4018/IJEBR.2016070101

Shams, S. M. (2016). Stakeholder Relationship Management in Online Business and Competitive Value Propositions: Evidence from the Sports Industry. *International Journal of Online Marketing, 6*(2), 1–17. doi:10.4018/IJOM.2016040101

Shamsuzzoha, A. (2016). Management of Risk and Resilience within Collaborative Business Network. In R. Addo-Tenkorang, J. Kantola, P. Helo, & A. Shamsuzzoha (Eds.), *Supply Chain Strategies and the Engineer-to-Order Approach* (pp. 143–159). Hershey, PA: IGI Global. doi:10.4018/978-1-5225-0021-6.ch008

Shaqrah, A. A. (2018). Analyzing Business Intelligence Systems Based on 7s Model of McKinsey. *International Journal of Business Intelligence Research, 9*(1), 53–63. doi:10.4018/IJBIR.2018010104

Sharma, A. J. (2017). Enhancing Sustainability through Experiential Learning in Management Education. In N. Baporikar (Ed.), *Management Education for Global Leadership* (pp. 256–274). Hershey, PA: IGI Global. doi:10.4018/978-1-5225-1013-0.ch013

Shetty, K. P. (2017). Responsible Global Leadership: Ethical Challenges in Management Education. In N. Baporikar (Ed.), *Innovation and Shifting Perspectives in Management Education* (pp. 194–223). Hershey, PA: IGI Global. doi:10.4018/978-1-5225-1019-2.ch009

Sinthupundaja, J., & Kohda, Y. (2017). Effects of Corporate Social Responsibility and Creating Shared Value on Sustainability. *International Journal of Sustainable Entrepreneurship and Corporate Social Responsibility, 2*(1), 27–38. doi:10.4018/IJSECSR.2017010103

Škarica, I., & Hrgović, A. V. (2018). Implementation of Total Quality Management Principles in Public Health Institutes in the Republic of Croatia. *International Journal of Productivity Management and Assessment Technologies, 6*(1), 1–16. doi:10.4018/IJPMAT.2018010101

Smuts, H., Kotzé, P., Van der Merwe, A., & Loock, M. (2017). Framework for Managing Shared Knowledge in an Information Systems Outsourcing Context. *International Journal of Knowledge Management, 13*(4), 1–30. doi:10.4018/IJKM.2017100101

Soares, E. R., & Zaidan, F. H. (2016). Information Architecture and Business Modeling in Modern Organizations of Information Technology: Professional Career Plan in Organizations IT. In G. Jamil, J. Poças Rascão, F. Ribeiro, & A. Malheiro da Silva (Eds.), *Handbook of Research on Information Architecture and Management in Modern Organizations* (pp. 439–457). Hershey, PA: IGI Global. doi:10.4018/978-1-4666-8637-3.ch020

Sousa, M. J., Cruz, R., Dias, I., & Caracol, C. (2017). Information Management Systems in the Supply Chain. In G. Jamil, A. Soares, & C. Pessoa (Eds.), *Handbook of Research on Information Management for Effective Logistics and Supply Chains* (pp. 469–485). Hershey, PA: IGI Global. doi:10.4018/978-1-5225-0973-8.ch025

Spremic, M., Turulja, L., & Bajgoric, N. (2018). Two Approaches in Assessing Business Continuity Management Attitudes in the Organizational Context. In N. Bajgoric (Ed.), *Always-On Enterprise Information Systems for Modern Organizations* (pp. 159–183). Hershey, PA: IGI Global. doi:10.4018/978-1-5225-3704-5.ch008

Steenkamp, A. L. (2018). Some Insights in Computer Science and Information Technology. In *Examining the Changing Role of Supervision in Doctoral Research Projects: Emerging Research and Opportunities* (pp. 113–133). Hershey, PA: IGI Global. doi:10.4018/978-1-5225-2610-0.ch005

Studdard, N., Dawson, M., Burton, S. L., Jackson, N., Leonard, B., Quisenberry, W., & Rahim, E. (2016). Nurturing Social Entrepreneurship and Building Social Entrepreneurial Self-Efficacy: Focusing on Primary and Secondary Schooling to Develop Future Social Entrepreneurs. In Z. Fields (Ed.), *Incorporating Business Models and Strategies into Social Entrepreneurship* (pp. 154–175). Hershey, PA: IGI Global. doi:10.4018/978-1-4666-8748-6.ch010

Sun, Z. (2016). A Framework for Developing Management Intelligent Systems. *International Journal of Systems and Service-Oriented Engineering*, 6(1), 37–53. doi:10.4018/IJSSOE.2016010103

Swami, B., & Mphele, G. T. (2016). Problems Preventing Growth of Small Entrepreneurs: A Case Study of a Few Small Entrepreneurs in Botswana Sub-Urban Areas. In N. Baporikar (Ed.), *Handbook of Research on Entrepreneurship in the Contemporary Knowledge-Based Global Economy* (pp. 479–508). Hershey, PA: IGI Global. doi:10.4018/978-1-4666-8798-1.ch020

Tabach, A., & Croteau, A. (2017). Configurations of Information Technology Governance Practices and Business Unit Performance. *International Journal of IT/Business Alignment and Governance*, 8(2), 1–27. doi:10.4018/IJITBAG.2017070101

Talaue, G. M., & Iqbal, T. (2017). Assessment of e-Business Mode of Selected Private Universities in the Philippines and Pakistan. *International Journal of Online Marketing*, 7(4), 63–77. doi:10.4018/IJOM.2017100105

Tam, G. C. (2017). Project Manager Sustainability Competence. In *Managerial Strategies and Green Solutions for Project Sustainability* (pp. 178–207). Hershey, PA: IGI Global. doi:10.4018/978-1-5225-2371-0.ch008

Tambo, T. (2018). Fashion Retail Innovation: About Context, Antecedents, and Outcome in Technological Change Projects. In I. Management Association (Ed.), Fashion and Textiles: Breakthroughs in Research and Practice (pp. 233-260). Hershey, PA: IGI Global. doi:10.4018/978-1-5225-3432-7.ch010

Tambo, T., & Mikkelsen, O. E. (2016). Fashion Supply Chain Optimization: Linking Make-to-Order Purchasing and B2B E-Commerce. In S. Joshi & R. Joshi (Eds.), *Designing and Implementing Global Supply Chain Management* (pp. 1–21). Hershey, PA: IGI Global. doi:10.4018/978-1-4666-9720-1.ch001

Tandon, K. (2016). Innovative Andragogy: The Paradigm Shift to Heutagogy. In S. Tiwari & L. Nafees (Eds.), *Innovative Management Education Pedagogies for Preparing Next-Generation Leaders* (pp. 238–257). Hershey, PA: IGI Global. doi:10.4018/978-1-4666-9691-4.ch014

Tantau, A. D., & Frăţilă, L. C. (2018). Information and Management System for Renewable Energy Business. In *Entrepreneurship and Business Development in the Renewable Energy Sector* (pp. 200–244). Hershey, PA: IGI Global. doi:10.4018/978-1-5225-3625-3.ch006

Teixeira, N., Pardal, P. N., & Rafael, B. G. (2018). Internationalization, Financial Performance, and Organizational Challenges: A Success Case in Portugal. In L. Carvalho (Ed.), *Handbook of Research on Entrepreneurial Ecosystems and Social Dynamics in a Globalized World* (pp. 379–423). Hershey, PA: IGI Global. doi:10.4018/978-1-5225-3525-6.ch017

Trad, A., & Kalpić, D. (2016). The E-Business Transformation Framework for E-Commerce Architecture-Modeling Projects. In I. Lee (Ed.), *Encyclopedia of E-Commerce Development, Implementation, and Management* (pp. 733–753). Hershey, PA: IGI Global. doi:10.4018/978-1-4666-9787-4.ch052

Trad, A., & Kalpić, D. (2016). The E-Business Transformation Framework for E-Commerce Control and Monitoring Pattern. In I. Lee (Ed.), *Encyclopedia of E-Commerce Development, Implementation, and Management* (pp. 754–777). Hershey, PA: IGI Global. doi:10.4018/978-1-4666-9787-4.ch053

Trad, A., & Kalpić, D. (2018). The Business Transformation Framework, Agile Project and Change Management. In M. Khosrow-Pour, D.B.A. (Ed.), Encyclopedia of Information Science and Technology, Fourth Edition (pp. 620-635). Hershey, PA: IGI Global. doi:10.4018/978-1-5225-2255-3.ch054

Trad, A., & Kalpić, D. (2018). The Business Transformation and Enterprise Architecture Framework: The Financial Engineering E-Risk Management and E-Law Integration. In B. Sergi, F. Fidanoski, M. Ziolo, & V. Naumovski (Eds.), *Regaining Global Stability After the Financial Crisis* (pp. 46–65). Hershey, PA: IGI Global. doi:10.4018/978-1-5225-4026-7.ch003

Turulja, L., & Bajgoric, N. (2018). Business Continuity and Information Systems: A Systematic Literature Review. In N. Bajgoric (Ed.), *Always-On Enterprise Information Systems for Modern Organizations* (pp. 60–87). Hershey, PA: IGI Global. doi:10.4018/978-1-5225-3704-5.ch004

van Wessel, R. M., de Vries, H. J., & Ribbers, P. M. (2016). Business Benefits through Company IT Standardization. In K. Jakobs (Ed.), *Effective Standardization Management in Corporate Settings* (pp. 34–53). Hershey, PA: IGI Global. doi:10.4018/978-1-4666-9737-9.ch003

Vargas-Hernández, J. G. (2017). Professional Integrity in Business Management Education. In N. Baporikar (Ed.), *Management Education for Global Leadership* (pp. 70–89). Hershey, PA: IGI Global. doi:10.4018/978-1-5225-1013-0.ch004

Vasista, T. G., & AlAbdullatif, A. M. (2017). Role of Electronic Customer Relationship Management in Demand Chain Management: A Predictive Analytic Approach. *International Journal of Information Systems and Supply Chain Management, 10*(1), 53–67. doi:10.4018/IJISSCM.2017010104

Vergidis, K. (2016). Rediscovering Business Processes: Definitions, Patterns, and Modelling Approaches. In P. Papajorgji, F. Pinet, A. Guimarães, & J. Papathanasiou (Eds.), *Automated Enterprise Systems for Maximizing Business Performance* (pp. 97–122). Hershey, PA: IGI Global. doi:10.4018/978-1-4666-8841-4.ch007

Vieru, D., & Bourdeau, S. (2017). Survival in the Digital Era: A Digital Competence-Based Multi-Case Study in the Canadian SME Clothing Industry. *International Journal of Social and Organizational Dynamics in IT, 6*(1), 17–34. doi:10.4018/IJSODIT.2017010102

Vijayan, G., & Kamarulzaman, N. H. (2017). An Introduction to Sustainable Supply Chain Management and Business Implications. In M. Khan, M. Hussain, & M. Ajmal (Eds.), *Green Supply Chain Management for Sustainable Business Practice* (pp. 27–50). Hershey, PA: IGI Global. doi:10.4018/978-1-5225-0635-5.ch002

Vlachvei, A., & Notta, O. (2017). Firm Competitiveness: Theories, Evidence, and Measurement. In A. Vlachvei, O. Notta, K. Karantininis, & N. Tsounis (Eds.), *Factors Affecting Firm Competitiveness and Performance in the Modern Business World* (pp. 1–42). Hershey, PA: IGI Global. doi:10.4018/978-1-5225-0843-4.ch001

von Rosing, M., Fullington, N., & Walker, J. (2016). Using the Business Ontology and Enterprise Standards to Transform Three Leading Organizations. *International Journal of Conceptual Structures and Smart Applications, 4*(1), 71–99. doi:10.4018/IJCSSA.2016010104

von Rosing, M., & von Scheel, H. (2016). Using the Business Ontology to Develop Enterprise Standards. *International Journal of Conceptual Structures and Smart Applications, 4*(1), 48–70. doi:10.4018/IJCSSA.2016010103

Walczak, S. (2016). Artificial Neural Networks and other AI Applications for Business Management Decision Support. *International Journal of Sociotechnology and Knowledge Development, 8*(4), 1–20. doi:10.4018/IJSKD.2016100101

Wamba, S. F., Akter, S., Kang, H., Bhattacharya, M., & Upal, M. (2016). The Primer of Social Media Analytics. *Journal of Organizational and End User Computing, 28*(2), 1–12. doi:10.4018/JOEUC.2016040101

Wang, C., Schofield, M., Li, X., & Ou, X. (2017). Do Chinese Students in Public and Private Higher Education Institutes Perform at Different Level in One of the Leadership Skills: Critical Thinking?: An Exploratory Comparison. In V. Wang (Ed.), *Encyclopedia of Strategic Leadership and Management* (pp. 160–181). Hershey, PA: IGI Global. doi:10.4018/978-1-5225-1049-9.ch013

Wang, F., Raisinghani, M. S., Mora, M., & Wang, X. (2016). Strategic E-Business Management through a Balanced Scored Card Approach. In I. Lee (Ed.), *Encyclopedia of E-Commerce Development, Implementation, and Management* (pp. 361–386). Hershey, PA: IGI Global. doi:10.4018/978-1-4666-9787-4.ch027

Wang, J. (2017). Multi-Agent based Production Management Decision System Modelling for the Textile Enterprise. *Journal of Global Information Management, 25*(4), 1–15. doi:10.4018/JGIM.2017100101

Wiedemann, A., & Gewald, H. (2017). Examining Cross-Domain Alignment: The Correlation of Business Strategy, IT Management, and IT Business Value. *International Journal of IT/Business Alignment and Governance, 8*(1), 17–31. doi:10.4018/IJITBAG.2017010102

Wolf, R., & Thiel, M. (2018). Advancing Global Business Ethics in China: Reducing Poverty Through Human and Social Welfare. In S. Hipsher (Ed.), *Examining the Private Sector's Role in Wealth Creation and Poverty Reduction* (pp. 67–84). Hershey, PA: IGI Global. doi:10.4018/978-1-5225-3117-3.ch004

Wu, J., Ding, F., Xu, M., Mo, Z., & Jin, A. (2016). Investigating the Determinants of Decision-Making on Adoption of Public Cloud Computing in E-government. *Journal of Global Information Management, 24*(3), 71–89. doi:10.4018/JGIM.2016070104

Xu, L., & de Vrieze, P. (2016). Building Situational Applications for Virtual Enterprises. In I. Lee (Ed.), *Encyclopedia of E-Commerce Development, Implementation, and Management* (pp. 715–724). Hershey, PA: IGI Global. doi:10.4018/978-1-4666-9787-4.ch050

Yablonsky, S. (2018). Innovation Platforms: Data and Analytics Platforms. In *Multi-Sided Platforms (MSPs) and Sharing Strategies in the Digital Economy: Emerging Research and Opportunities* (pp. 72–95). Hershey, PA: IGI Global. doi:10.4018/978-1-5225-5457-8.ch003

Yusoff, A., Ahmad, N. H., & Halim, H. A. (2017). Agropreneurship among Gen Y in Malaysia: The Role of Academic Institutions. In N. Ahmad, T. Ramayah, H. Halim, & S. Rahman (Eds.), *Handbook of Research on Small and Medium Enterprises in Developing Countries* (pp. 23–47). Hershey, PA: IGI Global. doi:10.4018/978-1-5225-2165-5.ch002

Zanin, F., Comuzzi, E., & Costantini, A. (2018). The Effect of Business Strategy and Stock Market Listing on the Use of Risk Assessment Tools. In *Management Control Systems in Complex Settings: Emerging Research and Opportunities* (pp. 145–168). Hershey, PA: IGI Global. doi:10.4018/978-1-5225-3987-2.ch007

Zgheib, P. W. (2017). Corporate Innovation and Intrapreneurship in the Middle East. In P. Zgheib (Ed.), *Entrepreneurship and Business Innovation in the Middle East* (pp. 37–56). Hershey, PA: IGI Global. doi:10.4018/978-1-5225-2066-5.ch003

About the Contributors

Tiko Iyamu is a Research Professor at the Faculty of Informatics and Design, Cape Peninsula University of Technology (CPUT), Cape Town, South Africa. He was previously with the Tshwane University of Technology, South Africa, and the Namibia University of Science and Technology, Windhoek, Namibia. Iyamu served as a Professor Extraordinaire at the Department of Computer Science, University of the Western Cape, South Africa. He was a visiting professor at the Flensburg University of Applied Sciences, Germany. Professor Iyamu's areas of focus include enterprise architecture, health informatics, big data analytics, and IT strategy. He has published over 120 research articles in journals, books and book chapters. Prior to joining academic, Professor Iyamu held several positions in both Public and Private Institutions in South Africa. He was Systems' Analyst at Nedcor Investment Bank, and Information Technologist at Metropolitan, an insurance company. Iyamu was the Chief Architect at the City of Cape Town; and IT Architect at Old Mutual. He was also at MWeb, a Telecommunication company, as Head of IT Architecture & Governance.

* * *

Nomathamsanqa (Thami) Batyashe is a professional with extensive experience in the IT industry. Her career started as an IT instructor in Microsoft products, advancing to software development, project management, software testing, IT governance, enterprise architecture, risk management, and strategy. She is currently an IT strategist. She held several positions in both the private and public sector. Her academic background entails a national diploma in software development, which she was awarded the best student over three years. This is followed by bachelor degree in the information systems, obtained cum laude for it. Further to this she obtained a Master degree in IT and a Master of Business Leadership degree. She is currently a doctoral candidate, studying towards a Ph.D in IT strategy.

Monica Nehemia has over fifteen years of experience in the field of Information Technology (IT). She is currently the Head of IT at the Office of the Prime Minister, Republic of Namibia. Prior to this appointment, Ms Nehemia worked in the Telecommunication industry as a technician, System Administrator, Networking Engineer and Manager of IT Customised solutions. Ms Nehemia is a part-time registered student for a PhD in Informatics at the Cape Peninsula University of Technology, Cape Town, South Africa. Her research focus include IT Governance, Enterprise Architecture, Data Management and Health Informatics.

Irja Shaanika holds Doctor of Philosophy degree in Informatics from Cape University Of Science and Technology from South Africa. She is currently a lecturer at Namibia University of Science and Technology. My research areas include health Informatics, Information Systems, IT, Enterprise architecture.

Index

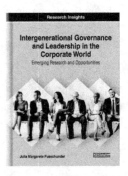

Ensure Quality Research is Introduced to the Academic Community

Become an IGI Global Reviewer for Authored Book Projects

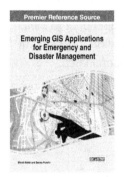
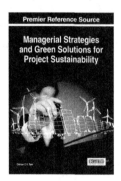

The overall success of an authored book project is dependent on quality and timely reviews.

In this competitive age of scholarly publishing, constructive and timely feedback significantly expedites the turnaround time of manuscripts from submission to acceptance, allowing the publication and discovery of forward-thinking research at a much more expeditious rate. Several IGI Global authored book projects are currently seeking highly-qualified experts in the field to fill vacancies on their respective editorial review boards:

Applications and Inquiries may be sent to:
development@igi-global.com

Applicants must have a doctorate (or an equivalent degree) as well as publishing and reviewing experience. Reviewers are asked to complete the open-ended evaluation questions with as much detail as possible in a timely, collegial, and constructive manner. All reviewers' tenures run for one-year terms on the editorial review boards and are expected to complete at least three reviews per term. Upon successful completion of this term, reviewers can be considered for an additional term.

If you have a colleague that may be interested in this opportunity, we encourage you to share this information with them.